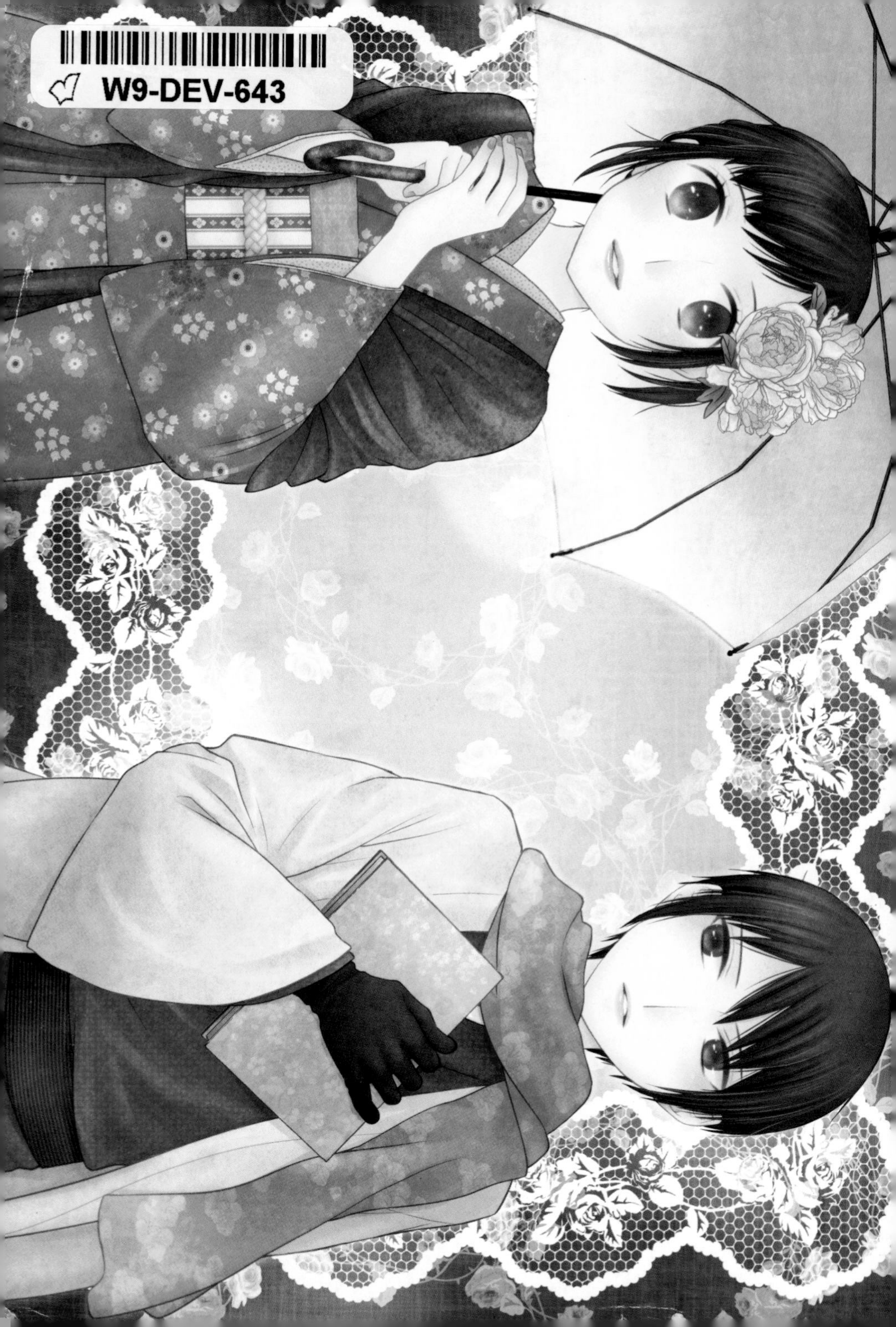

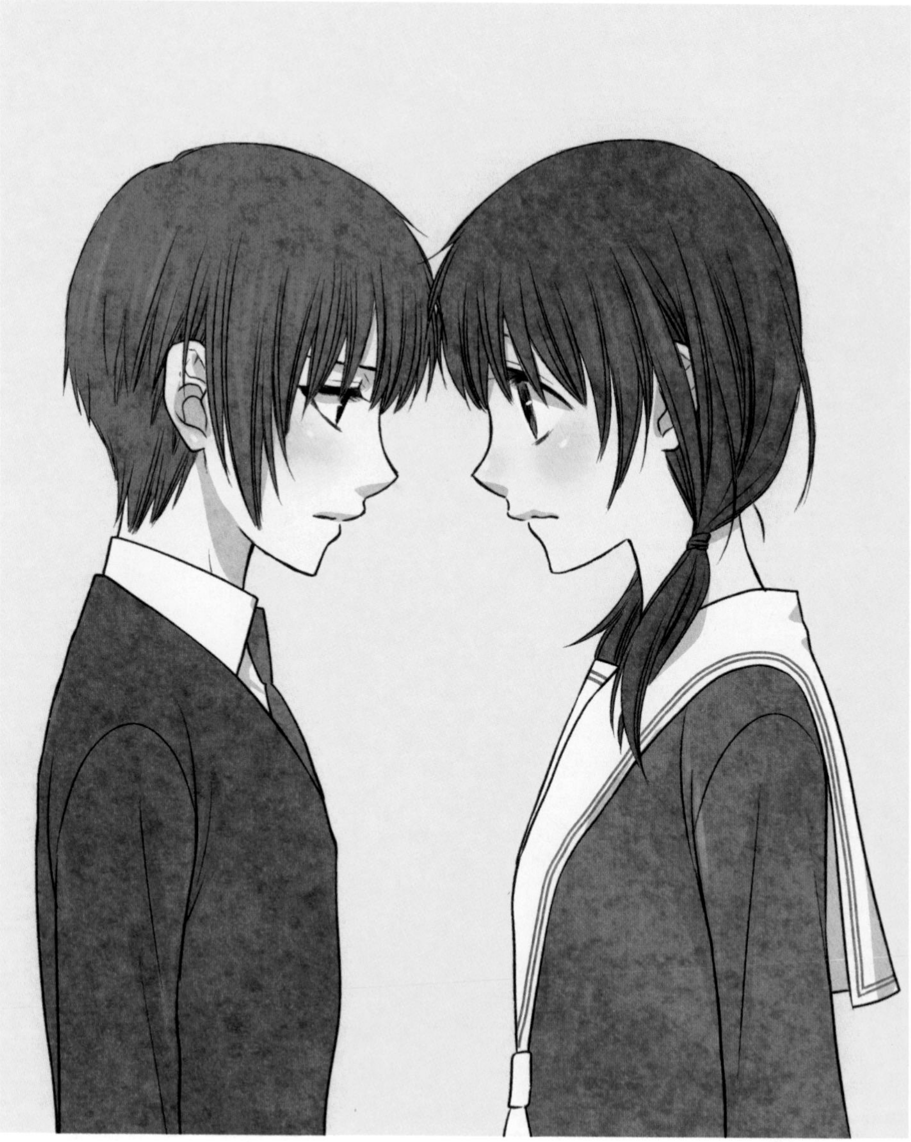

Fruits Basket another

NATSUKI TAKAYA

3

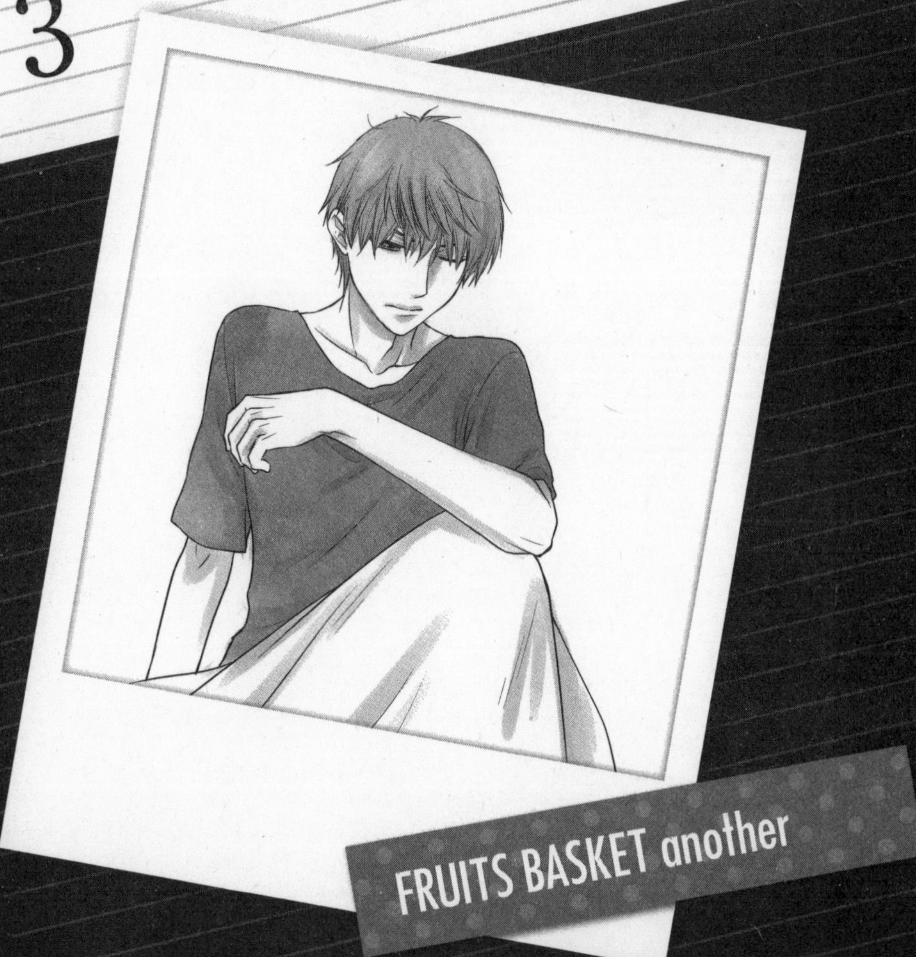
FRUITS BASKET another

Fruits Basket another

CONTENTS

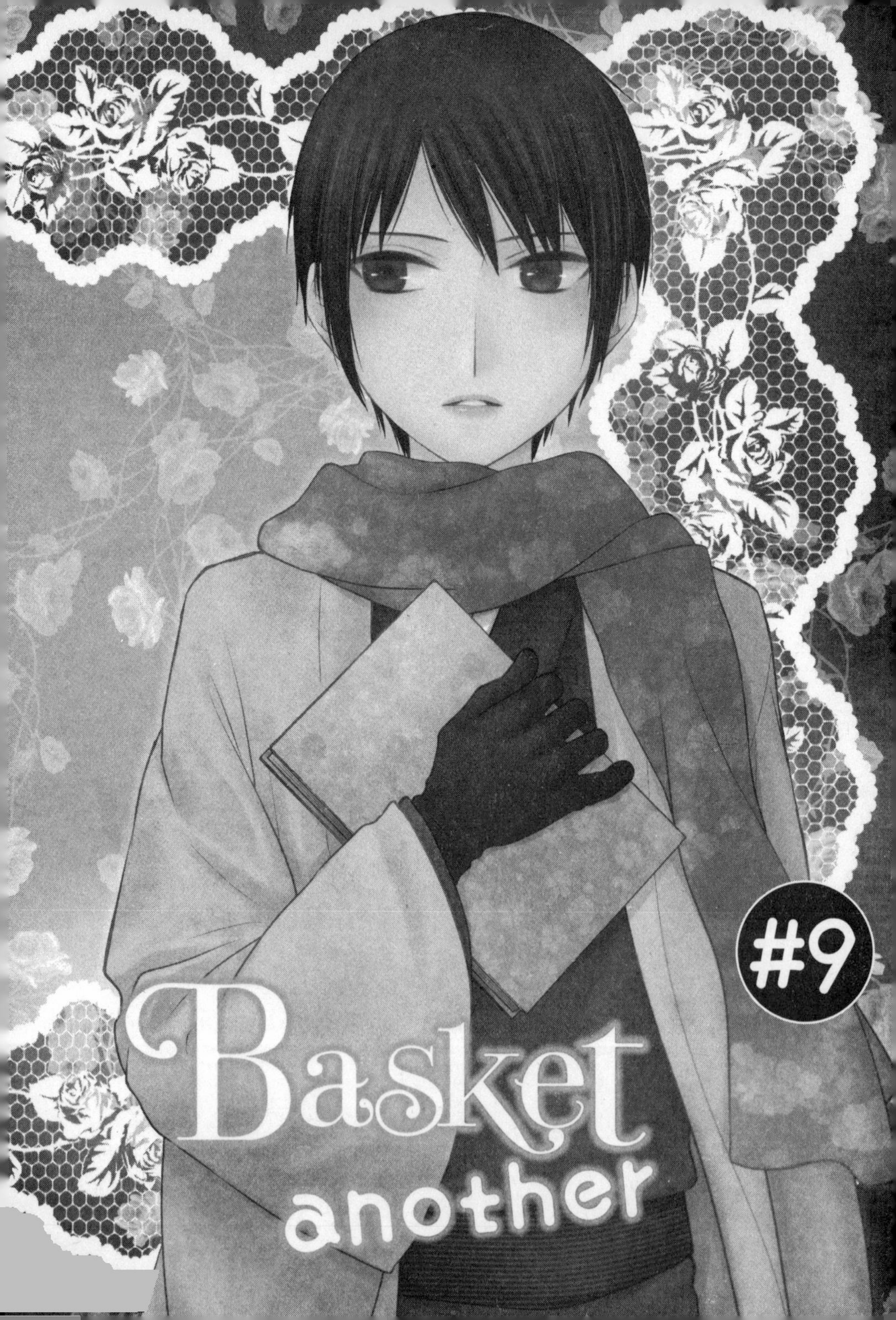
#9
Basket
another

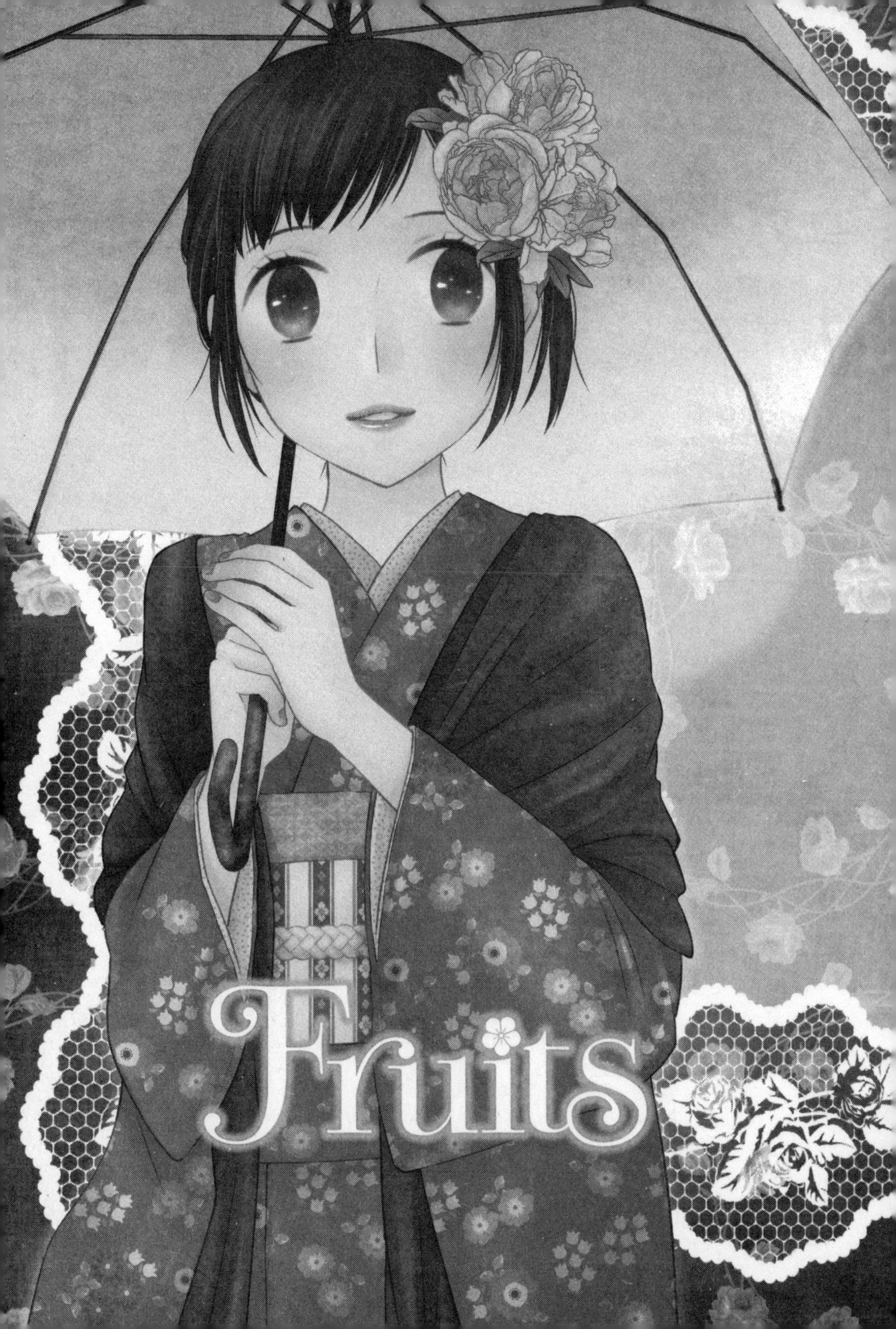
Fruits

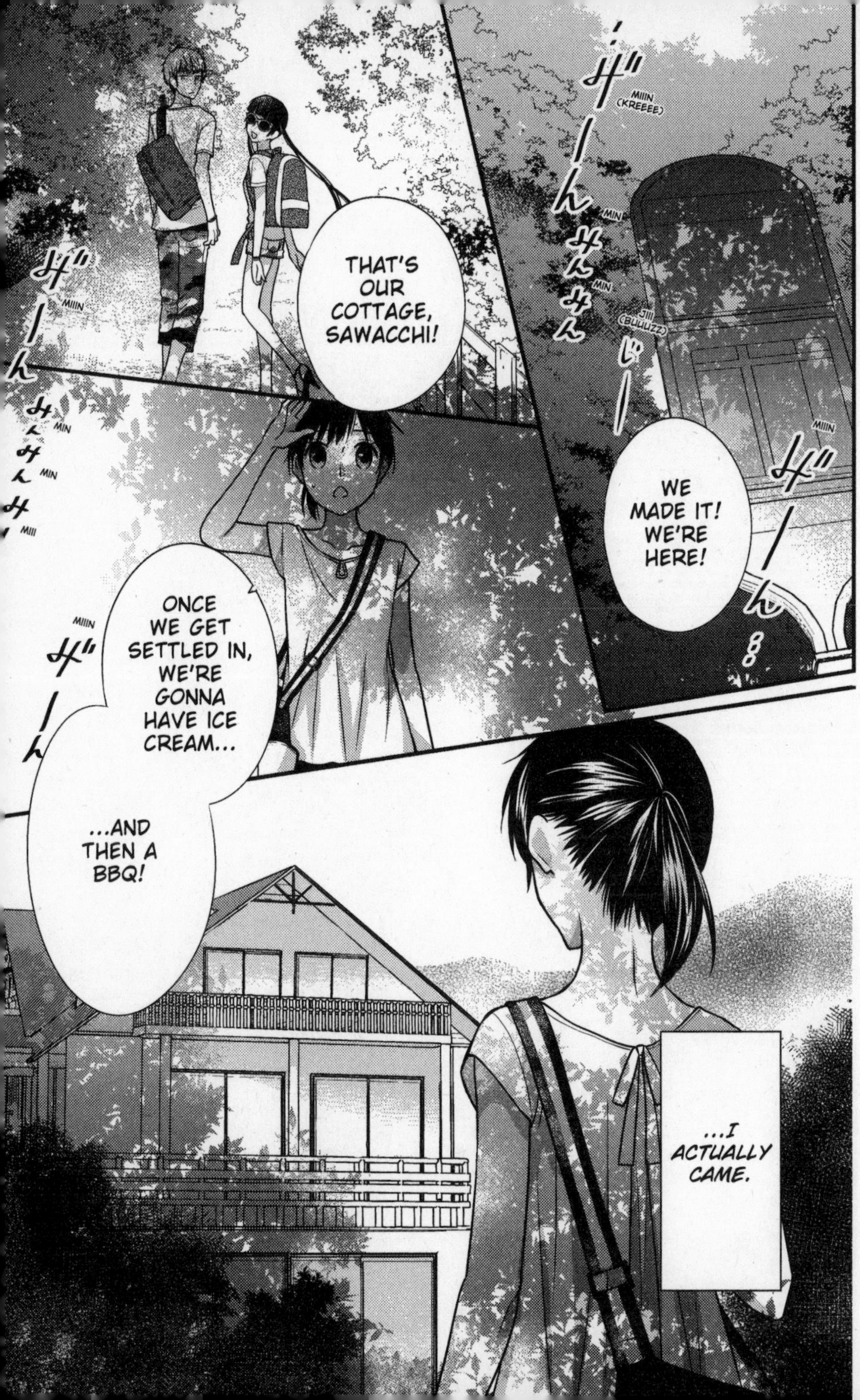

MIIN (KREEEE)
MIN
MIN
JIII (BUUUZZ)
MIIN
WE MADE IT! WE'RE HERE!
MIIN
THAT'S OUR COTTAGE, SAWACCHI!
MIN
MIN
MIII
MIIN
ONCE WE GET SETTLED IN, WE'RE GONNA HAVE ICE CREAM...
...AND THEN A BBQ!
...I ACTUALLY CAME.

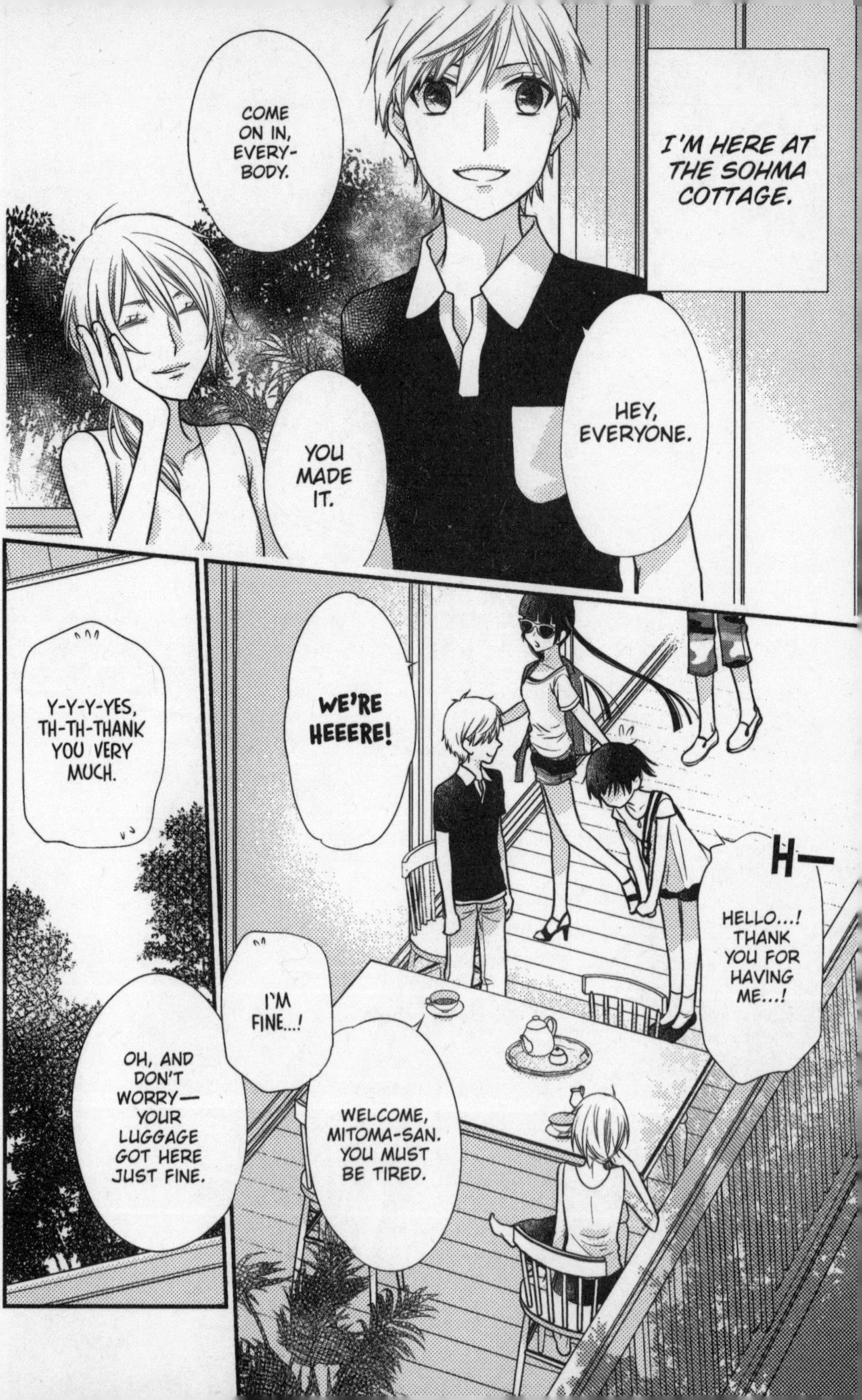
I'M HERE AT THE SOHMA COTTAGE.
COME ON IN, EVERYBODY.
HEY, EVERYONE.
YOU MADE IT.
H—
HELLO...! THANK YOU FOR HAVING ME...!
WE'RE HEEERE!
WELCOME, MITOMA-SAN. YOU MUST BE TIRED.
I'M FINE...!
OH, AND DON'T WORRY—YOUR LUGGAGE GOT HERE JUST FINE.
Y-Y-Y-YES, TH-TH-THANK YOU VERY MUCH.

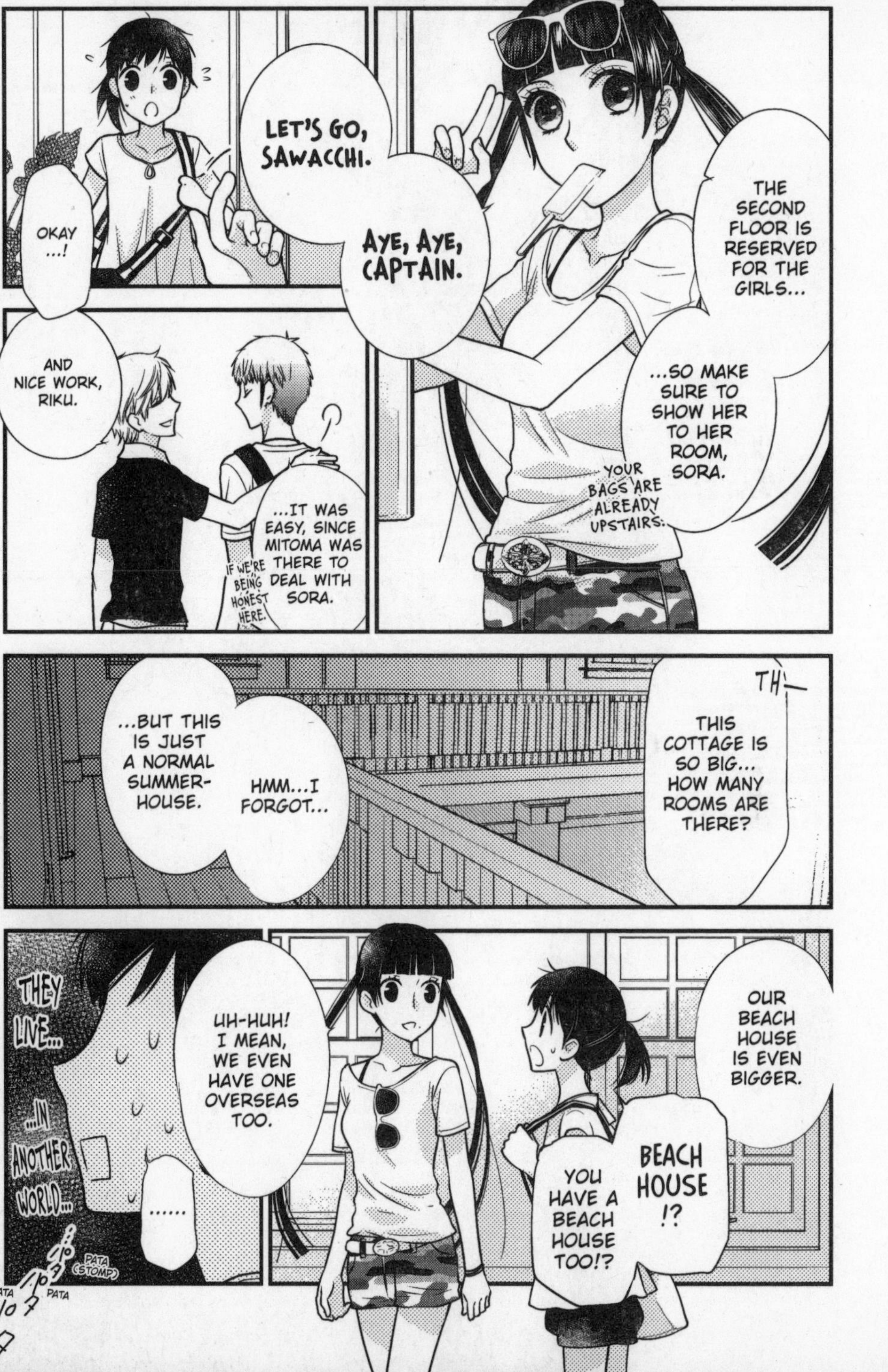
THE SECOND FLOOR IS RESERVED FOR THE GIRLS...
...SO MAKE SURE TO SHOW HER TO HER ROOM, SORA.
YOUR BAGS ARE ALREADY UPSTAIRS.
LET'S GO, SAWACCHI.
AYE, AYE, CAPTAIN.
OKAY ...!
AND NICE WORK, RIKU.
...IT WAS EASY, SINCE MITOMA WAS THERE TO DEAL WITH SORA.
IF WE'RE BEING HONEST HERE.
TH—
THIS COTTAGE IS SO BIG... HOW MANY ROOMS ARE THERE?
HMM...I FORGOT...
...BUT THIS IS JUST A NORMAL SUMMER-HOUSE.
OUR BEACH HOUSE IS EVEN BIGGER.
BEACH HOUSE !?
YOU HAVE A BEACH HOUSE TOO!?
UH-HUH! I MEAN, WE EVEN HAVE ONE OVERSEAS TOO.
THEY LIVE...
...IN ANOTHER WORLD...
......
PATA (STOMP)
PATA
PATA
PATA

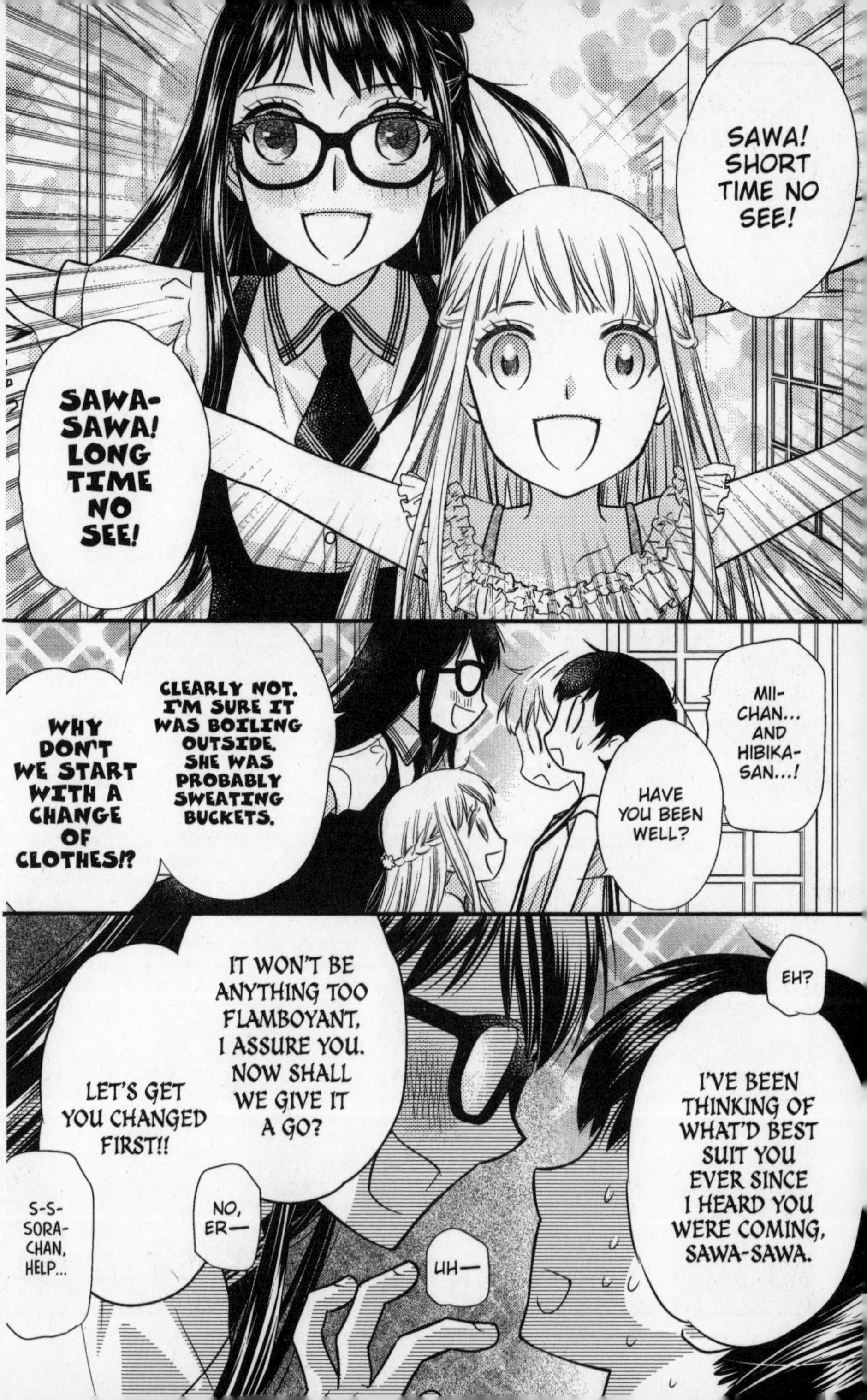
SAWA! SHORT TIME NO SEE!
SAWA-SAWA! LONG TIME NO SEE!
MII-CHAN... AND HIBIKA-SAN...!
HAVE YOU BEEN WELL?
CLEARLY NOT. I'M SURE IT WAS BOILING OUTSIDE. SHE WAS PROBABLY SWEATING BUCKETS.
WHY DON'T WE START WITH A CHANGE OF CLOTHES!?
EH?
I'VE BEEN THINKING OF WHAT'D BEST SUIT YOU EVER SINCE I HEARD YOU WERE COMING, SAWA-SAWA.
IT WON'T BE ANYTHING TOO FLAMBOYANT, I ASSURE YOU. NOW SHALL WE GIVE IT A GO?
LET'S GET YOU CHANGED FIRST!!
UH—
NO, ER—
S-S-SORA-CHAN, HELP...

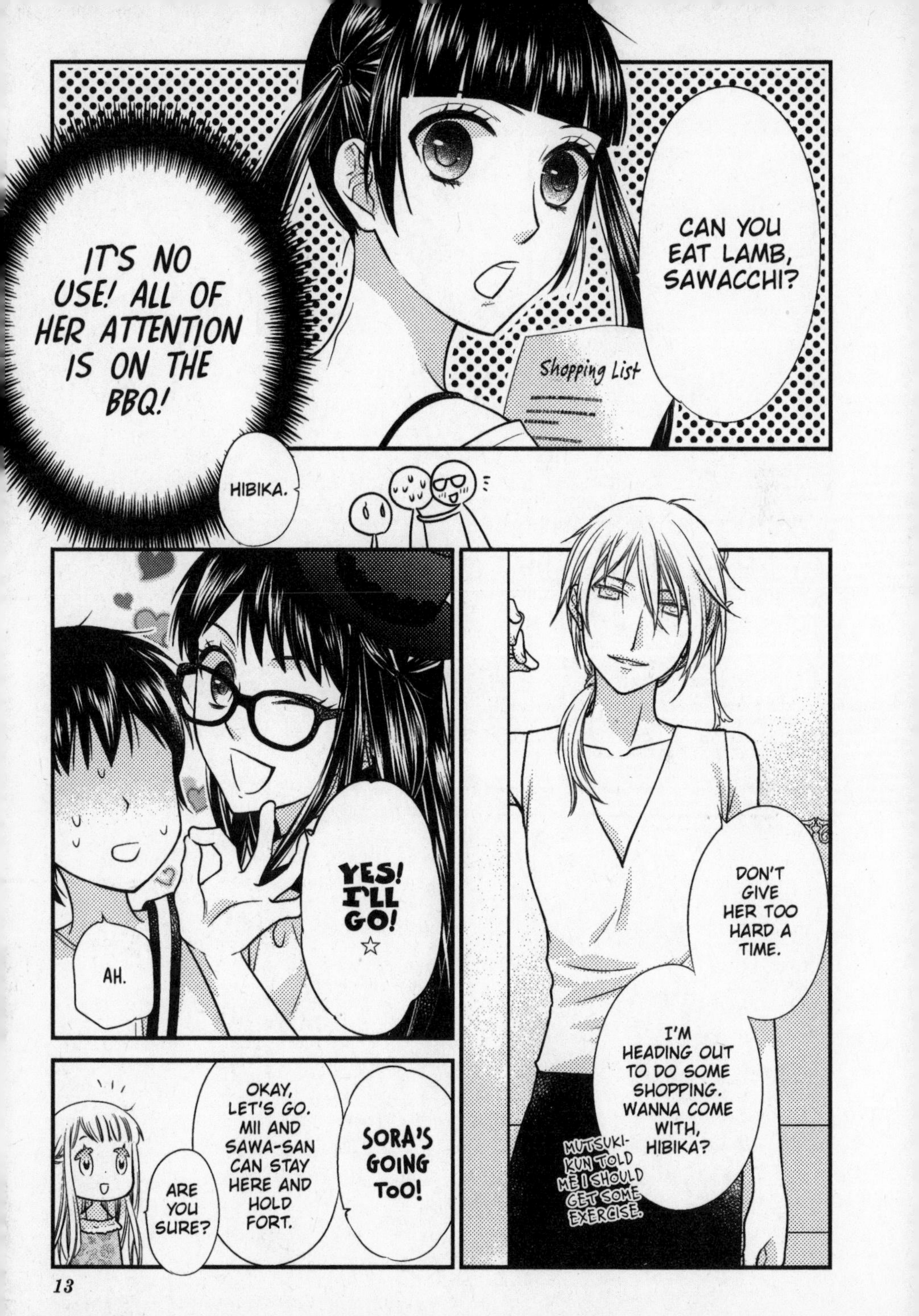
CAN YOU EAT LAMB, SAWACCHI?
Shopping List
IT'S NO USE! ALL OF HER ATTENTION IS ON THE BBQ!
HIBIKA.
DON'T GIVE HER TOO HARD A TIME.
I'M HEADING OUT TO DO SOME SHOPPING. WANNA COME WITH, HIBIKA?
MUTSUKI-KUN TOLD ME I SHOULD GET SOME EXERCISE.
YES! I'LL GO! ☆
AH.
SORA'S GOING TOO!
OKAY, LET'S GO. MII AND SAWA-SAN CAN STAY HERE AND HOLD FORT.
ARE YOU SURE?

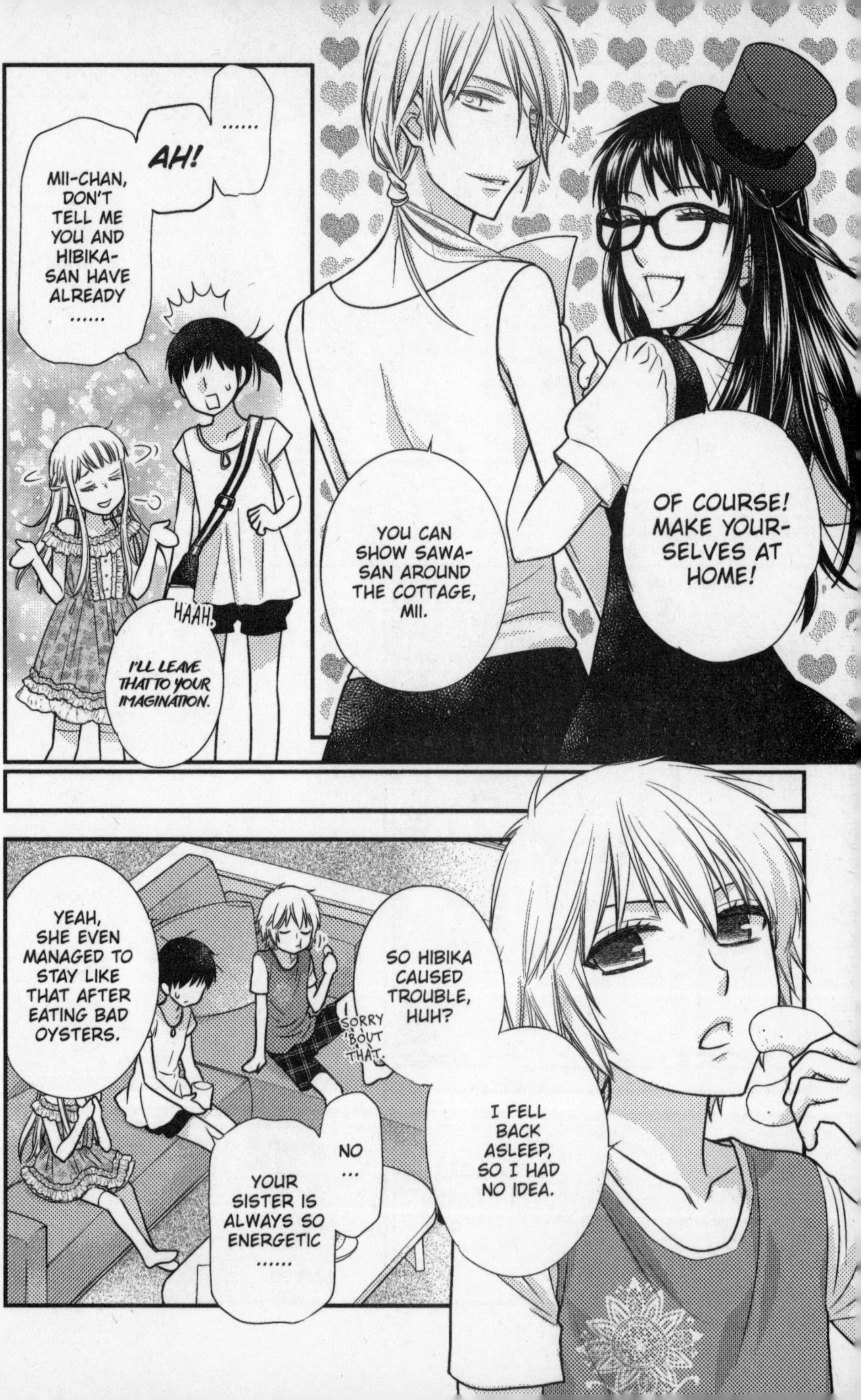
OF COURSE! MAKE YOUR-SELVES AT HOME!
YOU CAN SHOW SAWA-SAN AROUND THE COTTAGE, MII.
......
AH!
MII-CHAN, DON'T TELL ME YOU AND HIBIKA-SAN HAVE ALREADY ......
HAAH
I'LL LEAVE THAT TO YOUR IMAGINATION.
SO HIBIKA CAUSED TROUBLE, HUH?
SORRY 'BOUT THAT.
YEAH, SHE EVEN MANAGED TO STAY LIKE THAT AFTER EATING BAD OYSTERS.
I FELL BACK ASLEEP, SO I HAD NO IDEA.
NO ...
YOUR SISTER IS ALWAYS SO ENERGETIC ......

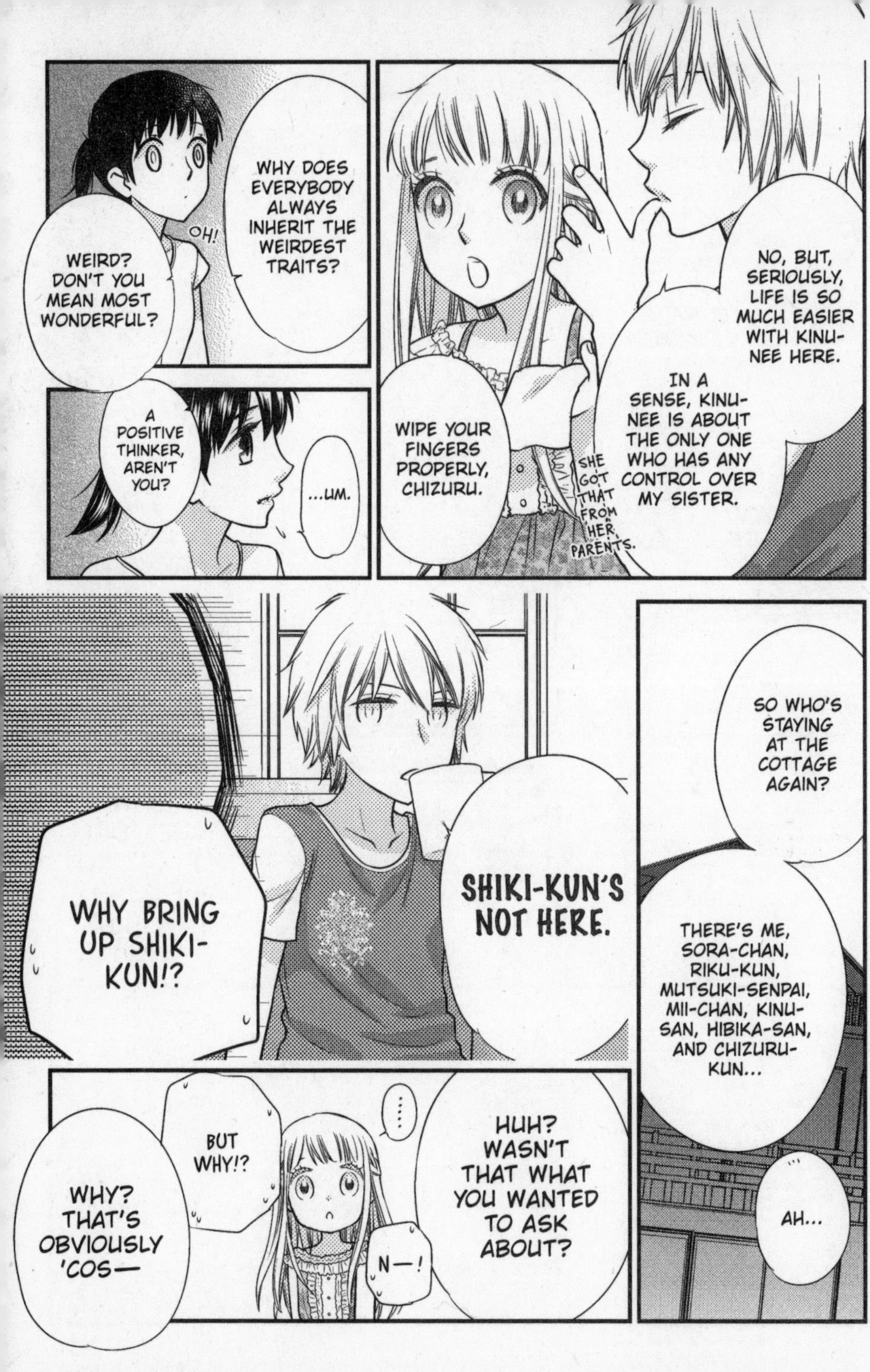
NO, BUT, SERIOUSLY, LIFE IS SO MUCH EASIER WITH KINU-NEE HERE.
IN A SENSE, KINU-NEE IS ABOUT THE ONLY ONE WHO HAS ANY CONTROL OVER MY SISTER.
SHE GOT THAT FROM HER PARENTS.
WIPE YOUR FINGERS PROPERLY, CHIZURU.
WHY DOES EVERYBODY ALWAYS INHERIT THE WEIRDEST TRAITS?
OH!
WEIRD? DON'T YOU MEAN MOST WONDERFUL?
...UM.
A POSITIVE THINKER, AREN'T YOU?
SO WHO'S STAYING AT THE COTTAGE AGAIN?
THERE'S ME, SORA-CHAN, RIKU-KUN, MUTSUKI-SENPAI, MII-CHAN, KINU-SAN, HIBIKA-SAN, AND CHIZURU-KUN...
...
AH...
SHIKI-KUN'S NOT HERE.
WHY BRING UP SHIKI-KUN!?
HUH? WASN'T THAT WHAT YOU WANTED TO ASK ABOUT?
......
N—!
BUT WHY!?
WHY? THAT'S OBVIOUSLY 'COS—

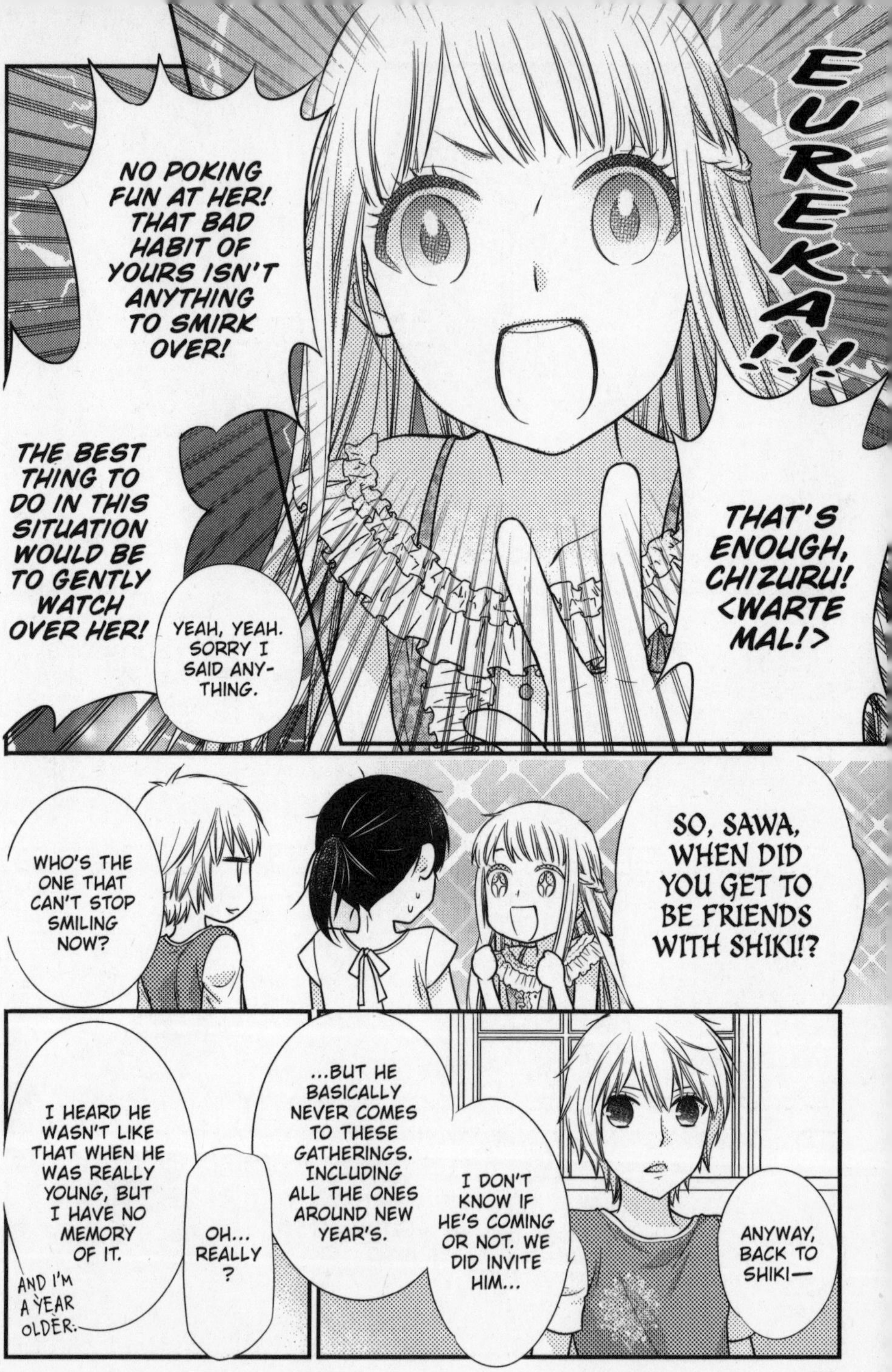
EUREKA!!!
THAT'S ENOUGH, CHIZURU! <WARTE MAL!>
NO POKING FUN AT HER! THAT BAD HABIT OF YOURS ISN'T ANYTHING TO SMIRK OVER!
THE BEST THING TO DO IN THIS SITUATION WOULD BE TO GENTLY WATCH OVER HER!
YEAH, YEAH. SORRY I SAID ANY-THING.
SO, SAWA, WHEN DID YOU GET TO BE FRIENDS WITH SHIKI!?
WHO'S THE ONE THAT CAN'T STOP SMILING NOW?
ANYWAY, BACK TO SHIKI—
I DON'T KNOW IF HE'S COMING OR NOT. WE DID INVITE HIM...
...BUT HE BASICALLY NEVER COMES TO THESE GATHERINGS. INCLUDING ALL THE ONES AROUND NEW YEAR'S.
OH... REALLY?
I HEARD HE WASN'T LIKE THAT WHEN HE WAS REALLY YOUNG, BUT I HAVE NO MEMORY OF IT.
AND I'M A YEAR OLDER.

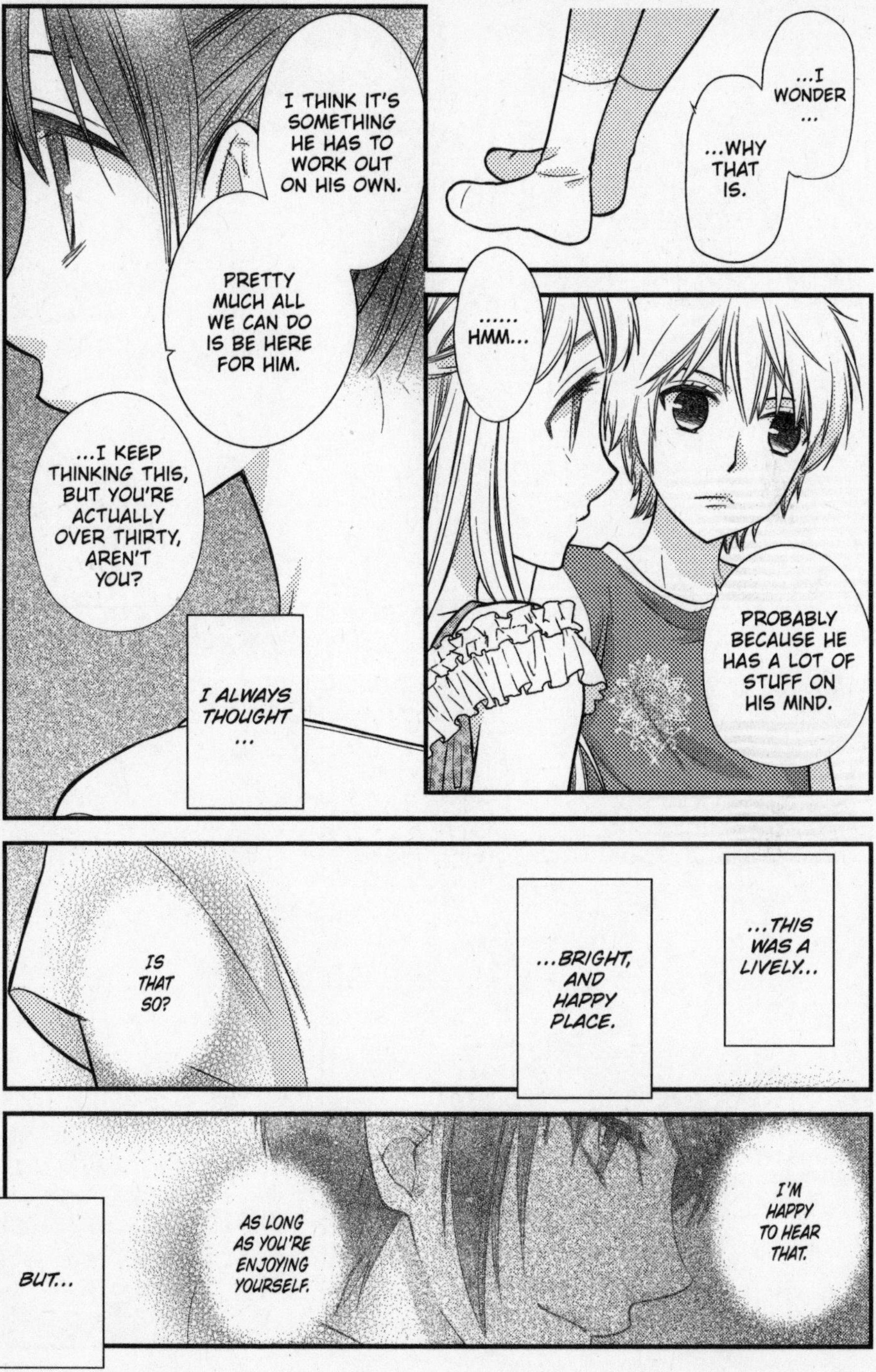
...I WONDER ...
...WHY THAT IS.
...... HMM...
PROBABLY BECAUSE HE HAS A LOT OF STUFF ON HIS MIND.
I THINK IT'S SOMETHING HE HAS TO WORK OUT ON HIS OWN.
PRETTY MUCH ALL WE CAN DO IS BE HERE FOR HIM.
...I KEEP THINKING THIS, BUT YOU'RE ACTUALLY OVER THIRTY, AREN'T YOU?
I ALWAYS THOUGHT ...
...THIS WAS A LIVELY...
...BRIGHT, AND HAPPY PLACE.
IS THAT SO?
I'M HAPPY TO HEAR THAT.
AS LONG AS YOU'RE ENJOYING YOURSELF.
BUT...

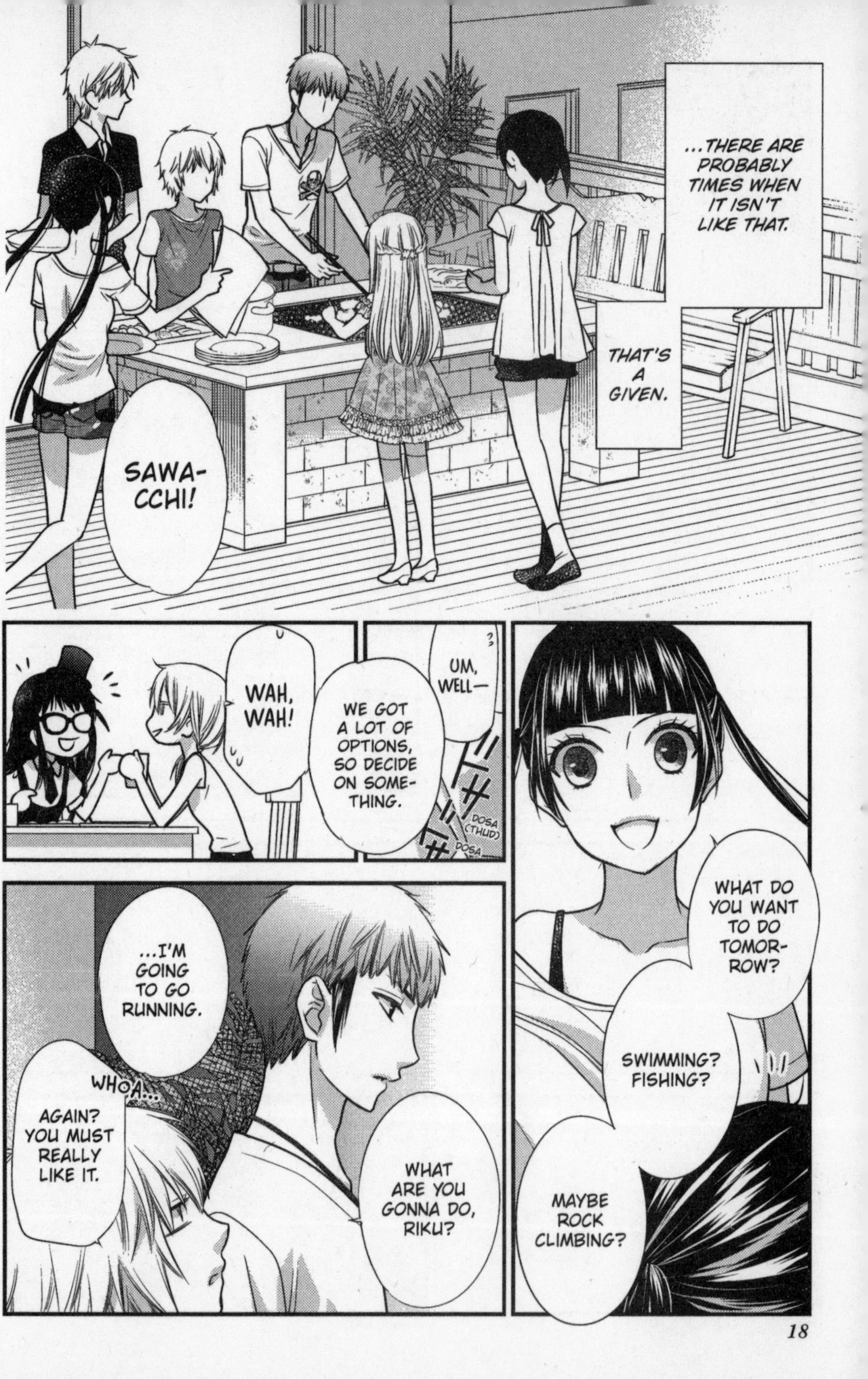
...THERE ARE PROBABLY TIMES WHEN IT ISN'T LIKE THAT.
THAT'S A GIVEN.
SAWA-CCHI!
WHAT DO YOU WANT TO DO TOMOR-ROW?
SWIMMING? FISHING?
MAYBE ROCK CLIMBING?
UM, WELL—
WE GOT A LOT OF OPTIONS, SO DECIDE ON SOME-THING.
DOSA (THUD)
DOSA
WAH, WAH!
WHAT ARE YOU GONNA DO, RIKU?
...I'M GOING TO GO RUNNING.
WHOA...
AGAIN? YOU MUST REALLY LIKE IT.

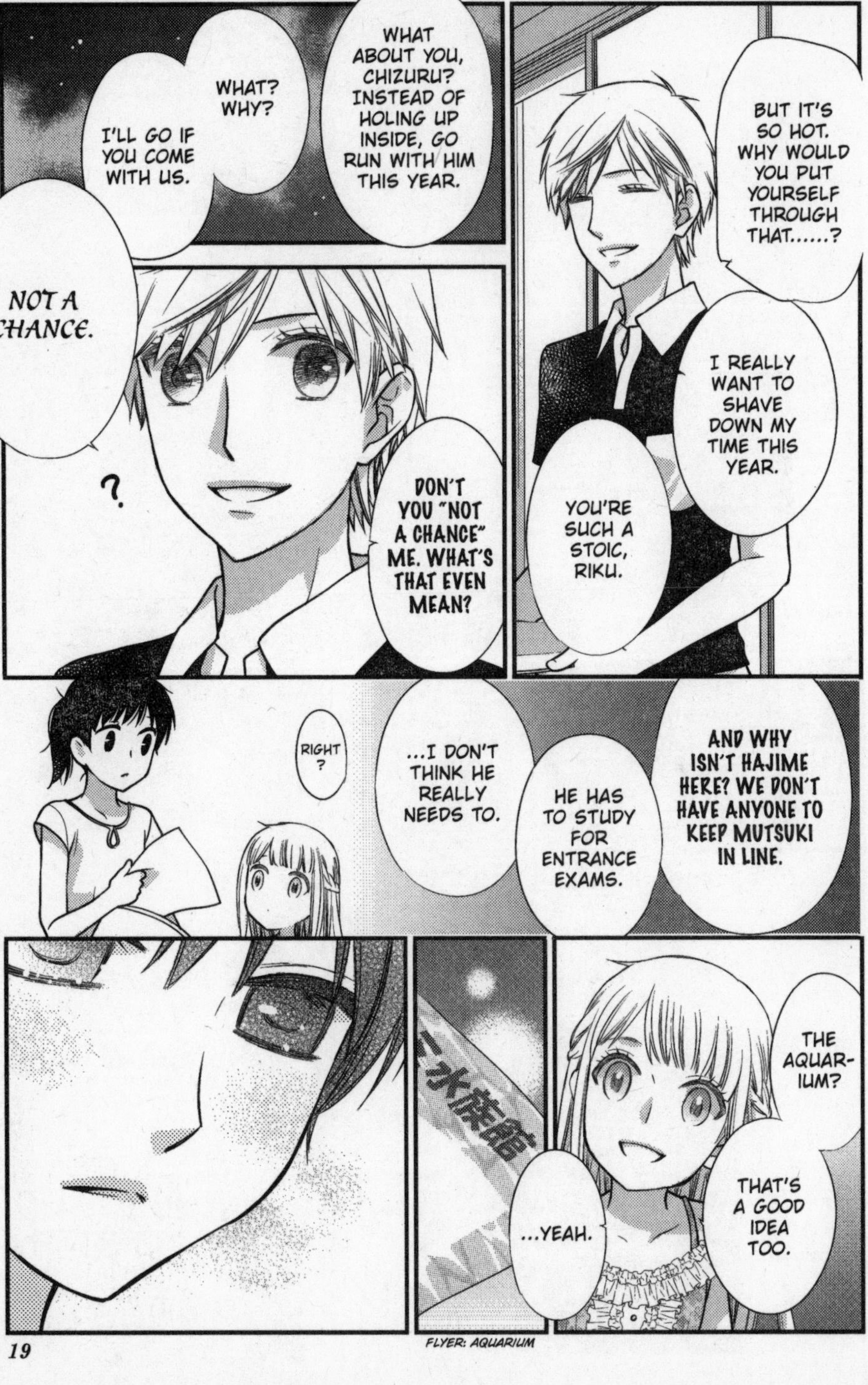
BUT IT'S SO HOT. WHY WOULD YOU PUT YOURSELF THROUGH THAT......?
I REALLY WANT TO SHAVE DOWN MY TIME THIS YEAR.
YOU'RE SUCH A STOIC, RIKU.
WHAT ABOUT YOU, CHIZURU? INSTEAD OF HOLING UP INSIDE, GO RUN WITH HIM THIS YEAR.
WHAT? WHY?
I'LL GO IF YOU COME WITH US.
NOT A CHANCE.
DON'T YOU "NOT A CHANCE" ME. WHAT'S THAT EVEN MEAN?
?
AND WHY ISN'T HAJIME HERE? WE DON'T HAVE ANYONE TO KEEP MUTSUKI IN LINE.
HE HAS TO STUDY FOR ENTRANCE EXAMS.
...I DON'T THINK HE REALLY NEEDS TO.
RIGHT?
THE AQUARIUM?
THAT'S A GOOD IDEA TOO.
...YEAH.
水族館
FLYER: AQUARIUM

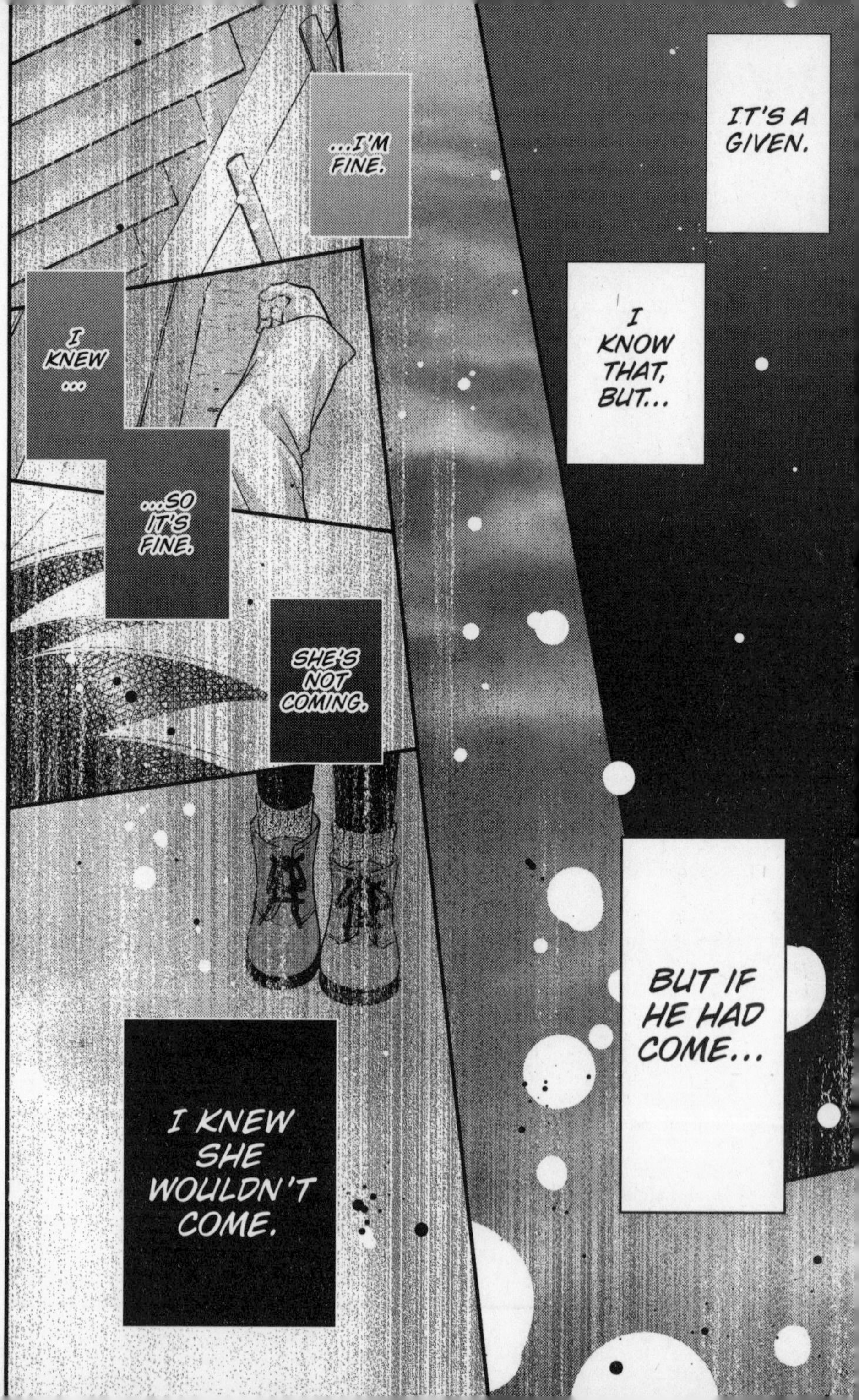
IT'S A GIVEN.
I KNOW THAT, BUT...
BUT IF HE HAD COME...
...I'M FINE.
I KNEW...
...SO IT'S FINE.
SHE'S NOT COMING.
I KNEW SHE WOULDN'T COME.

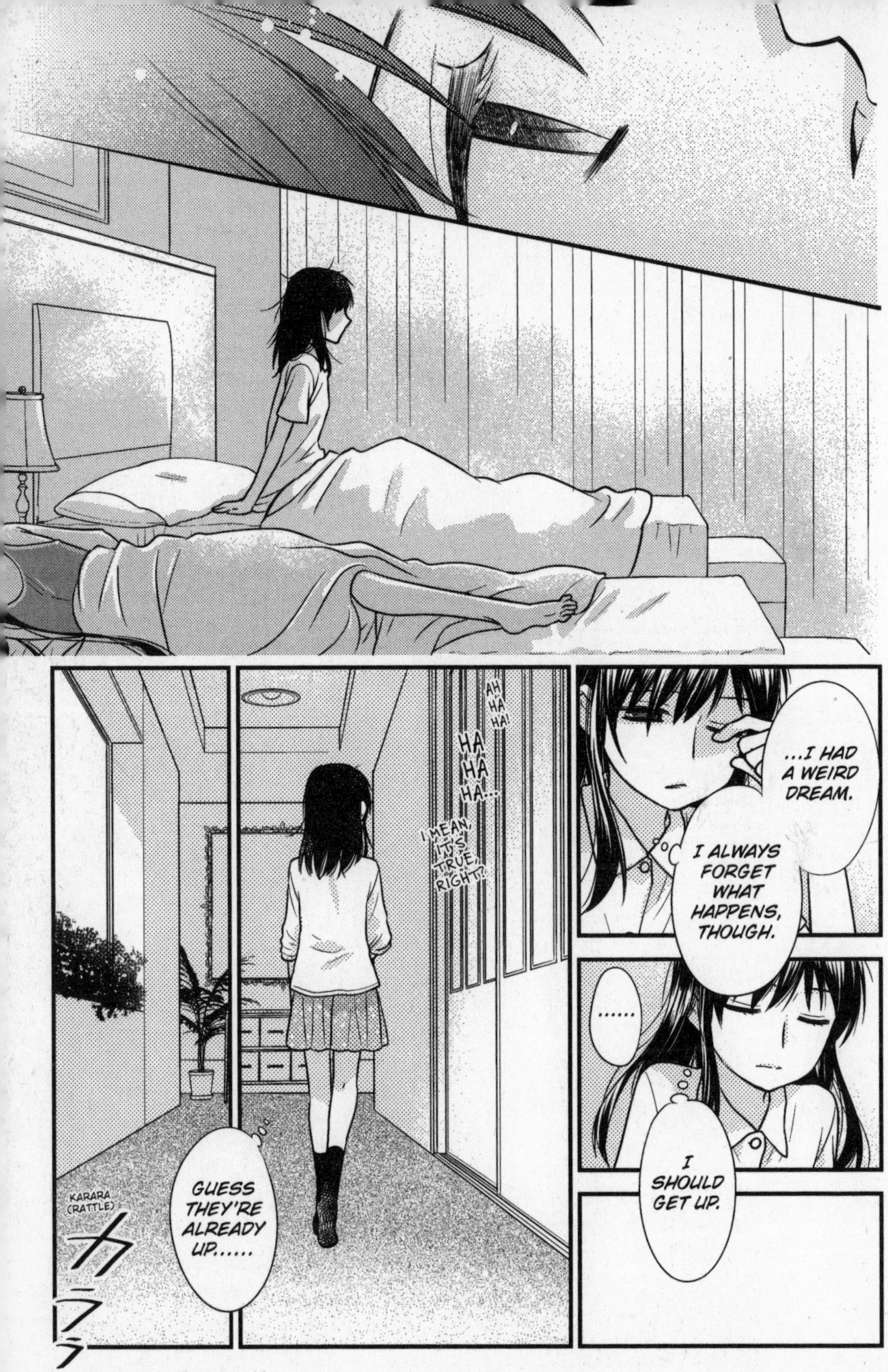
...I HAD A WEIRD DREAM.
I ALWAYS FORGET WHAT HAPPENS, THOUGH.
......
I SHOULD GET UP.
AH HA HA!
HA HA HA...
I MEAN, IT'S TRUE, RIGHT!?
GUESS THEY'RE ALREADY UP......
KARARA (RATTLE)

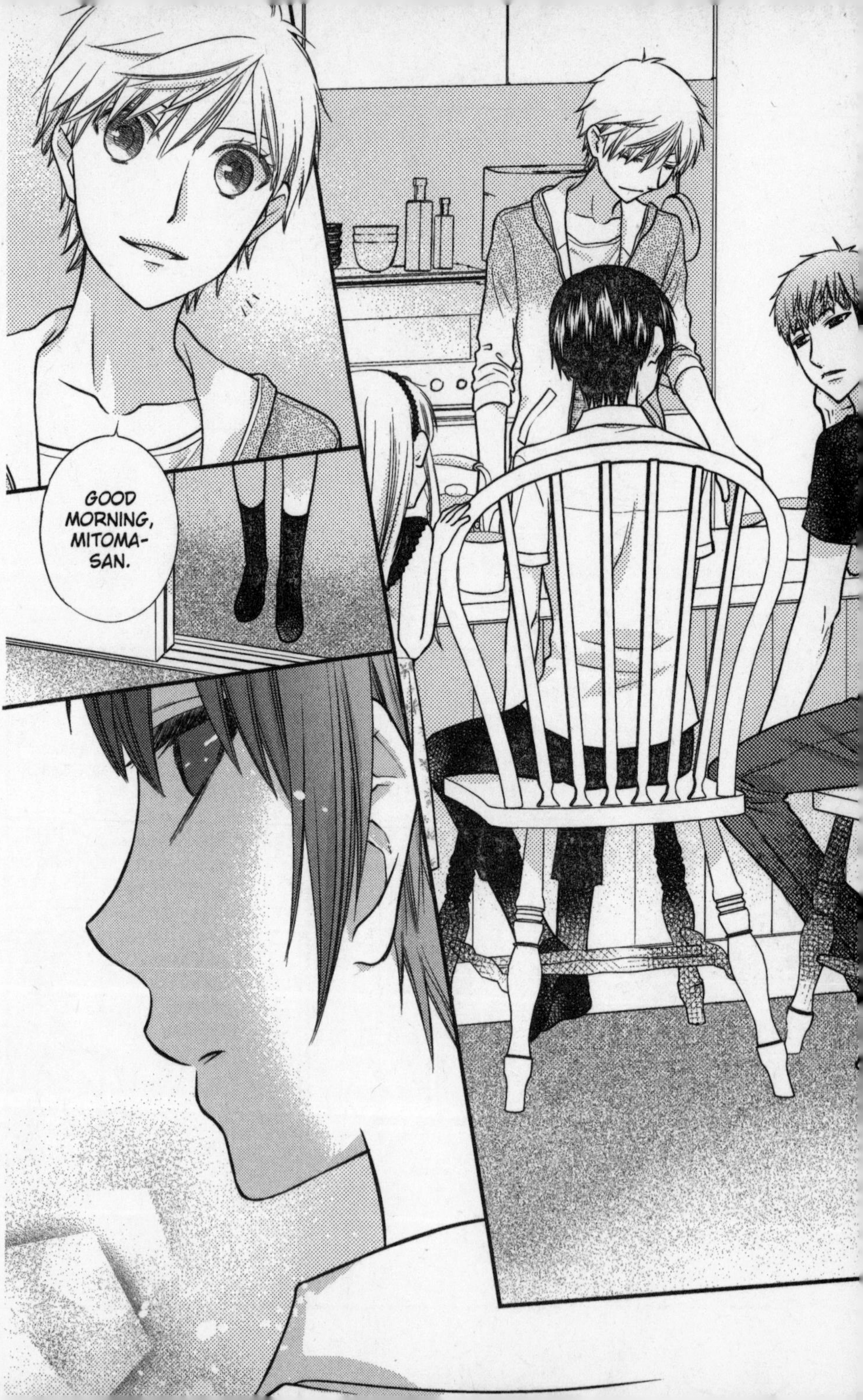
GOOD MORNING, MITOMA-SAN.

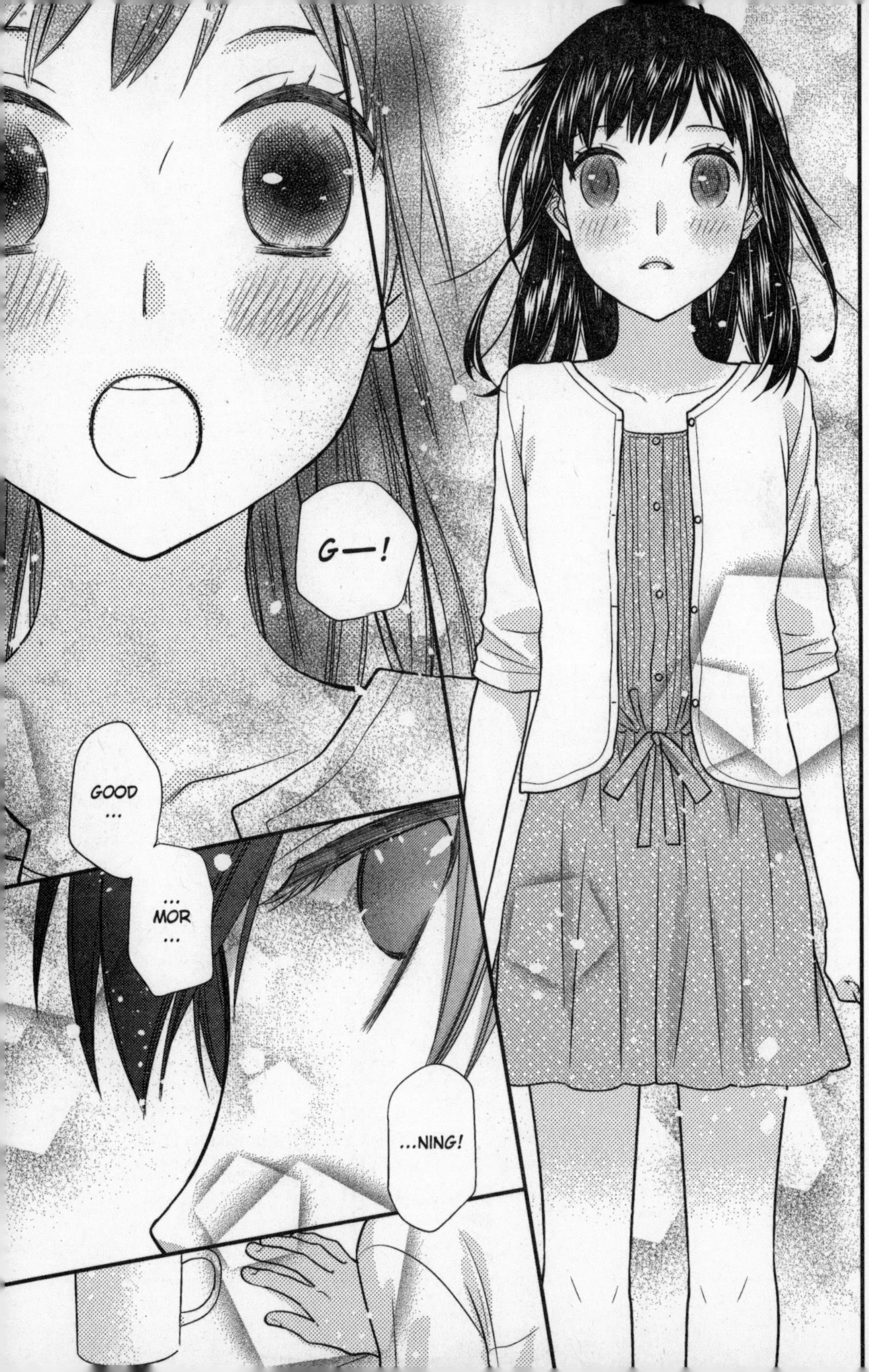
G—!
GOOD ...
... MOR ...
...NING!

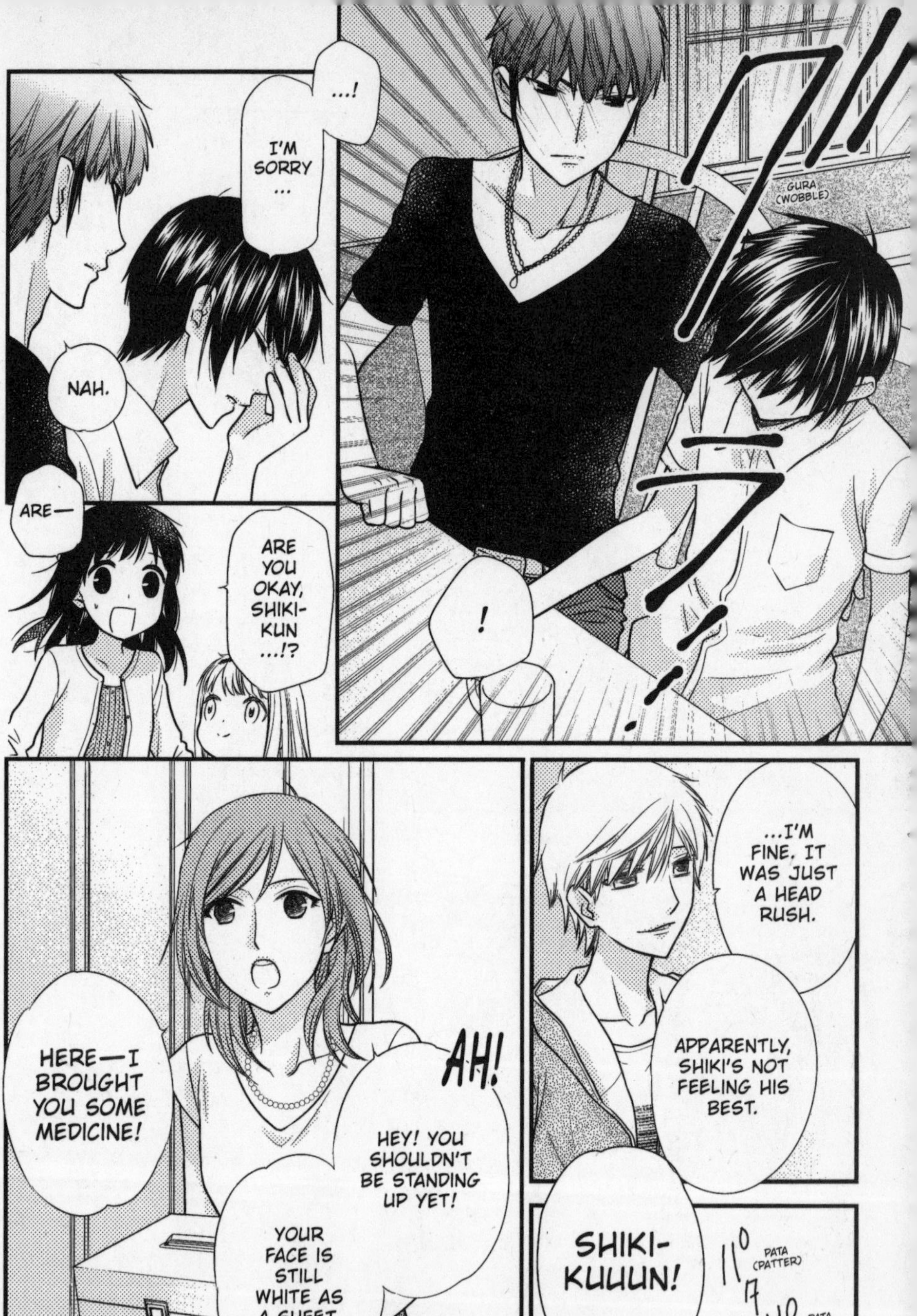
GURA (WOBBLE)
!
...!
I'M SORRY ...
NAH.
ARE—
ARE YOU OKAY, SHIKI-KUN ...!?
...I'M FINE. IT WAS JUST A HEAD RUSH.
APPARENTLY, SHIKI'S NOT FEELING HIS BEST.
PATA (PATTER)
PATA
SHIKI-KUUUN!
AH!
HEY! YOU SHOULDN'T BE STANDING UP YET!
YOUR FACE IS STILL WHITE AS A SHEET.
HERE—I BROUGHT YOU SOME MEDICINE!

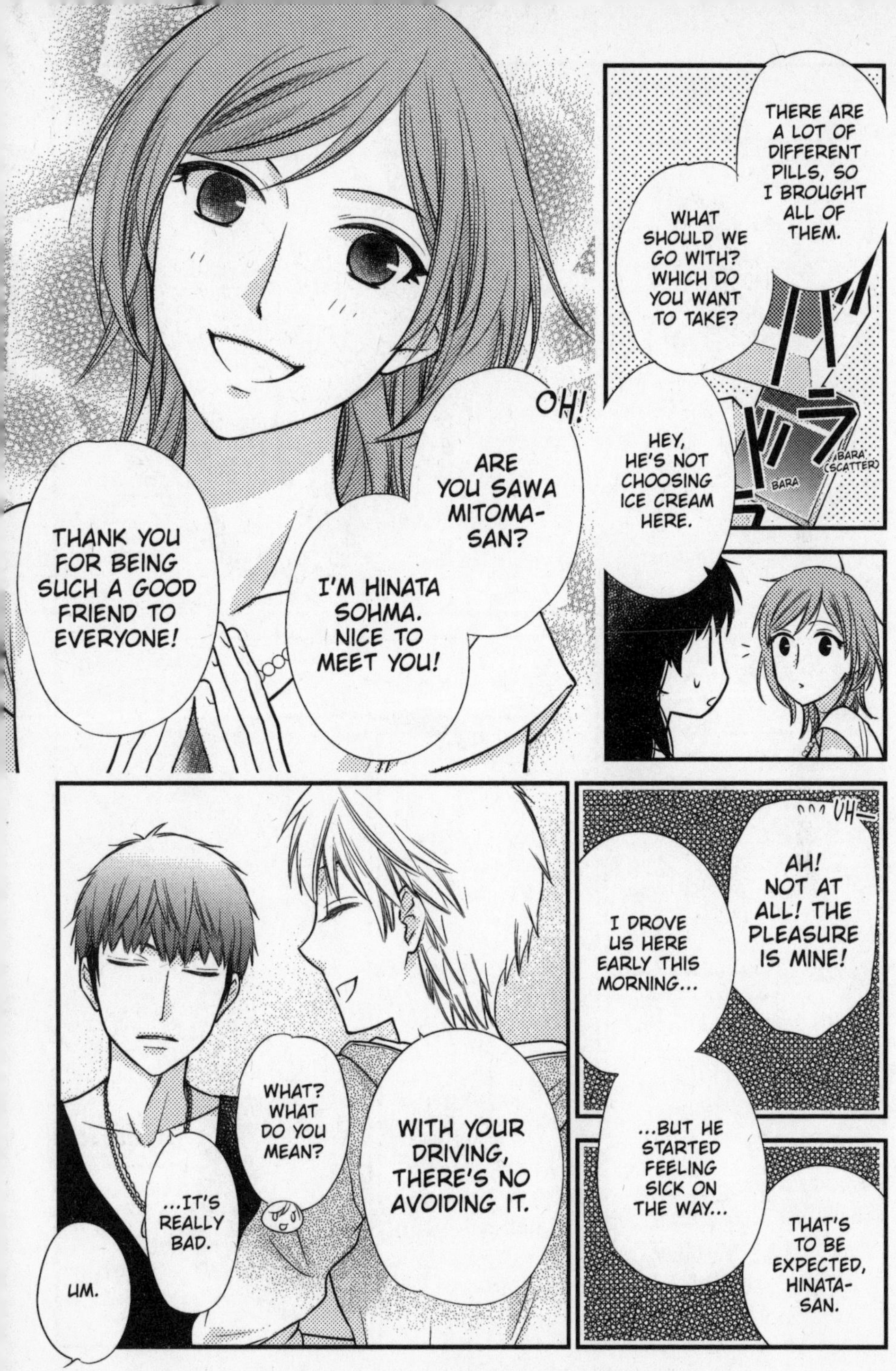
THERE ARE A LOT OF DIFFERENT PILLS, SO I BROUGHT ALL OF THEM.
WHAT SHOULD WE GO WITH? WHICH DO YOU WANT TO TAKE?
BARA (SCATTER)
BARA
HEY, HE'S NOT CHOOSING ICE CREAM HERE.
OH!
ARE YOU SAWA MITOMA-SAN?
I'M HINATA SOHMA. NICE TO MEET YOU!
THANK YOU FOR BEING SUCH A GOOD FRIEND TO EVERYONE!
UH—
AH! NOT AT ALL! THE PLEASURE IS MINE!
I DROVE US HERE EARLY THIS MORNING...
...BUT HE STARTED FEELING SICK ON THE WAY...
THAT'S TO BE EXPECTED, HINATA-SAN.
WITH YOUR DRIVING, THERE'S NO AVOIDING IT.
WHAT? WHAT DO YOU MEAN?
...IT'S REALLY BAD.
UM.

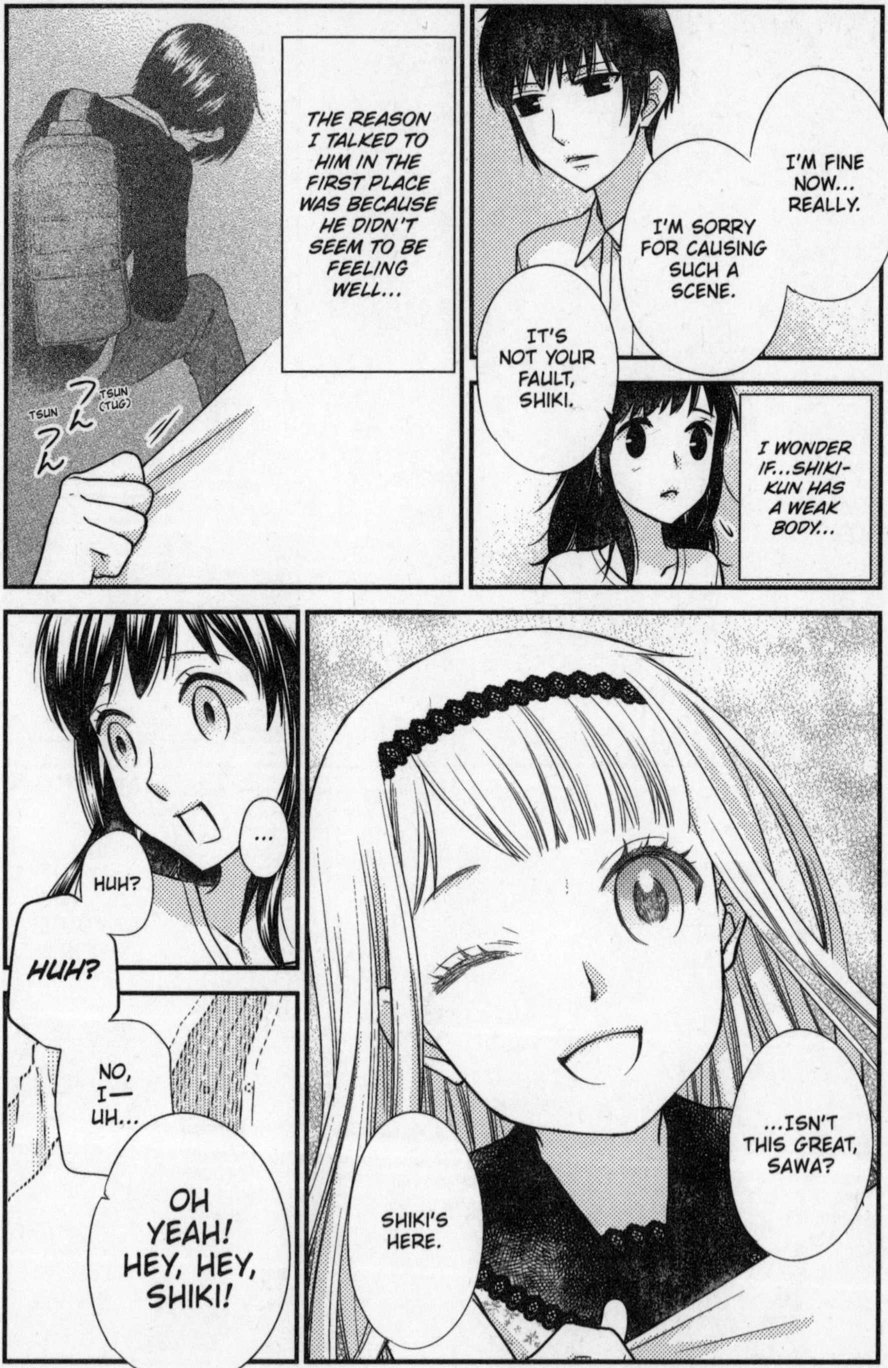
I'M FINE NOW... REALLY.
I'M SORRY FOR CAUSING SUCH A SCENE.
IT'S NOT YOUR FAULT, SHIKI.
I WONDER IF...SHIKI-KUN HAS A WEAK BODY...
THE REASON I TALKED TO HIM IN THE FIRST PLACE WAS BECAUSE HE DIDN'T SEEM TO BE FEELING WELL...
つん TSUN (TUG)
つん TSUN
...ISN'T THIS GREAT, SAWA?
SHIKI'S HERE.
...
HUH?
HUH?
NO, I— UH...
OH YEAH! HEY, HEY, SHIKI!

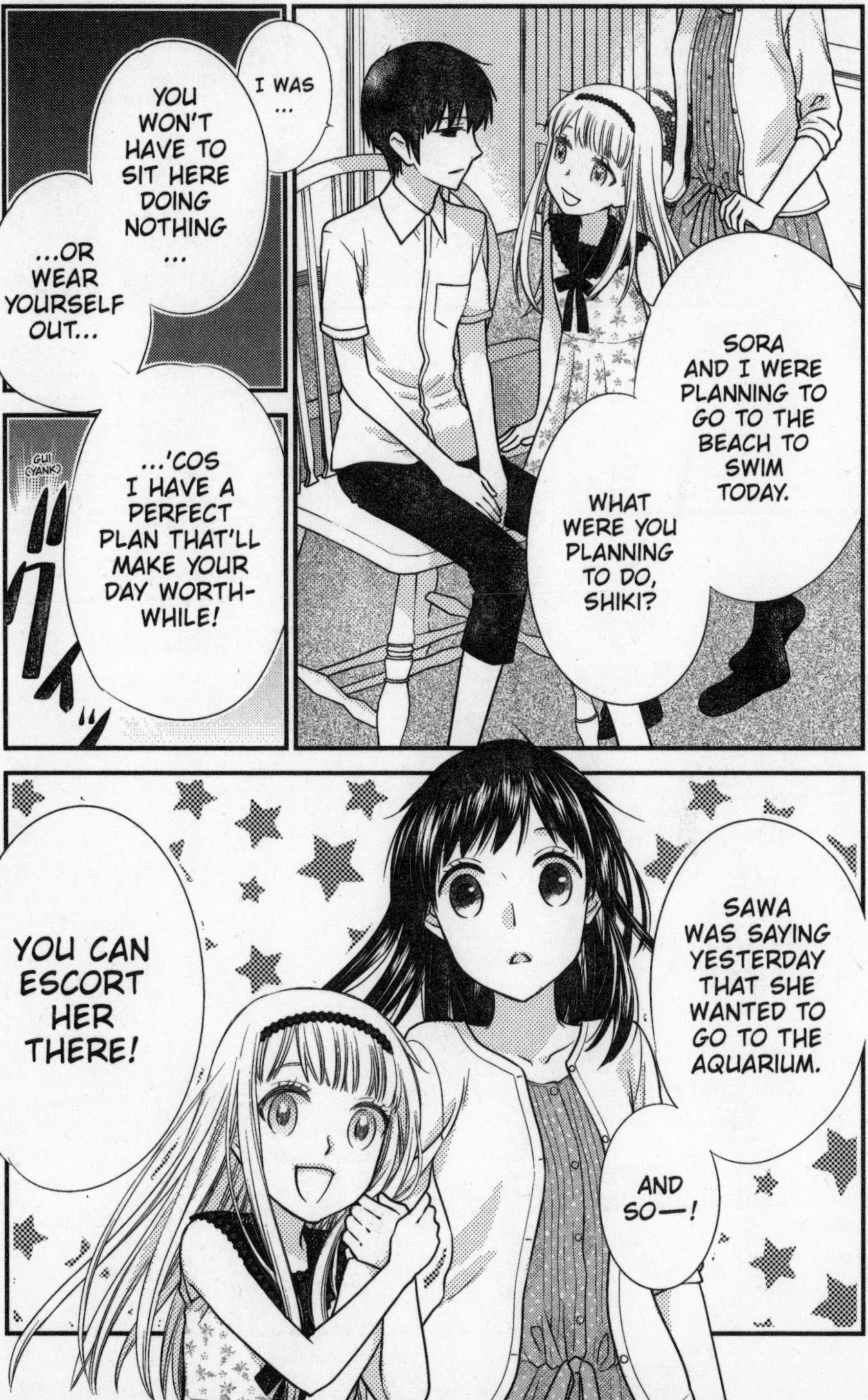
SORA AND I WERE PLANNING TO GO TO THE BEACH TO SWIM TODAY.
WHAT WERE YOU PLANNING TO DO, SHIKI?
I WAS ...
YOU WON'T HAVE TO SIT HERE DOING NOTHING ...
...OR WEAR YOURSELF OUT...
...'COS I HAVE A PERFECT PLAN THAT'LL MAKE YOUR DAY WORTH-WHILE!
GUI (YANK)
SAWA WAS SAYING YESTERDAY THAT SHE WANTED TO GO TO THE AQUARIUM.
AND SO—!
YOU CAN ESCORT HER THERE!

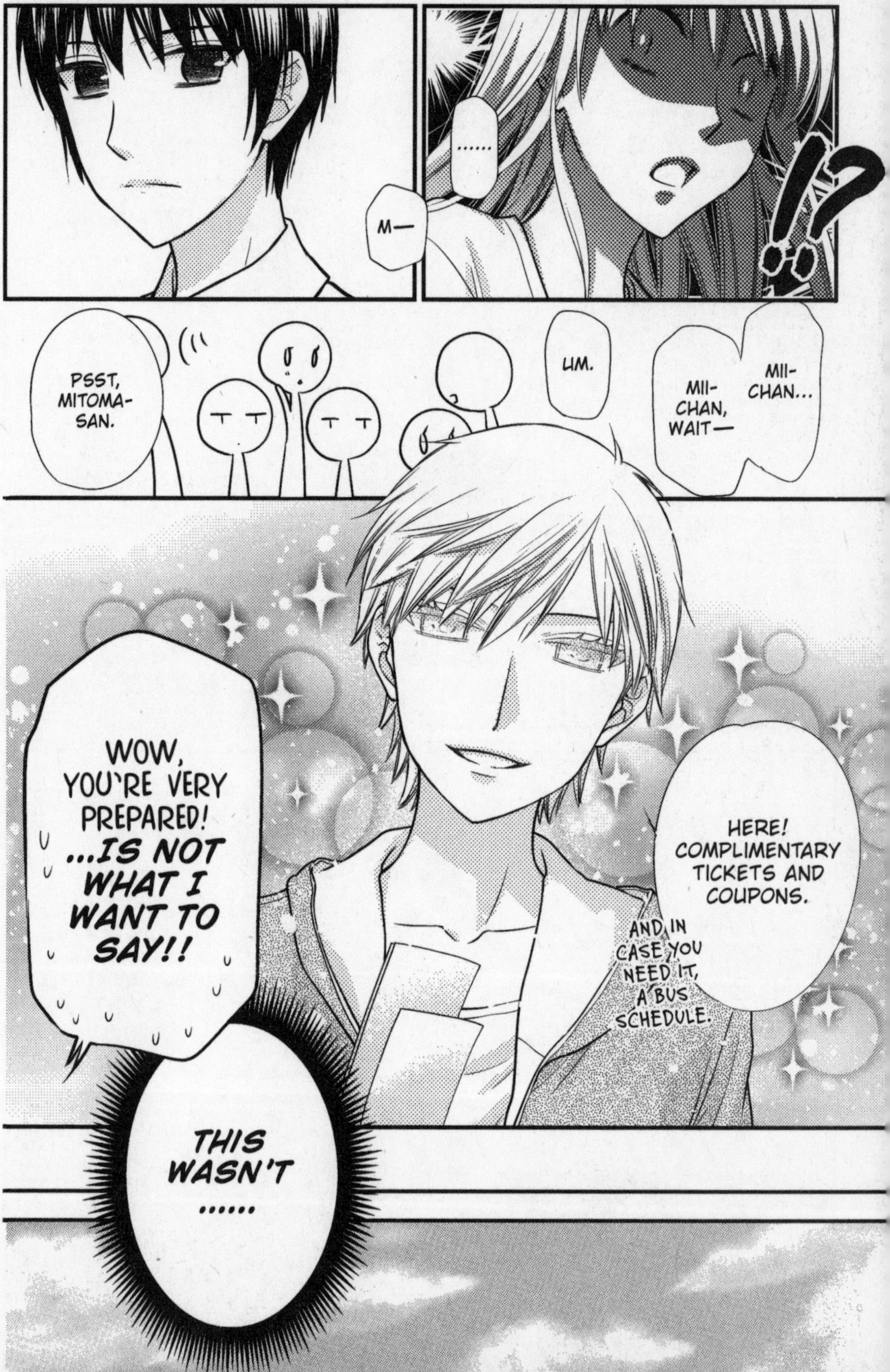
......
M—
!?
MII-CHAN...
MII-CHAN, WAIT—
UM.
PSST, MITOMA-SAN.
HERE! COMPLIMENTARY TICKETS AND COUPONS.
AND IN CASE YOU NEED IT, A BUS SCHEDULE.
WOW, YOU'RE VERY PREPARED! ...IS NOT WHAT I WANT TO SAY!!
THIS WASN'T ......

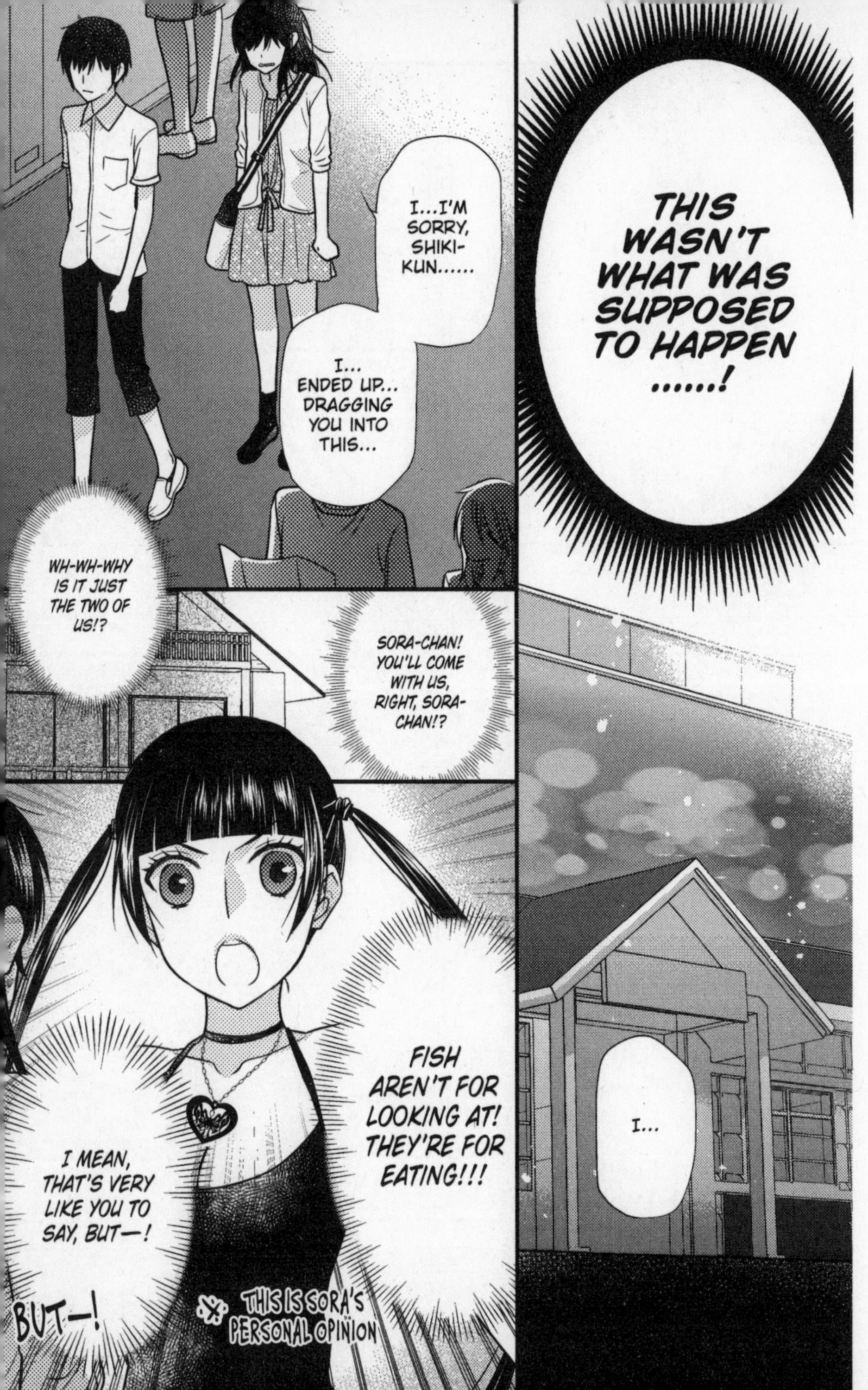
THIS WASN'T WHAT WAS SUPPOSED TO HAPPEN ......!
I...I'M SORRY, SHIKI-KUN......
I... ENDED UP... DRAGGING YOU INTO THIS...
I...
WH-WH-WHY IS IT JUST THE TWO OF US!?
SORA-CHAN! YOU'LL COME WITH US, RIGHT, SORA-CHAN!?
FISH AREN'T FOR LOOKING AT! THEY'RE FOR EATING!!!
I MEAN, THAT'S VERY LIKE YOU TO SAY, BUT—!
BUT—!
※ THIS IS SORA'S PERSONAL OPINION

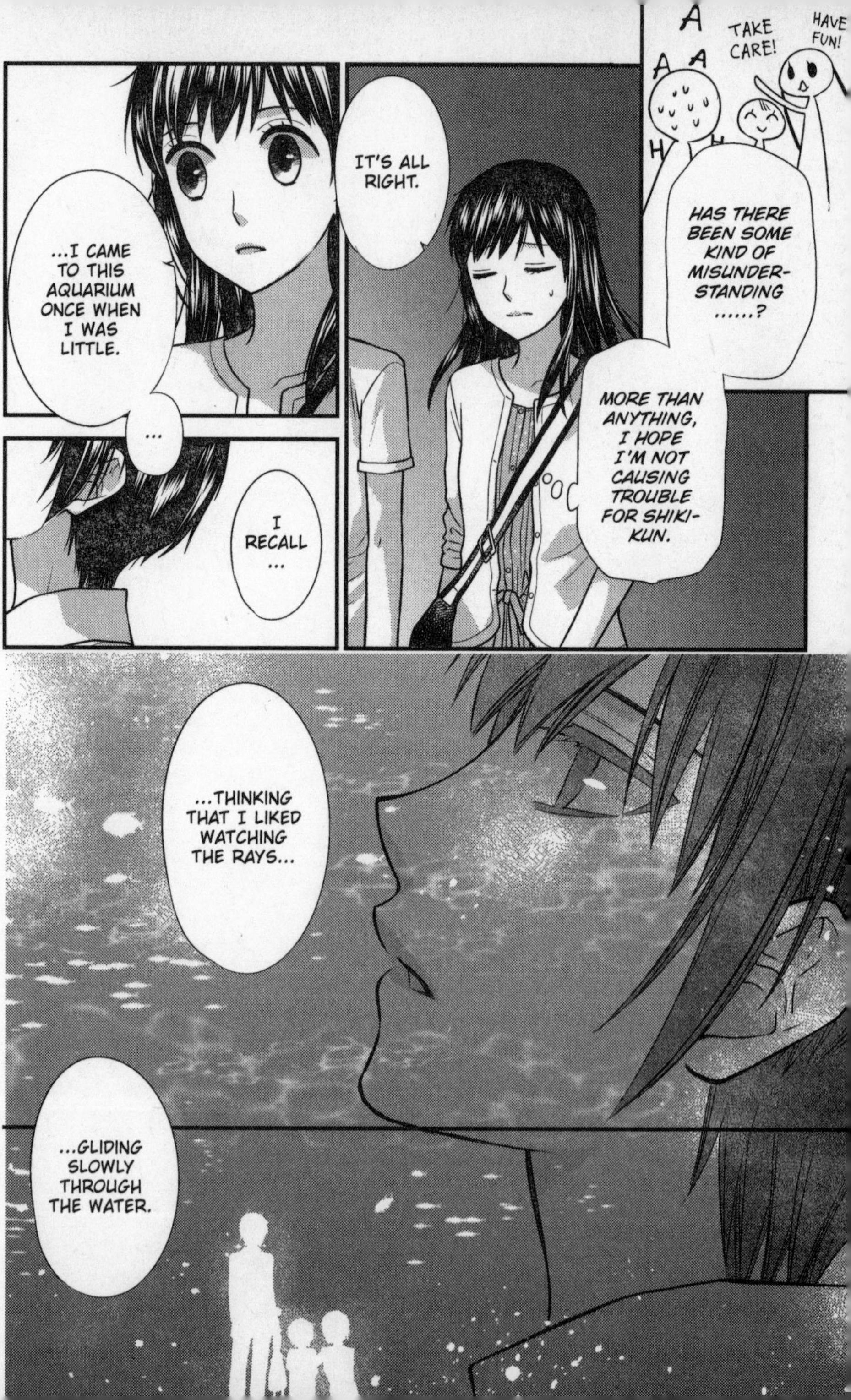
AAAH
TAKE CARE!
HAVE FUN!
HAS THERE BEEN SOME KIND OF MISUNDERSTANDING ......?
IT'S ALL RIGHT.
MORE THAN ANYTHING, I HOPE I'M NOT CAUSING TROUBLE FOR SHIKI-KUN.
...I CAME TO THIS AQUARIUM ONCE WHEN I WAS LITTLE.
...
I RECALL ...
...THINKING THAT I LIKED WATCHING THE RAYS...
...GLIDING SLOWLY THROUGH THE WATER.

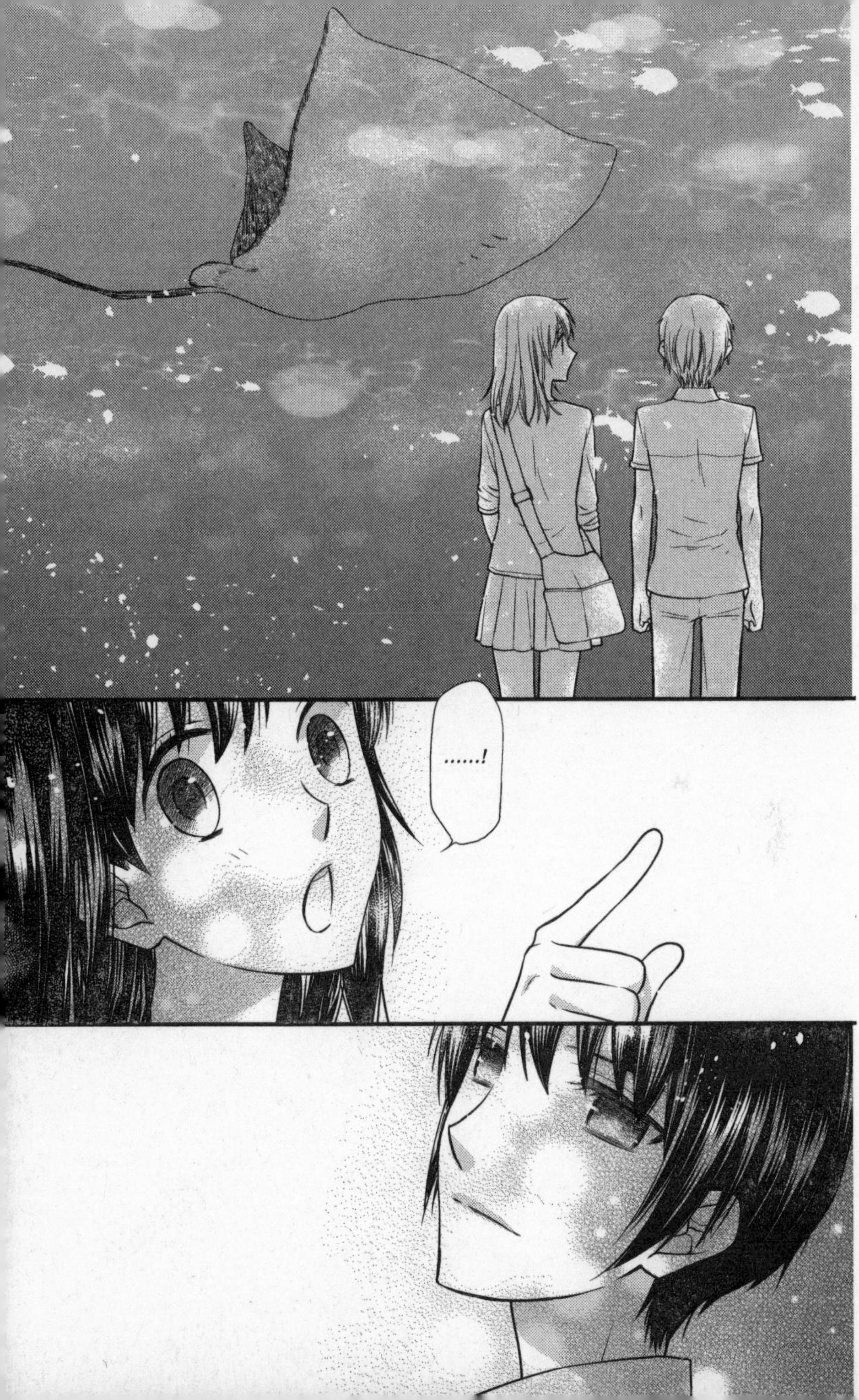

......!

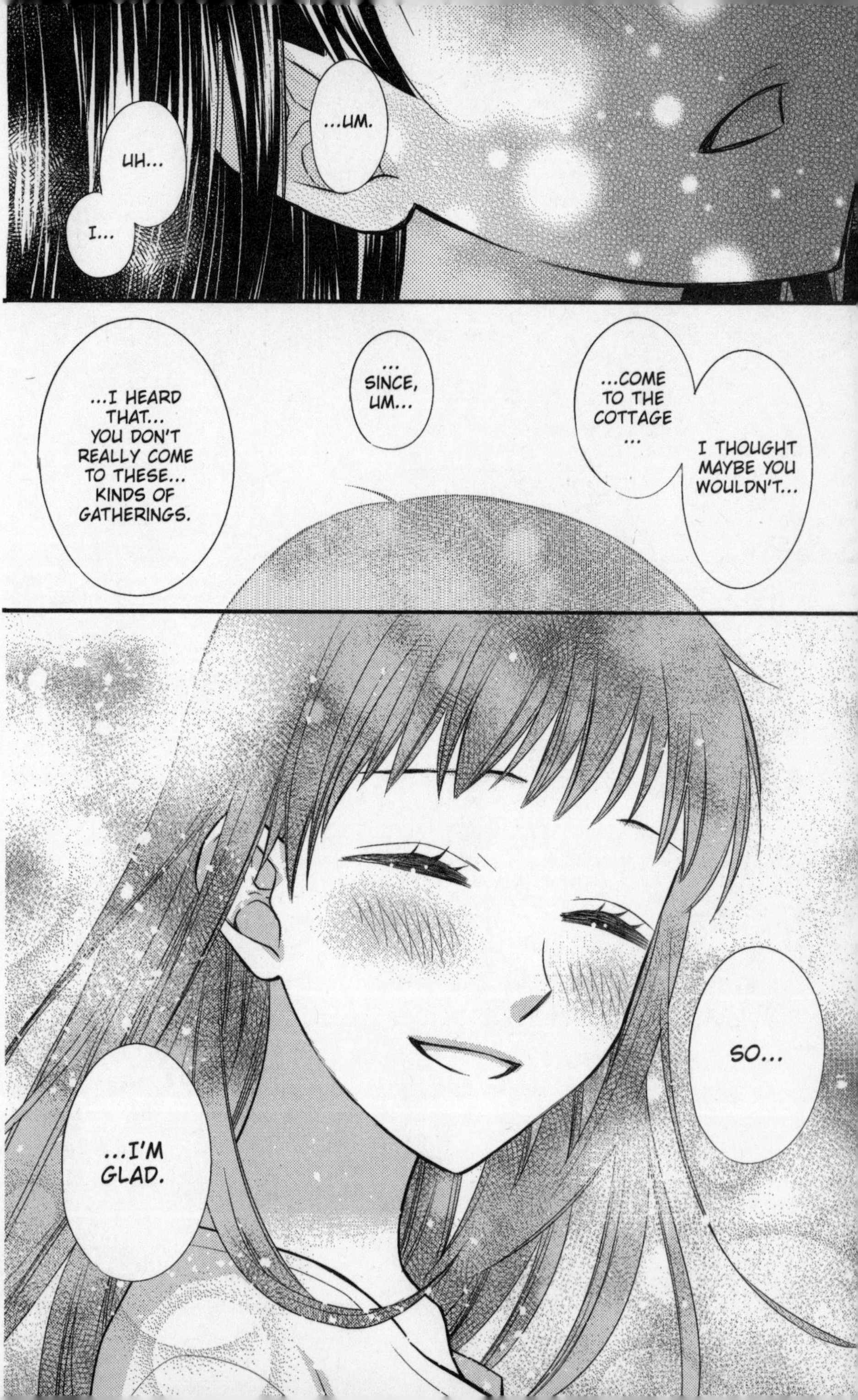
...UM.
UH...
I...
I THOUGHT MAYBE YOU WOULDN'T...
...COME TO THE COTTAGE ...
... SINCE, UM...
...I HEARD THAT... YOU DON'T REALLY COME TO THESE... KINDS OF GATHERINGS.
SO...
...I'M GLAD.

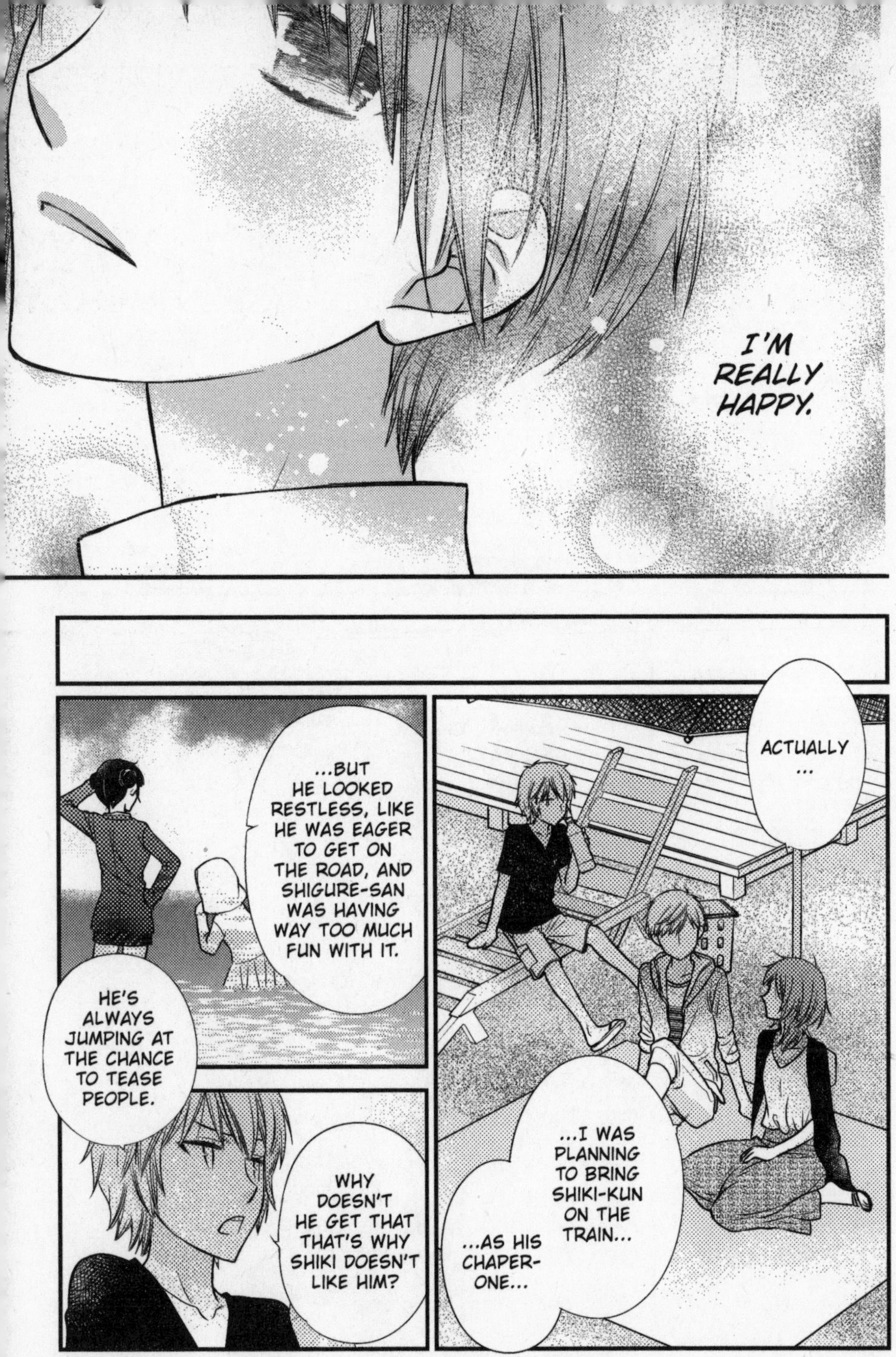
I'M REALLY HAPPY.
ACTUALLY ...
...I WAS PLANNING TO BRING SHIKI-KUN ON THE TRAIN...
...AS HIS CHAPER-ONE...
...BUT HE LOOKED RESTLESS, LIKE HE WAS EAGER TO GET ON THE ROAD, AND SHIGURE-SAN WAS HAVING WAY TOO MUCH FUN WITH IT.
HE'S ALWAYS JUMPING AT THE CHANCE TO TEASE PEOPLE.
WHY DOESN'T HE GET THAT THAT'S WHY SHIKI DOESN'T LIKE HIM?

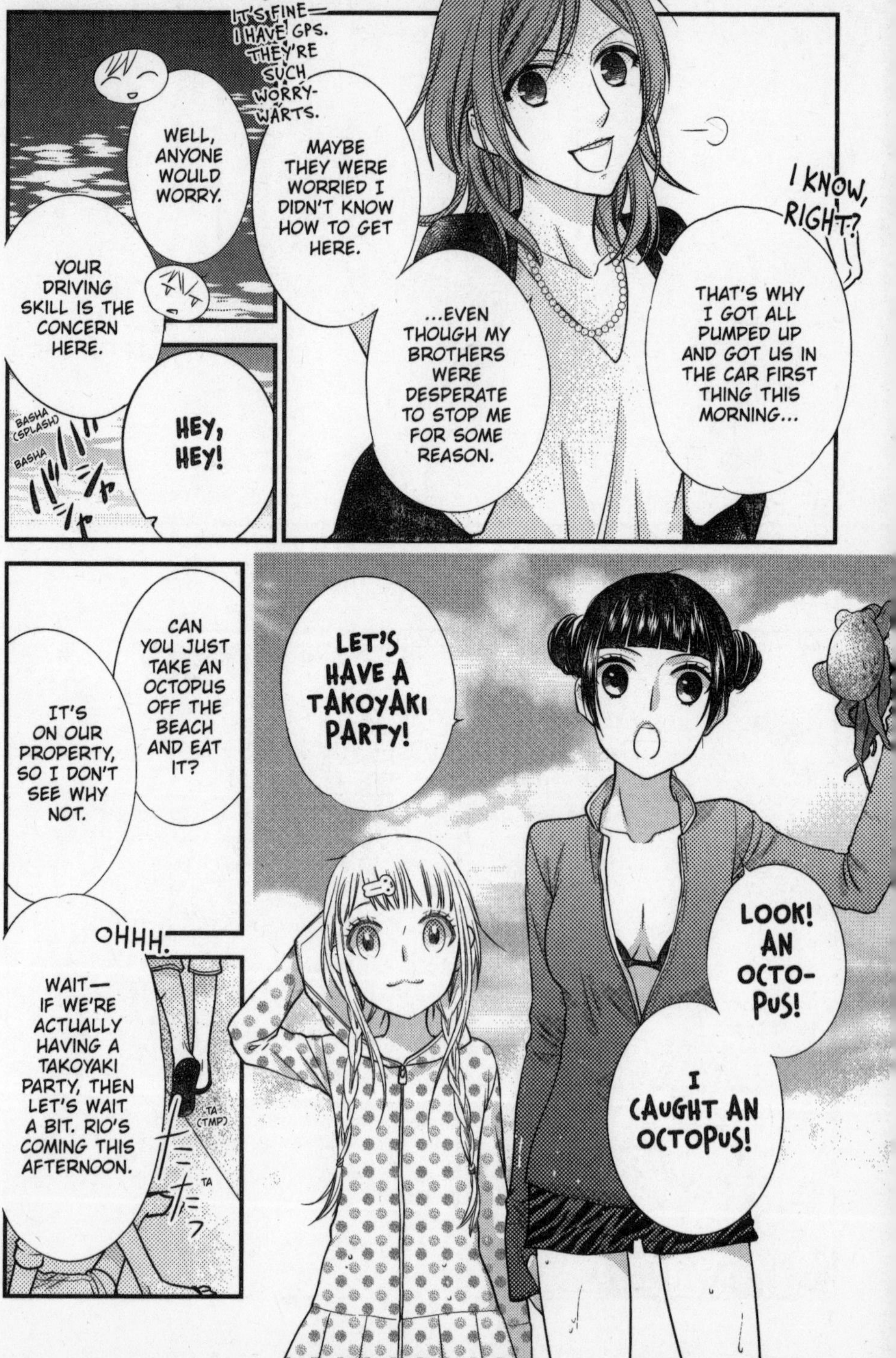
I KNOW, RIGHT?
THAT'S WHY I GOT ALL PUMPED UP AND GOT US IN THE CAR FIRST THING THIS MORNING...
...EVEN THOUGH MY BROTHERS WERE DESPERATE TO STOP ME FOR SOME REASON.
MAYBE THEY WERE WORRIED I DIDN'T KNOW HOW TO GET HERE.
BUT IT'S FINE— I HAVE GPS. THEY'RE SUCH WORRY-WARTS.
WELL, ANYONE WOULD WORRY.
YOUR DRIVING SKILL IS THE CONCERN HERE.
HEY, HEY!
BASHA (SPLASH)
BASHA
LOOK! AN OCTO-PUS!
I CAUGHT AN OCTOPUS!
LET'S HAVE A TAKOYAKI PARTY!
CAN YOU JUST TAKE AN OCTOPUS OFF THE BEACH AND EAT IT?
IT'S ON OUR PROPERTY, SO I DON'T SEE WHY NOT.
OHHH.
WAIT— IF WE'RE ACTUALLY HAVING A TAKOYAKI PARTY, THEN LET'S WAIT A BIT. RIO'S COMING THIS AFTERNOON.
TA (TMP)
TA

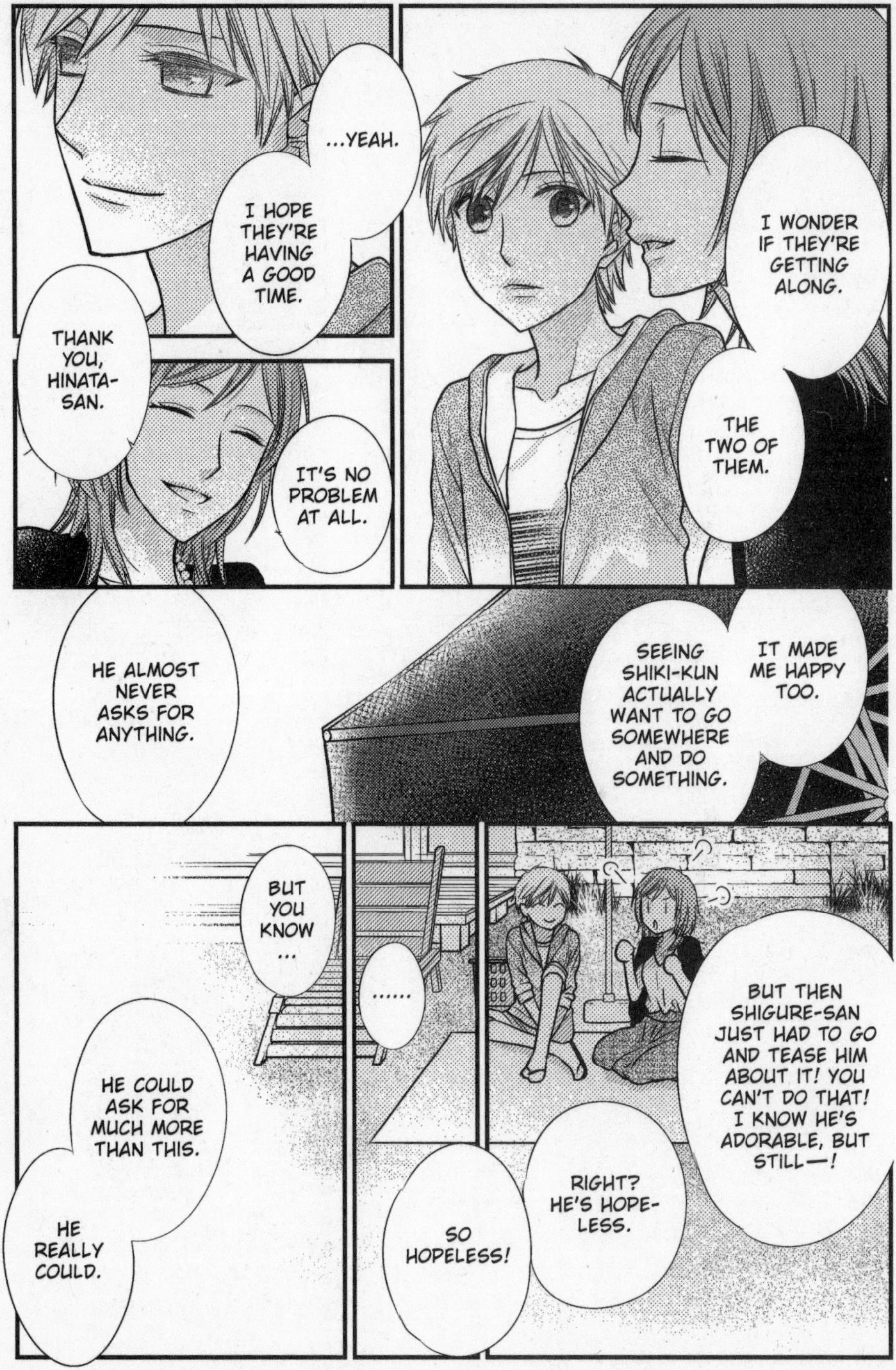
I WONDER IF THEY'RE GETTING ALONG.
THE TWO OF THEM.
...YEAH.
I HOPE THEY'RE HAVING A GOOD TIME.
THANK YOU, HINATA-SAN.
IT'S NO PROBLEM AT ALL.
IT MADE ME HAPPY TOO.
SEEING SHIKI-KUN ACTUALLY WANT TO GO SOMEWHERE AND DO SOMETHING.
HE ALMOST NEVER ASKS FOR ANYTHING.
BUT THEN SHIGURE-SAN JUST HAD TO GO AND TEASE HIM ABOUT IT! YOU CAN'T DO THAT! I KNOW HE'S ADORABLE, BUT STILL—!
RIGHT? HE'S HOPE-LESS.
SO HOPELESS!
......
BUT YOU KNOW ...
HE COULD ASK FOR MUCH MORE THAN THIS.
HE REALLY COULD.

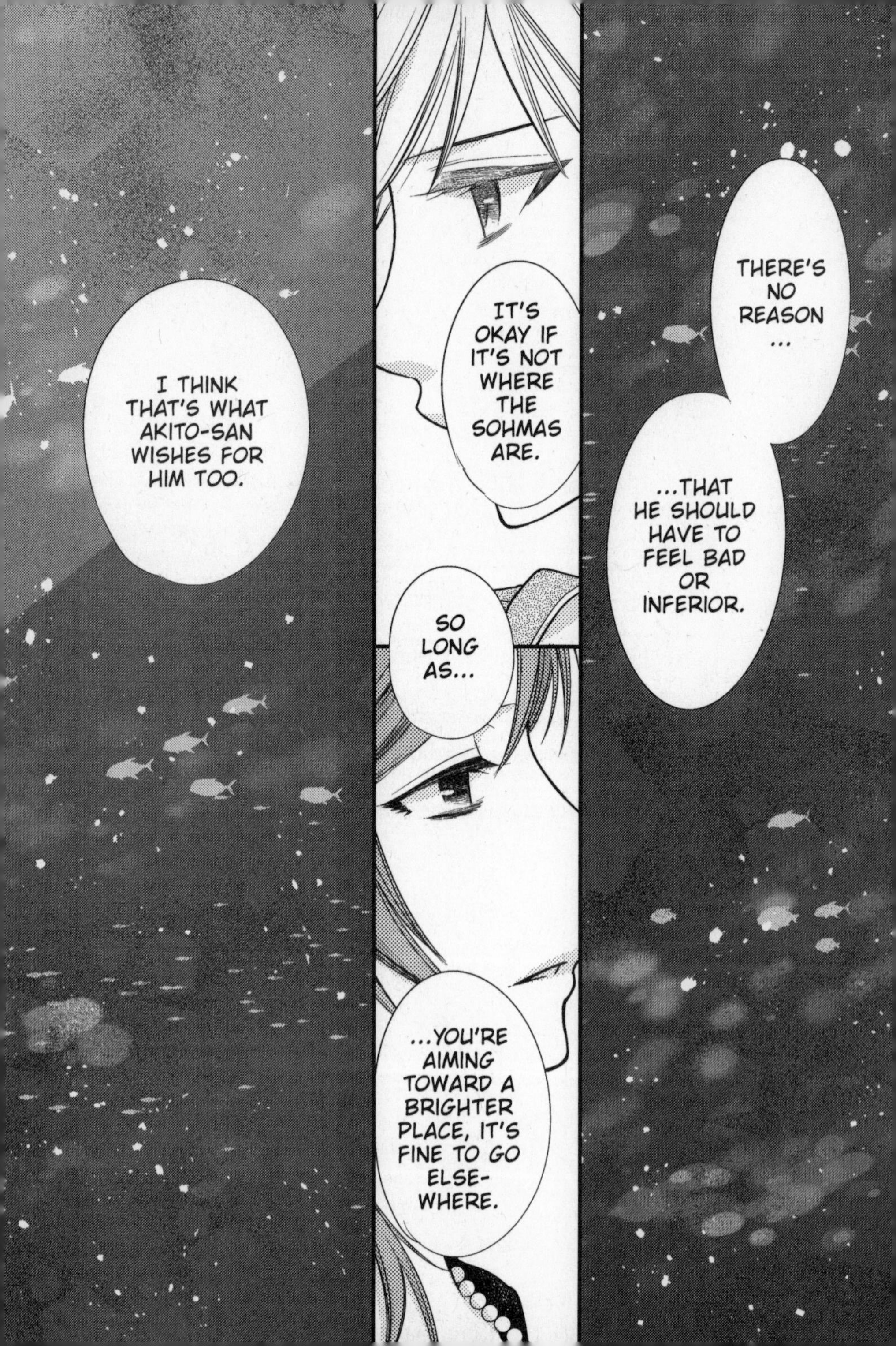
THERE'S NO REASON ...
...THAT HE SHOULD HAVE TO FEEL BAD OR INFERIOR.
IT'S OKAY IF IT'S NOT WHERE THE SOHMAS ARE.
SO LONG AS...
...YOU'RE AIMING TOWARD A BRIGHTER PLACE, IT'S FINE TO GO ELSE-WHERE.
I THINK THAT'S WHAT AKITO-SAN WISHES FOR HIM TOO.

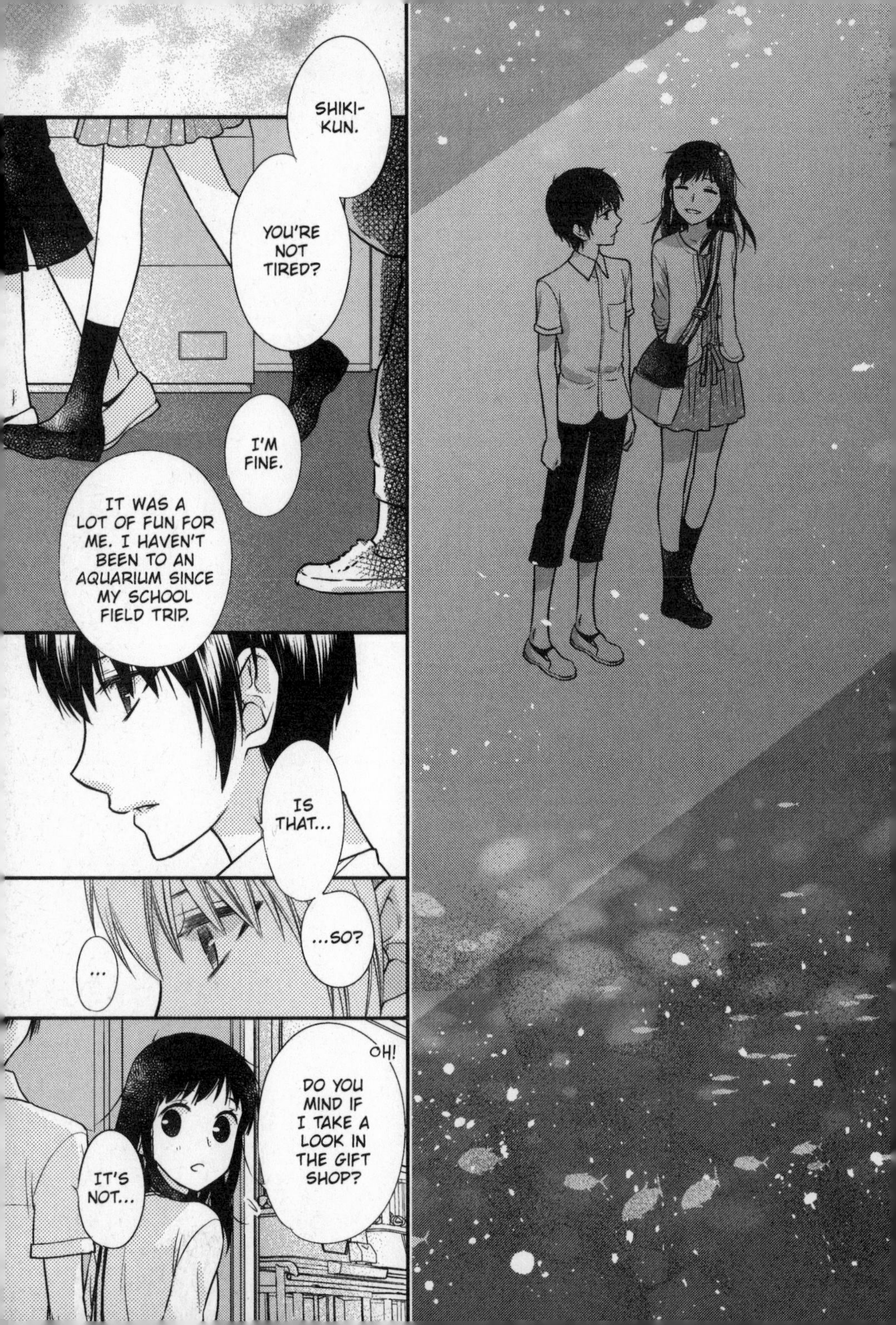
SHIKI-KUN.
YOU'RE NOT TIRED?
I'M FINE.
IT WAS A LOT OF FUN FOR ME. I HAVEN'T BEEN TO AN AQUARIUM SINCE MY SCHOOL FIELD TRIP.
IS THAT...
...SO?
...
OH!
DO YOU MIND IF I TAKE A LOOK IN THE GIFT SHOP?
IT'S NOT...

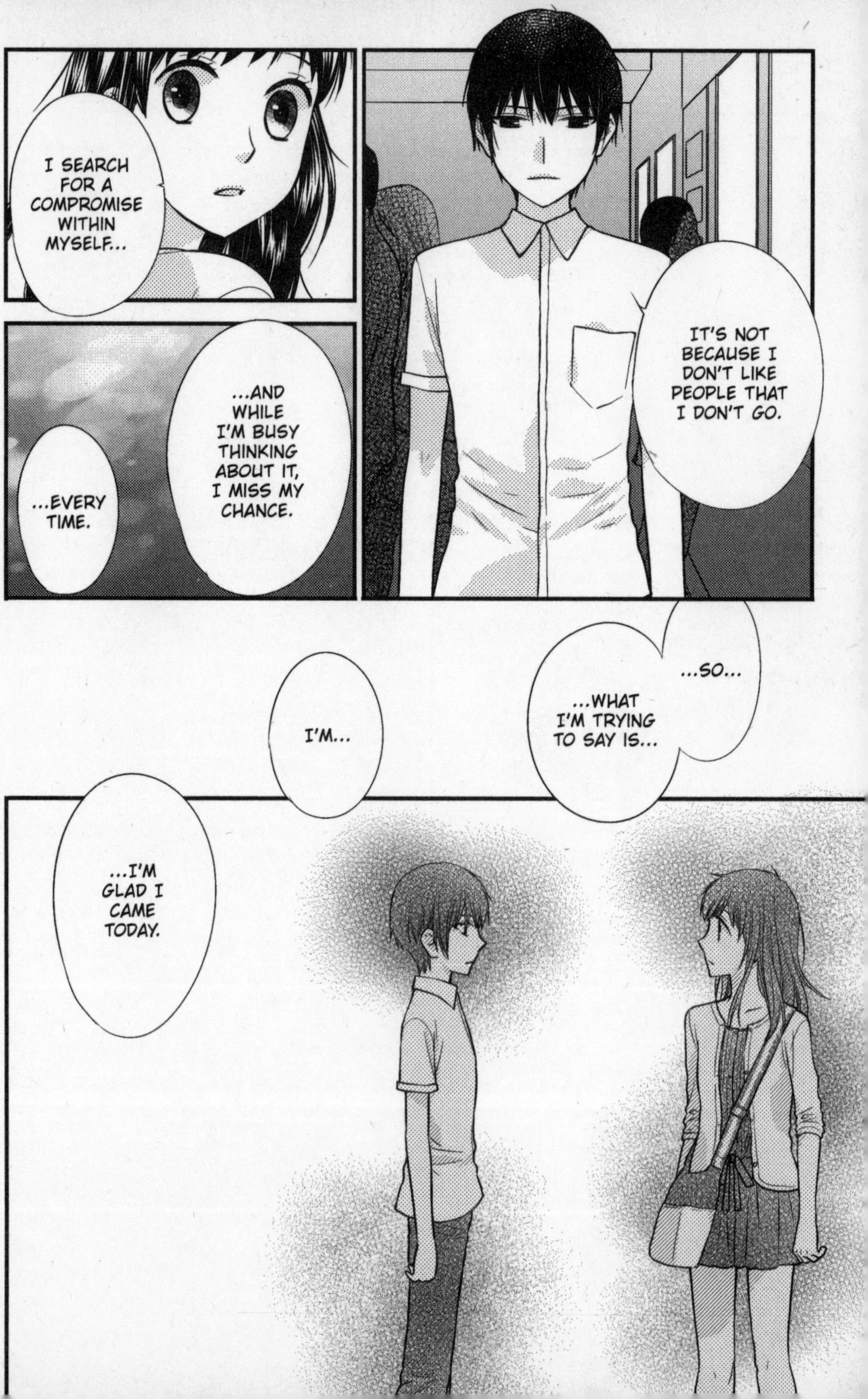
IT'S NOT BECAUSE I DON'T LIKE PEOPLE THAT I DON'T GO.
I SEARCH FOR A COMPROMISE WITHIN MYSELF...
...AND WHILE I'M BUSY THINKING ABOUT IT, I MISS MY CHANCE.
...EVERY TIME.
...SO...
...WHAT I'M TRYING TO SAY IS...
I'M...
...I'M GLAD I CAME TODAY.

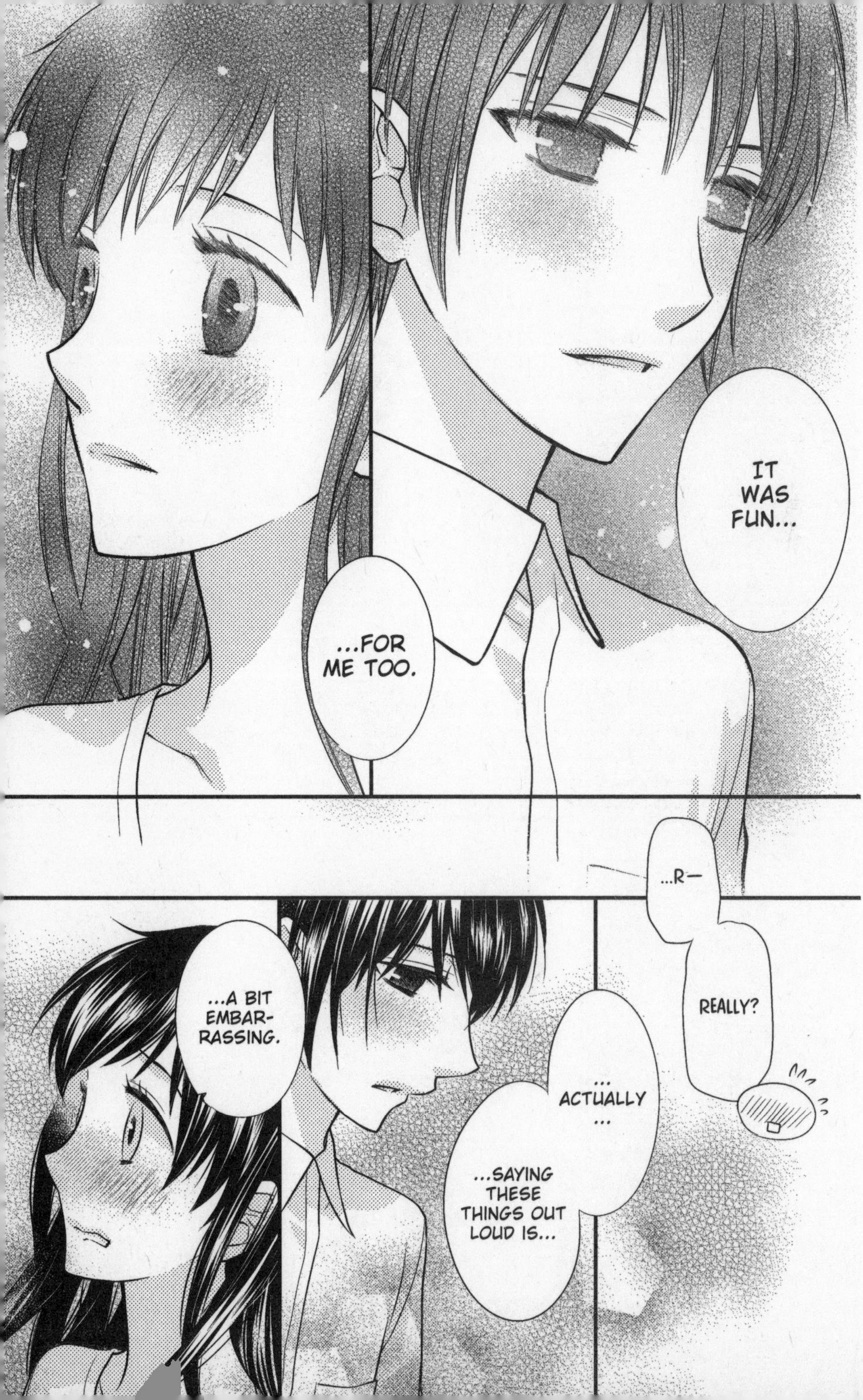
IT WAS FUN...
...FOR ME TOO.
...R—
REALLY?
... ACTUALLY ...
...SAYING THESE THINGS OUT LOUD IS...
...A BIT EMBAR-RASSING.

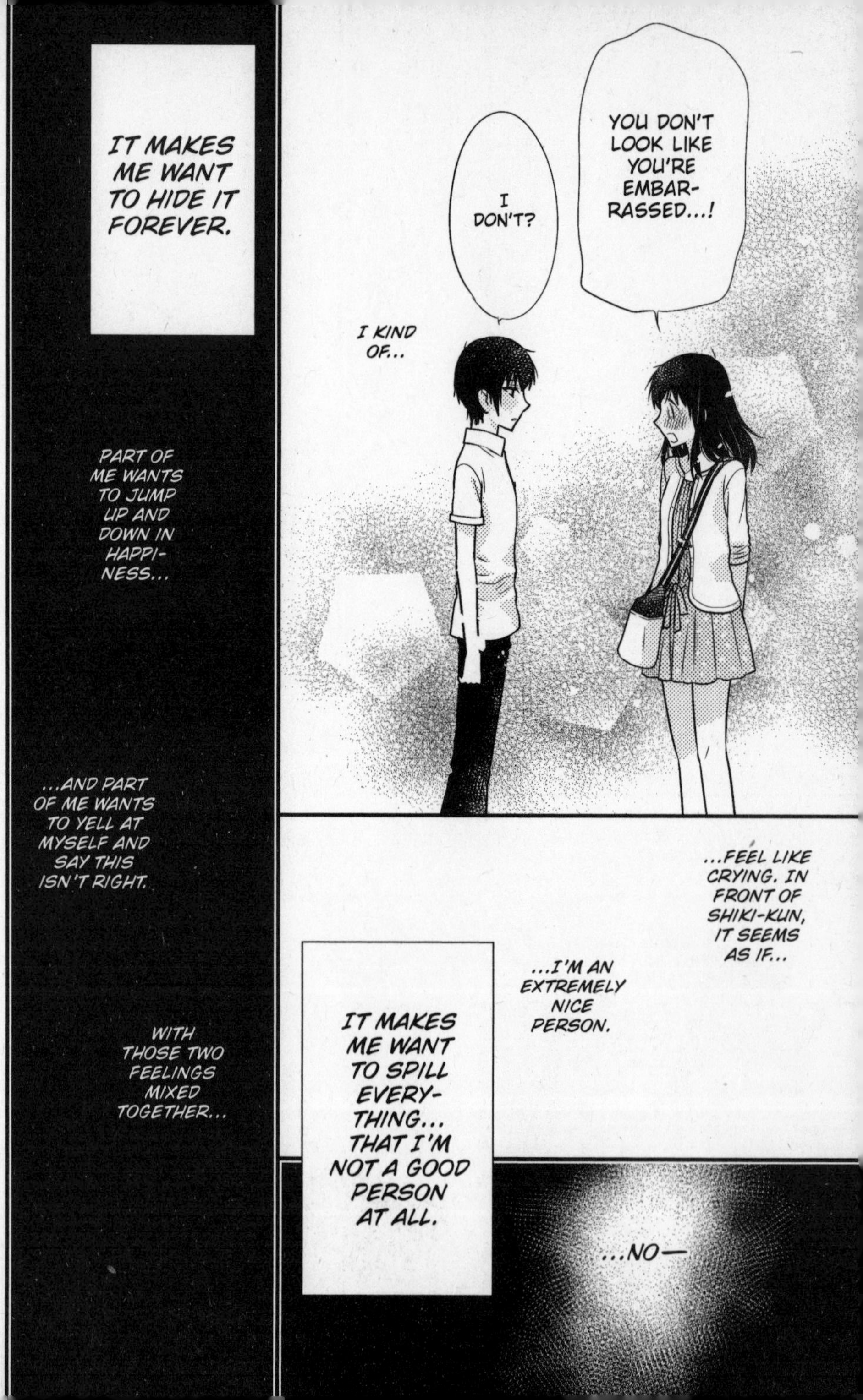
YOU DON'T LOOK LIKE YOU'RE EMBARRASSED...!
I DON'T?
I KIND OF...
...FEEL LIKE CRYING. IN FRONT OF SHIKI-KUN, IT SEEMS AS IF...
...I'M AN EXTREMELY NICE PERSON.
IT MAKES ME WANT TO SPILL EVERYTHING... THAT I'M NOT A GOOD PERSON AT ALL.
...NO—
IT MAKES ME WANT TO HIDE IT FOREVER.
PART OF ME WANTS TO JUMP UP AND DOWN IN HAPPINESS...
...AND PART OF ME WANTS TO YELL AT MYSELF AND SAY THIS ISN'T RIGHT.
WITH THOSE TWO FEELINGS MIXED TOGETHER...

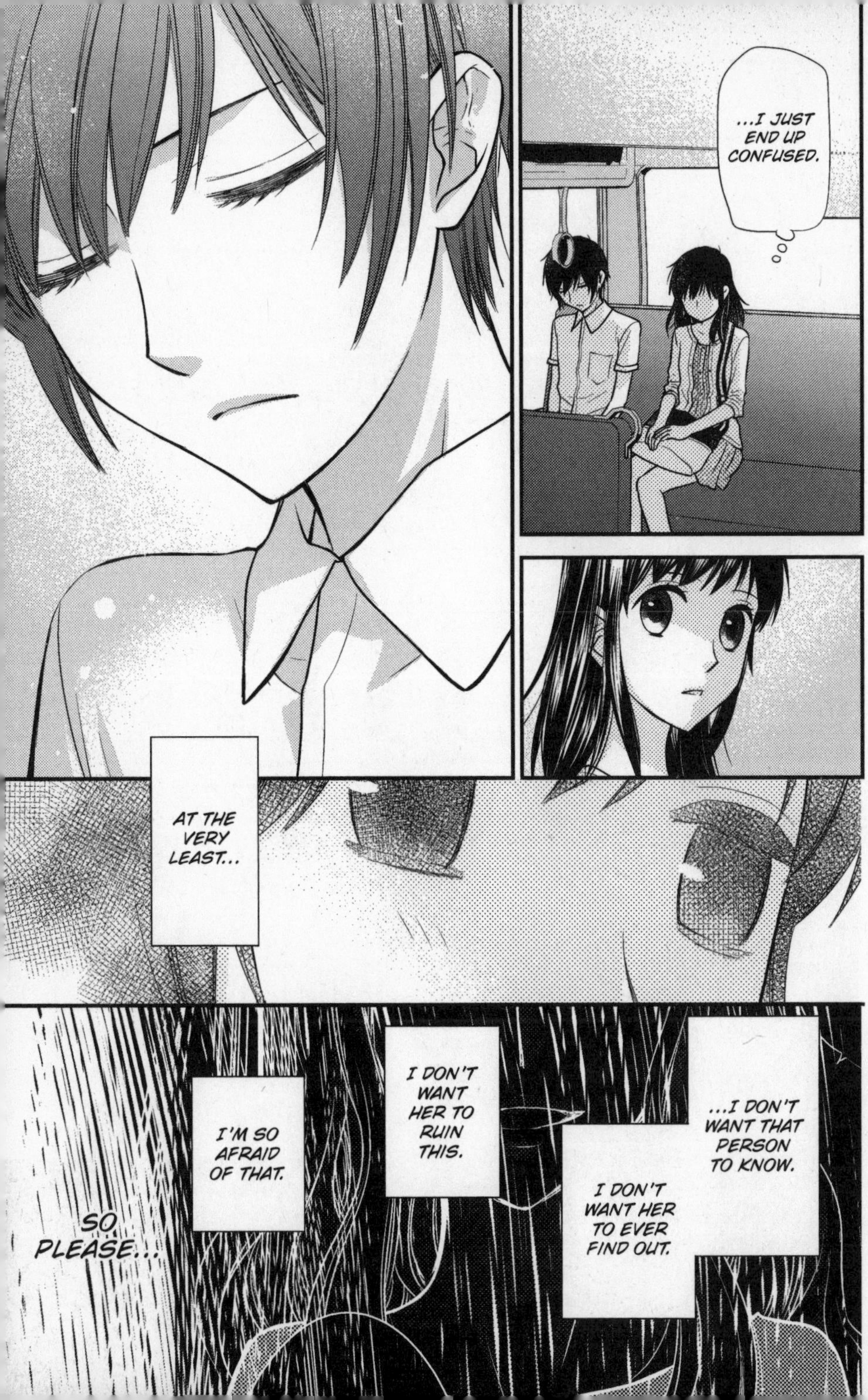
...I JUST END UP CONFUSED.
AT THE VERY LEAST...
...I DON'T WANT THAT PERSON TO KNOW.
I DON'T WANT HER TO EVER FIND OUT.
I DON'T WANT HER TO RUIN THIS.
I'M SO AFRAID OF THAT.
SO PLEASE...

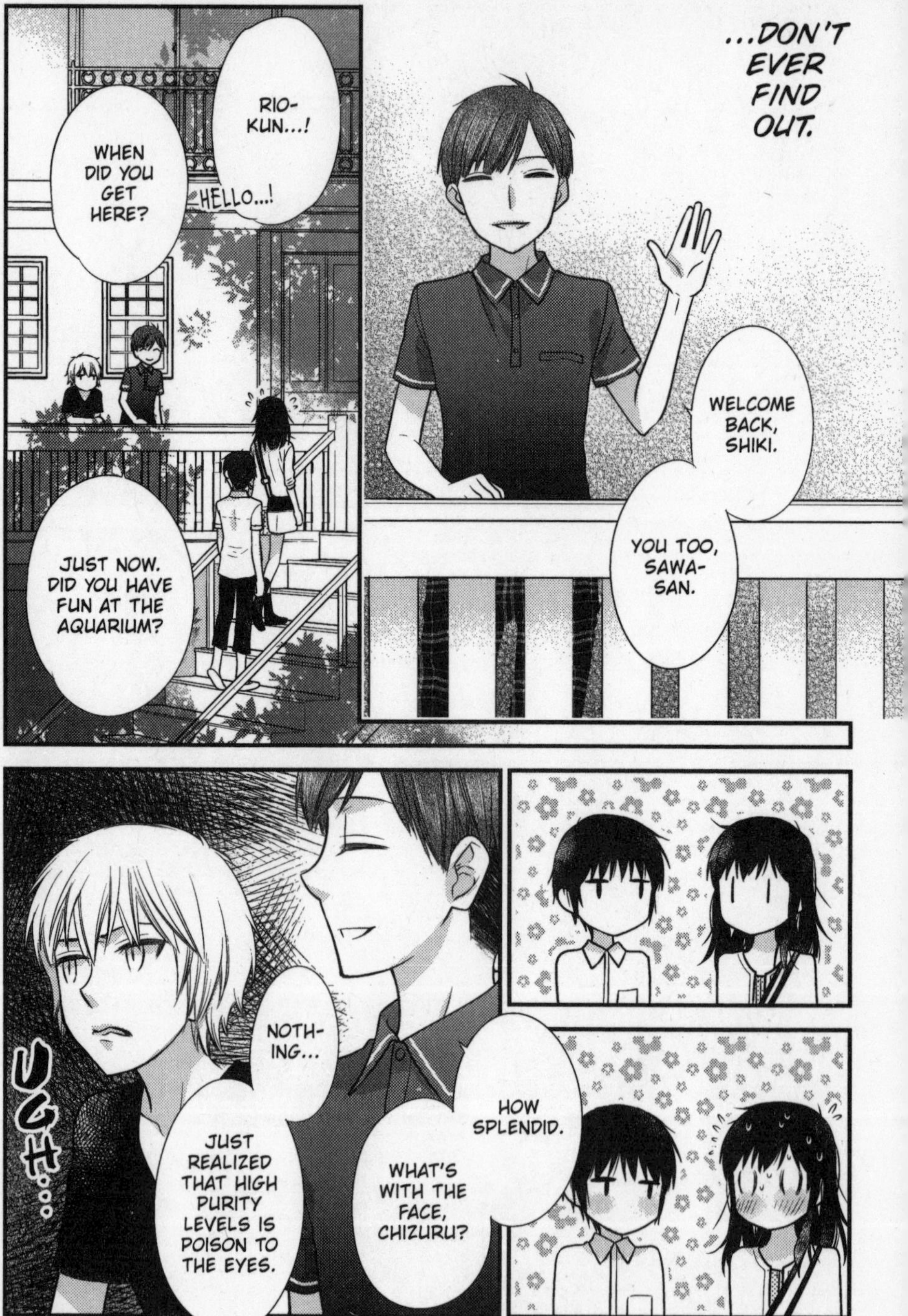
...DON'T EVER FIND OUT.
WELCOME BACK, SHIKI.
YOU TOO, SAWA-SAN.
RIO-KUN...!
HELLO...!
WHEN DID YOU GET HERE?
JUST NOW. DID YOU HAVE FUN AT THE AQUARIUM?
HOW SPLENDID.
WHAT'S WITH THE FACE, CHIZURU?
NOTH-ING...
JUST REALIZED THAT HIGH PURITY LEVELS IS POISON TO THE EYES.
UGH...

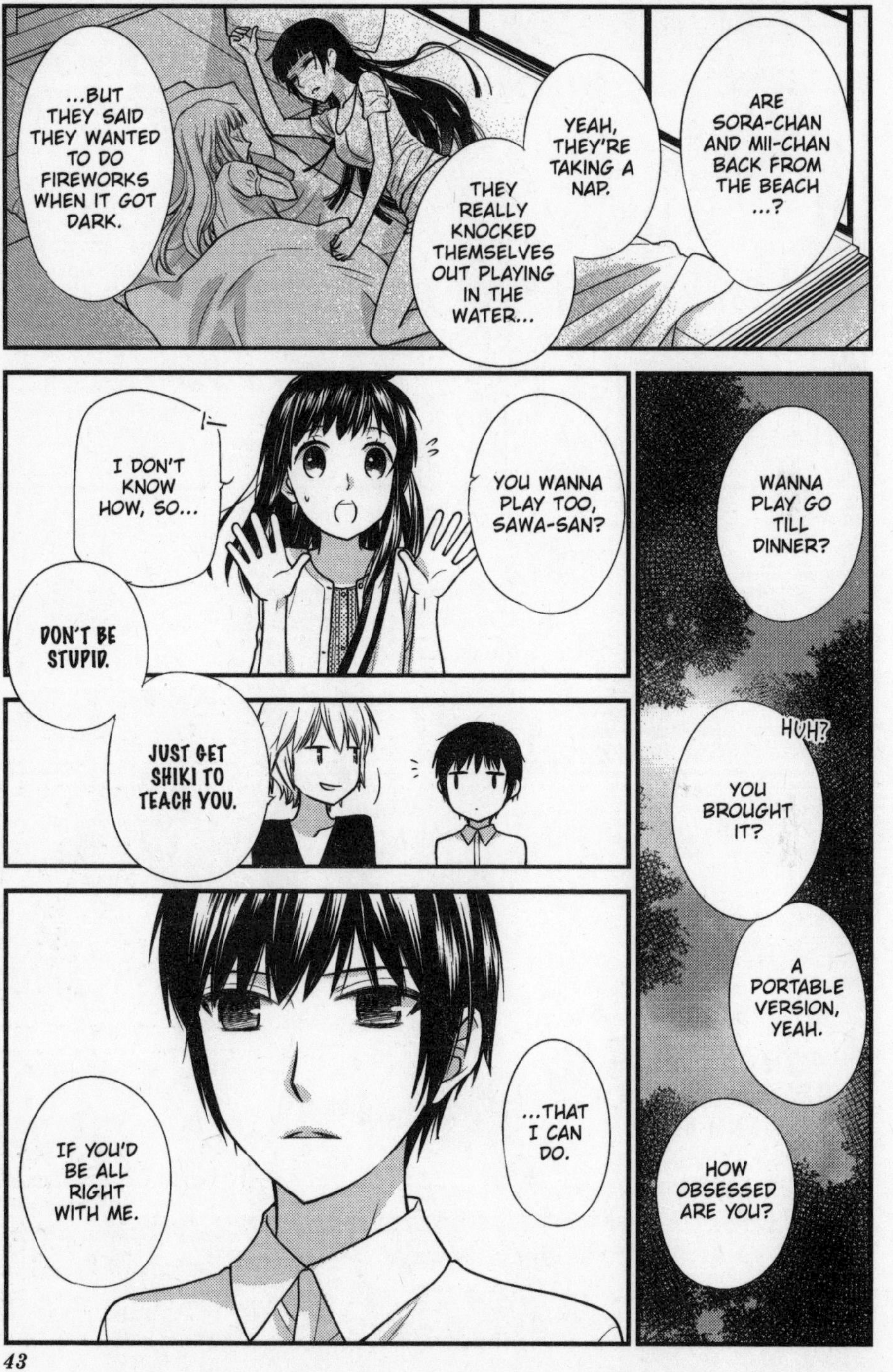
ARE SORA-CHAN AND MII-CHAN BACK FROM THE BEACH ...?
YEAH, THEY'RE TAKING A NAP.
THEY REALLY KNOCKED THEMSELVES OUT PLAYING IN THE WATER...
...BUT THEY SAID THEY WANTED TO DO FIREWORKS WHEN IT GOT DARK.
WANNA PLAY GO TILL DINNER?
HUH?
YOU BROUGHT IT?
A PORTABLE VERSION, YEAH.
HOW OBSESSED ARE YOU?
YOU WANNA PLAY TOO, SAWA-SAN?
I DON'T KNOW HOW, SO...
DON'T BE STUPID.
JUST GET SHIKI TO TEACH YOU.
...THAT I CAN DO.
IF YOU'D BE ALL RIGHT WITH ME.

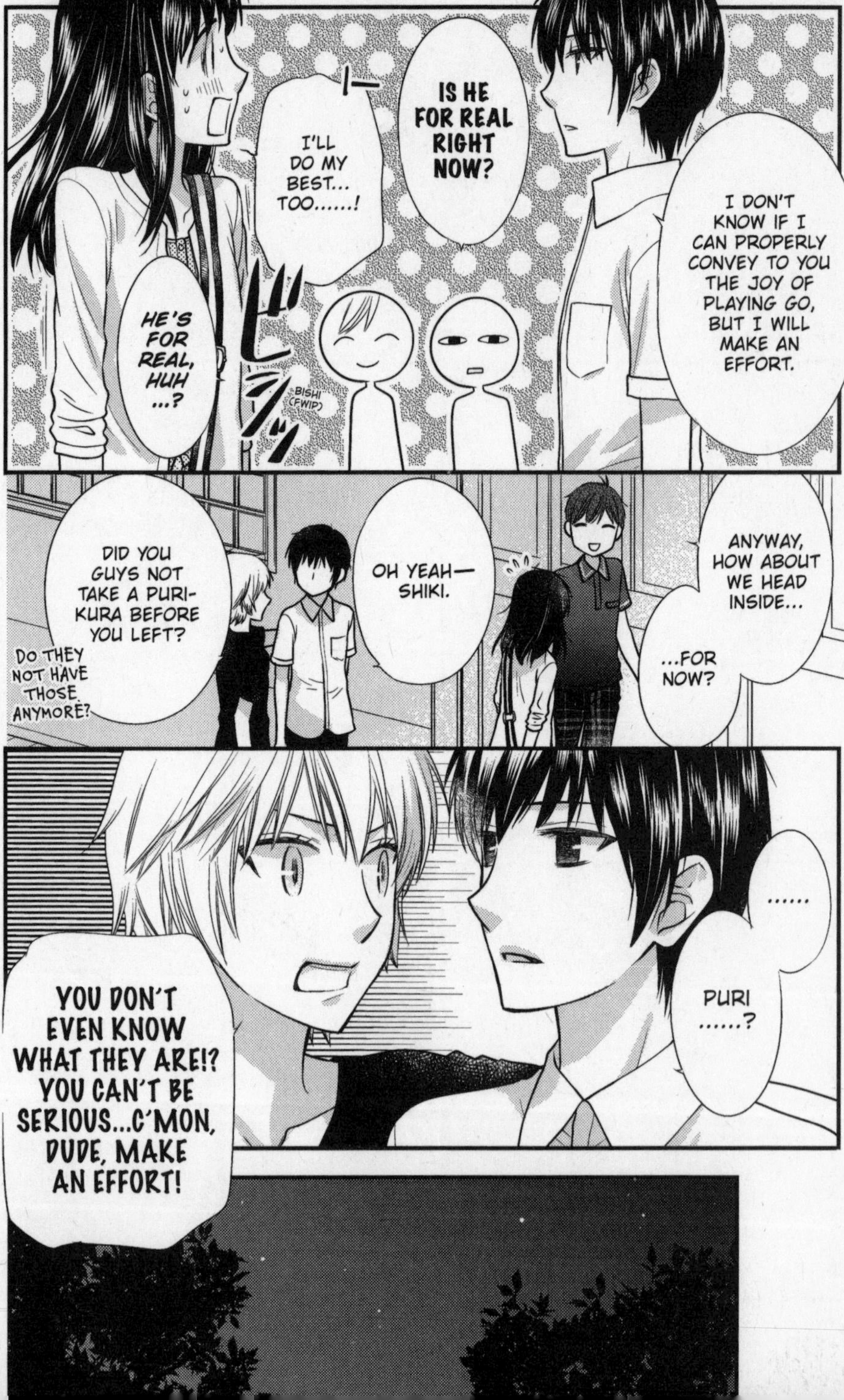
I DON'T KNOW IF I CAN PROPERLY CONVEY TO YOU THE JOY OF PLAYING GO, BUT I WILL MAKE AN EFFORT.
IS HE FOR REAL RIGHT NOW?
I'LL DO MY BEST... TOO......!
BISHI (FWIP)
HE'S FOR REAL, HUH ...?
ANYWAY, HOW ABOUT WE HEAD INSIDE...
...FOR NOW?
OH YEAH— SHIKI.
DID YOU GUYS NOT TAKE A PURI-KURA BEFORE YOU LEFT?
DO THEY NOT HAVE THOSE ANYMORE?
......
PURI ......?
YOU DON'T EVEN KNOW WHAT THEY ARE!? YOU CAN'T BE SERIOUS...C'MON, DUDE, MAKE AN EFFORT!

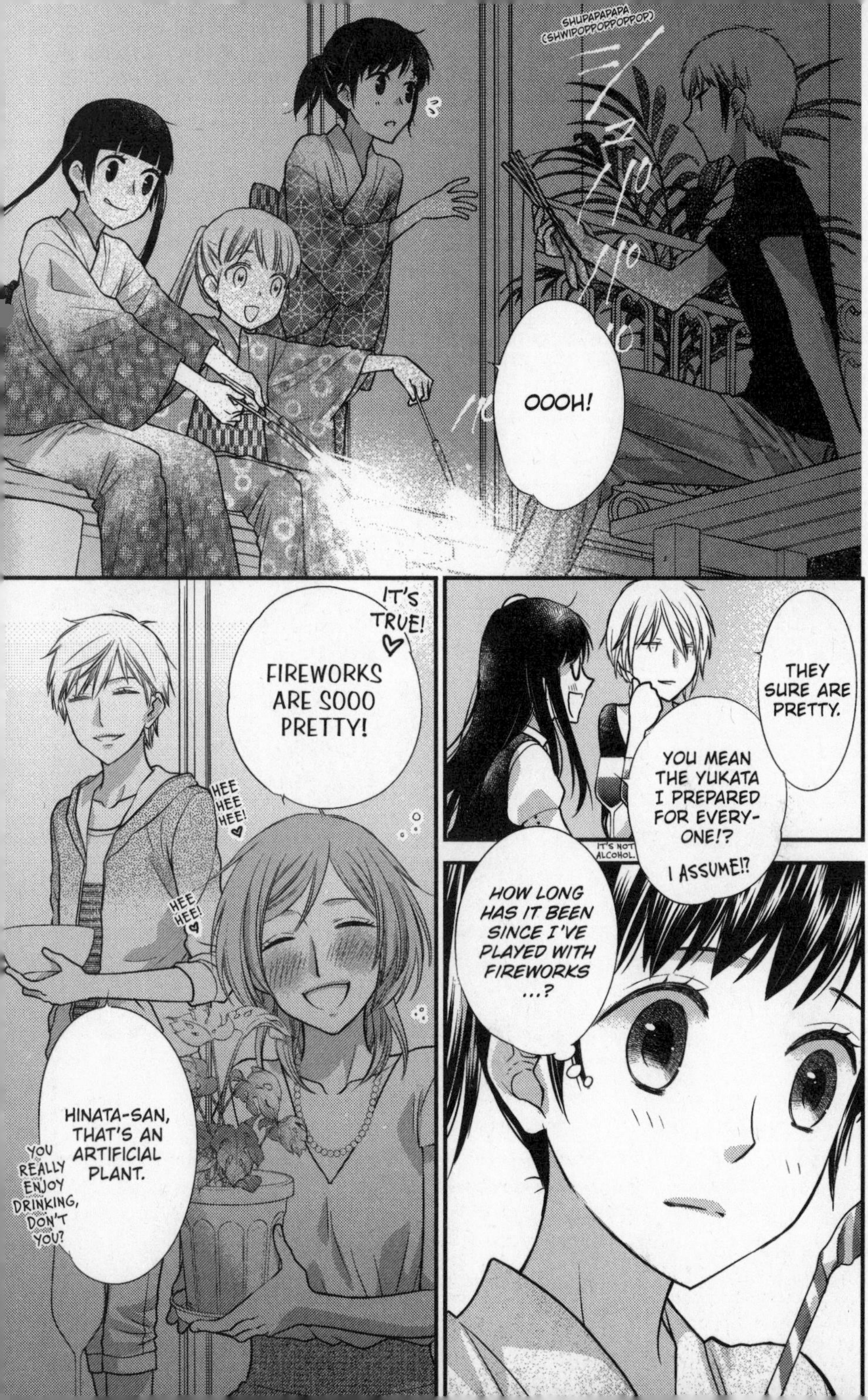
SHUPAPAPAPA (SHWIPOPPOPPOPPOP)
OOOH!
THEY SURE ARE PRETTY.
YOU MEAN THE YUKATA I PREPARED FOR EVERY-ONE!? I ASSUME!?
IT'S NOT ALCOHOL.
HOW LONG HAS IT BEEN SINCE I'VE PLAYED WITH FIREWORKS ...?
IT'S TRUE!
FIREWORKS ARE SOOO PRETTY!
HEE HEE HEE!
HEE HEE!
HINATA-SAN, THAT'S AN ARTIFICIAL PLANT.
YOU REALLY ENJOY DRINKING, DON'T YOU?

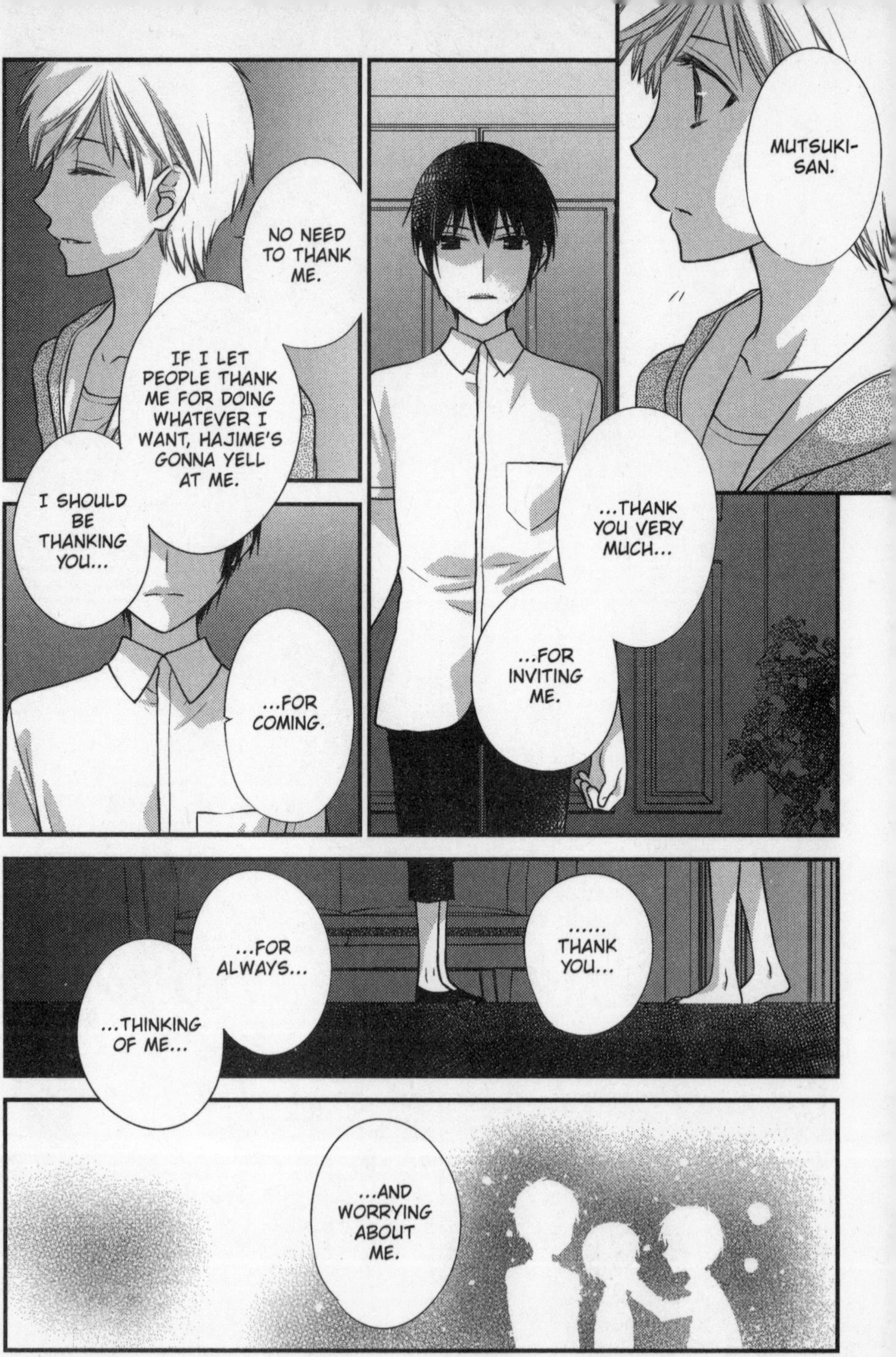
MUTSUKI-SAN.
...THANK YOU VERY MUCH...
...FOR INVITING ME.
NO NEED TO THANK ME.
IF I LET PEOPLE THANK ME FOR DOING WHATEVER I WANT, HAJIME'S GONNA YELL AT ME.
I SHOULD BE THANKING YOU...
...FOR COMING.
......THANK YOU...
...FOR ALWAYS...
...THINKING OF ME...
...AND WORRYING ABOUT ME.

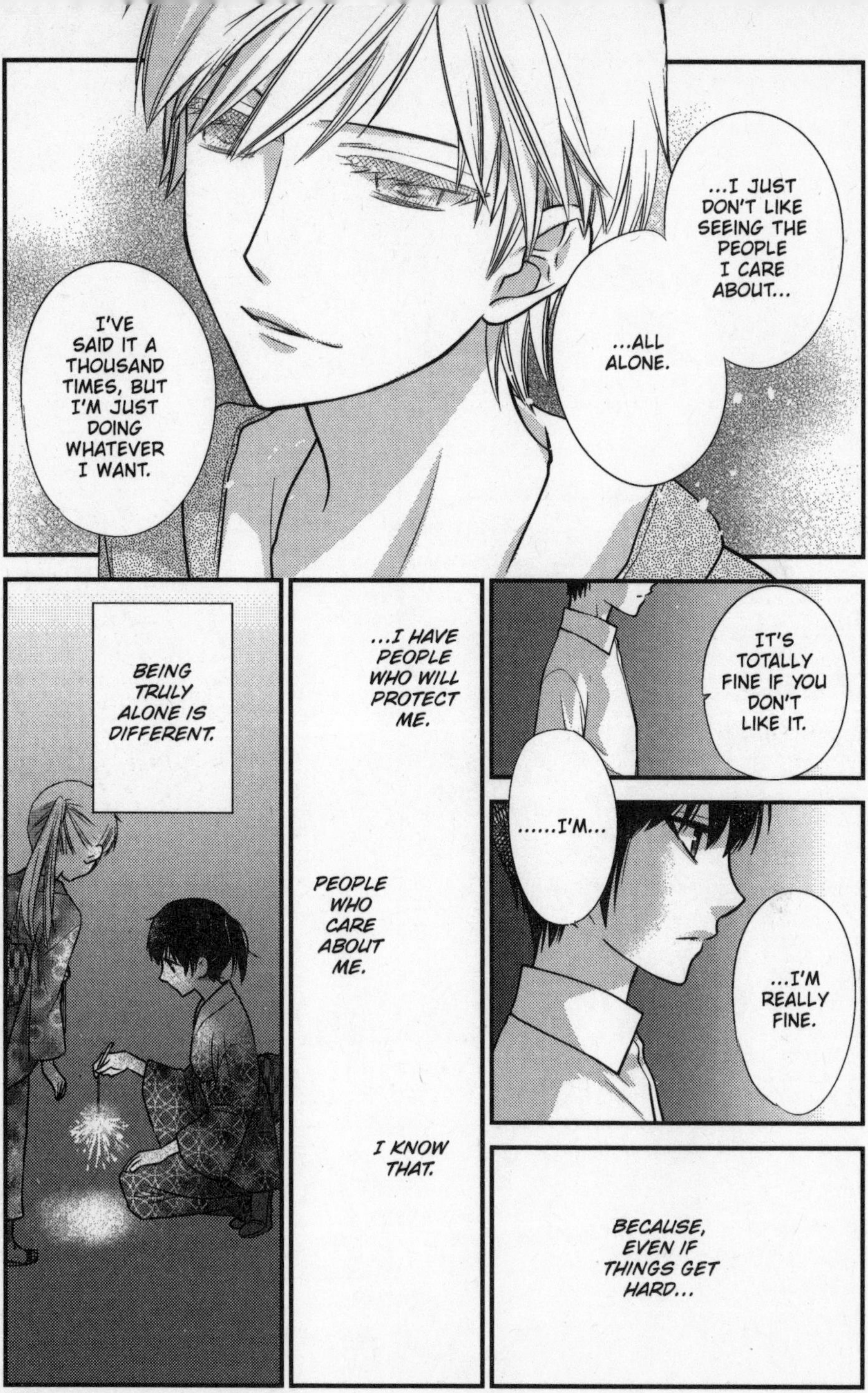
...I JUST DON'T LIKE SEEING THE PEOPLE I CARE ABOUT...
...ALL ALONE.
I'VE SAID IT A THOUSAND TIMES, BUT I'M JUST DOING WHATEVER I WANT.
IT'S TOTALLY FINE IF YOU DON'T LIKE IT.
......I'M...
...I'M REALLY FINE.
BECAUSE, EVEN IF THINGS GET HARD...
...I HAVE PEOPLE WHO WILL PROTECT ME.
PEOPLE WHO CARE ABOUT ME.
I KNOW THAT.
BEING TRULY ALONE IS DIFFERENT.

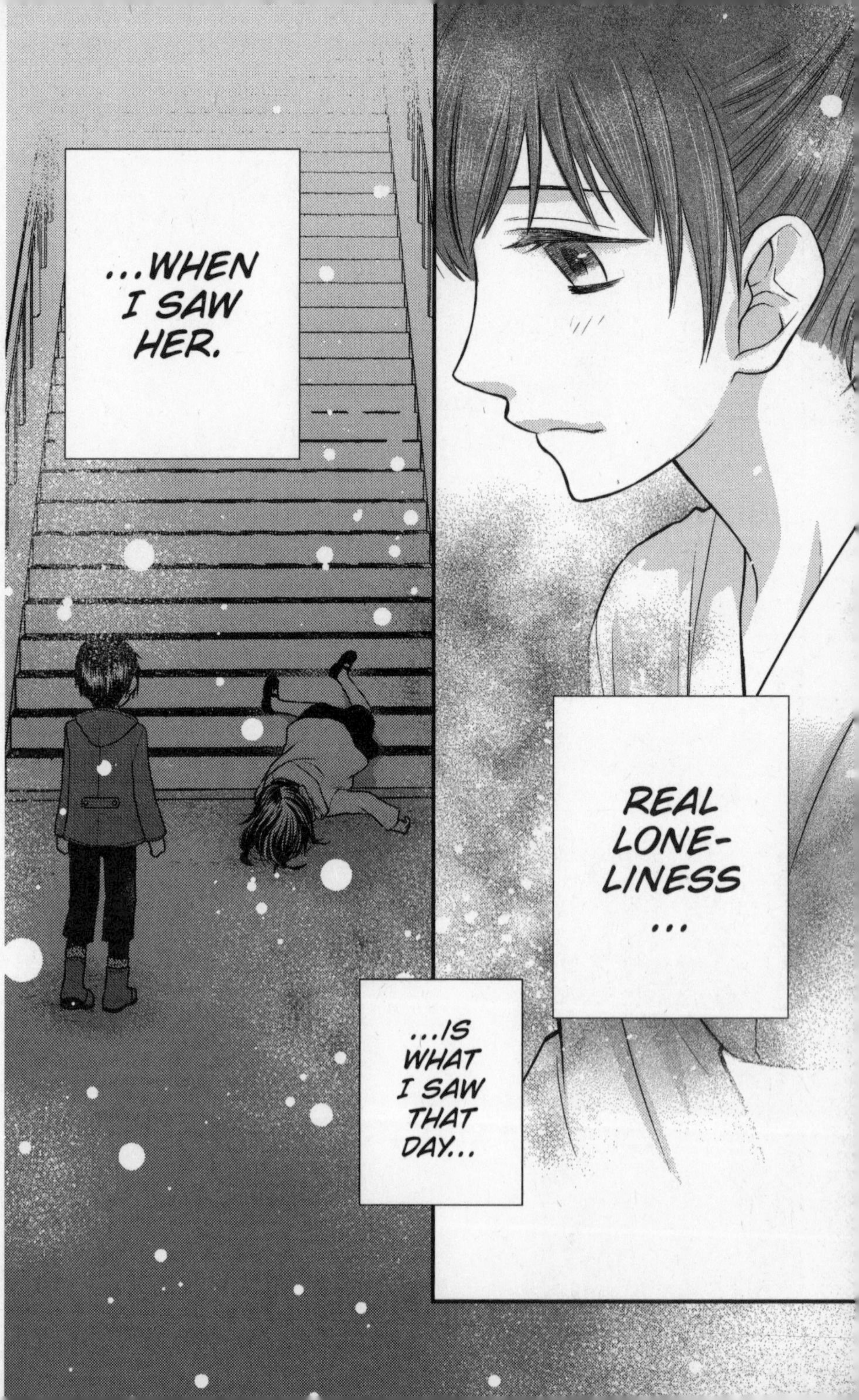
REAL LONE-LINESS...
...IS WHAT I SAW THAT DAY...
...WHEN I SAW HER.

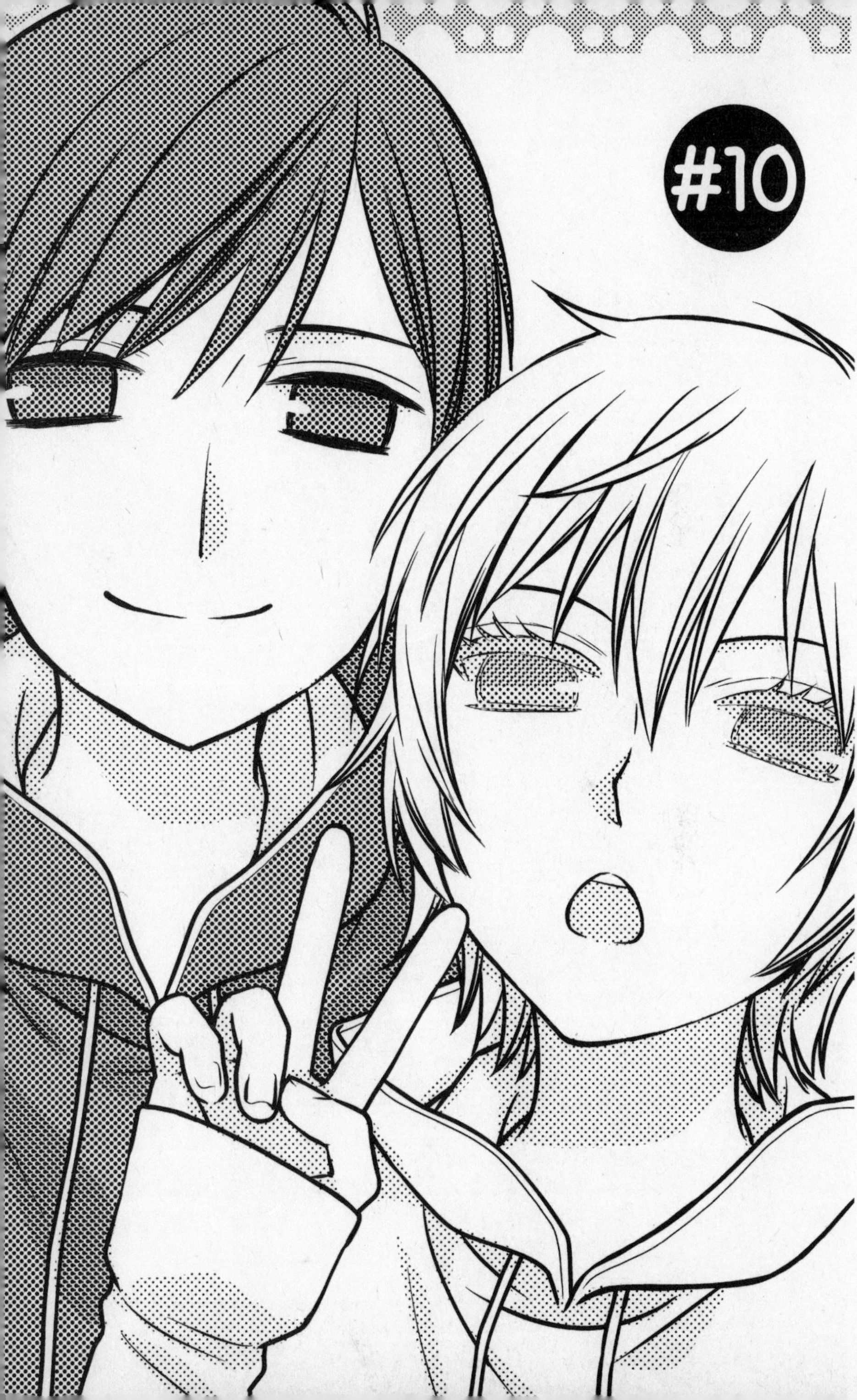
#10

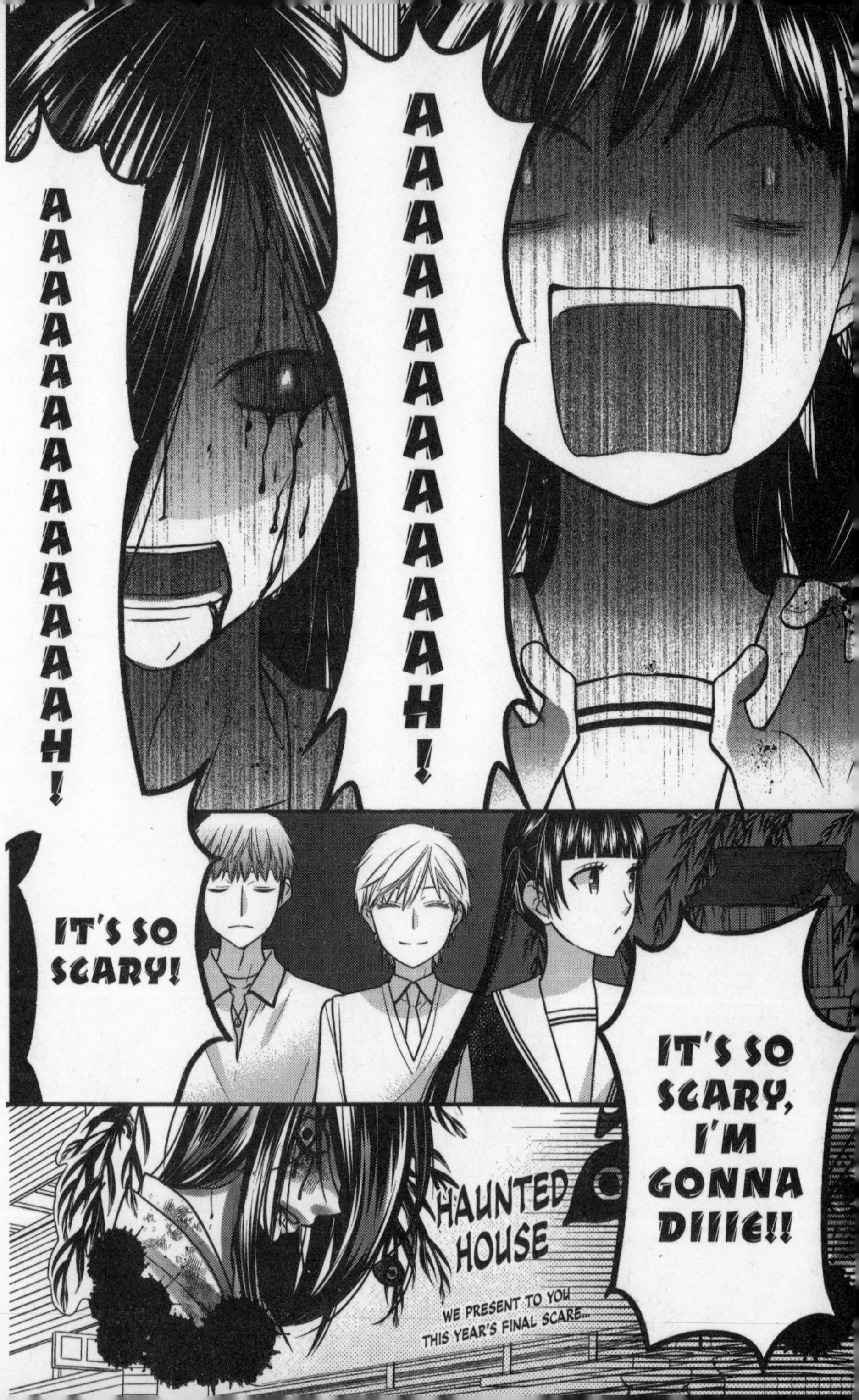
AAAAAAAAAAAAH!
AAAAAAAAAAAAAH!
IT'S SO SCARY, I'M GONNA DIIIE!!
IT'S SO SCARY!
HAUNTED HOUSE
WE PRESENT TO YOU THIS YEAR'S FINAL SCARE...

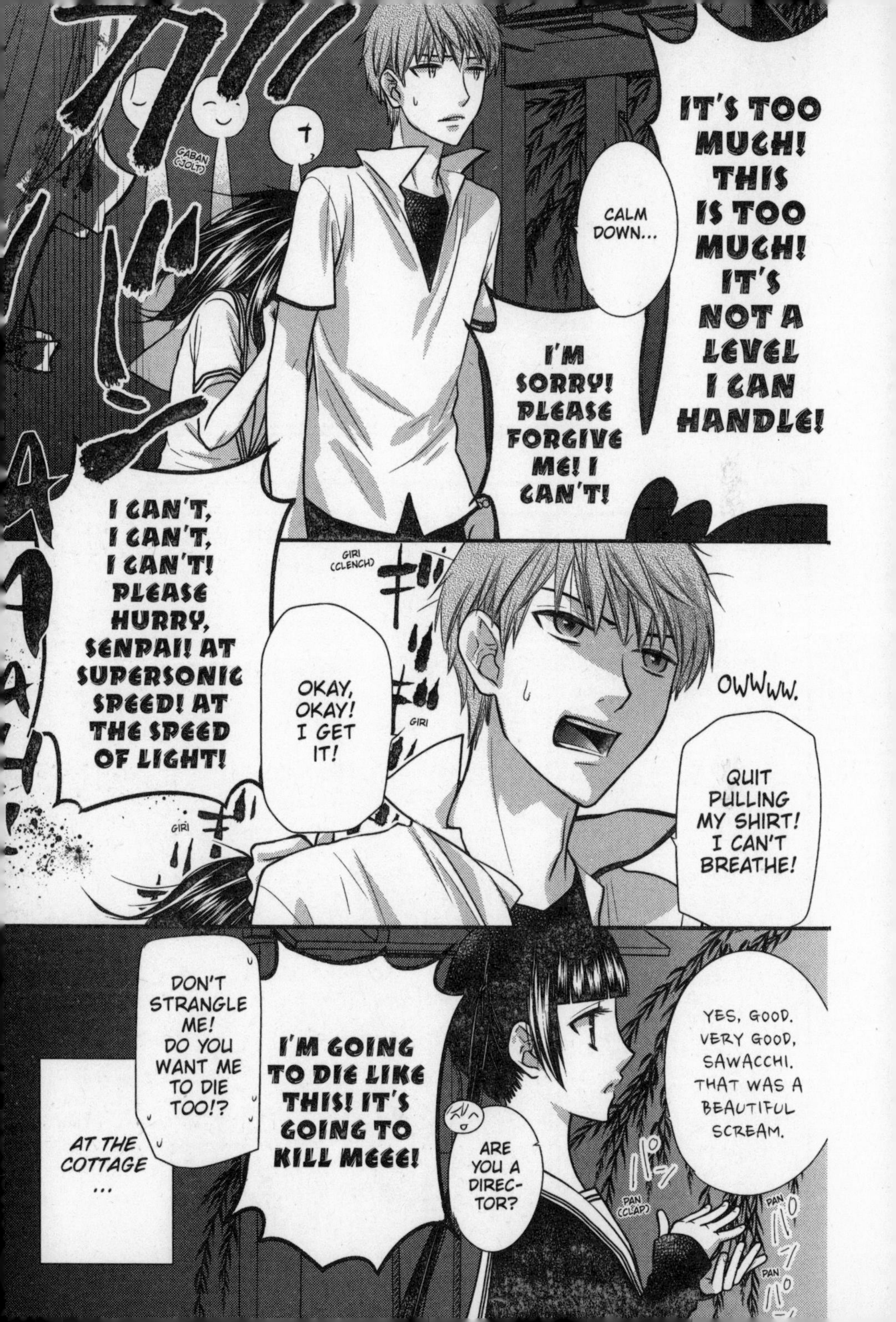
IT'S TOO MUCH! THIS IS TOO MUCH! IT'S NOT A LEVEL I CAN HANDLE!
CALM DOWN...
I'M SORRY! PLEASE FORGIVE ME! I CAN'T!
GABAN (JOLT)
OWWWW.
QUIT PULLING MY SHIRT! I CAN'T BREATHE!
GIRI (CLENCH)
OKAY, OKAY! I GET IT!
GIRI
GIRI
I CAN'T, I CAN'T, I CAN'T! PLEASE HURRY, SENPAI! AT SUPERSONIC SPEED! AT THE SPEED OF LIGHT!
YES, GOOD. VERY GOOD, SAWACCHI. THAT WAS A BEAUTIFUL SCREAM.
PAN (CLAP)
PAN
PAN
ARE YOU A DIRECTOR?
I'M GOING TO DIE LIKE THIS! IT'S GOING TO KILL MEEE!
DON'T STRANGLE ME! DO YOU WANT ME TO DIE TOO!?
AT THE COTTAGE ...

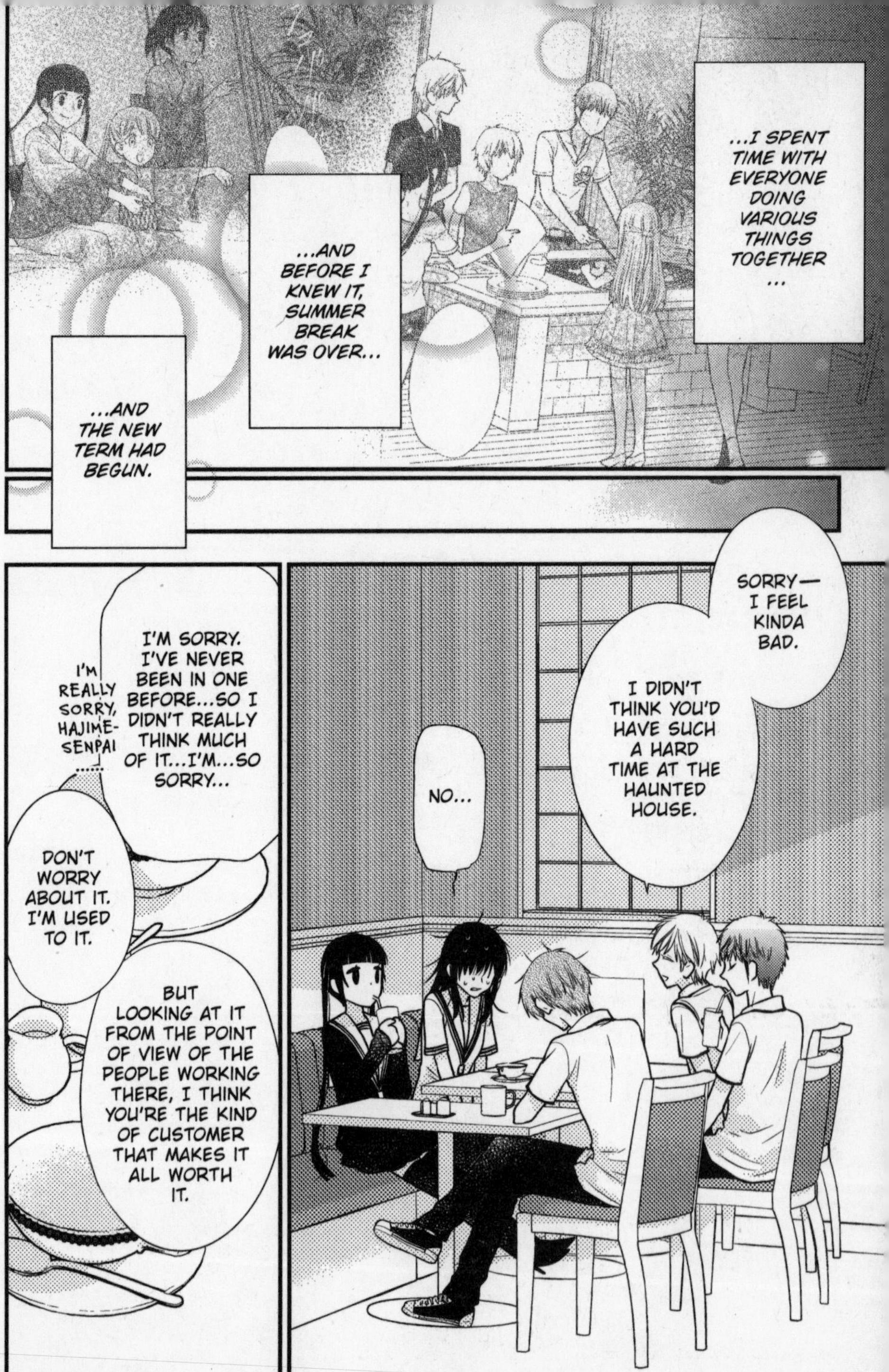
...I SPENT TIME WITH EVERYONE DOING VARIOUS THINGS TOGETHER...
...AND BEFORE I KNEW IT, SUMMER BREAK WAS OVER...
...AND THE NEW TERM HAD BEGUN.
SORRY— I FEEL KINDA BAD.
I DIDN'T THINK YOU'D HAVE SUCH A HARD TIME AT THE HAUNTED HOUSE.
NO...
I'M SORRY. I'VE NEVER BEEN IN ONE BEFORE...SO I DIDN'T REALLY THINK MUCH OF IT...I'M...SO SORRY...
I'M REALLY SORRY, HAJIME-SENPAI......
DON'T WORRY ABOUT IT. I'M USED TO IT.
BUT LOOKING AT IT FROM THE POINT OF VIEW OF THE PEOPLE WORKING THERE, I THINK YOU'RE THE KIND OF CUSTOMER THAT MAKES IT ALL WORTH IT.

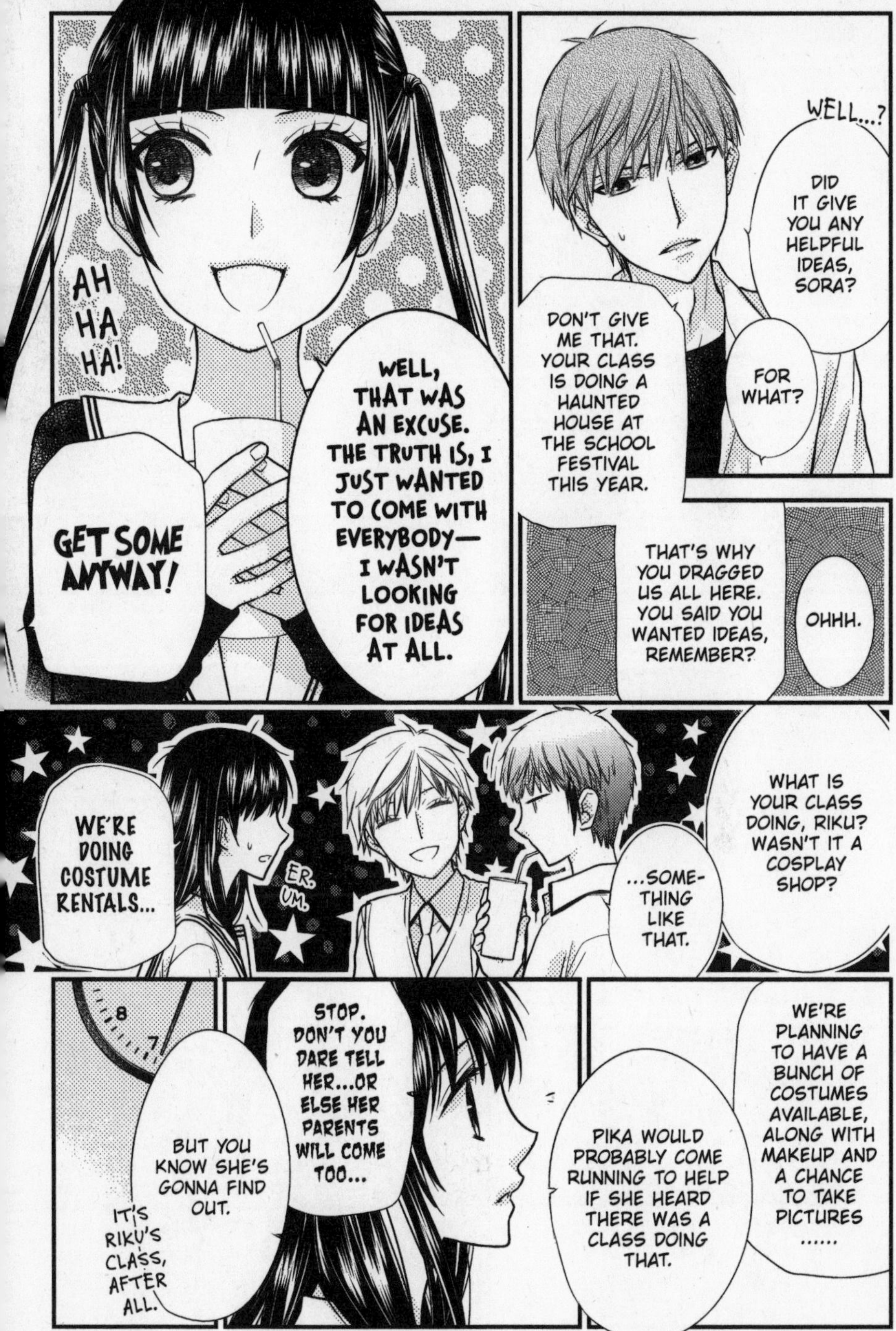
WELL...?
DID IT GIVE YOU ANY HELPFUL IDEAS, SORA?
FOR WHAT?
DON'T GIVE ME THAT. YOUR CLASS IS DOING A HAUNTED HOUSE AT THE SCHOOL FESTIVAL THIS YEAR.
OHHH.
THAT'S WHY YOU DRAGGED US ALL HERE. YOU SAID YOU WANTED IDEAS, REMEMBER?
WELL, THAT WAS AN EXCUSE. THE TRUTH IS, I JUST WANTED TO COME WITH EVERYBODY— I WASN'T LOOKING FOR IDEAS AT ALL.
AH HA HA!
GET SOME ANYWAY!
WHAT IS YOUR CLASS DOING, RIKU? WASN'T IT A COSPLAY SHOP?
...SOME-THING LIKE THAT.
ER. UM.
WE'RE DOING COSTUME RENTALS...
WE'RE PLANNING TO HAVE A BUNCH OF COSTUMES AVAILABLE, ALONG WITH MAKEUP AND A CHANCE TO TAKE PICTURES ......
PIKA WOULD PROBABLY COME RUNNING TO HELP IF SHE HEARD THERE WAS A CLASS DOING THAT.
STOP. DON'T YOU DARE TELL HER...OR ELSE HER PARENTS WILL COME TOO...
BUT YOU KNOW SHE'S GONNA FIND OUT.
IT'S RIKU'S CLASS, AFTER ALL.

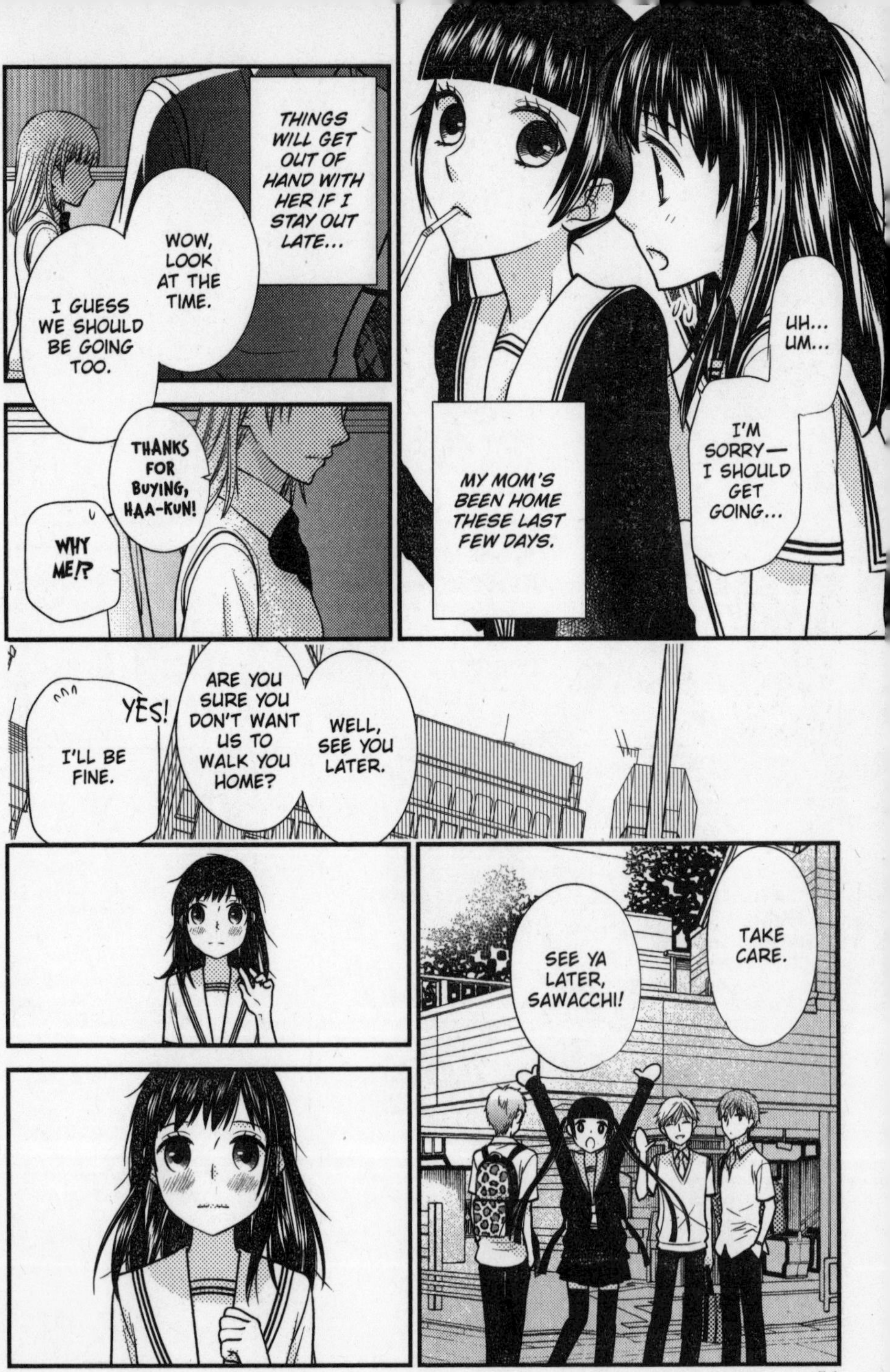
UH... UM...
I'M SORRY— I SHOULD GET GOING...
MY MOM'S BEEN HOME THESE LAST FEW DAYS.
THINGS WILL GET OUT OF HAND WITH HER IF I STAY OUT LATE...
WOW, LOOK AT THE TIME.
I GUESS WE SHOULD BE GOING TOO.
THANKS FOR BUYING, HAA-KUN!
WHY ME!?
WELL, SEE YOU LATER.
ARE YOU SURE YOU DON'T WANT US TO WALK YOU HOME?
YES!
I'LL BE FINE.
TAKE CARE.
SEE YA LATER, SAWACCHI!

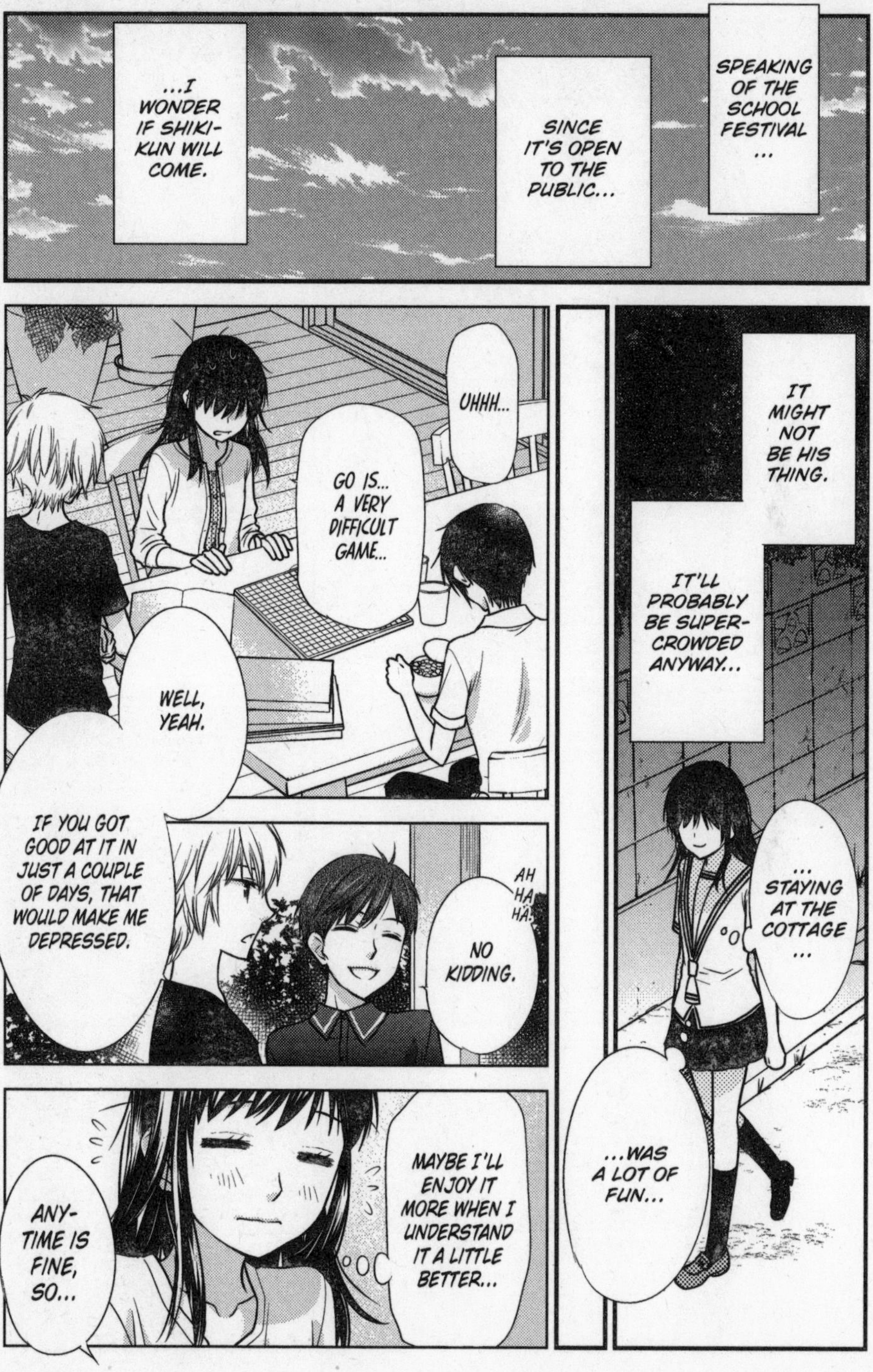
SPEAKING OF THE SCHOOL FESTIVAL...
SINCE IT'S OPEN TO THE PUBLIC...
...I WONDER IF SHIKI-KUN WILL COME.
IT MIGHT NOT BE HIS THING.
IT'LL PROBABLY BE SUPER-CROWDED ANYWAY...
...STAYING AT THE COTTAGE...
...WAS A LOT OF FUN...
UHHH...
GO IS... A VERY DIFFICULT GAME...
WELL, YEAH.
IF YOU GOT GOOD AT IT IN JUST A COUPLE OF DAYS, THAT WOULD MAKE ME DEPRESSED.
AH HA HA.
NO KIDDING.
MAYBE I'LL ENJOY IT MORE WHEN I UNDERSTAND IT A LITTLE BETTER...
ANY-TIME IS FINE, SO...

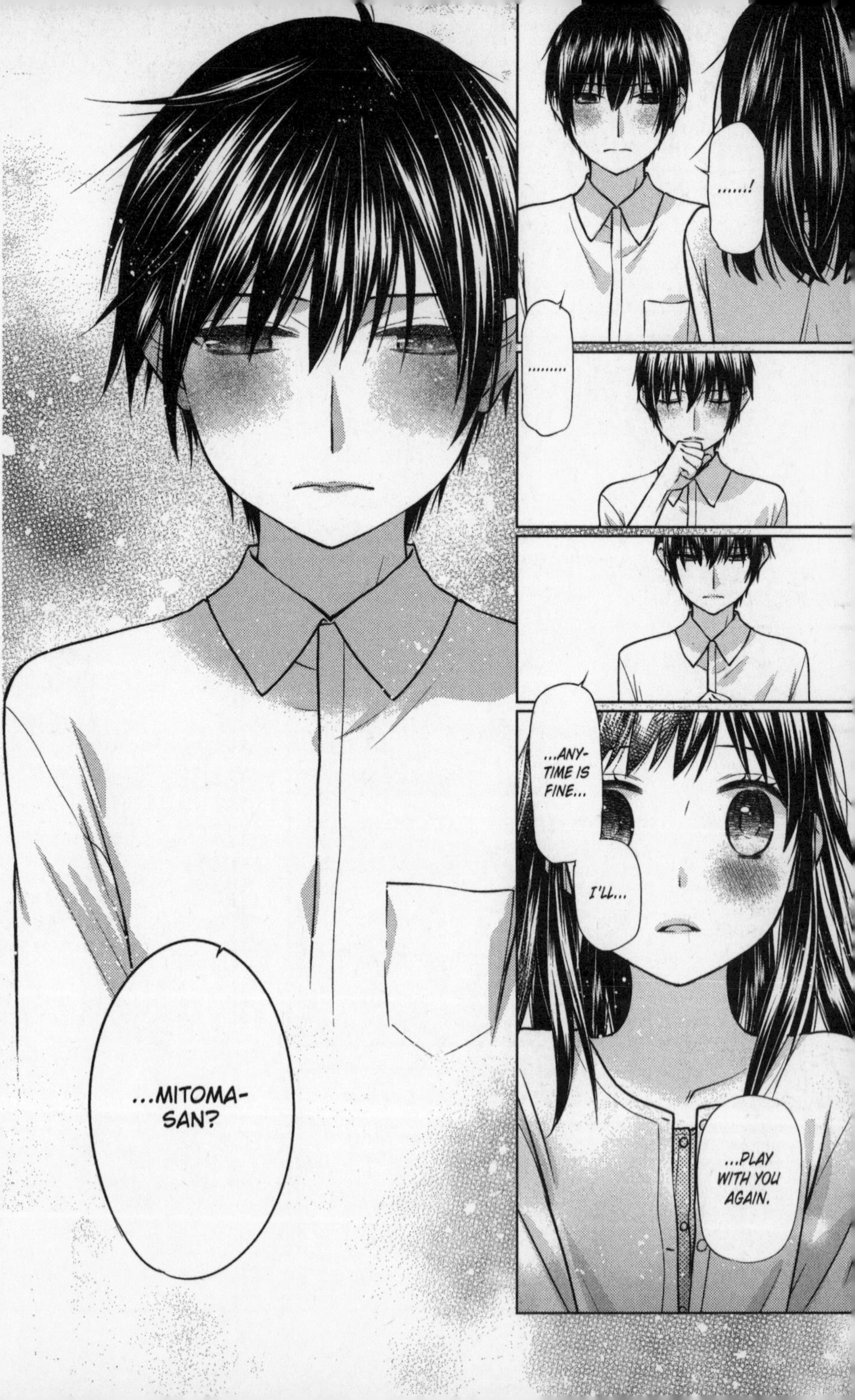
......!
....
...ANY-TIME IS FINE...
I'LL...
...PLAY WITH YOU AGAIN.
...MITOMA-SAN?

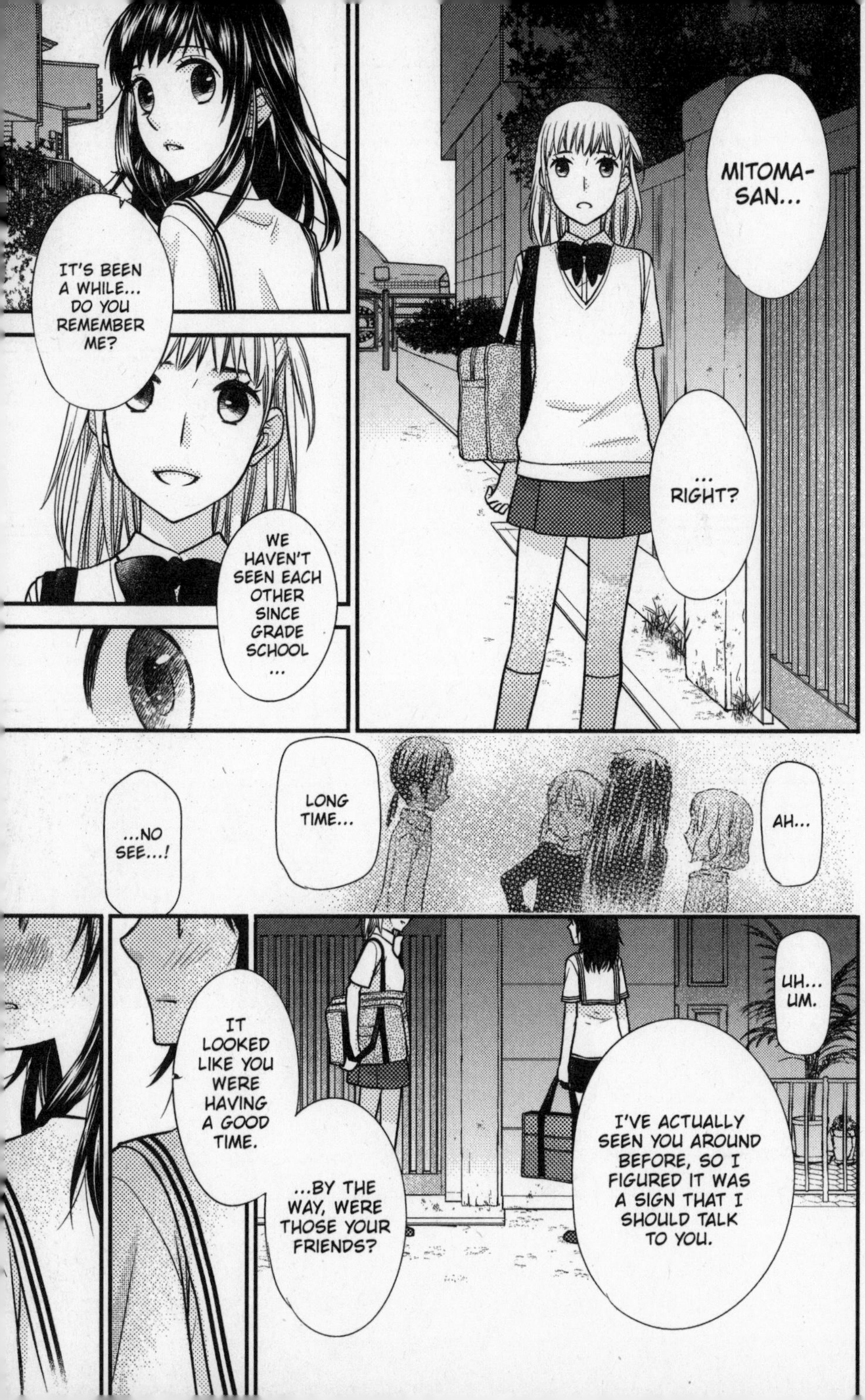
MITOMA-SAN...
... RIGHT?
IT'S BEEN A WHILE... DO YOU REMEMBER ME?
WE HAVEN'T SEEN EACH OTHER SINCE GRADE SCHOOL ...
AH...
LONG TIME...
...NO SEE...!
UH... UM.
I'VE ACTUALLY SEEN YOU AROUND BEFORE, SO I FIGURED IT WAS A SIGN THAT I SHOULD TALK TO YOU.
IT LOOKED LIKE YOU WERE HAVING A GOOD TIME.
...BY THE WAY, WERE THOSE YOUR FRIENDS?

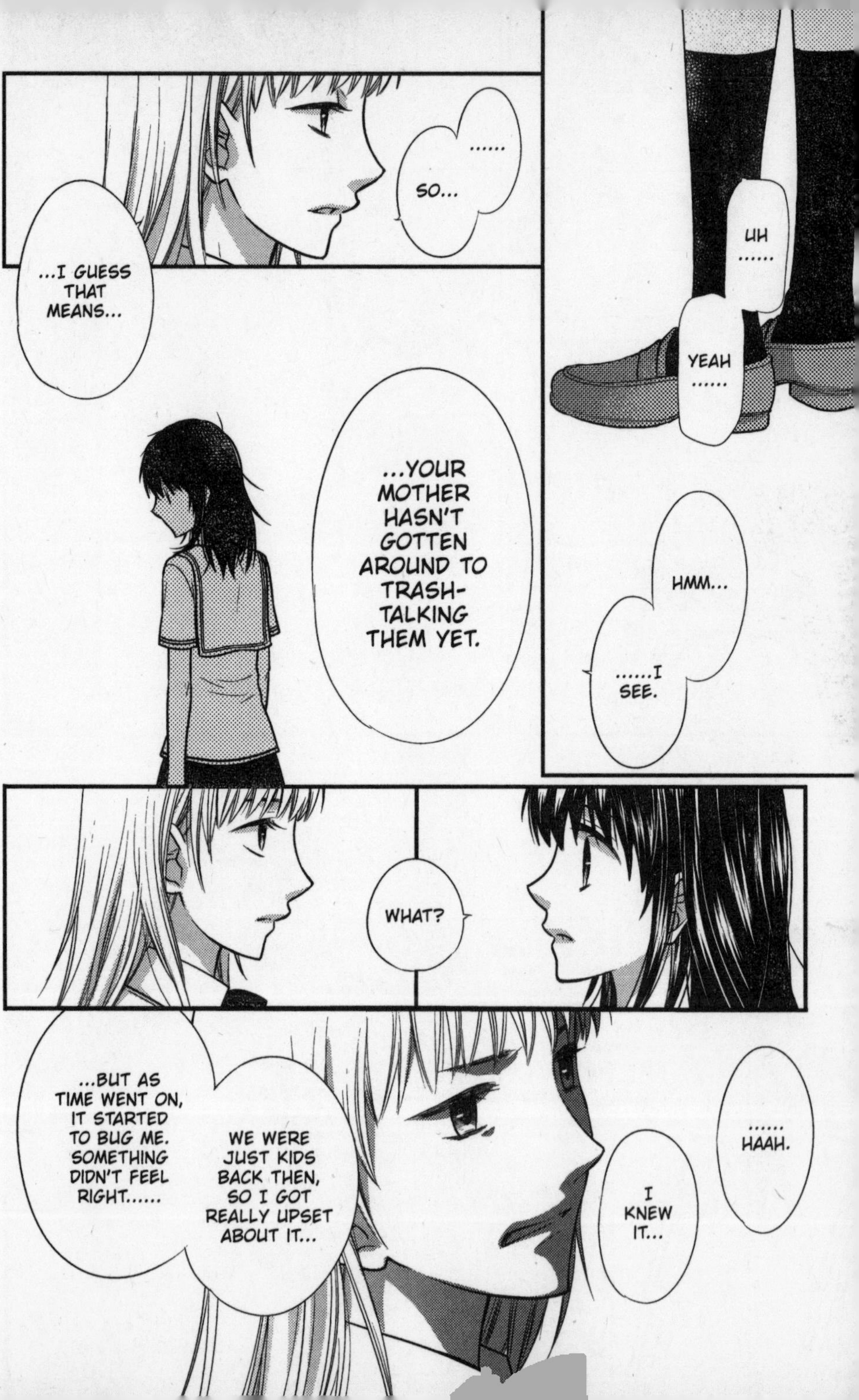
UH ......
YEAH ......
HMM...
......I SEE.
......
SO...
...I GUESS THAT MEANS...
...YOUR MOTHER HASN'T GOTTEN AROUND TO TRASH-TALKING THEM YET.
WHAT?
...... HAAH.
I KNEW IT...
WE WERE JUST KIDS BACK THEN, SO I GOT REALLY UPSET ABOUT IT...
...BUT AS TIME WENT ON, IT STARTED TO BUG ME. SOMETHING DIDN'T FEEL RIGHT......

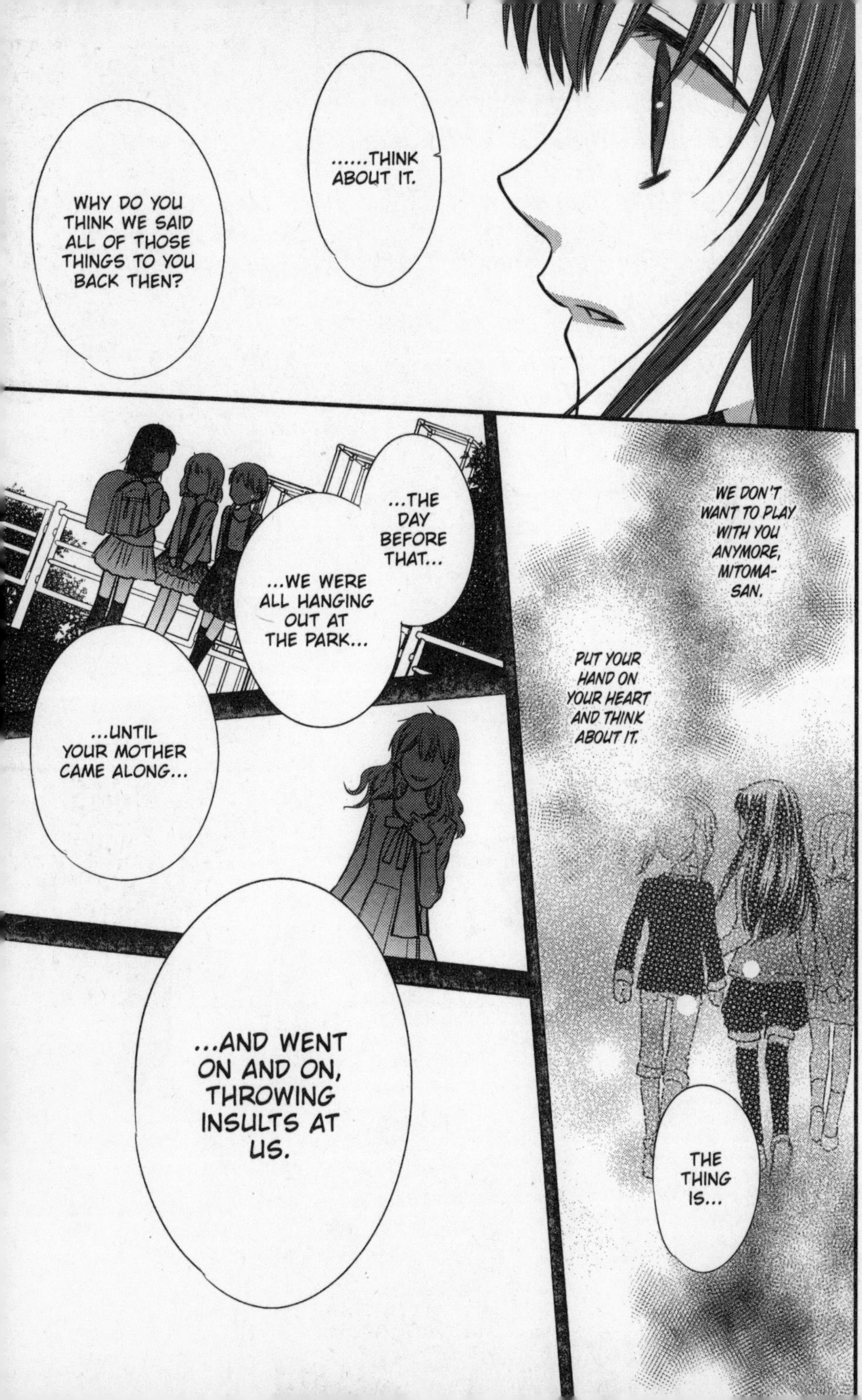
......THINK ABOUT IT.
WHY DO YOU THINK WE SAID ALL OF THOSE THINGS TO YOU BACK THEN?
WE DON'T WANT TO PLAY WITH YOU ANYMORE, MITOMA-SAN.
PUT YOUR HAND ON YOUR HEART AND THINK ABOUT IT.
THE THING IS...
...THE DAY BEFORE THAT...
...WE WERE ALL HANGING OUT AT THE PARK...
...UNTIL YOUR MOTHER CAME ALONG...
...AND WENT ON AND ON, THROWING INSULTS AT US.

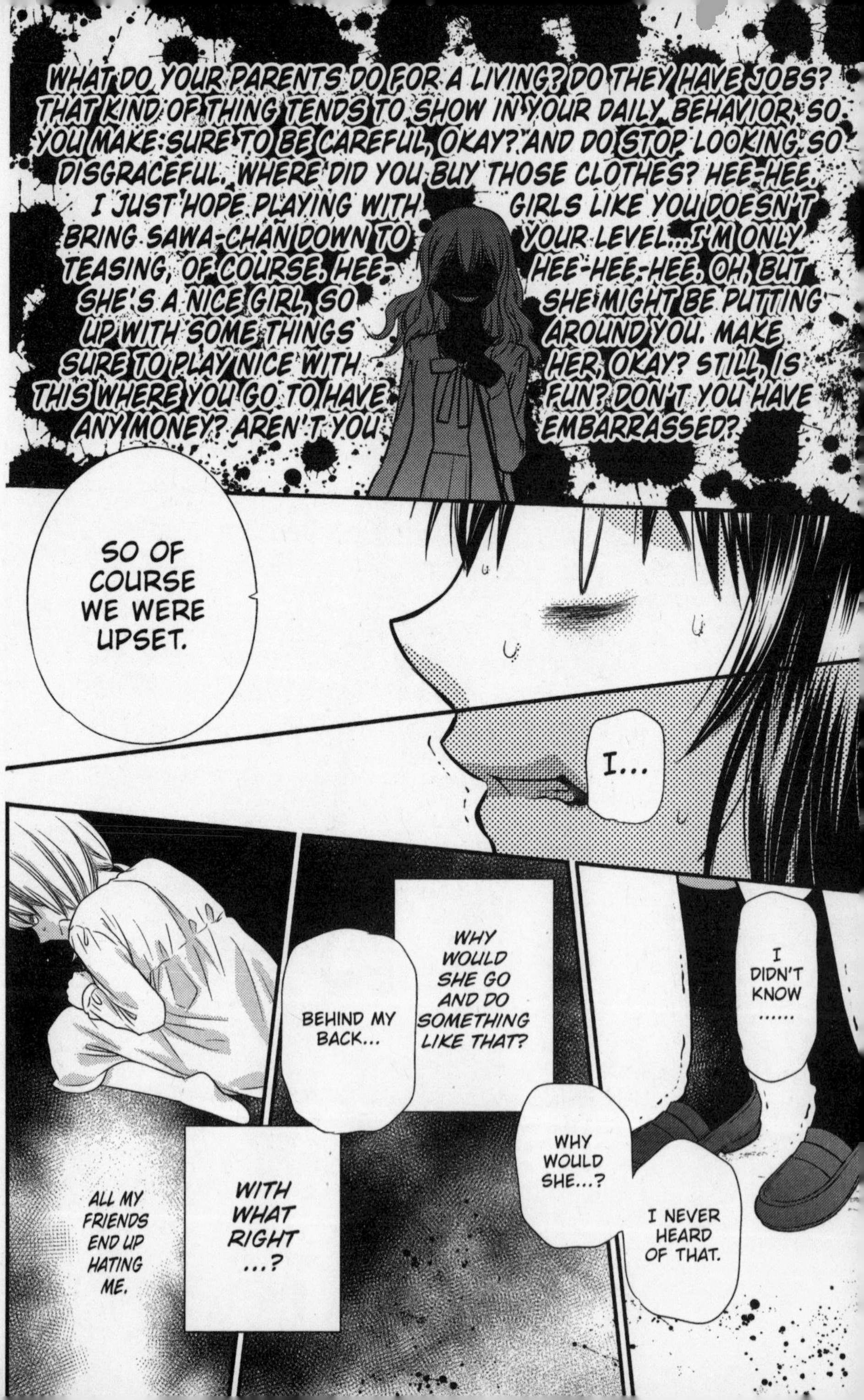
WHAT DO YOUR PARENTS DO FOR A LIVING? DO THEY HAVE JOBS? THAT KIND OF THING TENDS TO SHOW IN YOUR DAILY BEHAVIOR, SO YOU MAKE SURE TO BE CAREFUL, OKAY? AND DO STOP LOOKING SO DISGRACEFUL. WHERE DID YOU BUY THOSE CLOTHES? HEE-HEE. I JUST HOPE PLAYING WITH GIRLS LIKE YOU DOESN'T BRING SAWA-CHAN DOWN TO YOUR LEVEL... I'M ONLY TEASING, OF COURSE. HEE-HEE-HEE-HEE. OH, BUT SHE'S A NICE GIRL, SO SHE MIGHT BE PUTTING UP WITH SOME THINGS AROUND YOU. MAKE SURE TO PLAY NICE WITH HER, OKAY? STILL, IS THIS WHERE YOU GO TO HAVE FUN? DON'T YOU HAVE ANY MONEY? AREN'T YOU EMBARRASSED?
SO OF COURSE WE WERE UPSET.
I...
I DIDN'T KNOW ......
WHY WOULD SHE...?
I NEVER HEARD OF THAT.
WHY WOULD SHE GO AND DO SOMETHING LIKE THAT?
BEHIND MY BACK...
WITH WHAT RIGHT ...?
ALL MY FRIENDS END UP HATING ME.

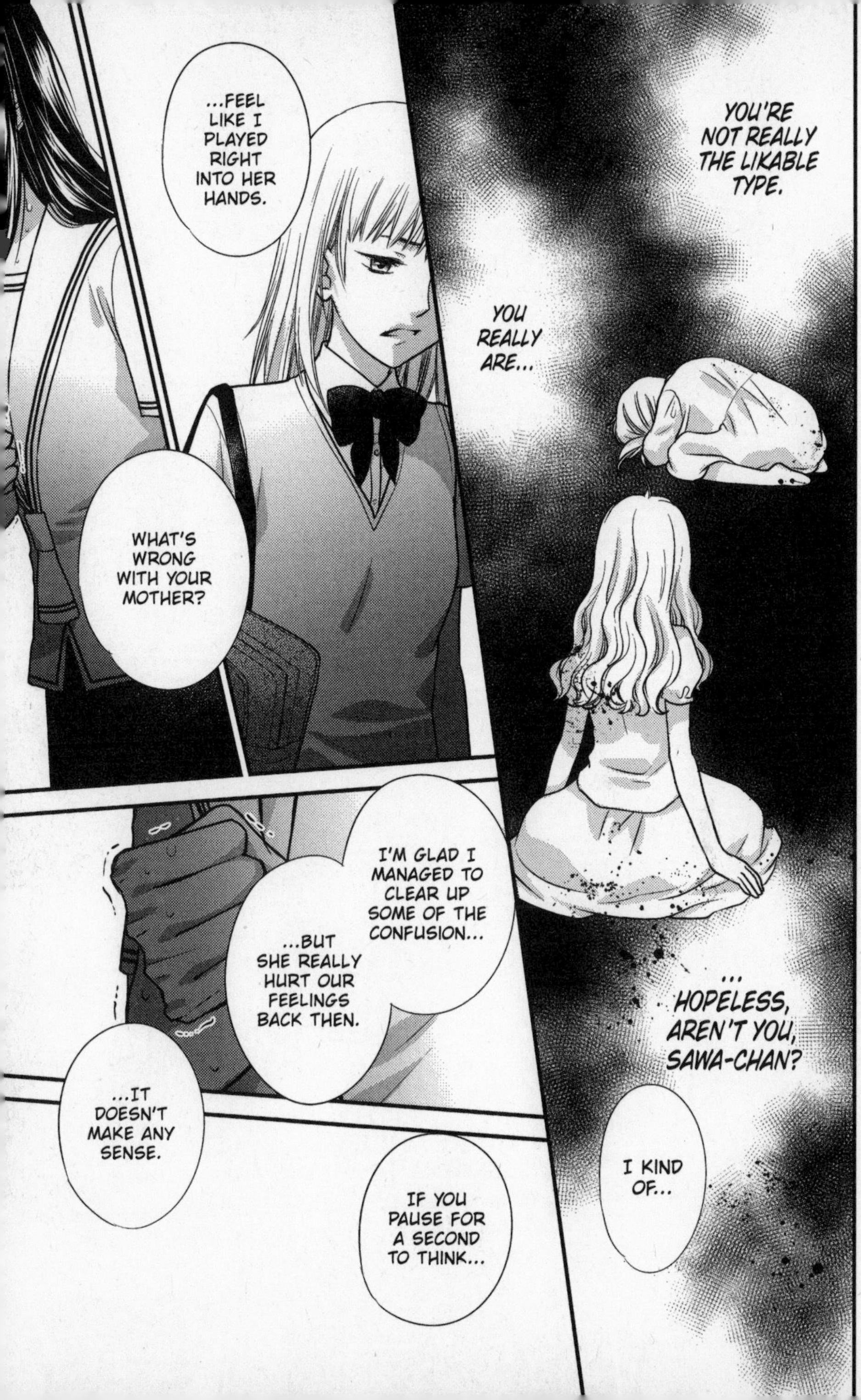
YOU'RE NOT REALLY THE LIKABLE TYPE.
YOU REALLY ARE...
...HOPELESS, AREN'T YOU, SAWA-CHAN?
I KIND OF...
...FEEL LIKE I PLAYED RIGHT INTO HER HANDS.
WHAT'S WRONG WITH YOUR MOTHER?
I'M GLAD I MANAGED TO CLEAR UP SOME OF THE CONFUSION...
...BUT SHE REALLY HURT OUR FEELINGS BACK THEN.
IF YOU PAUSE FOR A SECOND TO THINK...
...IT DOESN'T MAKE ANY SENSE.

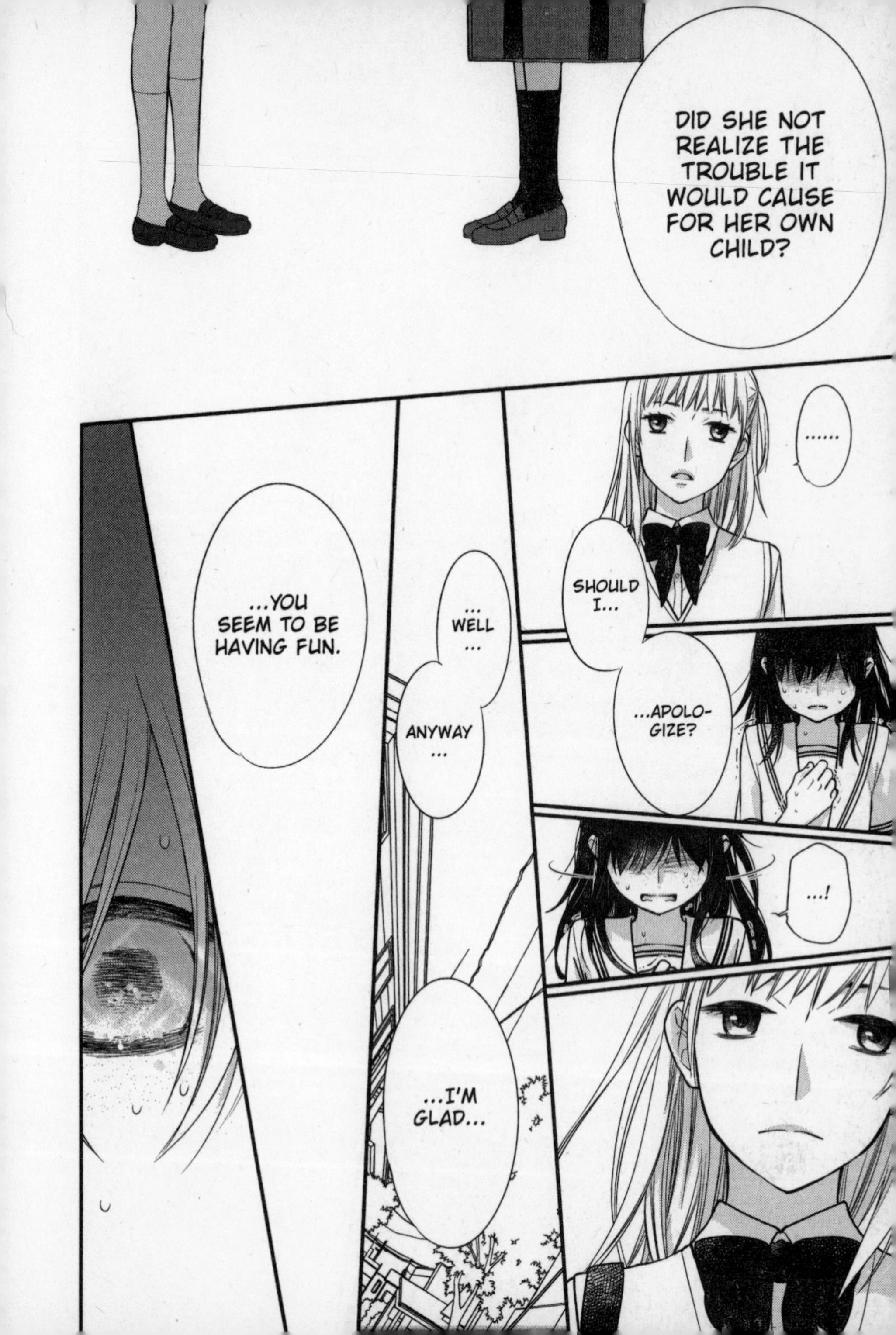
DID SHE NOT REALIZE THE TROUBLE IT WOULD CAUSE FOR HER OWN CHILD?
......
SHOULD I...
...APOLOGIZE?
...!
... WELL ...
ANYWAY ...
...I'M GLAD...
...YOU SEEM TO BE HAVING FUN.

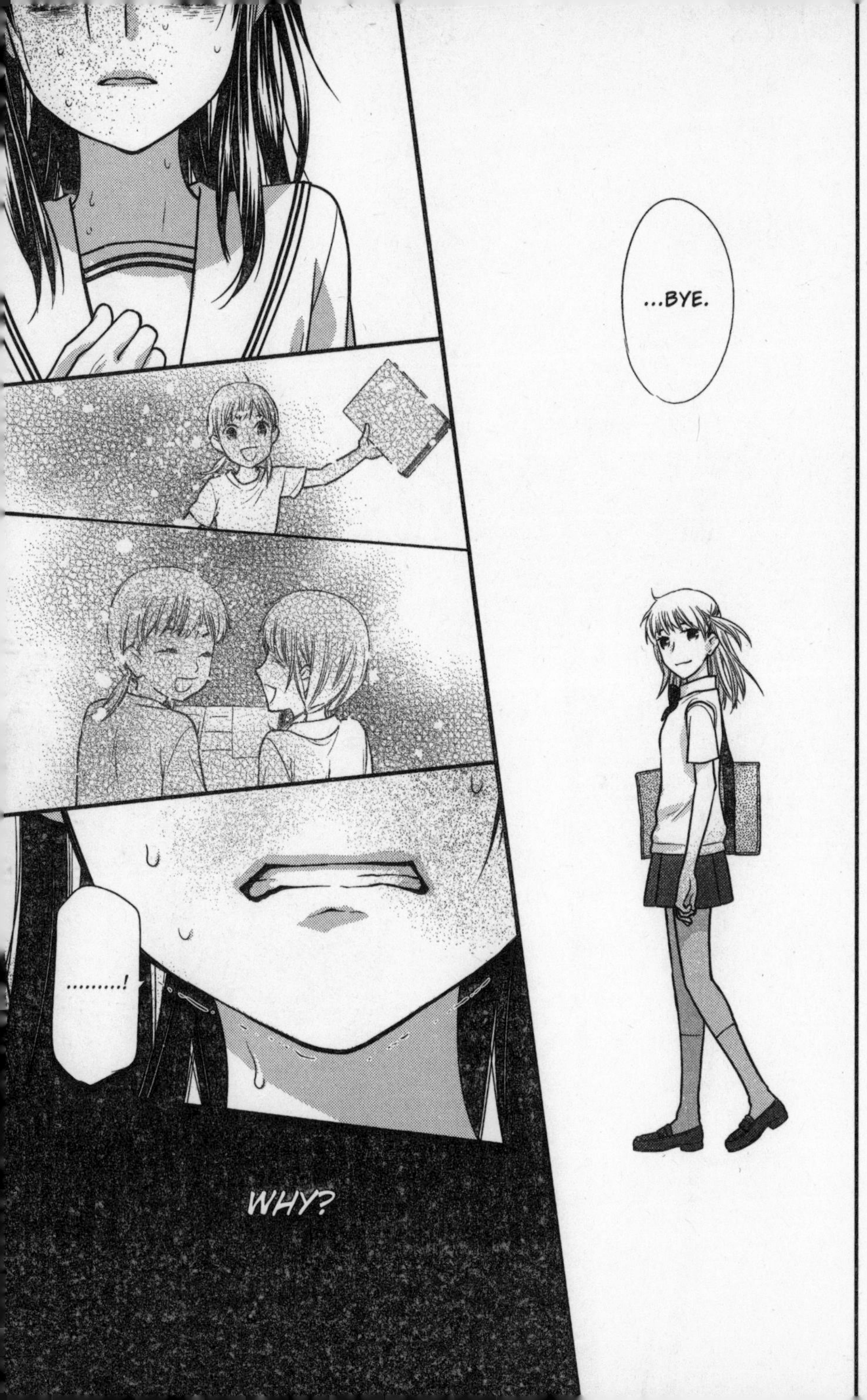
...BYE.
.........!
WHY?

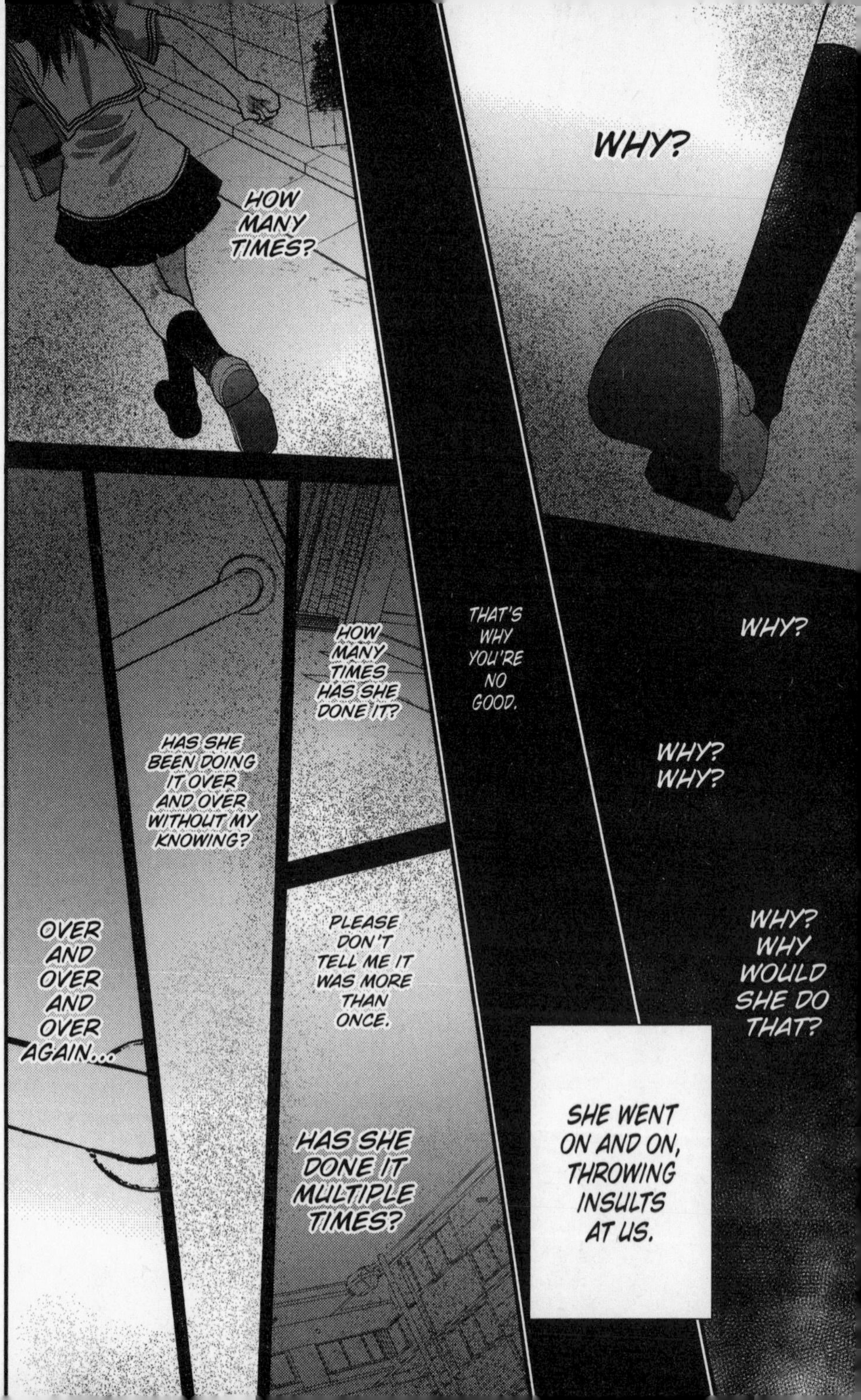
WHY?
WHY?
WHY? WHY?
THAT'S WHY YOU'RE NO GOOD.
WHY? WHY WOULD SHE DO THAT?
SHE WENT ON AND ON, THROWING INSULTS AT US.
HOW MANY TIMES?
HOW MANY TIMES HAS SHE DONE IT?
HAS SHE BEEN DOING IT OVER AND OVER WITHOUT MY KNOWING?
PLEASE DON'T TELL ME IT WAS MORE THAN ONCE.
OVER AND OVER AND OVER AGAIN...
HAS SHE DONE IT MULTIPLE TIMES?

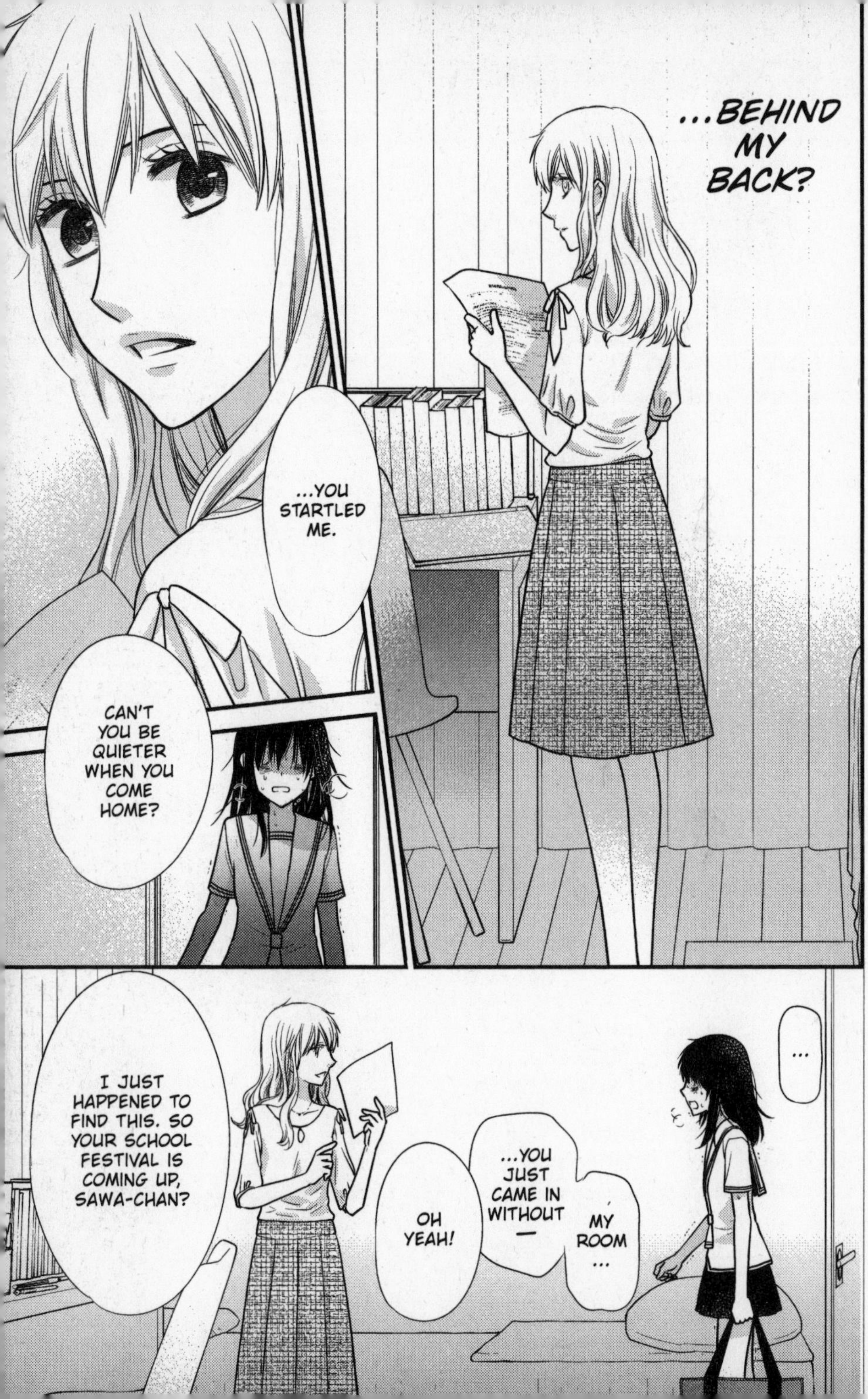
...BEHIND MY BACK?
...YOU STARTLED ME.
CAN'T YOU BE QUIETER WHEN YOU COME HOME?
...
...YOU JUST CAME IN WITHOUT —
MY ROOM ...
OH YEAH!
I JUST HAPPENED TO FIND THIS. SO YOUR SCHOOL FESTIVAL IS COMING UP, SAWA-CHAN?

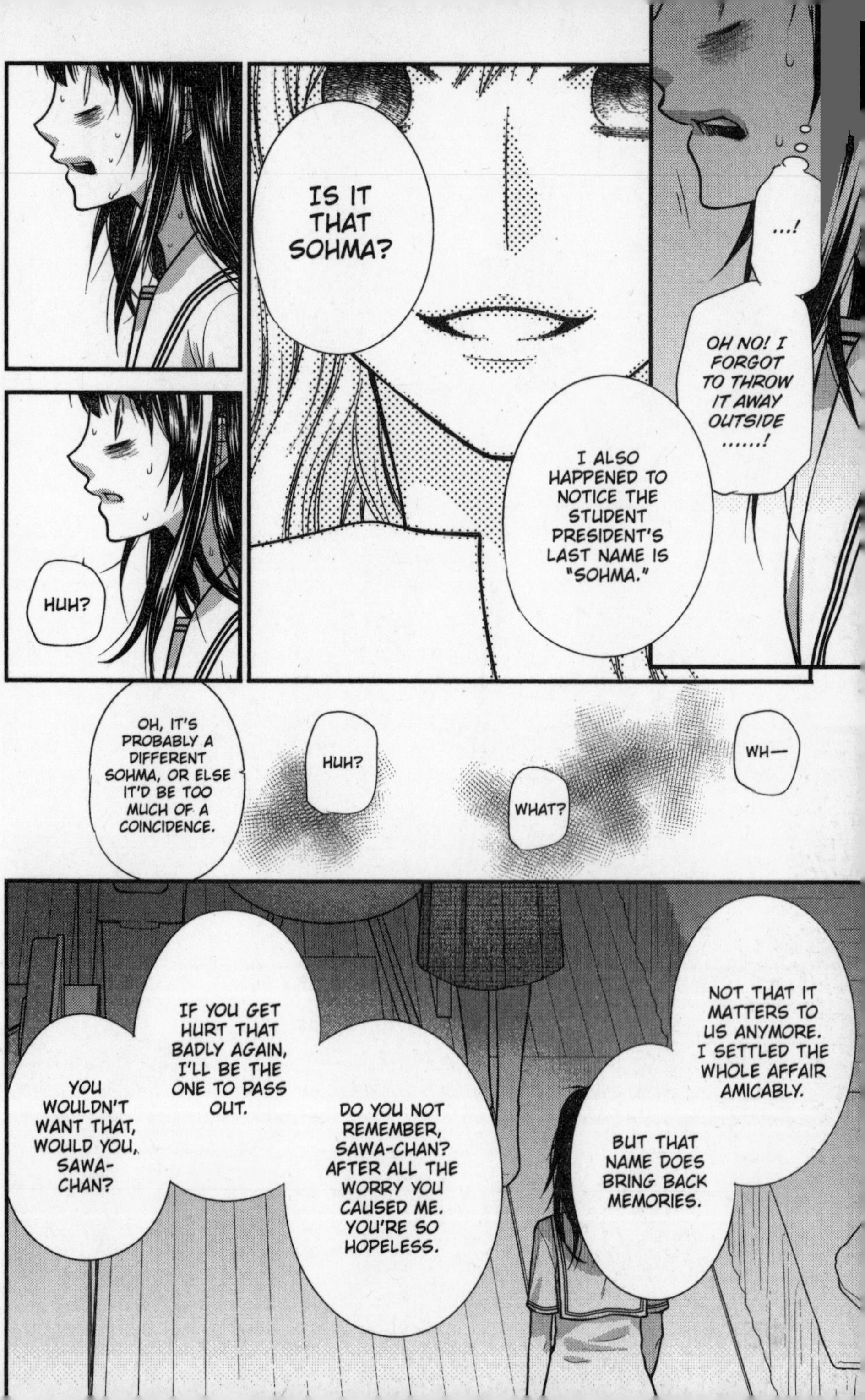
...!
OH NO! I FORGOT TO THROW IT AWAY OUTSIDE ......!
I ALSO HAPPENED TO NOTICE THE STUDENT PRESIDENT'S LAST NAME IS "SOHMA."
IS IT THAT SOHMA?
HUH?
WH—
WHAT?
HUH?
OH, IT'S PROBABLY A DIFFERENT SOHMA, OR ELSE IT'D BE TOO MUCH OF A COINCIDENCE.
NOT THAT IT MATTERS TO US ANYMORE. I SETTLED THE WHOLE AFFAIR AMICABLY.
BUT THAT NAME DOES BRING BACK MEMORIES.
DO YOU NOT REMEMBER, SAWA-CHAN? AFTER ALL THE WORRY YOU CAUSED ME. YOU'RE SO HOPELESS.
IF YOU GET HURT THAT BADLY AGAIN, I'LL BE THE ONE TO PASS OUT.
YOU WOULDN'T WANT THAT, WOULD YOU, SAWA-CHAN?

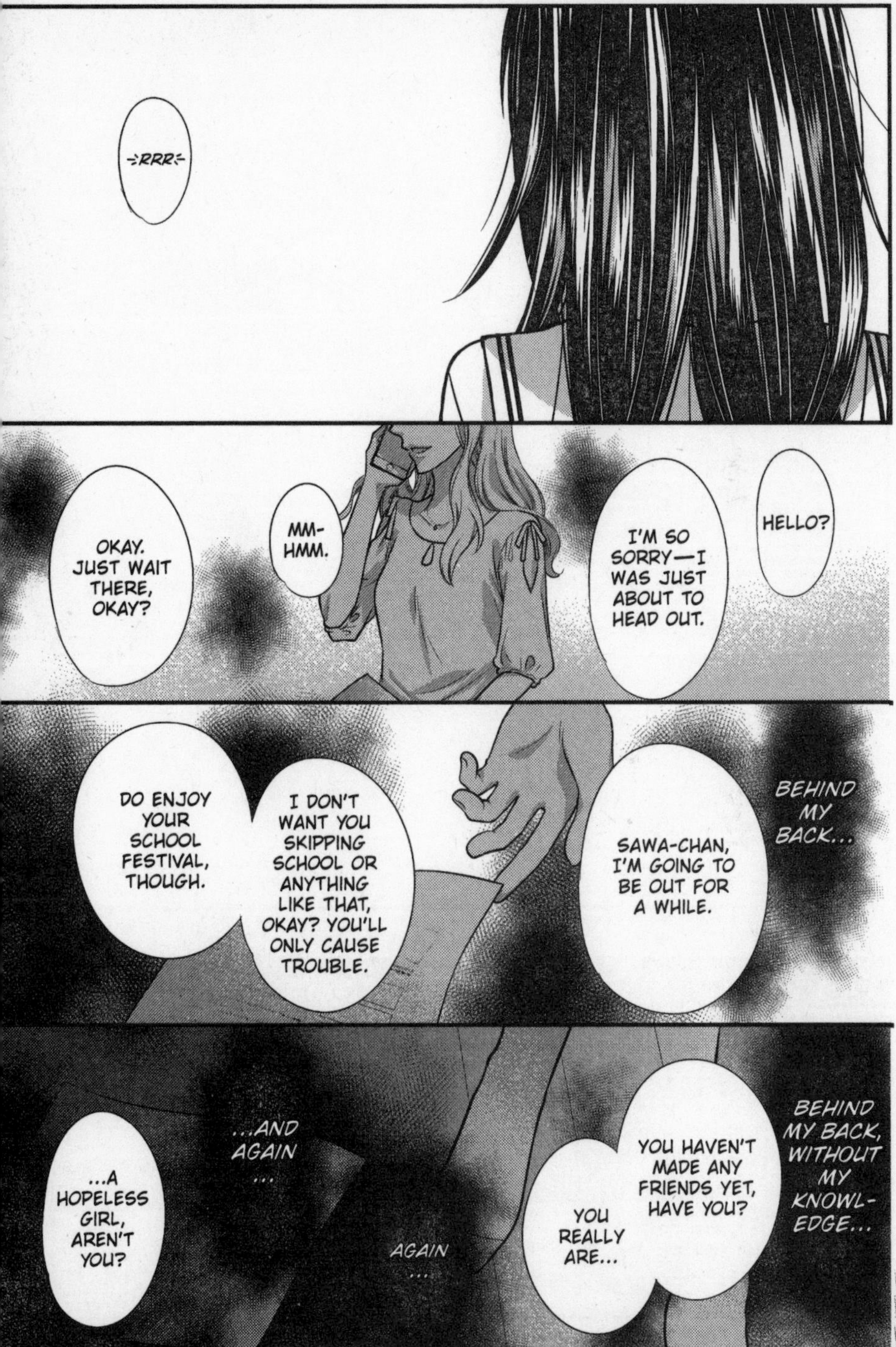
RRR
HELLO?
I'M SO SORRY—I WAS JUST ABOUT TO HEAD OUT.
MM-HMM.
OKAY. JUST WAIT THERE, OKAY?
BEHIND MY BACK...
SAWA-CHAN, I'M GOING TO BE OUT FOR A WHILE.
I DON'T WANT YOU SKIPPING SCHOOL OR ANYTHING LIKE THAT, OKAY? YOU'LL ONLY CAUSE TROUBLE.
DO ENJOY YOUR SCHOOL FESTIVAL, THOUGH.
BEHIND MY BACK, WITHOUT MY KNOWL-EDGE...
YOU HAVEN'T MADE ANY FRIENDS YET, HAVE YOU?
YOU REALLY ARE...
AGAIN...
...AND AGAIN...
...A HOPELESS GIRL, AREN'T YOU?

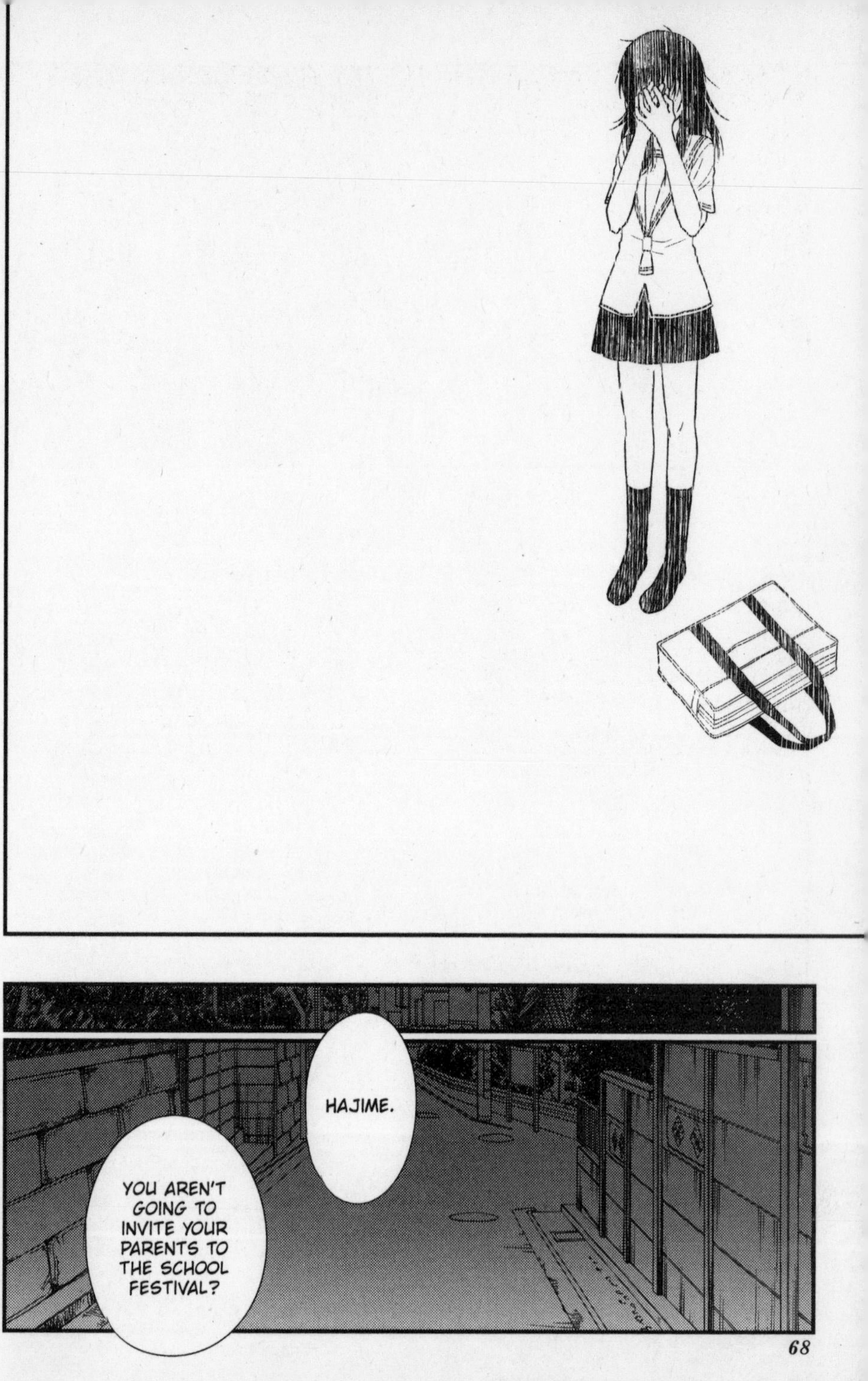
HAJIME.
YOU AREN'T GOING TO INVITE YOUR PARENTS TO THE SCHOOL FESTIVAL?

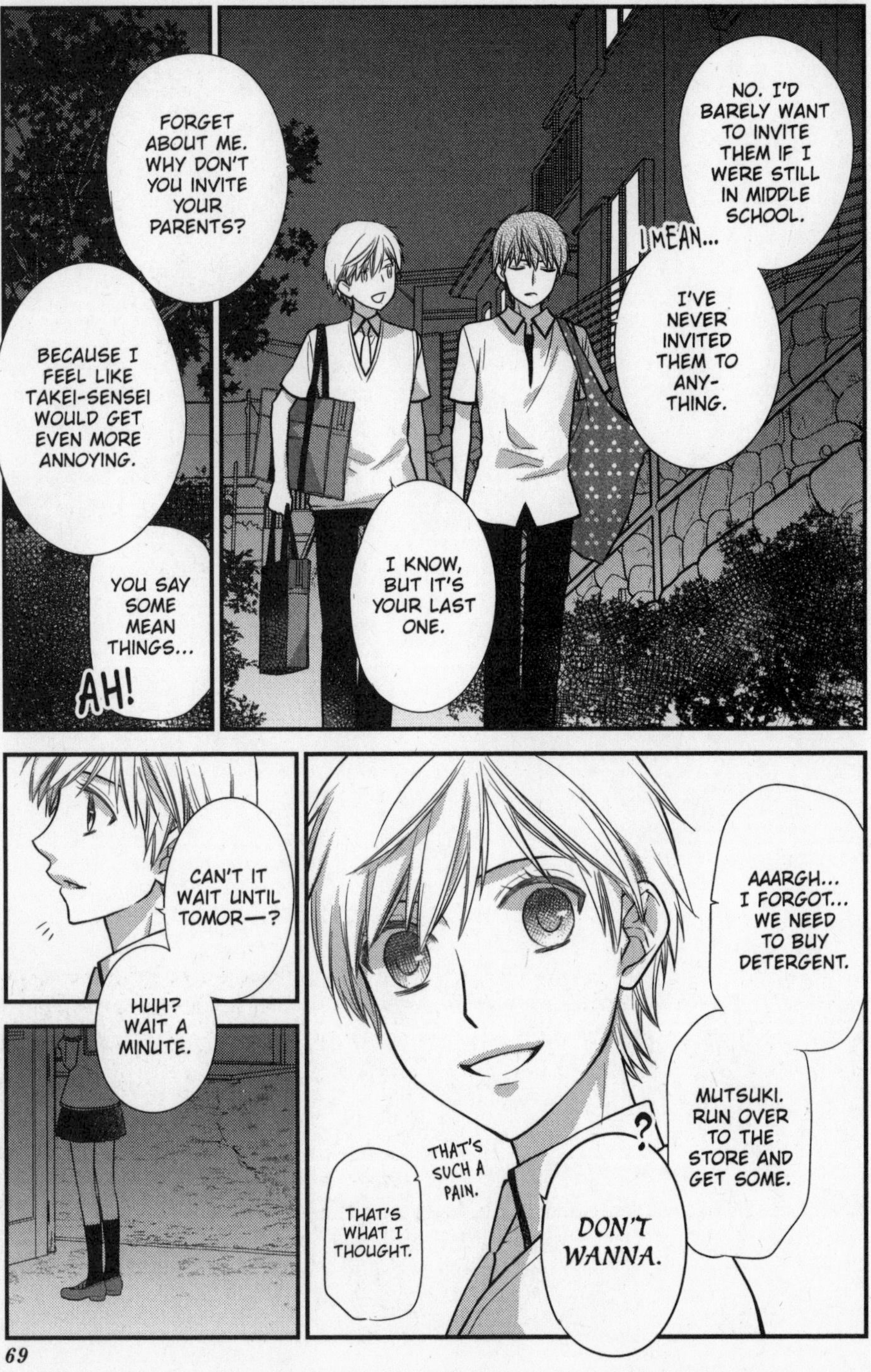
NO. I'D BARELY WANT TO INVITE THEM IF I WERE STILL IN MIDDLE SCHOOL.
I MEAN...
I'VE NEVER INVITED THEM TO ANY-THING.
I KNOW, BUT IT'S YOUR LAST ONE.
FORGET ABOUT ME. WHY DON'T YOU INVITE YOUR PARENTS?
BECAUSE I FEEL LIKE TAKEI-SENSEI WOULD GET EVEN MORE ANNOYING.
YOU SAY SOME MEAN THINGS...
AH!
AAARGH... I FORGOT... WE NEED TO BUY DETERGENT.
MUTSUKI. RUN OVER TO THE STORE AND GET SOME.
?
DON'T WANNA.
THAT'S SUCH A PAIN.
THAT'S WHAT I THOUGHT.
CAN'T IT WAIT UNTIL TOMOR—?
HUH? WAIT A MINUTE.

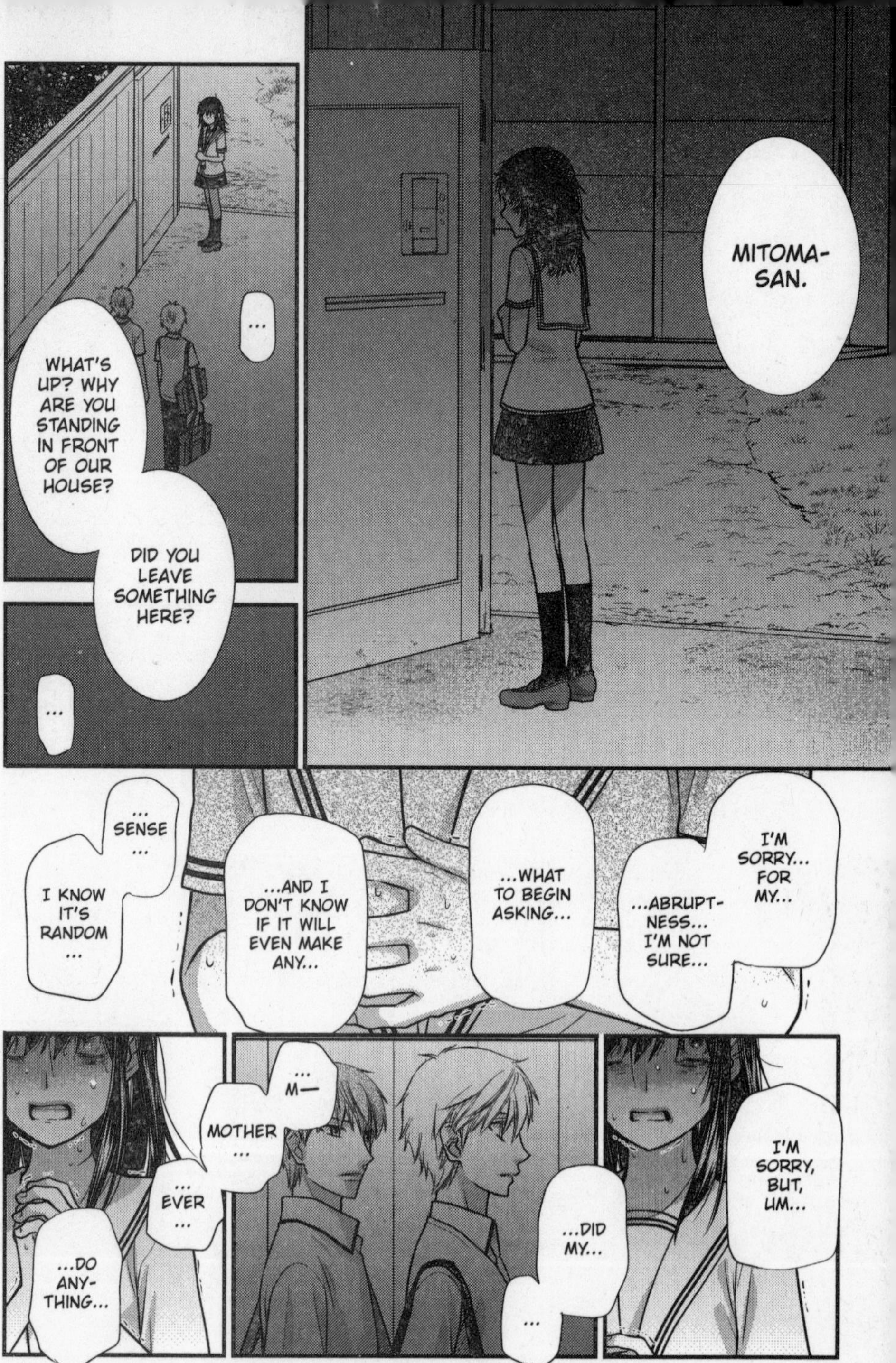
MITOMA-SAN.
...
WHAT'S UP? WHY ARE YOU STANDING IN FRONT OF OUR HOUSE?
DID YOU LEAVE SOMETHING HERE?
...
I'M SORRY... FOR MY...
...ABRUPTNESS... I'M NOT SURE...
...WHAT TO BEGIN ASKING...
...AND I DON'T KNOW IF IT WILL EVEN MAKE ANY...
... SENSE ...
I KNOW IT'S RANDOM ...
I'M SORRY, BUT, UM...
...DID MY...
...
... M—
MOTHER ...
... EVER ...
...DO ANYTHING...

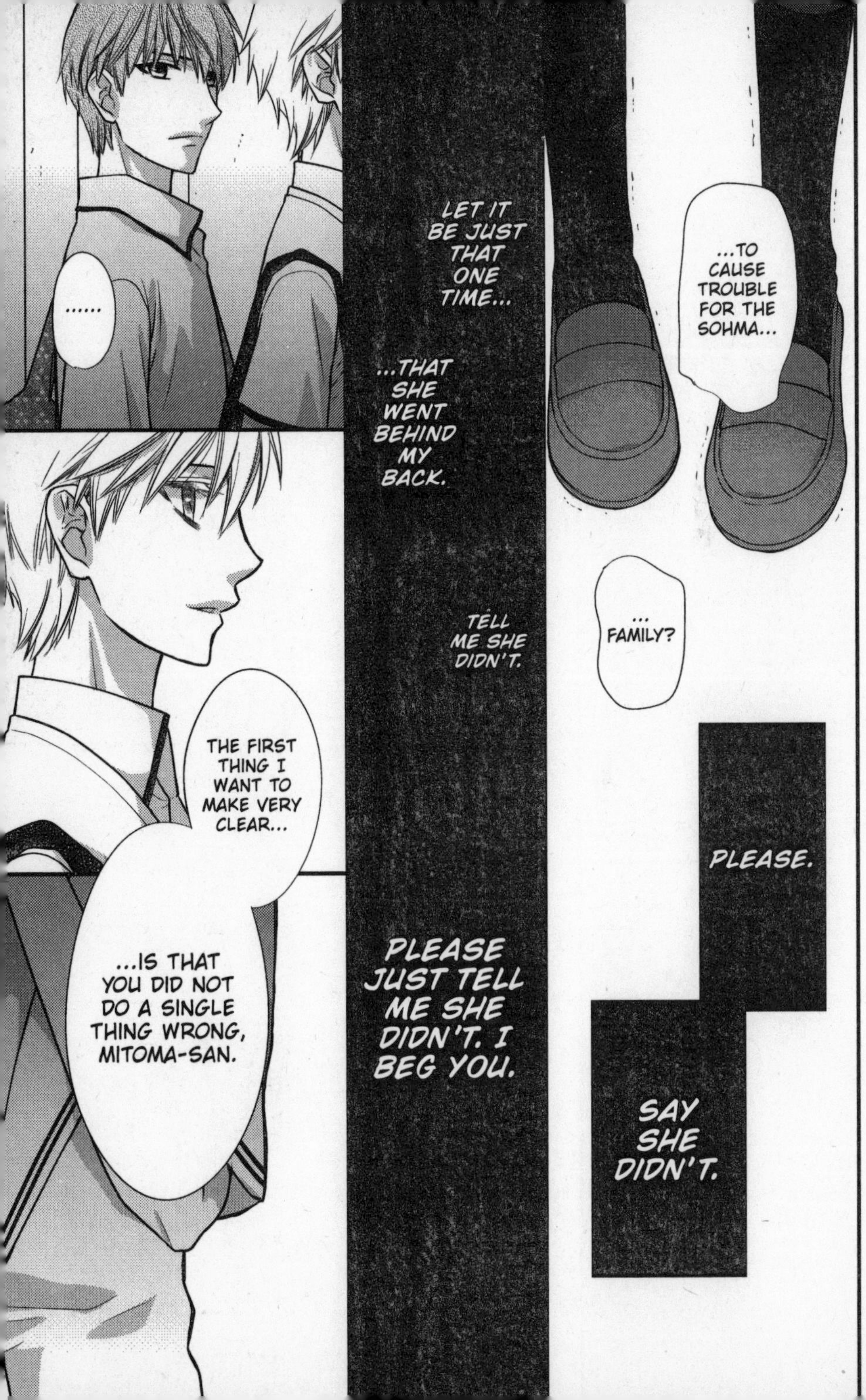
...TO CAUSE TROUBLE FOR THE SOHMA...
...FAMILY?
PLEASE.
SAY SHE DIDN'T.
LET IT BE JUST THAT ONE TIME...
...THAT SHE WENT BEHIND MY BACK.
TELL ME SHE DIDN'T.
PLEASE JUST TELL ME SHE DIDN'T. I BEG YOU.
......
THE FIRST THING I WANT TO MAKE VERY CLEAR...
...IS THAT YOU DID NOT DO A SINGLE THING WRONG, MITOMA-SAN.

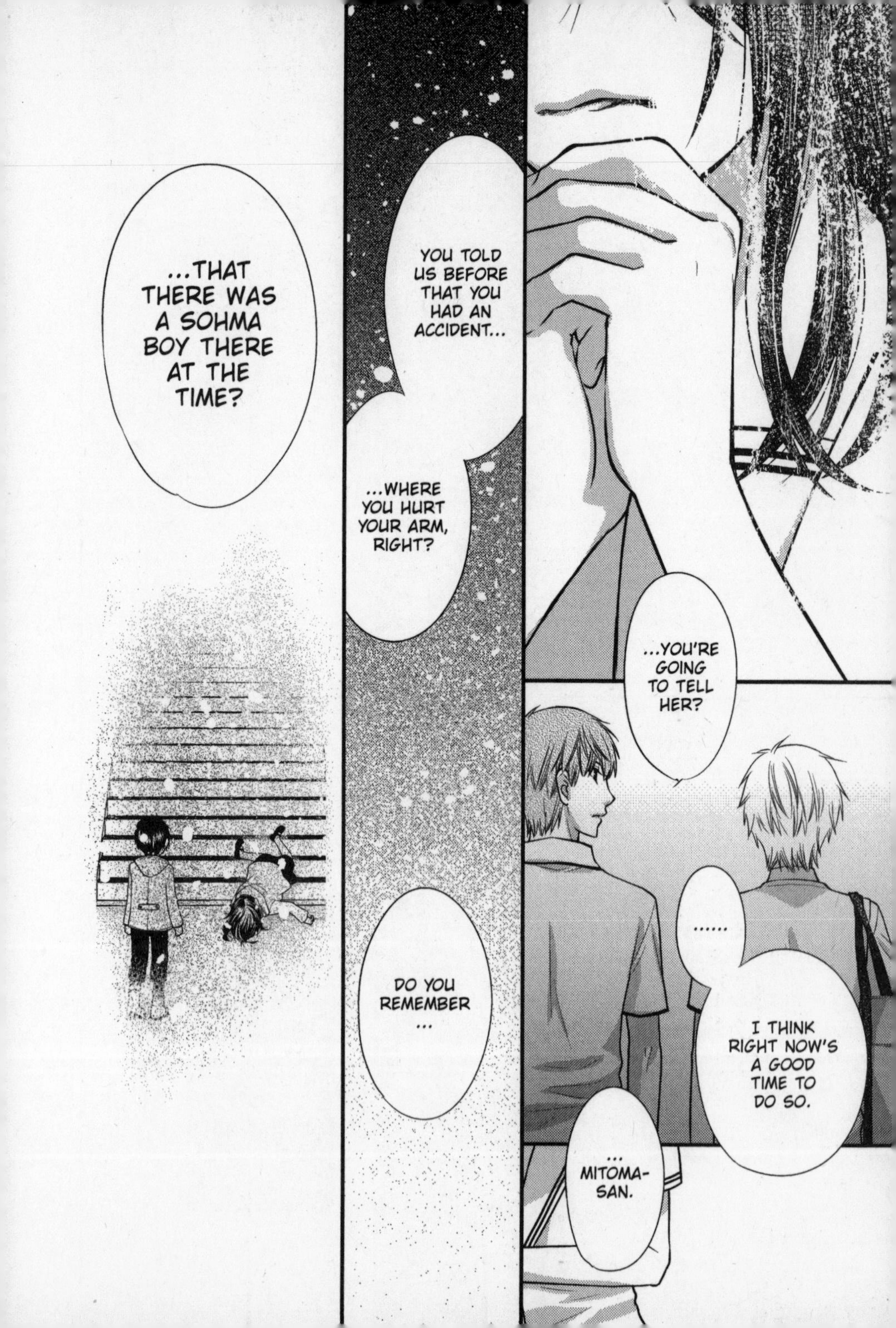
...YOU'RE GOING TO TELL HER?
......
I THINK RIGHT NOW'S A GOOD TIME TO DO SO.
...MITOMA-SAN.
YOU TOLD US BEFORE THAT YOU HAD AN ACCIDENT...
...WHERE YOU HURT YOUR ARM, RIGHT?
DO YOU REMEMBER ...
...THAT THERE WAS A SOHMA BOY THERE AT THE TIME?

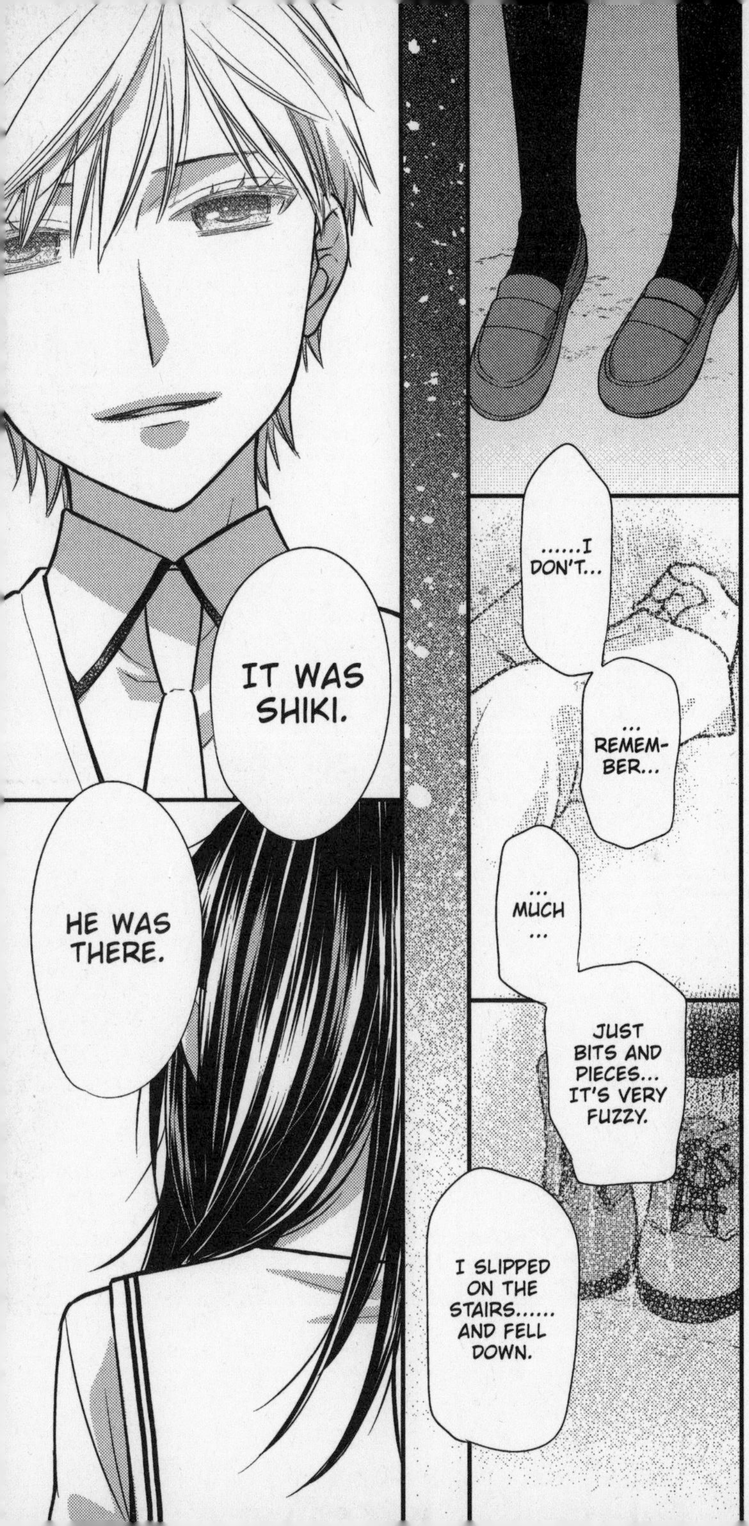
......I DON'T...
...REMEMBER...
...MUCH...
JUST BITS AND PIECES... IT'S VERY FUZZY.
I SLIPPED ON THE STAIRS...... AND FELL DOWN.
IT WAS SHIKI.
HE WAS THERE.

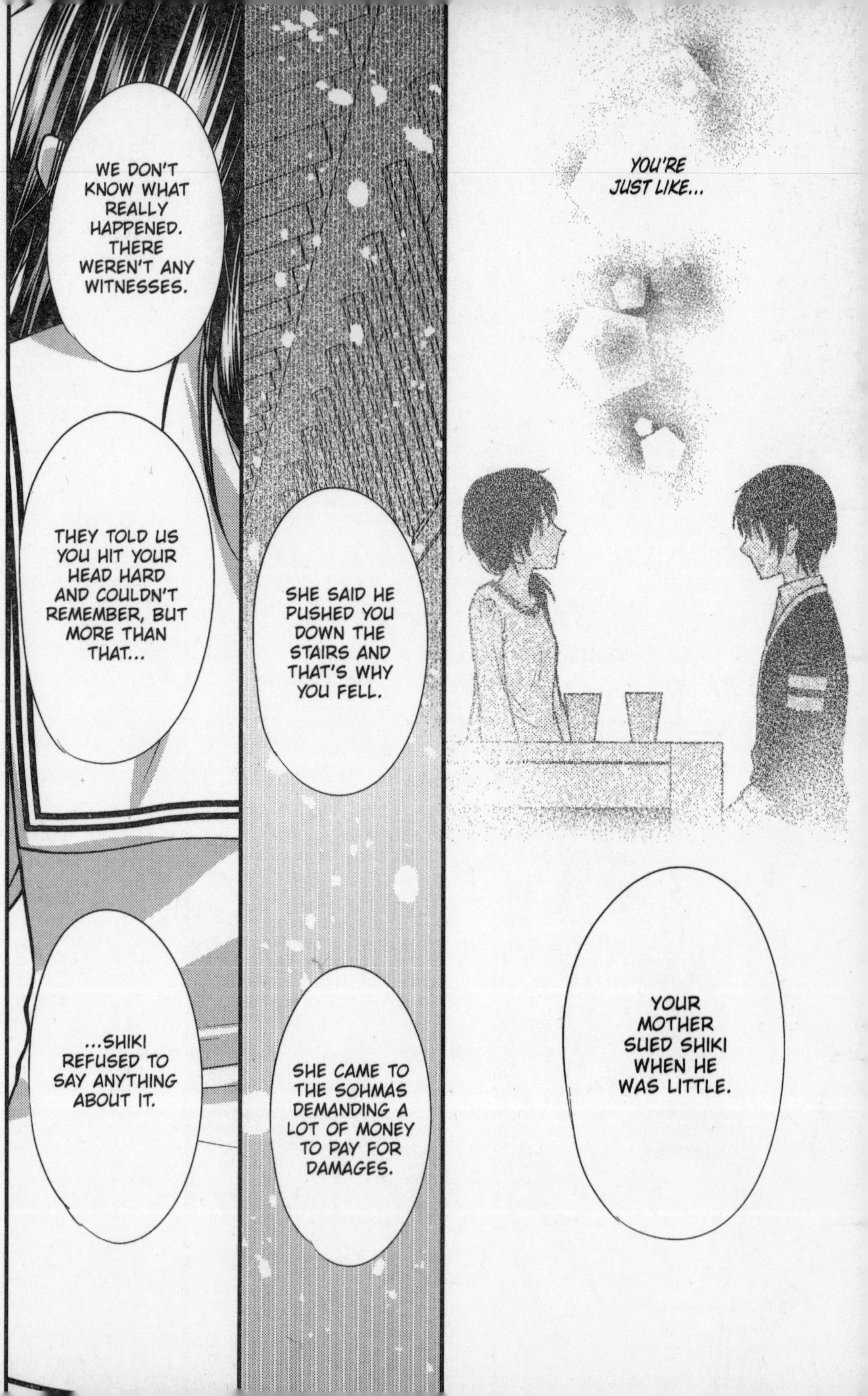
YOU'RE JUST LIKE...
YOUR MOTHER SUED SHIKI WHEN HE WAS LITTLE.
SHE SAID HE PUSHED YOU DOWN THE STAIRS AND THAT'S WHY YOU FELL.
SHE CAME TO THE SOHMAS DEMANDING A LOT OF MONEY TO PAY FOR DAMAGES.
WE DON'T KNOW WHAT REALLY HAPPENED. THERE WEREN'T ANY WITNESSES.
THEY TOLD US YOU HIT YOUR HEAD HARD AND COULDN'T REMEMBER, BUT MORE THAN THAT...
...SHIKI REFUSED TO SAY ANYTHING ABOUT IT.

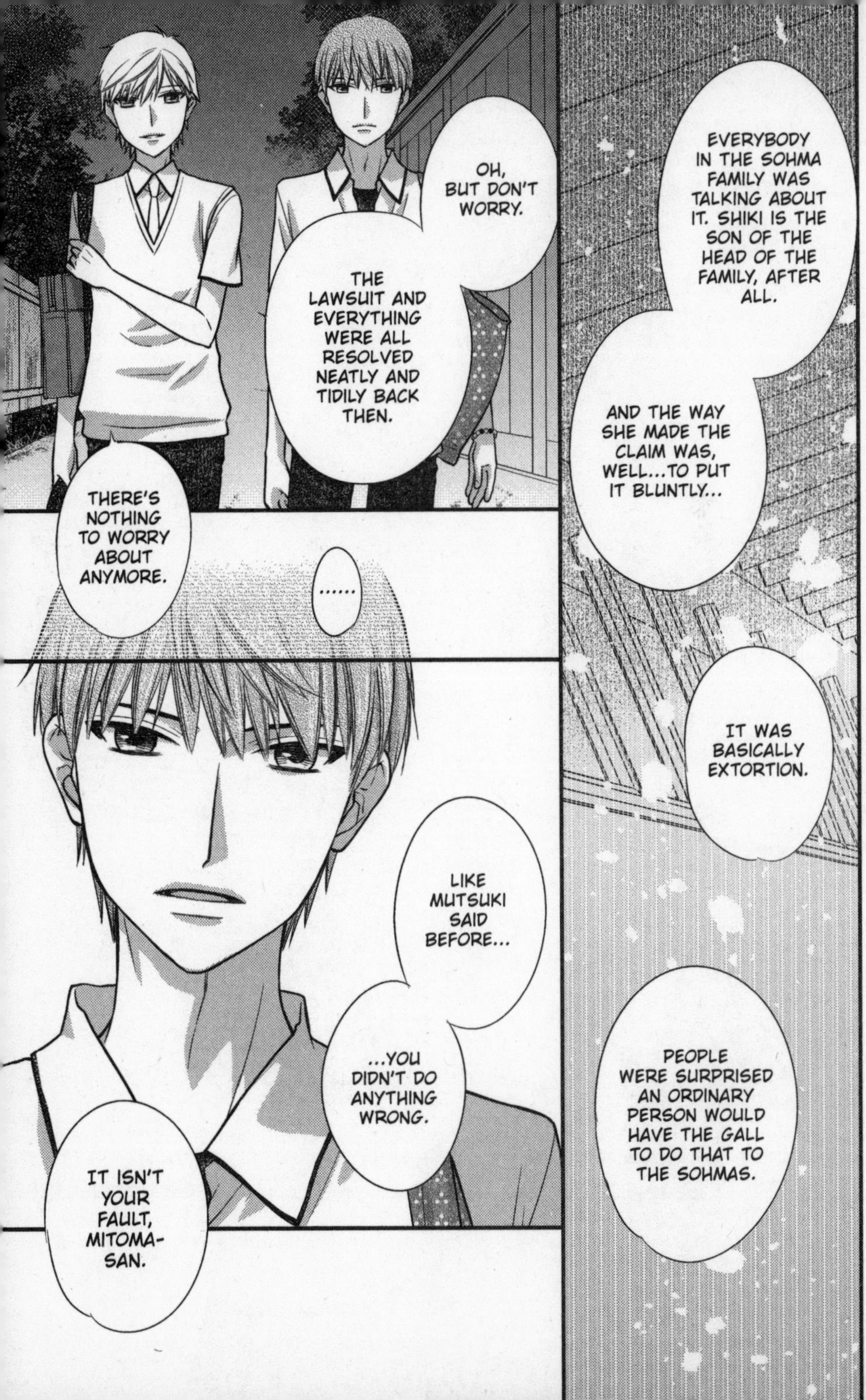
EVERYBODY IN THE SOHMA FAMILY WAS TALKING ABOUT IT. SHIKI IS THE SON OF THE HEAD OF THE FAMILY, AFTER ALL.
AND THE WAY SHE MADE THE CLAIM WAS, WELL...TO PUT IT BLUNTLY...
IT WAS BASICALLY EXTORTION.
PEOPLE WERE SURPRISED AN ORDINARY PERSON WOULD HAVE THE GALL TO DO THAT TO THE SOHMAS.
OH, BUT DON'T WORRY.
THE LAWSUIT AND EVERYTHING WERE ALL RESOLVED NEATLY AND TIDILY BACK THEN.
THERE'S NOTHING TO WORRY ABOUT ANYMORE.
......
LIKE MUTSUKI SAID BEFORE...
...YOU DIDN'T DO ANYTHING WRONG.
IT ISN'T YOUR FAULT, MITOMA-SAN.

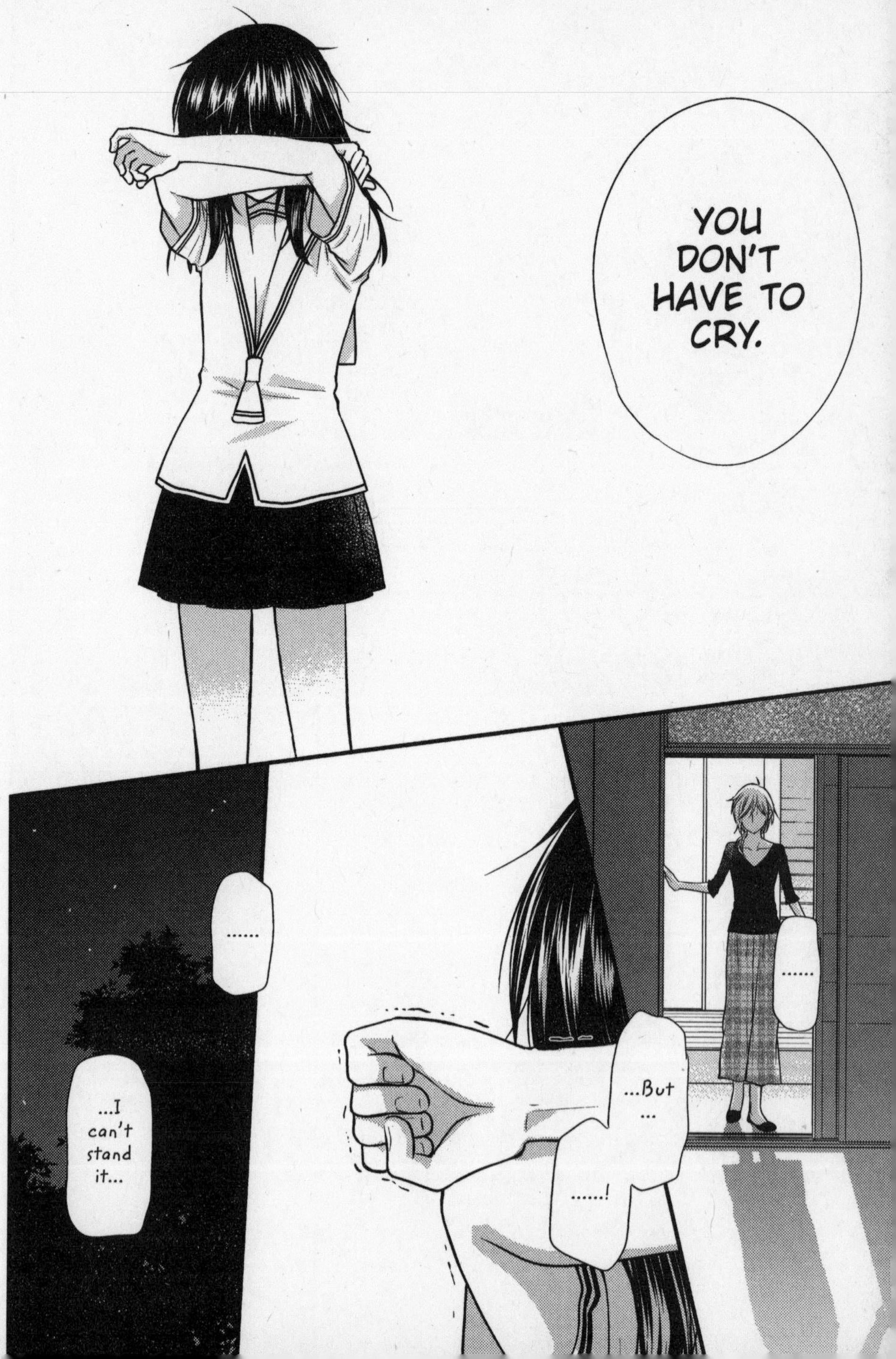
YOU DON'T HAVE TO CRY.
......
...But ...
......!
......
...I can't stand it...

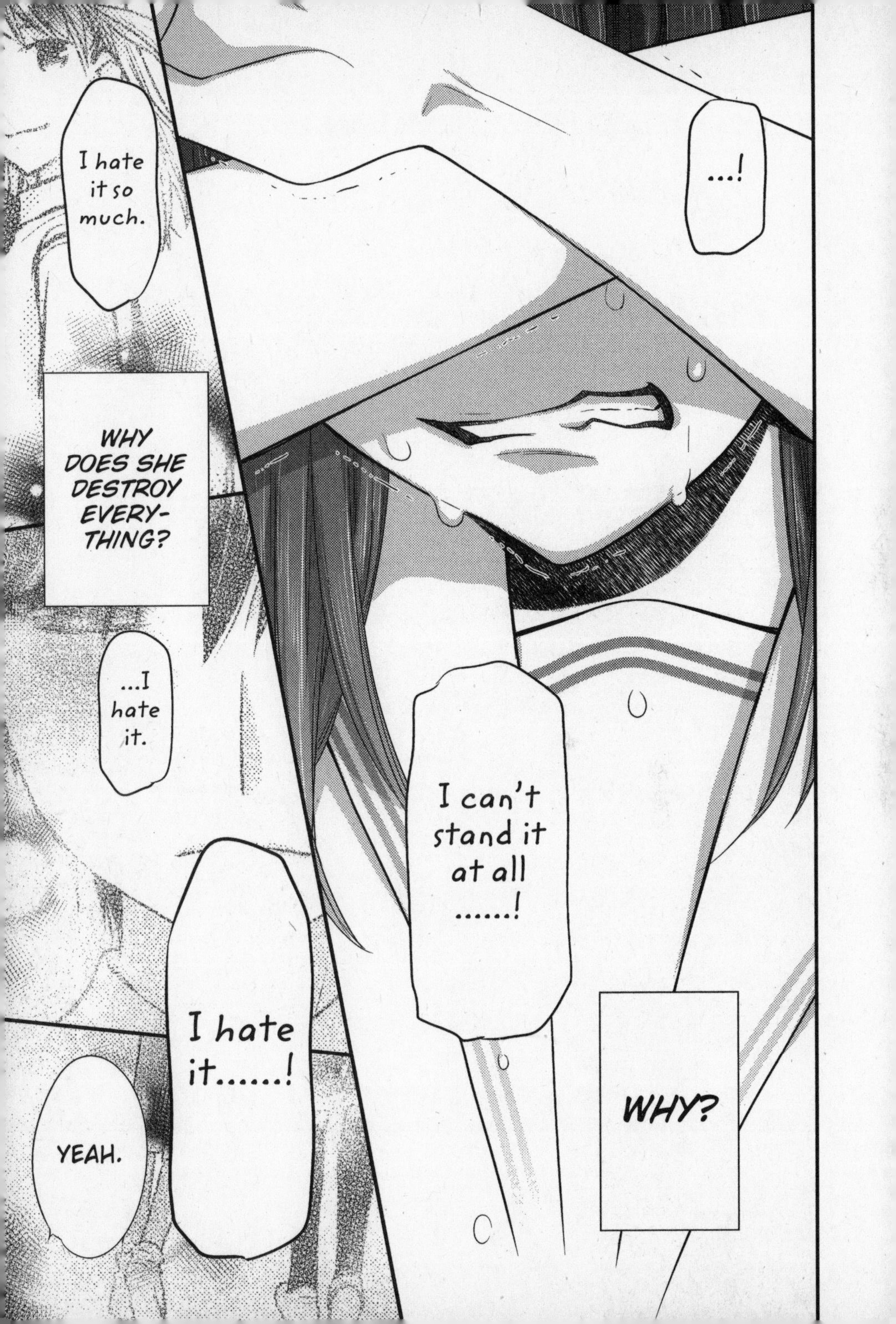
...!
I hate it so much.
WHY DOES SHE DESTROY EVERYTHING?
...I hate it.
I can't stand it at all ......!
WHY?
I hate it......!
YEAH.

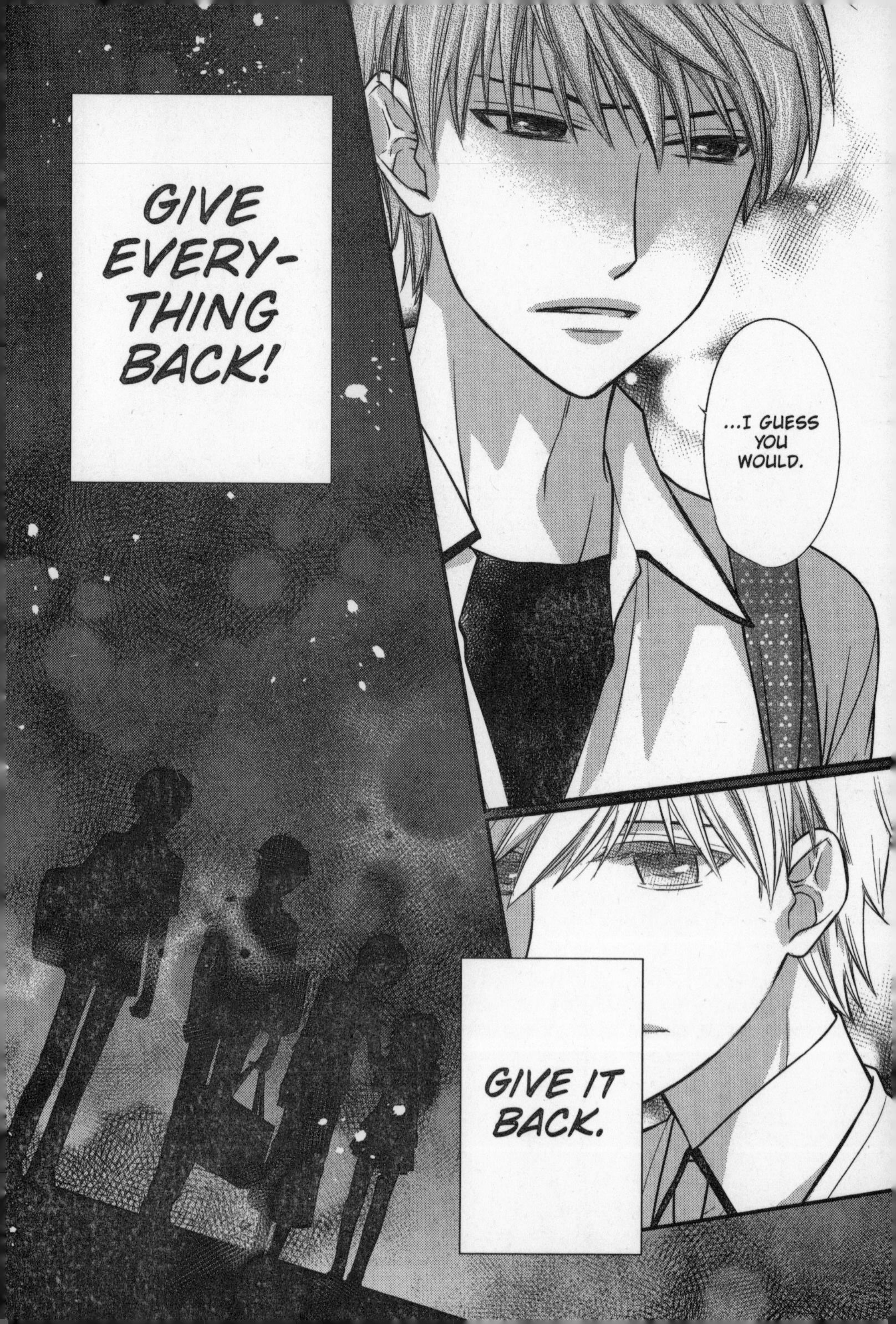
...I GUESS YOU WOULD.
GIVE IT BACK.
GIVE EVERY-THING BACK!

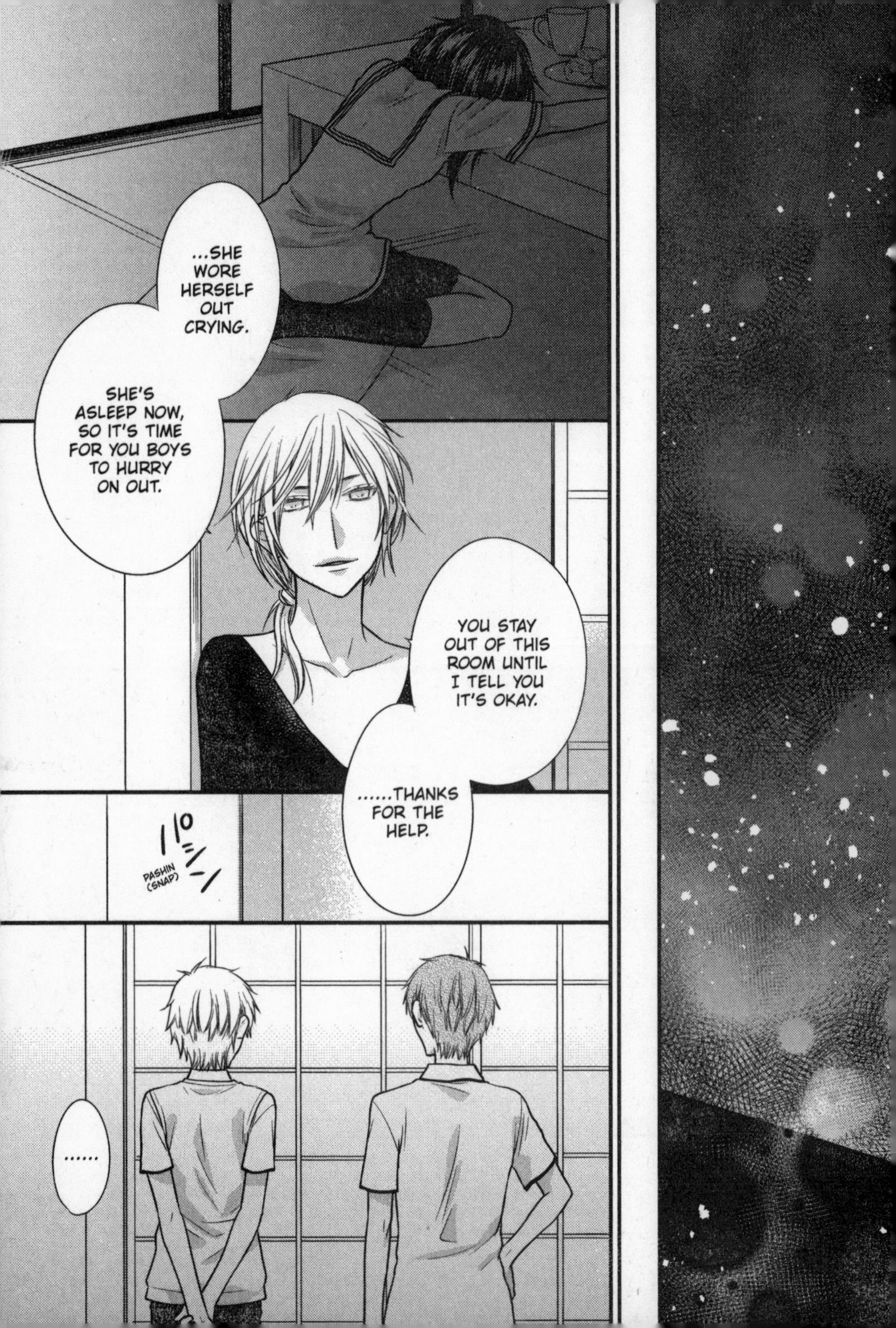
...SHE WORE HERSELF OUT CRYING.
SHE'S ASLEEP NOW, SO IT'S TIME FOR YOU BOYS TO HURRY ON OUT.
YOU STAY OUT OF THIS ROOM UNTIL I TELL YOU IT'S OKAY.
......THANKS FOR THE HELP.
PASHIN (SNAP)
......

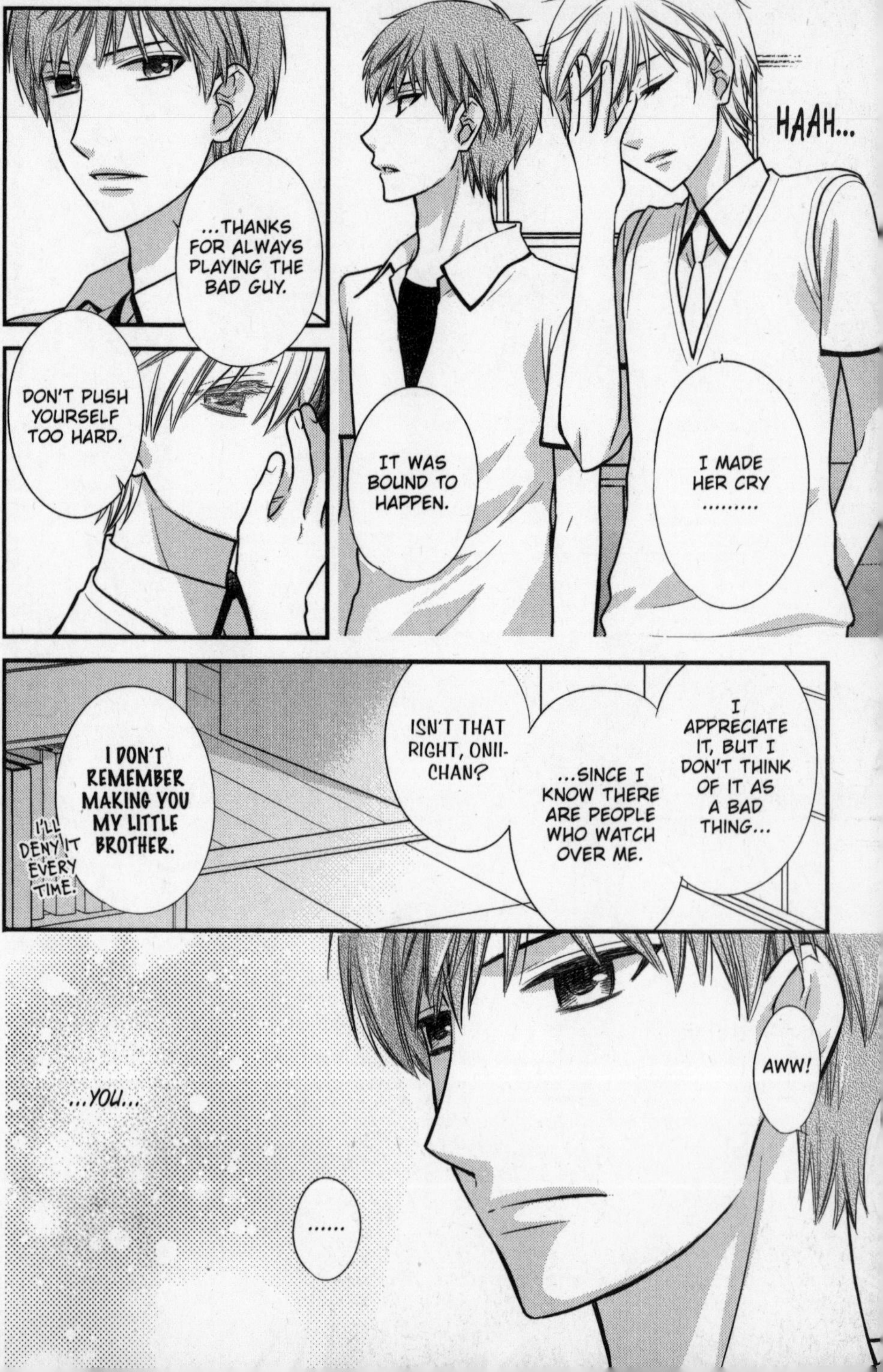
HAAH...
I MADE HER CRY ....
IT WAS BOUND TO HAPPEN.
...THANKS FOR ALWAYS PLAYING THE BAD GUY.
DON'T PUSH YOURSELF TOO HARD.
I APPRECIATE IT, BUT I DON'T THINK OF IT AS A BAD THING...
...SINCE I KNOW THERE ARE PEOPLE WHO WATCH OVER ME.
ISN'T THAT RIGHT, ONII-CHAN?
I DON'T REMEMBER MAKING YOU MY LITTLE BROTHER.
I'LL DENY IT EVERY TIME.
AWW!
...YOU...
......

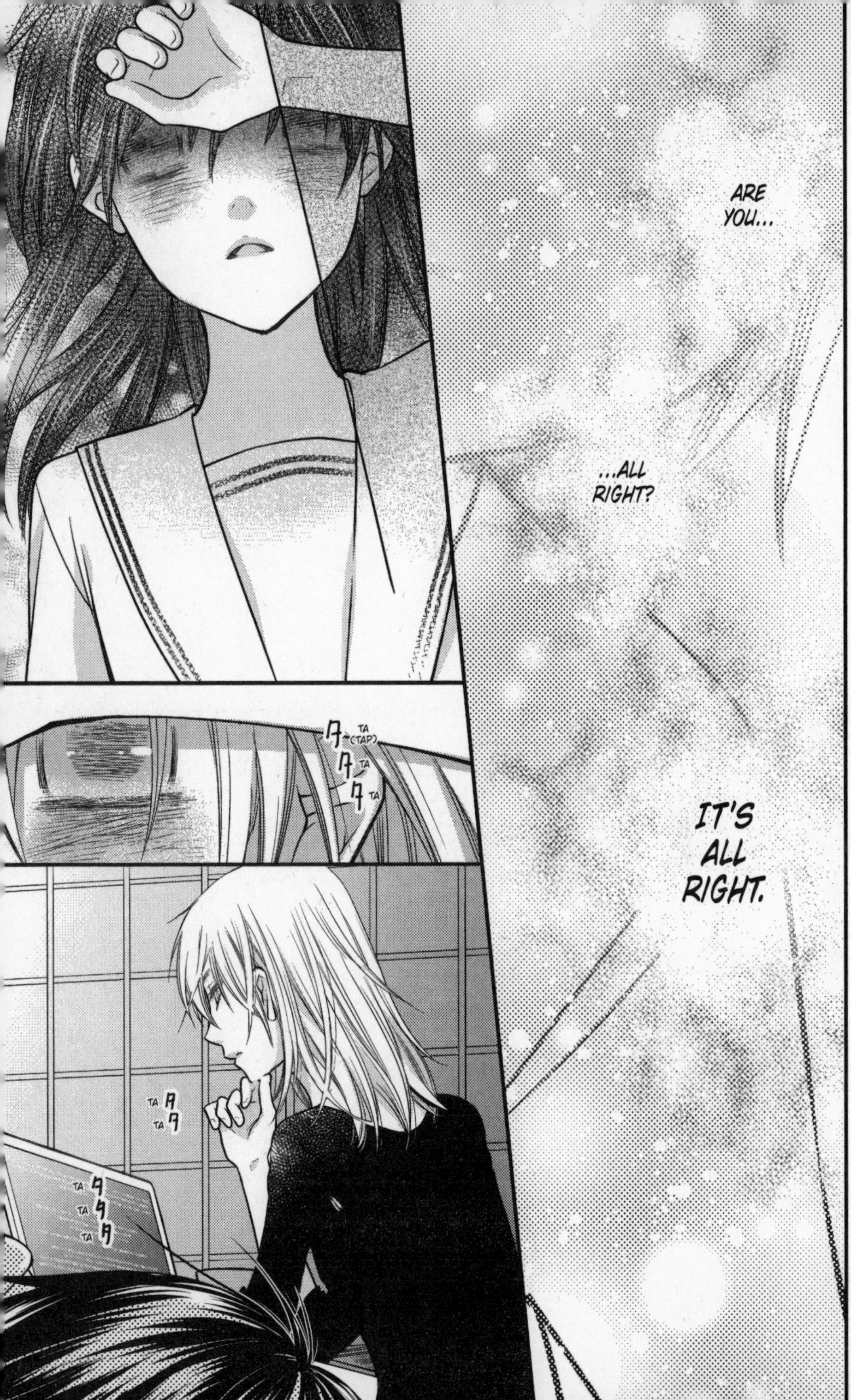
ARE YOU...
...ALL RIGHT?
IT'S ALL RIGHT.
タ TA (TAP)
タ TA
タ TA
TA タ
TA タ
TA タ
TA タ
TA タ

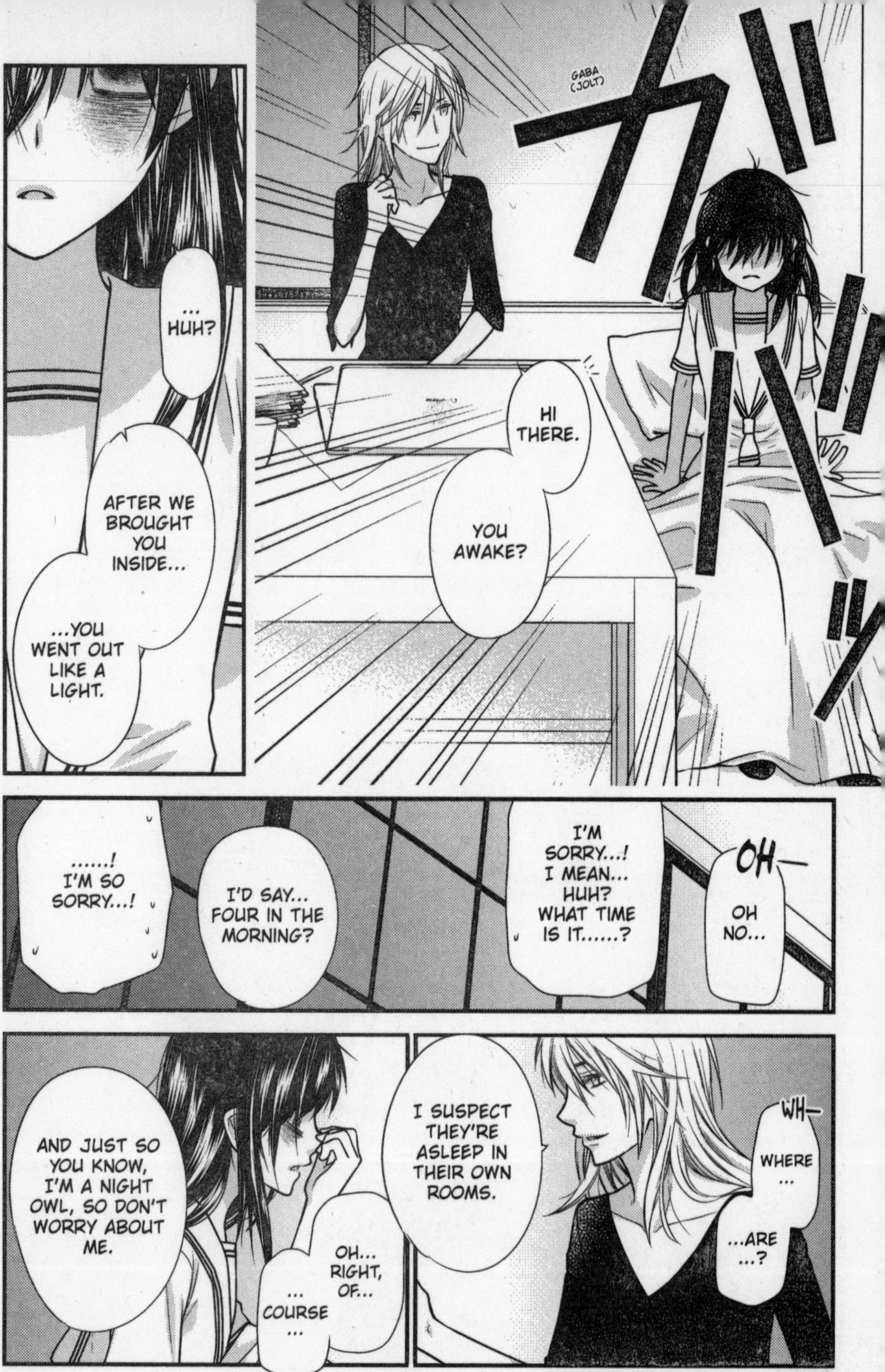
ガバッ
GABA (JOLT)
HI THERE.
YOU AWAKE?
... HUH?
AFTER WE BROUGHT YOU INSIDE...
...YOU WENT OUT LIKE A LIGHT.
OH—
OH NO...
I'M SORRY...! I MEAN... HUH? WHAT TIME IS IT......?
I'D SAY... FOUR IN THE MORNING?
......! I'M SO SORRY...!
WH—
WHERE ...
...ARE ...?
I SUSPECT THEY'RE ASLEEP IN THEIR OWN ROOMS.
AND JUST SO YOU KNOW, I'M A NIGHT OWL, SO DON'T WORRY ABOUT ME.
OH... RIGHT, OF...
... COURSE ...

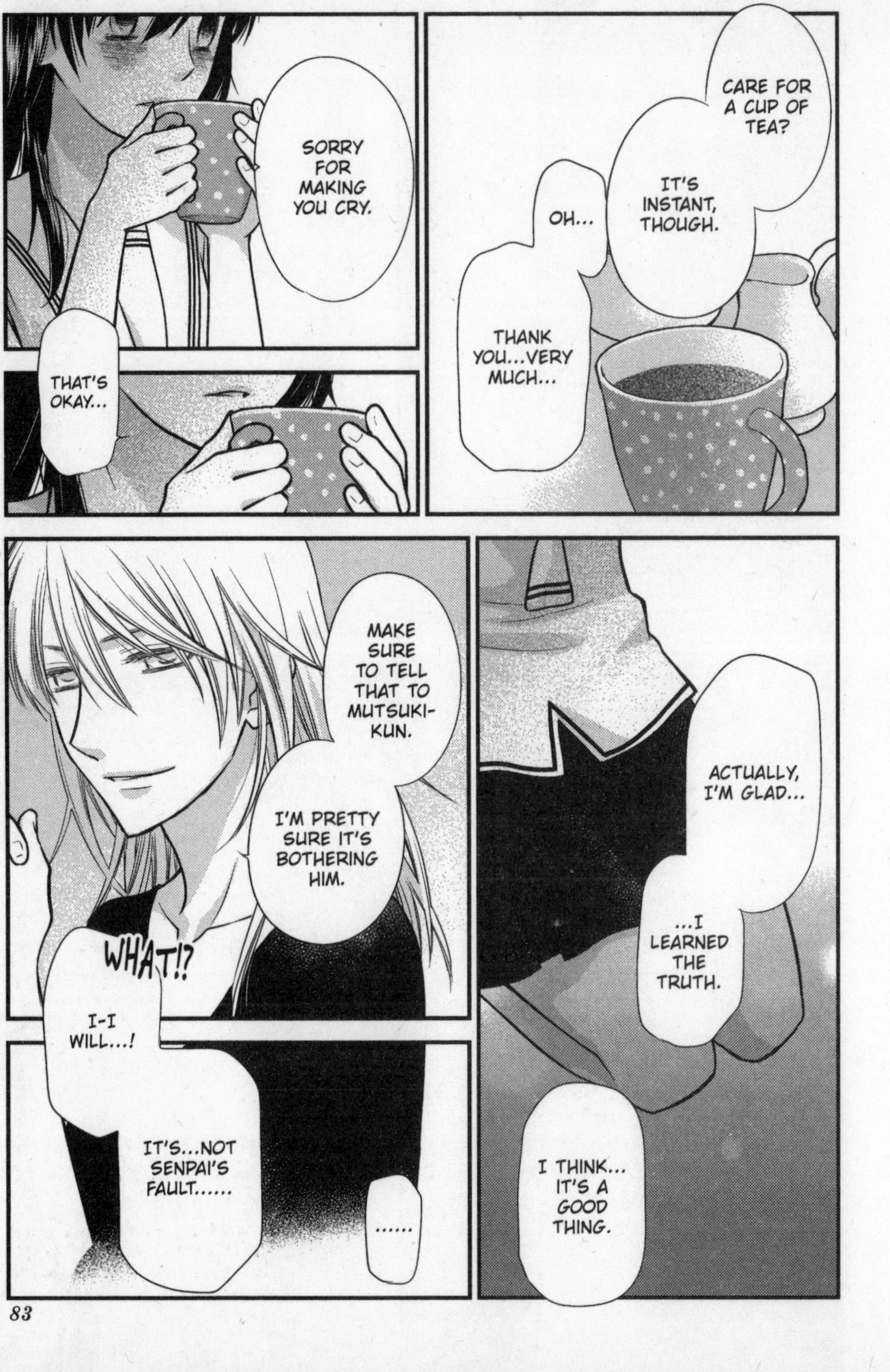
CARE FOR A CUP OF TEA?
IT'S INSTANT, THOUGH.
OH...
THANK YOU...VERY MUCH...
SORRY FOR MAKING YOU CRY.
THAT'S OKAY...
ACTUALLY, I'M GLAD...
...I LEARNED THE TRUTH.
I THINK... IT'S A GOOD THING.
MAKE SURE TO TELL THAT TO MUTSUKI-KUN.
I'M PRETTY SURE IT'S BOTHERING HIM.
WHAT!?
I-I WILL...!
IT'S...NOT SENPAI'S FAULT......
......

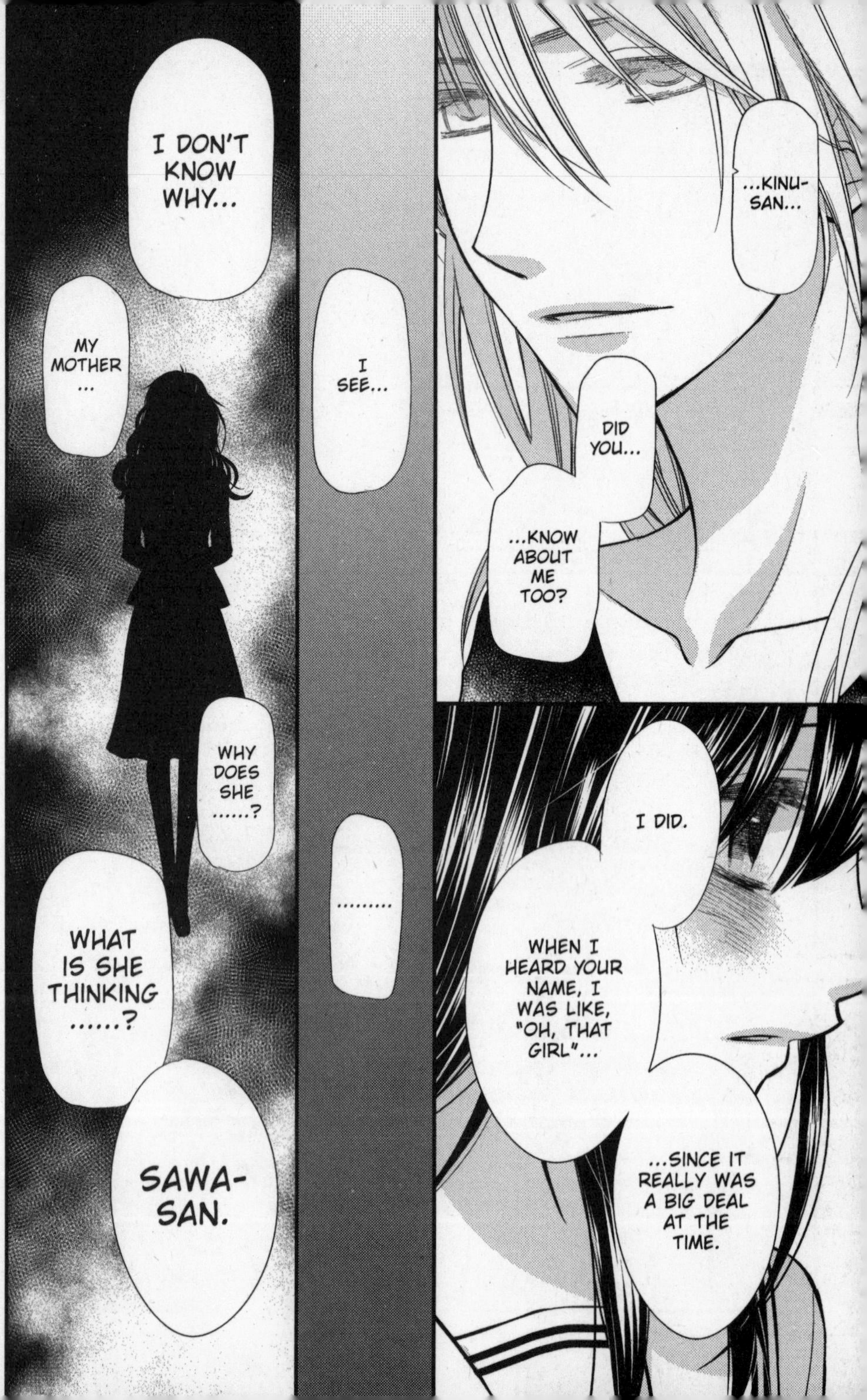
...KINU-SAN...
DID YOU...
...KNOW ABOUT ME TOO?
I DID.
WHEN I HEARD YOUR NAME, I WAS LIKE, "OH, THAT GIRL"...
...SINCE IT REALLY WAS A BIG DEAL AT THE TIME.
I SEE...
....
I DON'T KNOW WHY...
MY MOTHER ...
WHY DOES SHE ......?
WHAT IS SHE THINKING ......?
SAWA-SAN.

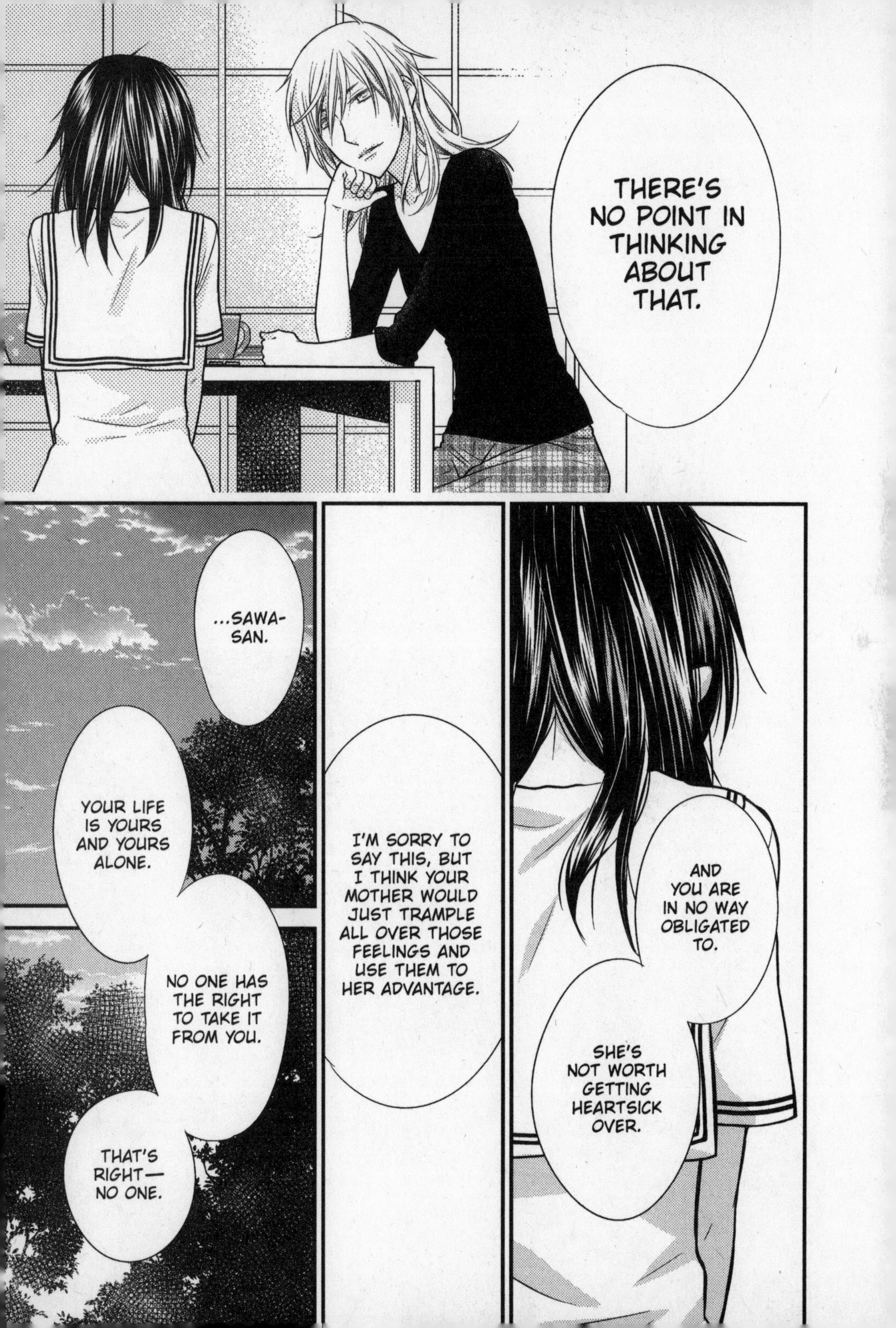
THERE'S NO POINT IN THINKING ABOUT THAT.
AND YOU ARE IN NO WAY OBLIGATED TO.
SHE'S NOT WORTH GETTING HEARTSICK OVER.
I'M SORRY TO SAY THIS, BUT I THINK YOUR MOTHER WOULD JUST TRAMPLE ALL OVER THOSE FEELINGS AND USE THEM TO HER ADVANTAGE.
...SAWA-SAN.
YOUR LIFE IS YOURS AND YOURS ALONE.
NO ONE HAS THE RIGHT TO TAKE IT FROM YOU.
THAT'S RIGHT— NO ONE.

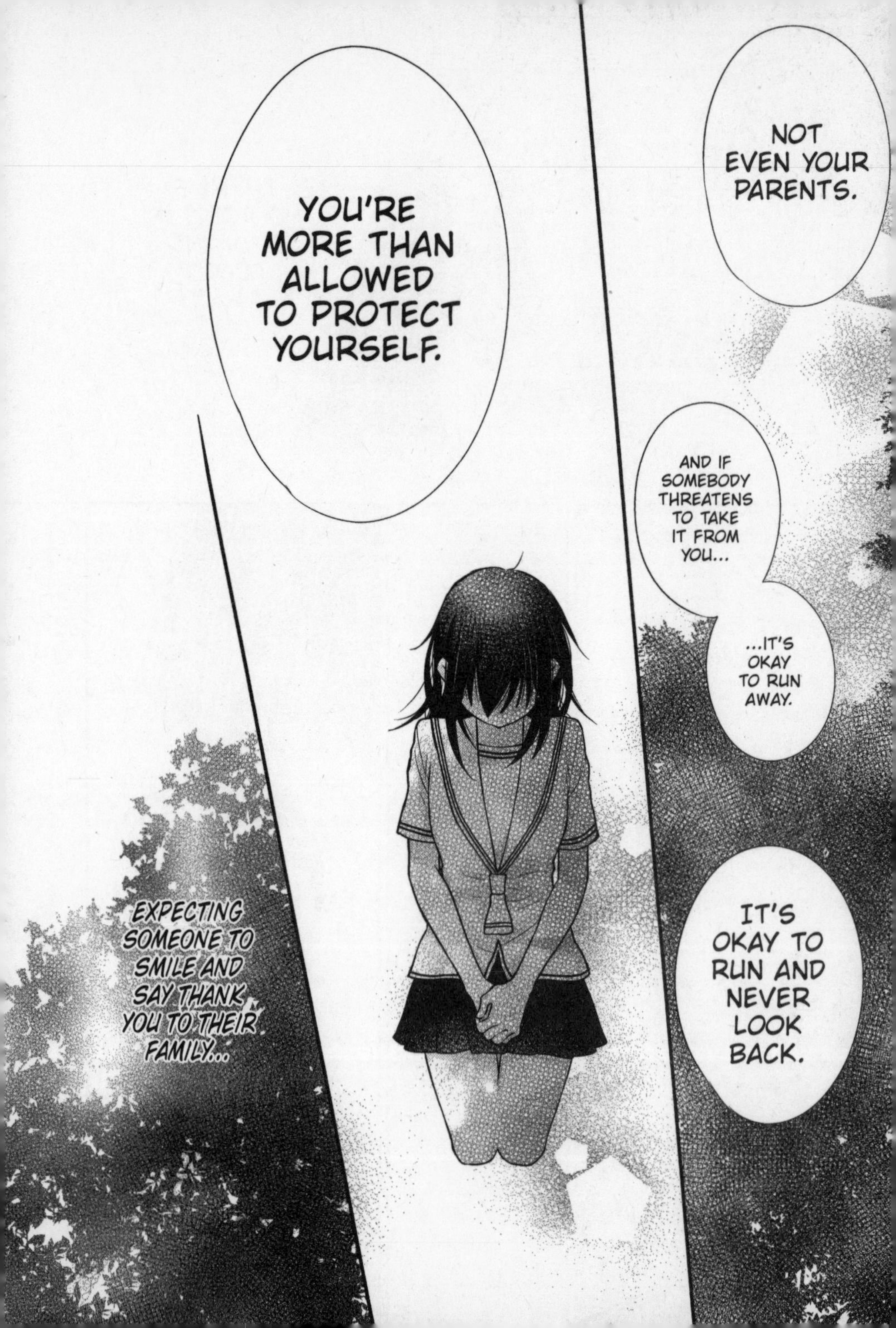
NOT EVEN YOUR PARENTS.
AND IF SOMEBODY THREATENS TO TAKE IT FROM YOU...
...IT'S OKAY TO RUN AWAY.
IT'S OKAY TO RUN AND NEVER LOOK BACK.
YOU'RE MORE THAN ALLOWED TO PROTECT YOURSELF.
EXPECTING SOMEONE TO SMILE AND SAY THANK YOU TO THEIR FAMILY...

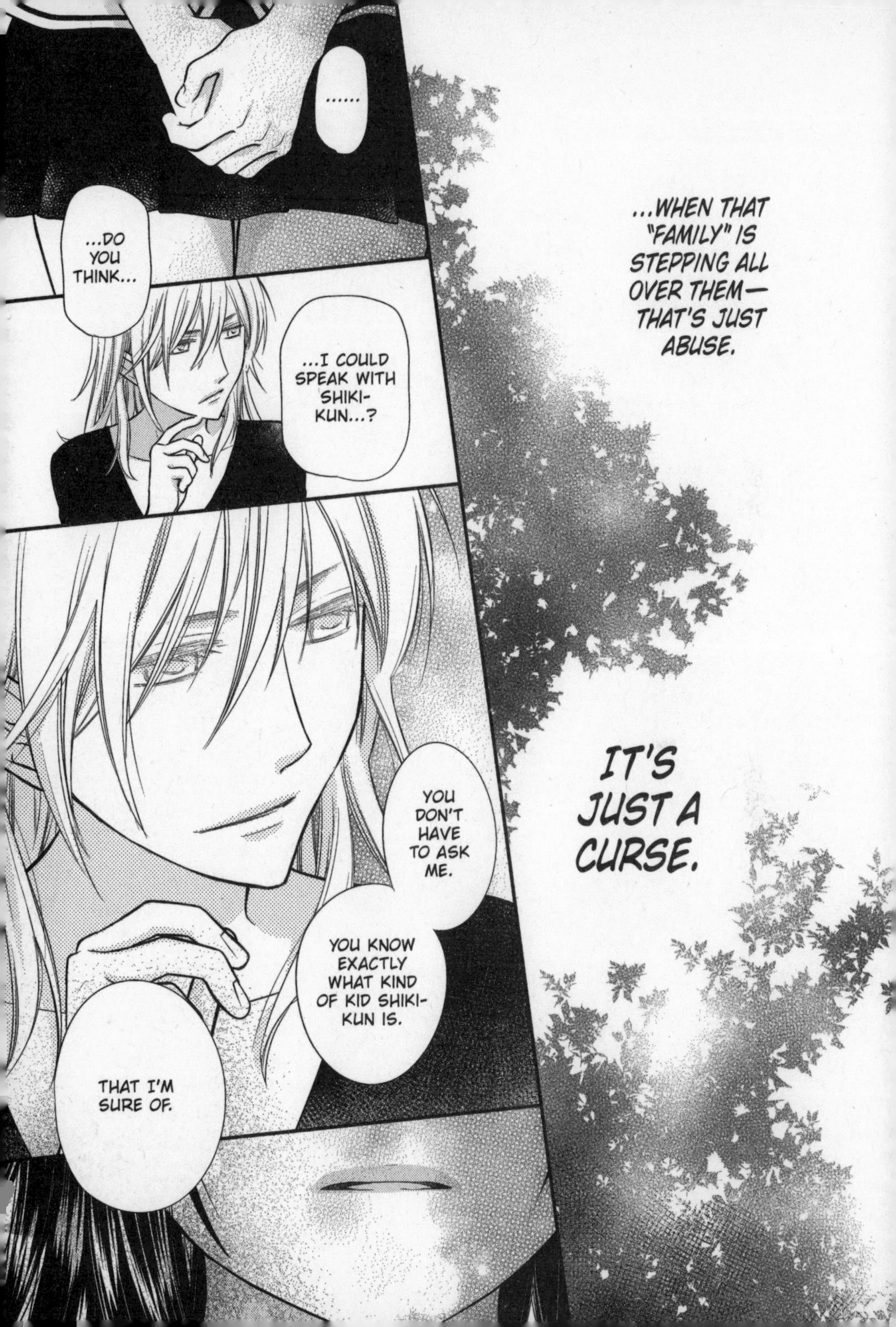
...WHEN THAT "FAMILY" IS STEPPING ALL OVER THEM—THAT'S JUST ABUSE.
IT'S JUST A CURSE.
......
...DO YOU THINK...
...I COULD SPEAK WITH SHIKI-KUN...?
YOU DON'T HAVE TO ASK ME.
YOU KNOW EXACTLY WHAT KIND OF KID SHIKI-KUN IS.
THAT I'M SURE OF.

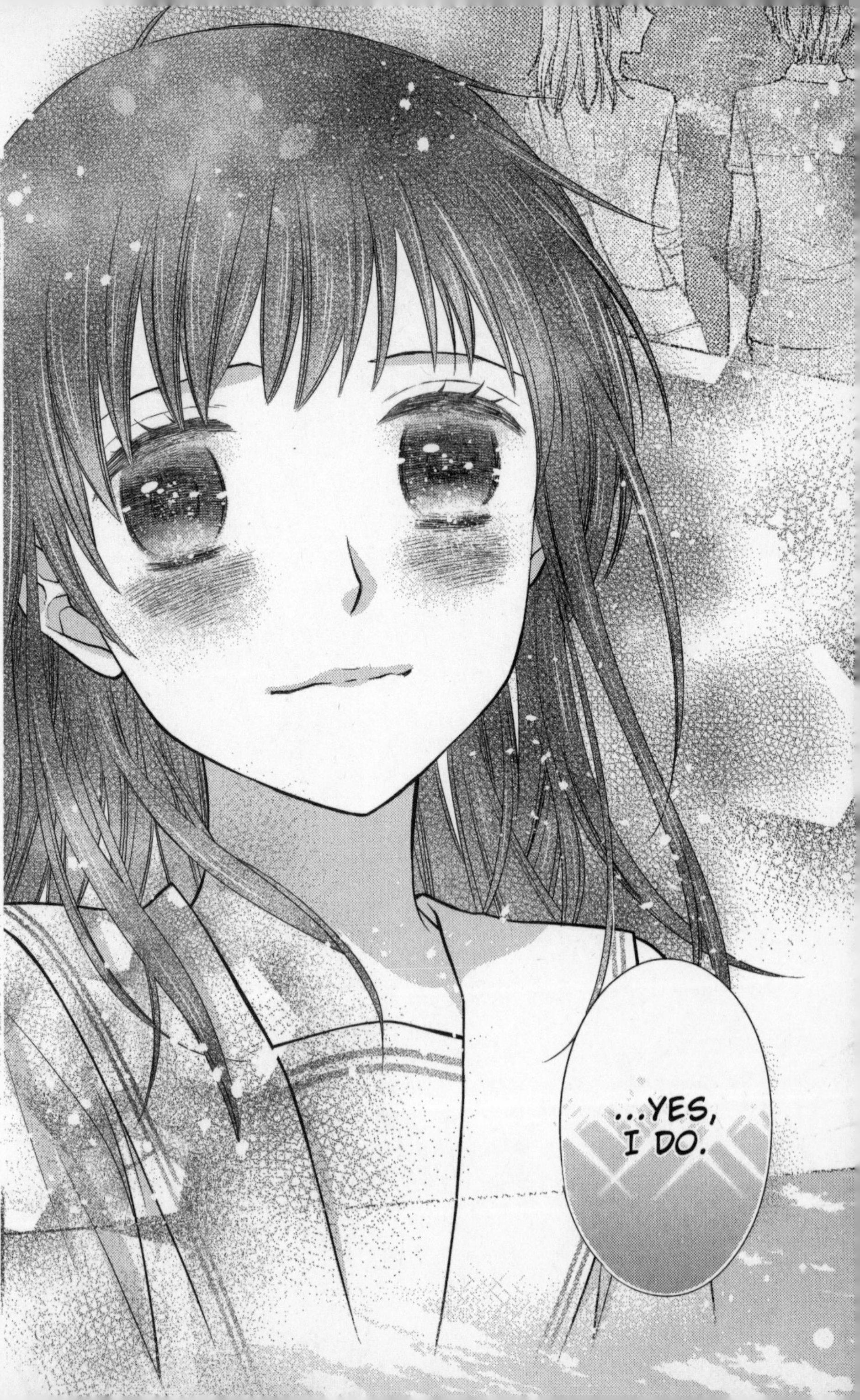
...YES, I DO.

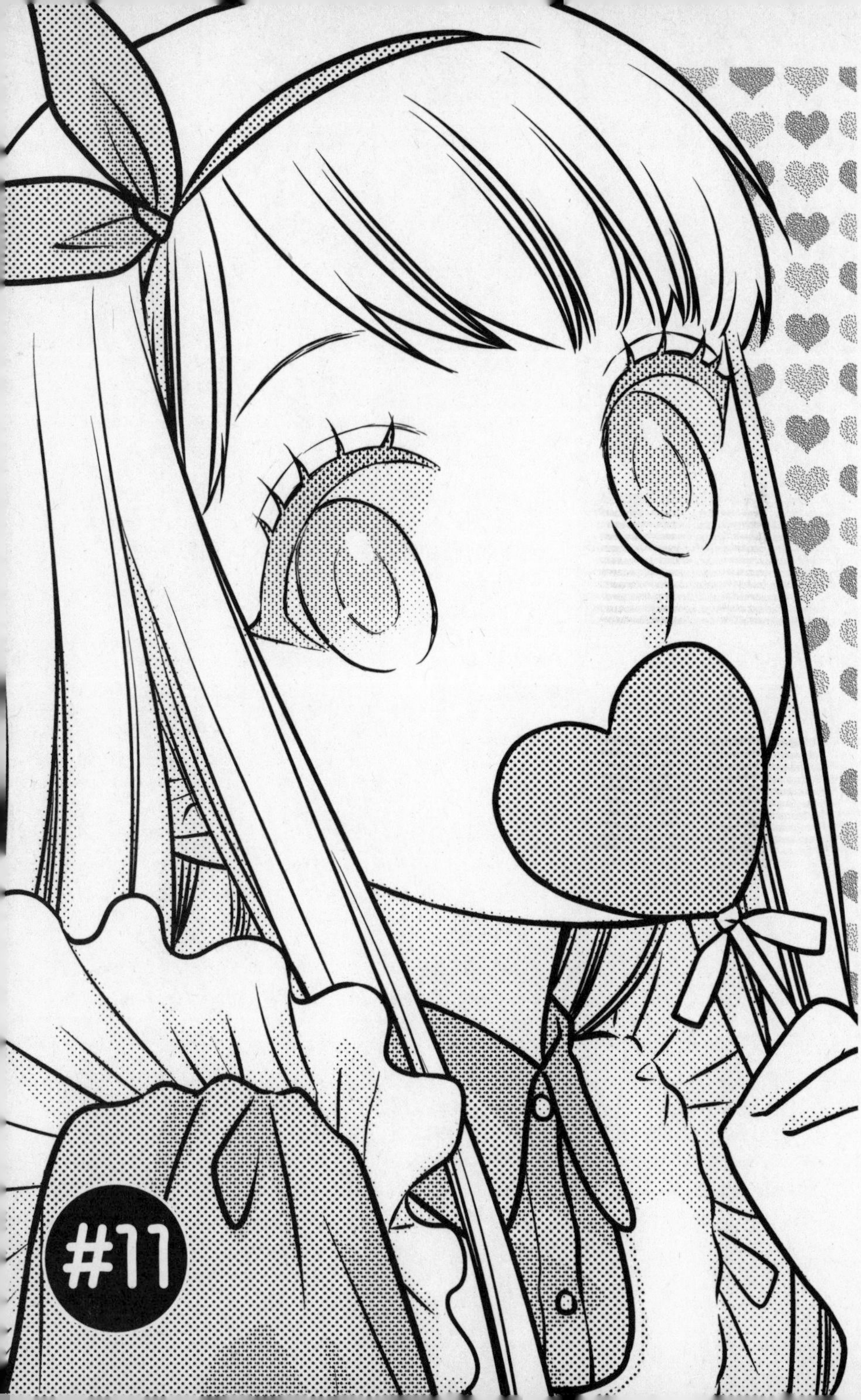
#11

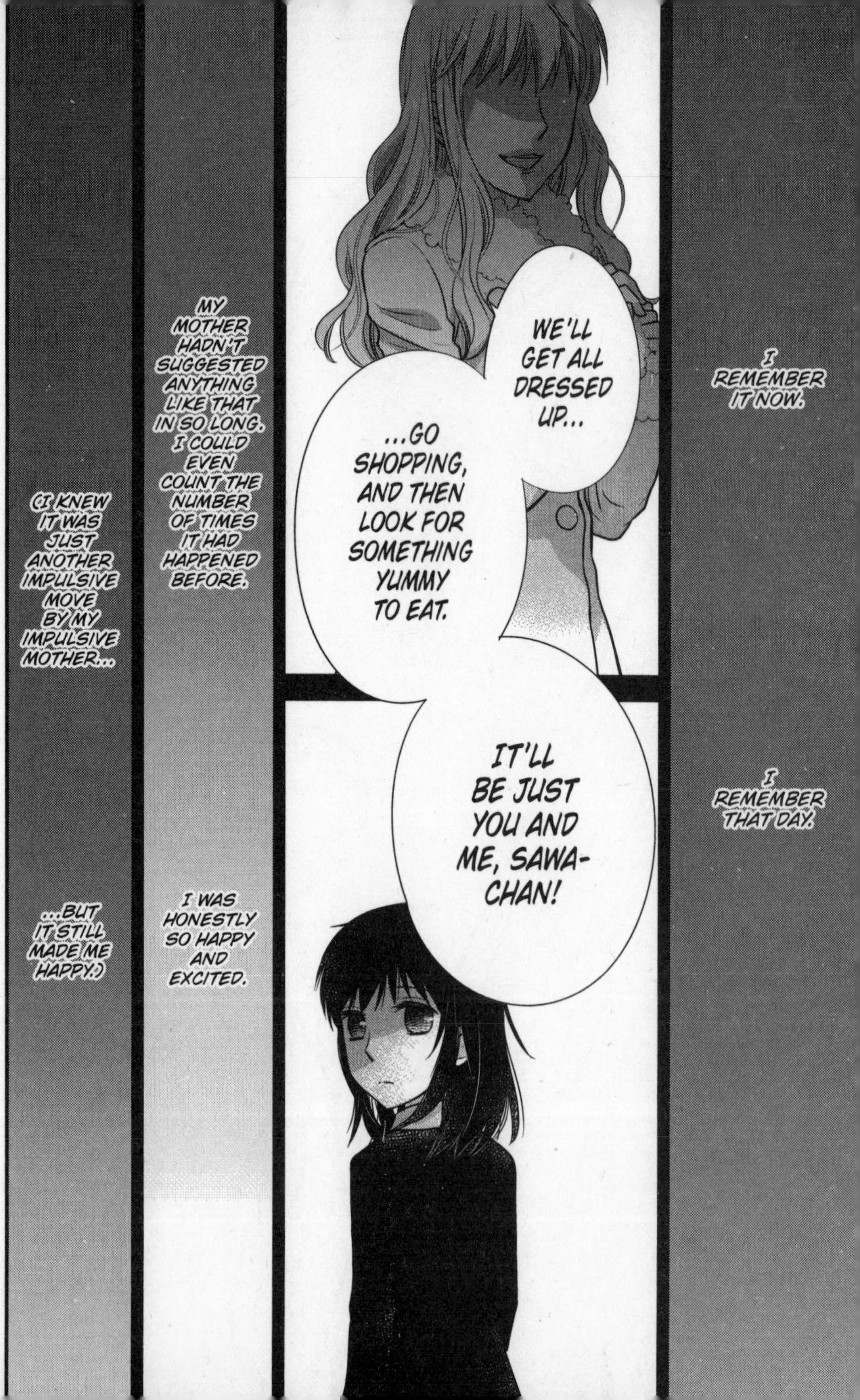
I REMEMBER IT NOW.
I REMEMBER THAT DAY.
WE'LL GET ALL DRESSED UP...
...GO SHOPPING, AND THEN LOOK FOR SOMETHING YUMMY TO EAT.
IT'LL BE JUST YOU AND ME, SAWA-CHAN!
MY MOTHER HADN'T SUGGESTED ANYTHING LIKE THAT IN SO LONG. I COULD EVEN COUNT THE NUMBER OF TIMES IT HAD HAPPENED BEFORE.
I WAS HONESTLY SO HAPPY AND EXCITED.
(I KNEW IT WAS JUST ANOTHER IMPULSIVE MOVE BY MY IMPULSIVE MOTHER...
...BUT IT STILL MADE ME HAPPY.)

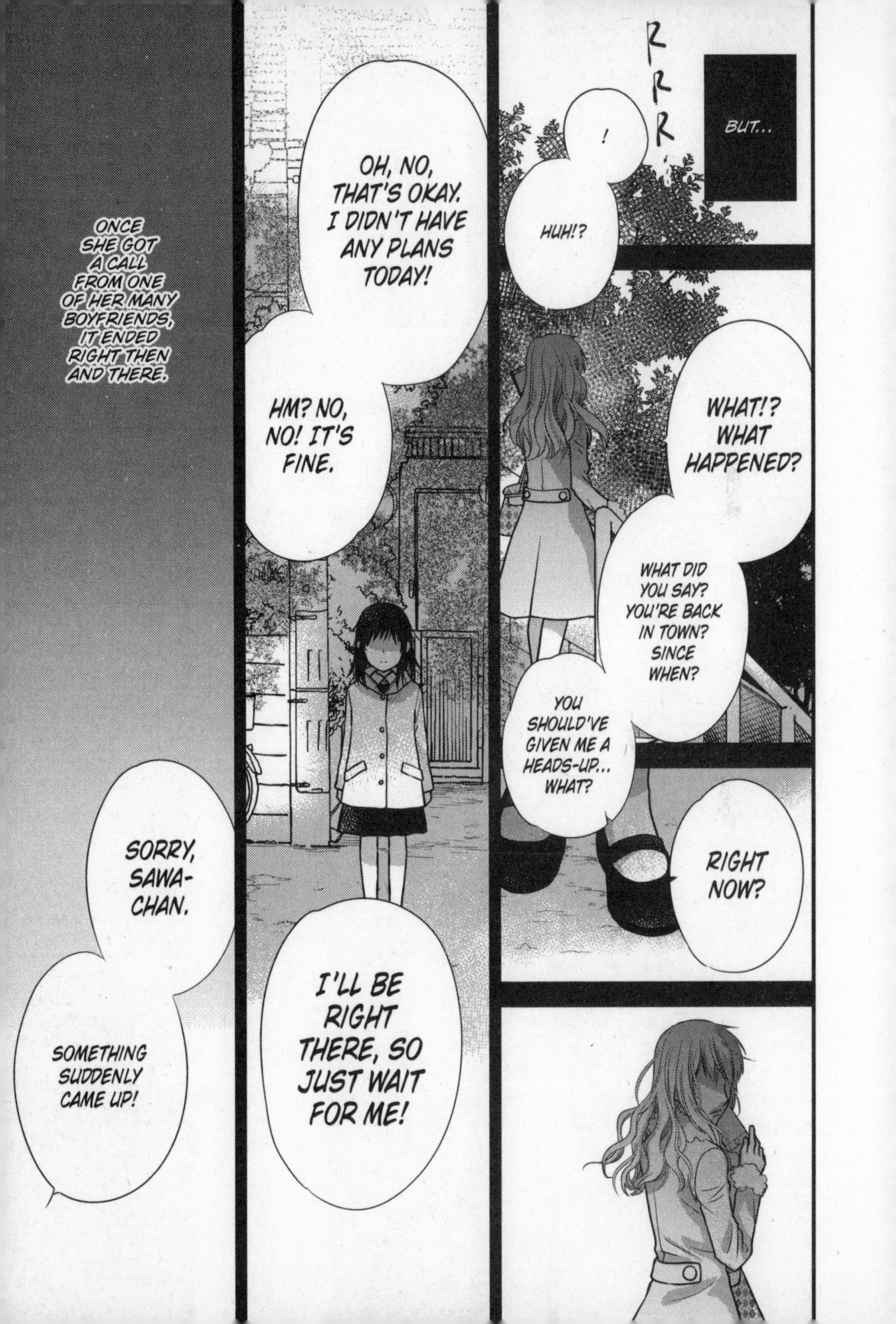
BUT...
RRR
!
HUH!?
WHAT!? WHAT HAPPENED?
WHAT DID YOU SAY? YOU'RE BACK IN TOWN? SINCE WHEN?
YOU SHOULD'VE GIVEN ME A HEADS-UP... WHAT?
RIGHT NOW?
OH, NO, THAT'S OKAY. I DIDN'T HAVE ANY PLANS TODAY!
HM? NO, NO! IT'S FINE.
I'LL BE RIGHT THERE, SO JUST WAIT FOR ME!
ONCE SHE GOT A CALL FROM ONE OF HER MANY BOYFRIENDS, IT ENDED RIGHT THEN AND THERE.
SORRY, SAWA-CHAN.
SOMETHING SUDDENLY CAME UP!

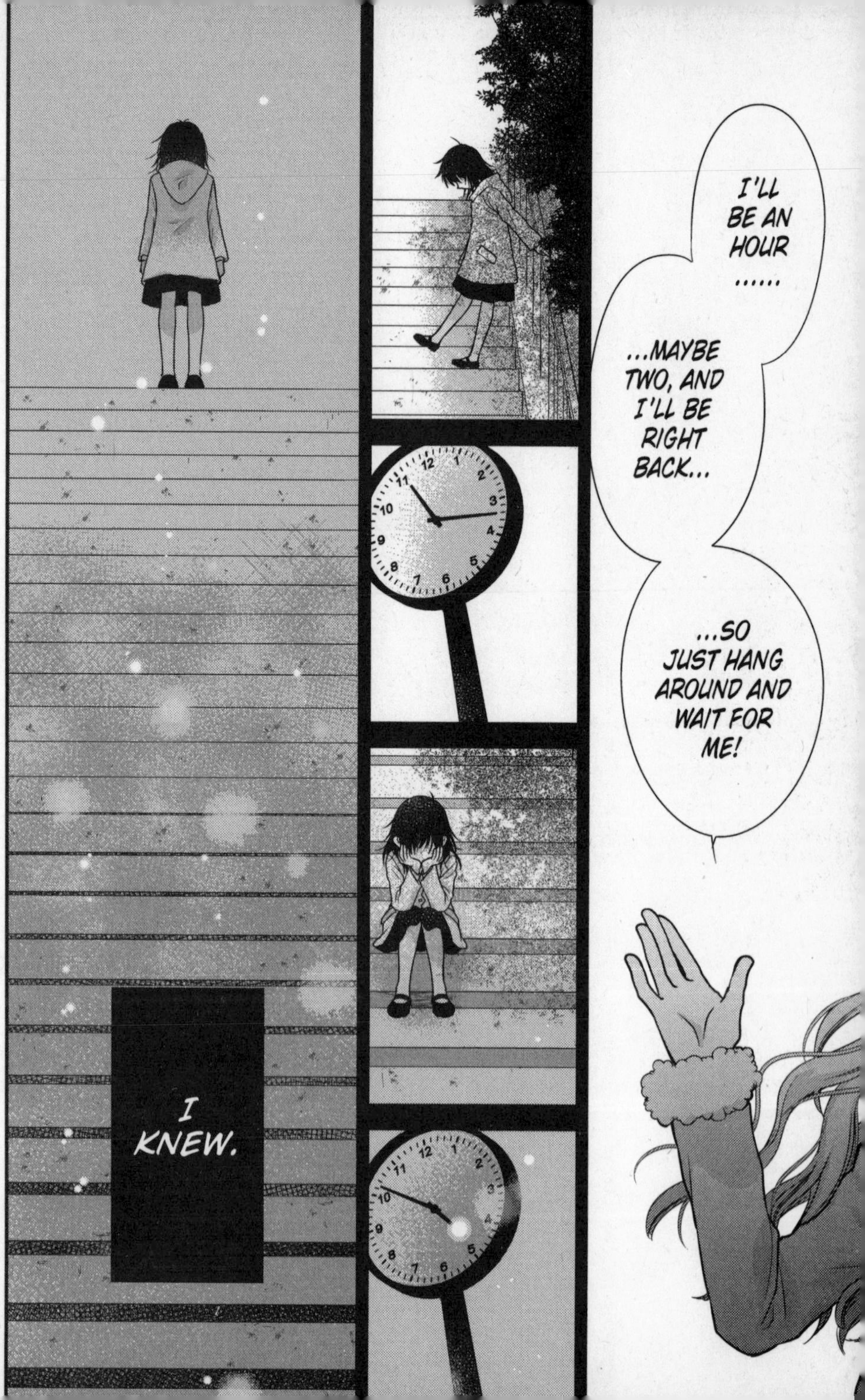
I'LL BE AN HOUR ......
...MAYBE TWO, AND I'LL BE RIGHT BACK...
...SO JUST HANG AROUND AND WAIT FOR ME!
I KNEW.

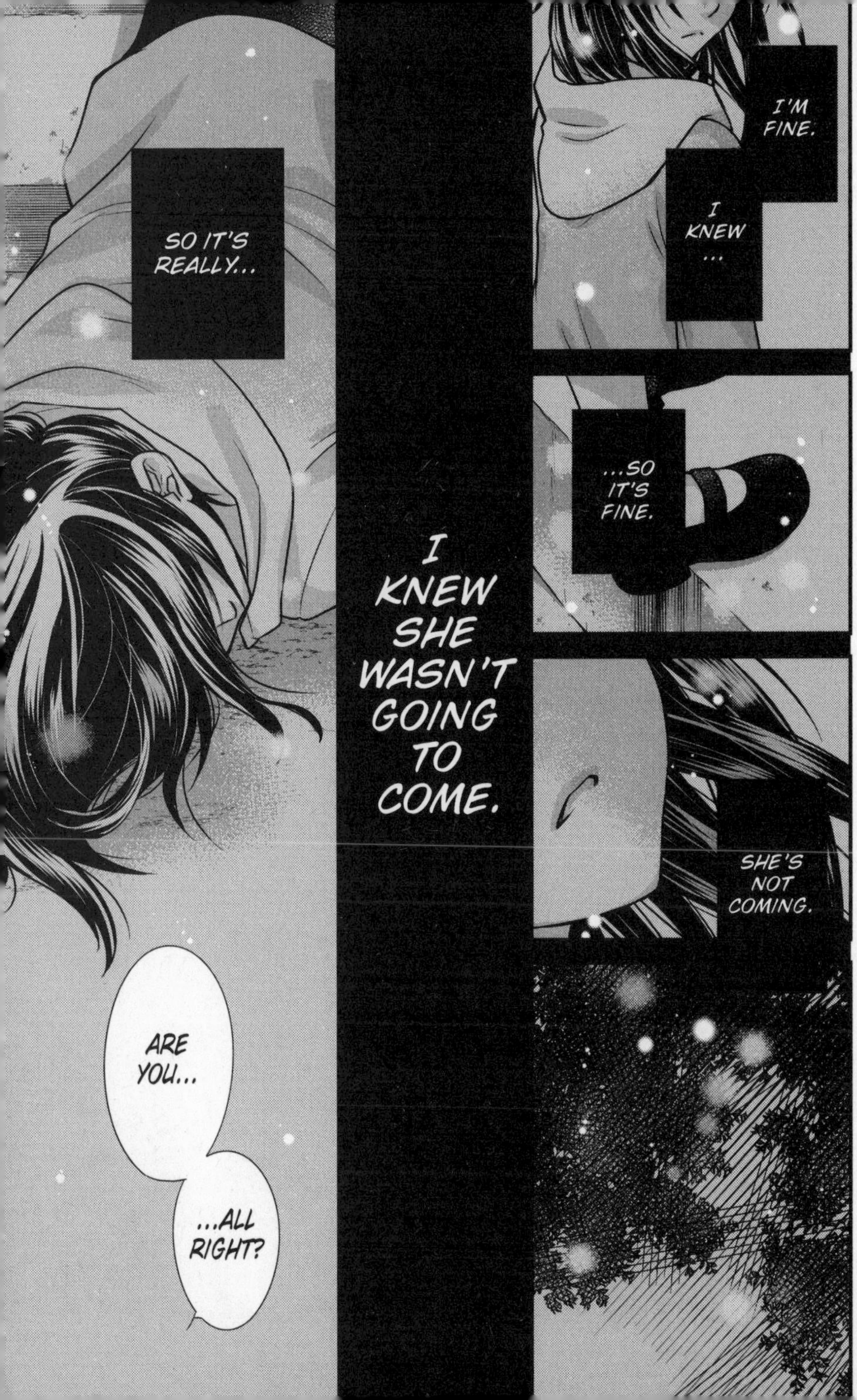
I'M FINE.
I KNEW...
...SO IT'S FINE.
SHE'S NOT COMING.
I KNEW SHE WASN'T GOING TO COME.
SO IT'S REALLY...
ARE YOU...
...ALL RIGHT?

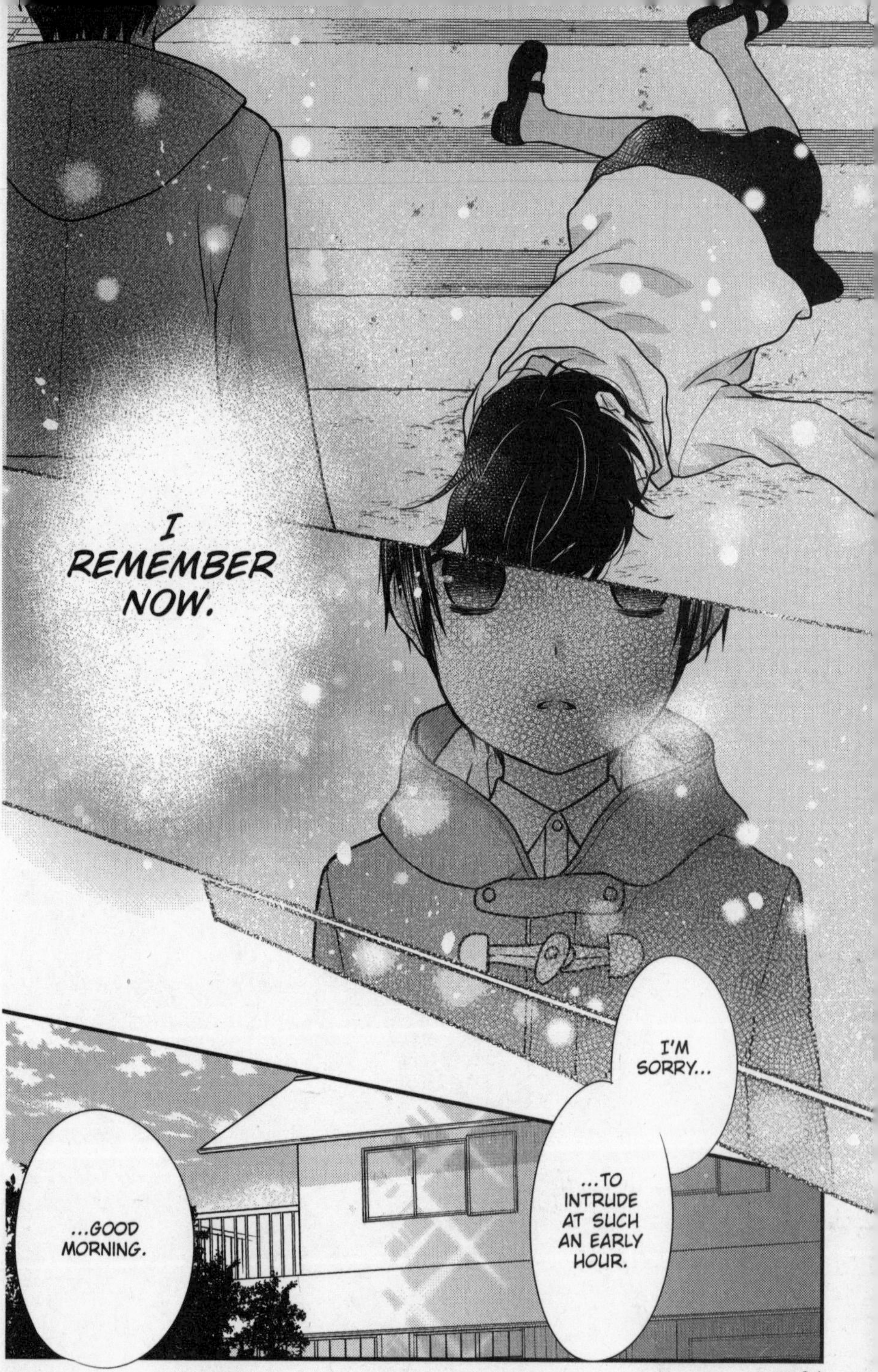
I REMEMBER NOW.
I'M SORRY...
...TO INTRUDE AT SUCH AN EARLY HOUR.
...GOOD MORNING.

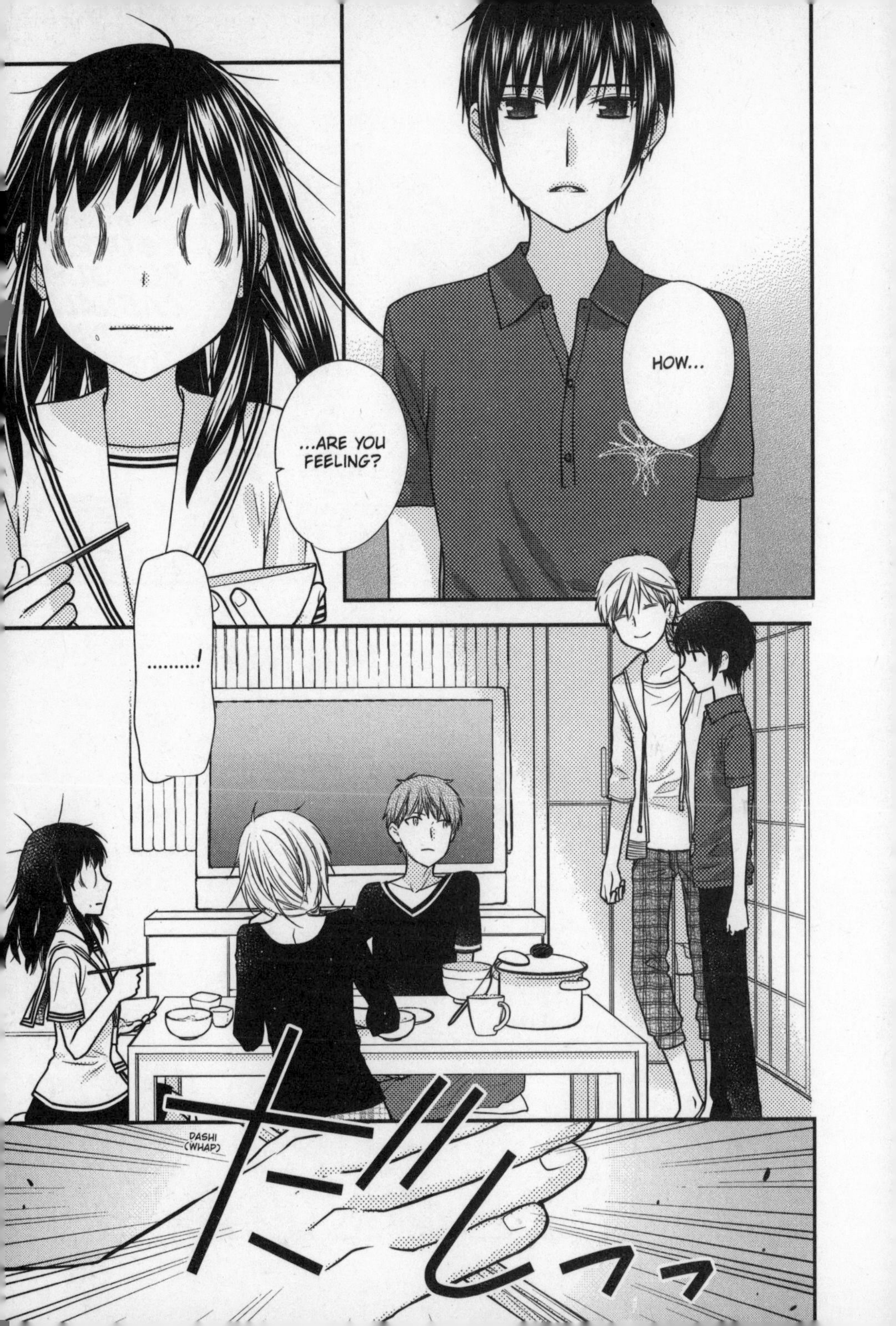
HOW...
...ARE YOU FEELING?
..........!
DASHI (WHAP)

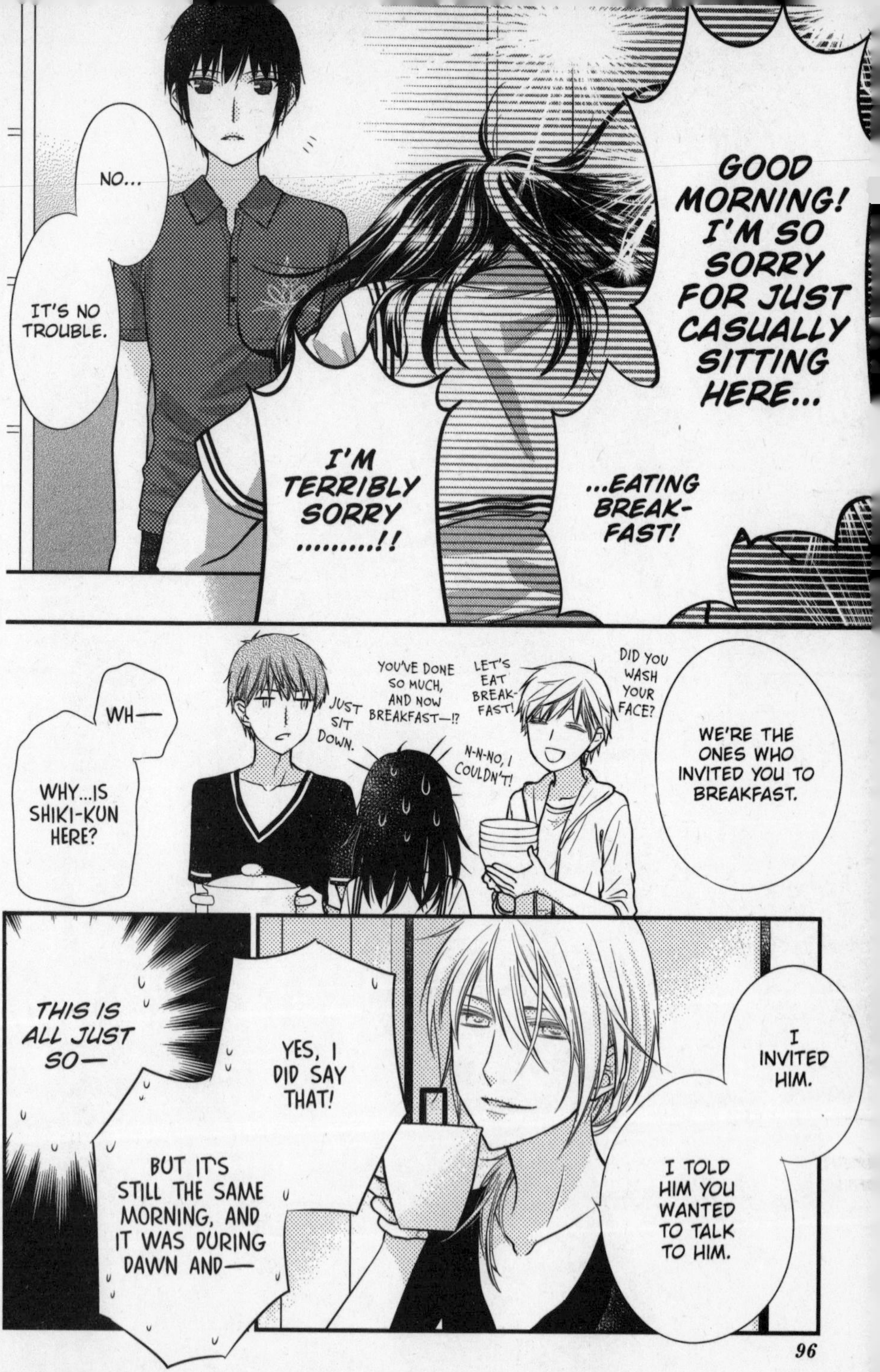
GOOD MORNING! I'M SO SORRY FOR JUST CASUALLY SITTING HERE...
...EATING BREAK-FAST!
I'M TERRIBLY SORRY ....!!
NO...
IT'S NO TROUBLE.
WE'RE THE ONES WHO INVITED YOU TO BREAKFAST.
DID YOU WASH YOUR FACE?
LET'S EAT BREAK-FAST!
N-N-NO, I COULDN'T!
YOU'VE DONE SO MUCH, AND NOW BREAKFAST—!?
JUST SIT DOWN.
WH—
WHY...IS SHIKI-KUN HERE?
I INVITED HIM.
I TOLD HIM YOU WANTED TO TALK TO HIM.
YES, I DID SAY THAT!
BUT IT'S STILL THE SAME MORNING, AND IT WAS DURING DAWN AND—
THIS IS ALL JUST SO—

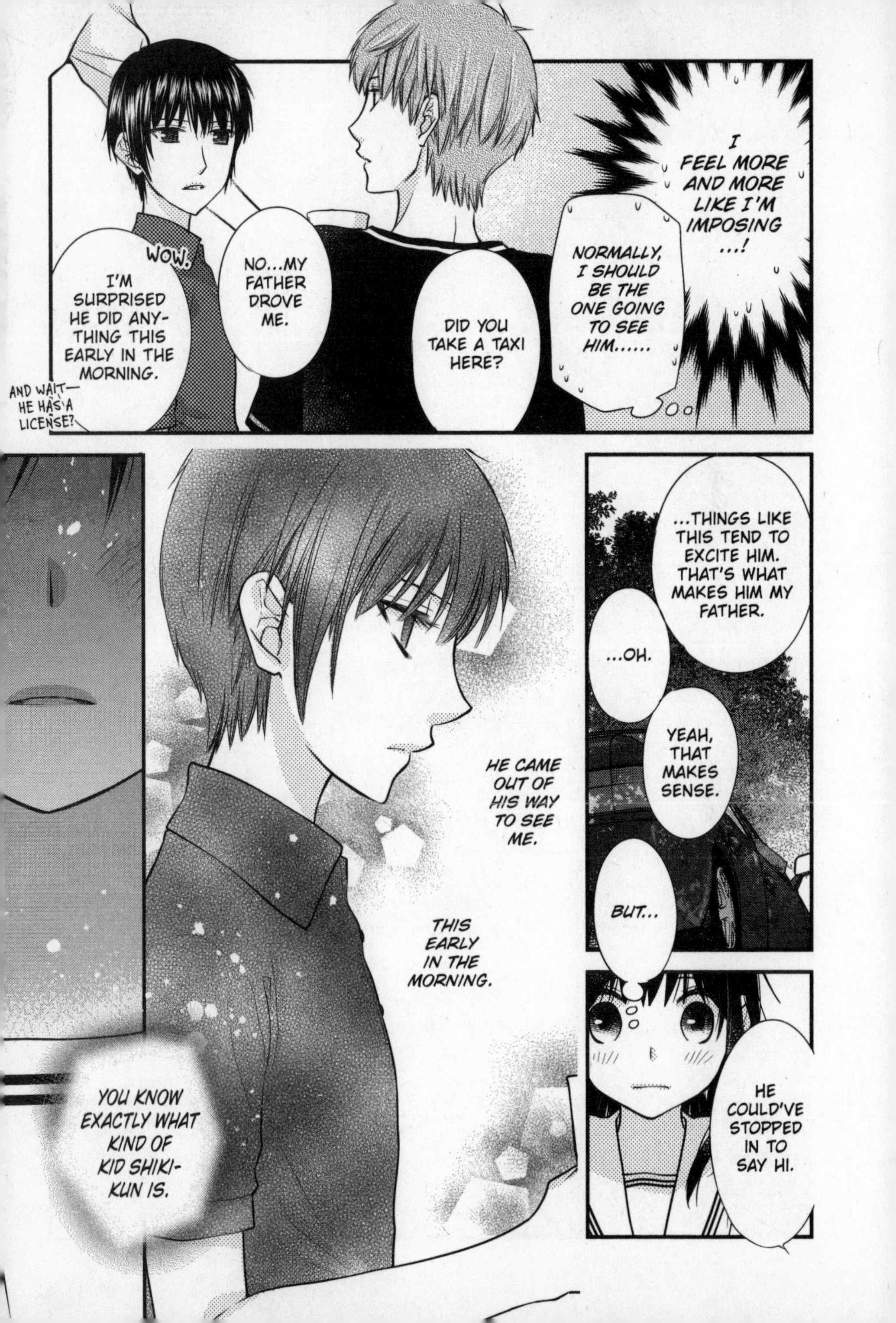
I FEEL MORE AND MORE LIKE I'M IMPOSING ...!
NORMALLY, I SHOULD BE THE ONE GOING TO SEE HIM......
DID YOU TAKE A TAXI HERE?
NO...MY FATHER DROVE ME.
WOW.
I'M SURPRISED HE DID ANYTHING THIS EARLY IN THE MORNING.
AND WAIT— HE HAS A LICENSE?
...THINGS LIKE THIS TEND TO EXCITE HIM. THAT'S WHAT MAKES HIM MY FATHER.
...OH.
YEAH, THAT MAKES SENSE.
BUT...
HE COULD'VE STOPPED IN TO SAY HI.
HE CAME OUT OF HIS WAY TO SEE ME.
THIS EARLY IN THE MORNING.
YOU KNOW EXACTLY WHAT KIND OF KID SHIKI-KUN IS.

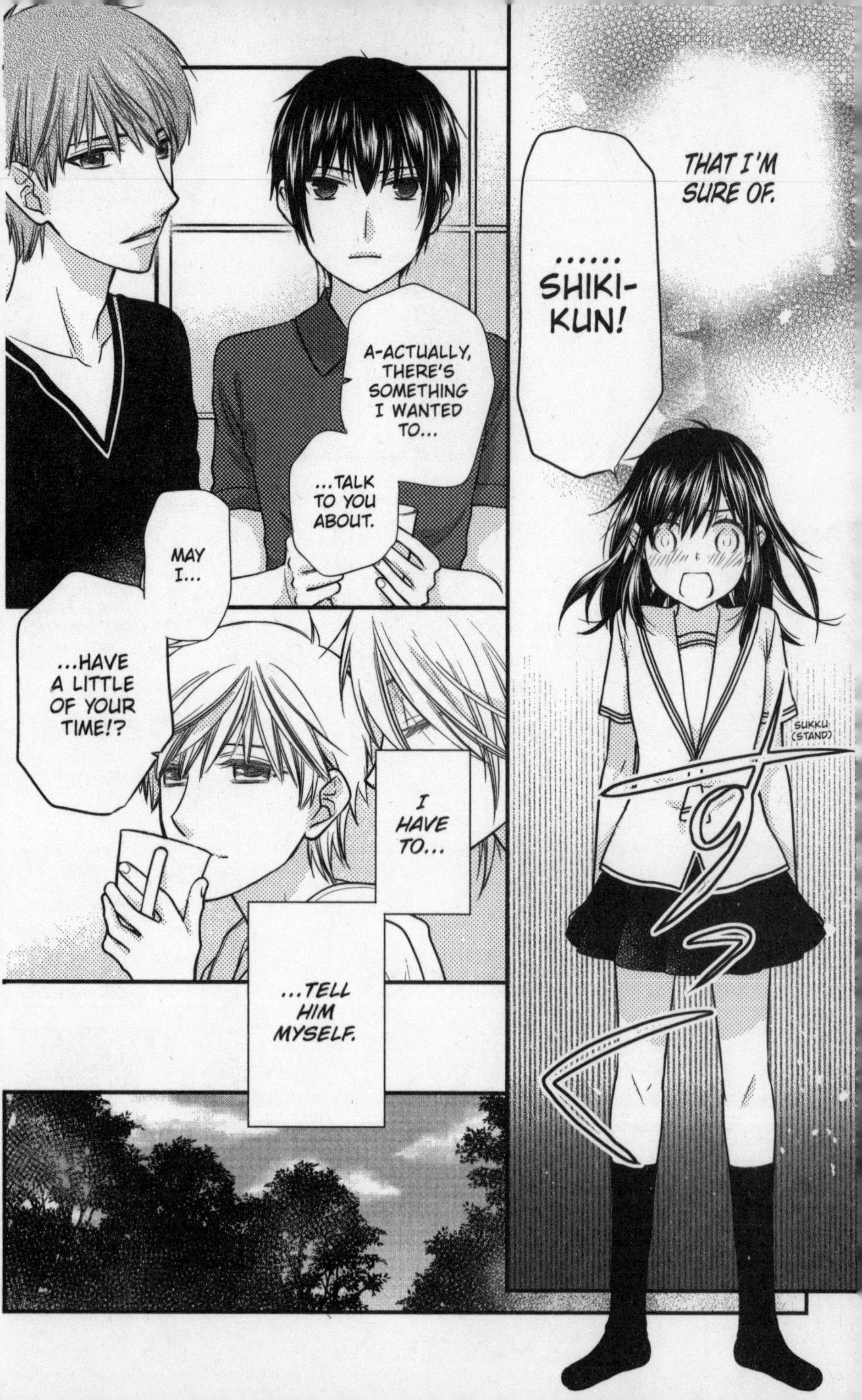
THAT I'M SURE OF.
......SHIKI-KUN!
SUKKU (STAND)
A-ACTUALLY, THERE'S SOMETHING I WANTED TO...
...TALK TO YOU ABOUT.
MAY I...
...HAVE A LITTLE OF YOUR TIME!?
I HAVE TO...
...TELL HIM MYSELF.

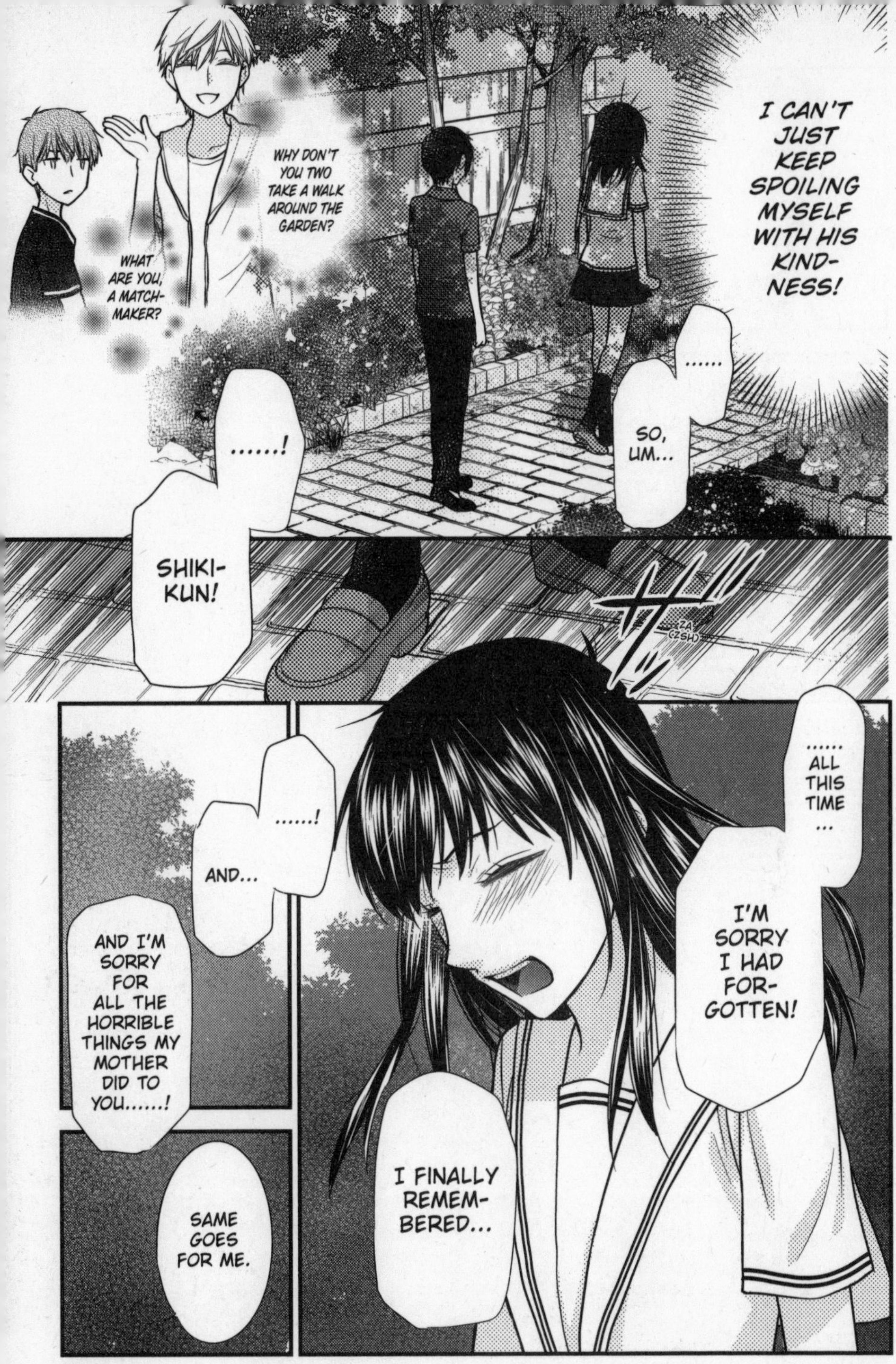
I CAN'T JUST KEEP SPOILING MYSELF WITH HIS KINDNESS!
WHY DON'T YOU TWO TAKE A WALK AROUND THE GARDEN?
WHAT ARE YOU, A MATCH-MAKER?
......
SO, UM...
......!
SHIKI-KUN!
ZA (ZSH)
...... ALL THIS TIME ...
I'M SORRY I HAD FOR-GOTTEN!
I FINALLY REMEM-BERED...
......!
AND...
AND I'M SORRY FOR ALL THE HORRIBLE THINGS MY MOTHER DID TO YOU......!
SAME GOES FOR ME.

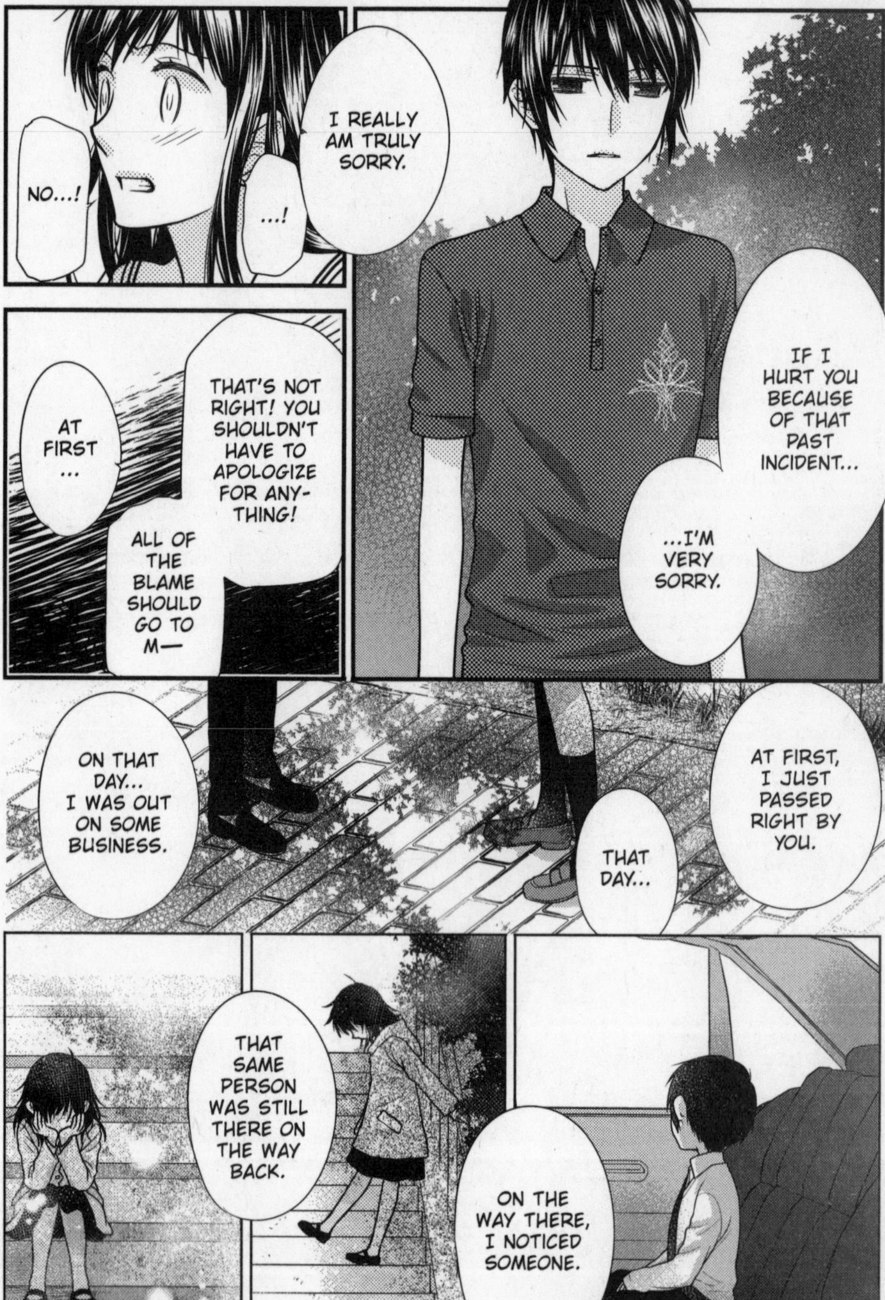
IF I HURT YOU BECAUSE OF THAT PAST INCIDENT...
...I'M VERY SORRY.
I REALLY AM TRULY SORRY.
...!
NO...!
THAT'S NOT RIGHT! YOU SHOULDN'T HAVE TO APOLOGIZE FOR ANY-THING!
ALL OF THE BLAME SHOULD GO TO M—
AT FIRST ...
AT FIRST, I JUST PASSED RIGHT BY YOU.
THAT DAY...
ON THAT DAY... I WAS OUT ON SOME BUSINESS.
ON THE WAY THERE, I NOTICED SOMEONE.
THAT SAME PERSON WAS STILL THERE ON THE WAY BACK.

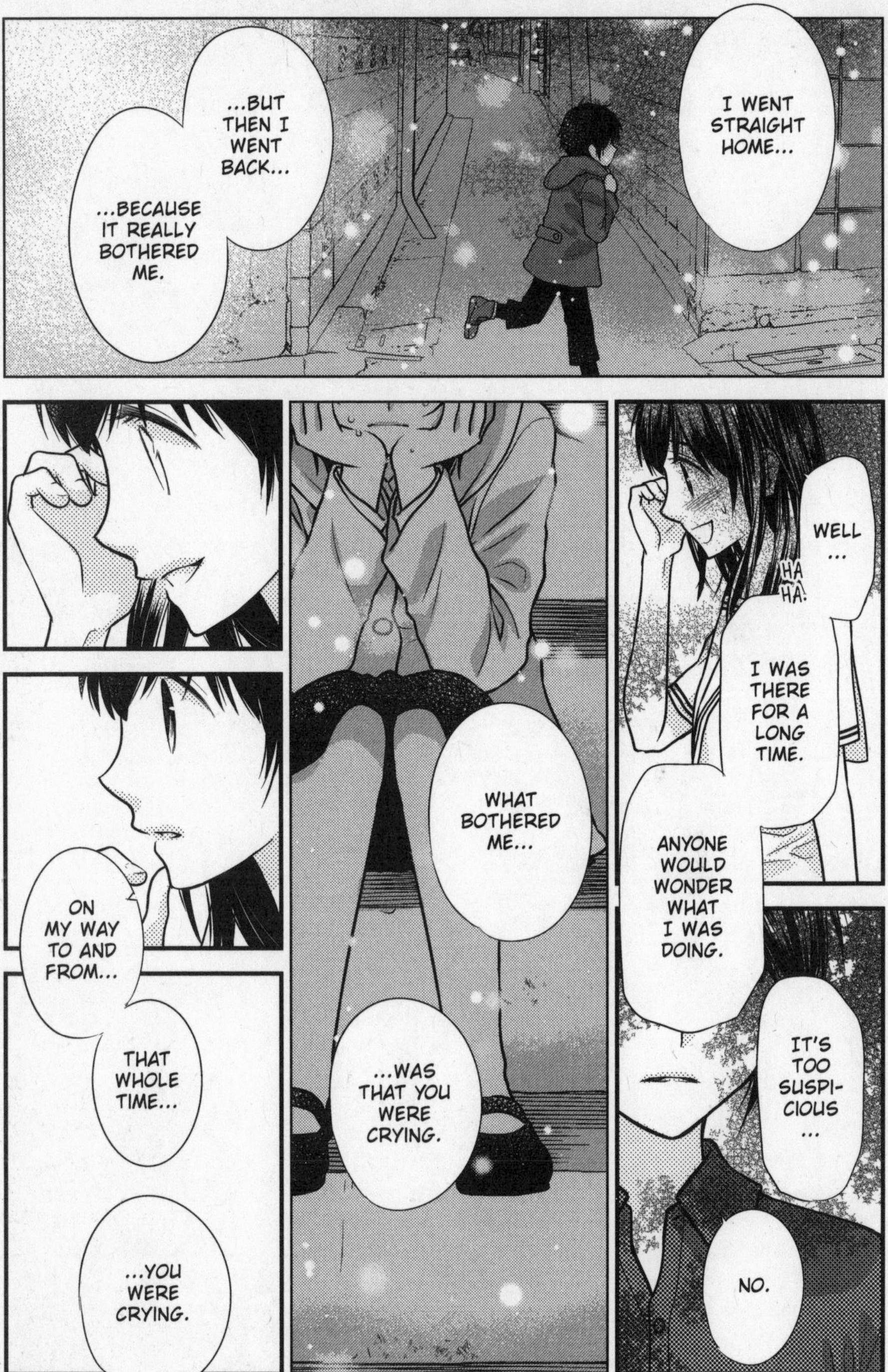
I WENT STRAIGHT HOME...
...BUT THEN I WENT BACK...
...BECAUSE IT REALLY BOTHERED ME.
WELL...
HA HA!
I WAS THERE FOR A LONG TIME.
ANYONE WOULD WONDER WHAT I WAS DOING.
IT'S TOO SUSPICIOUS...
NO.
WHAT BOTHERED ME...
...WAS THAT YOU WERE CRYING.
ON MY WAY TO AND FROM...
THAT WHOLE TIME...
...YOU WERE CRYING.

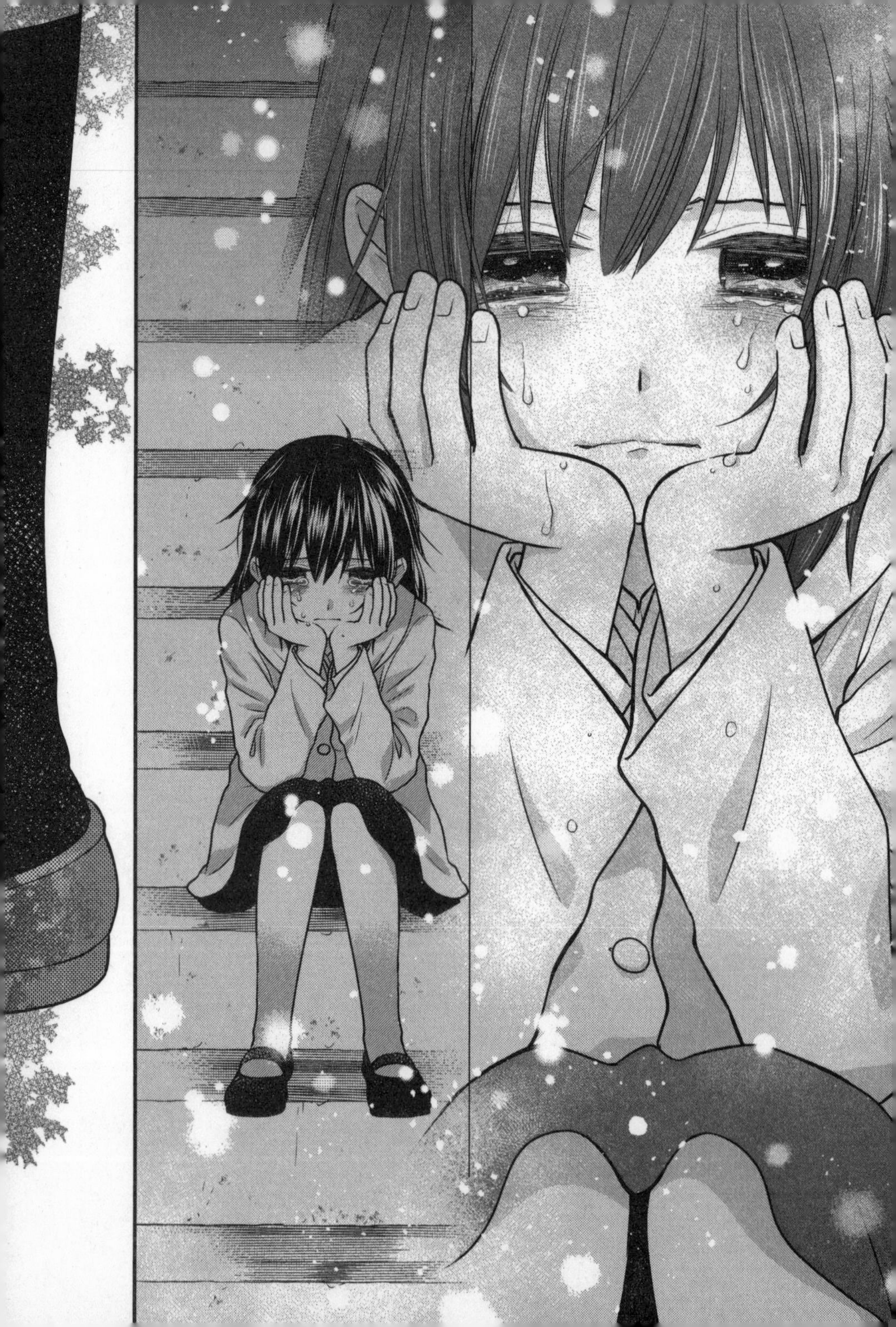

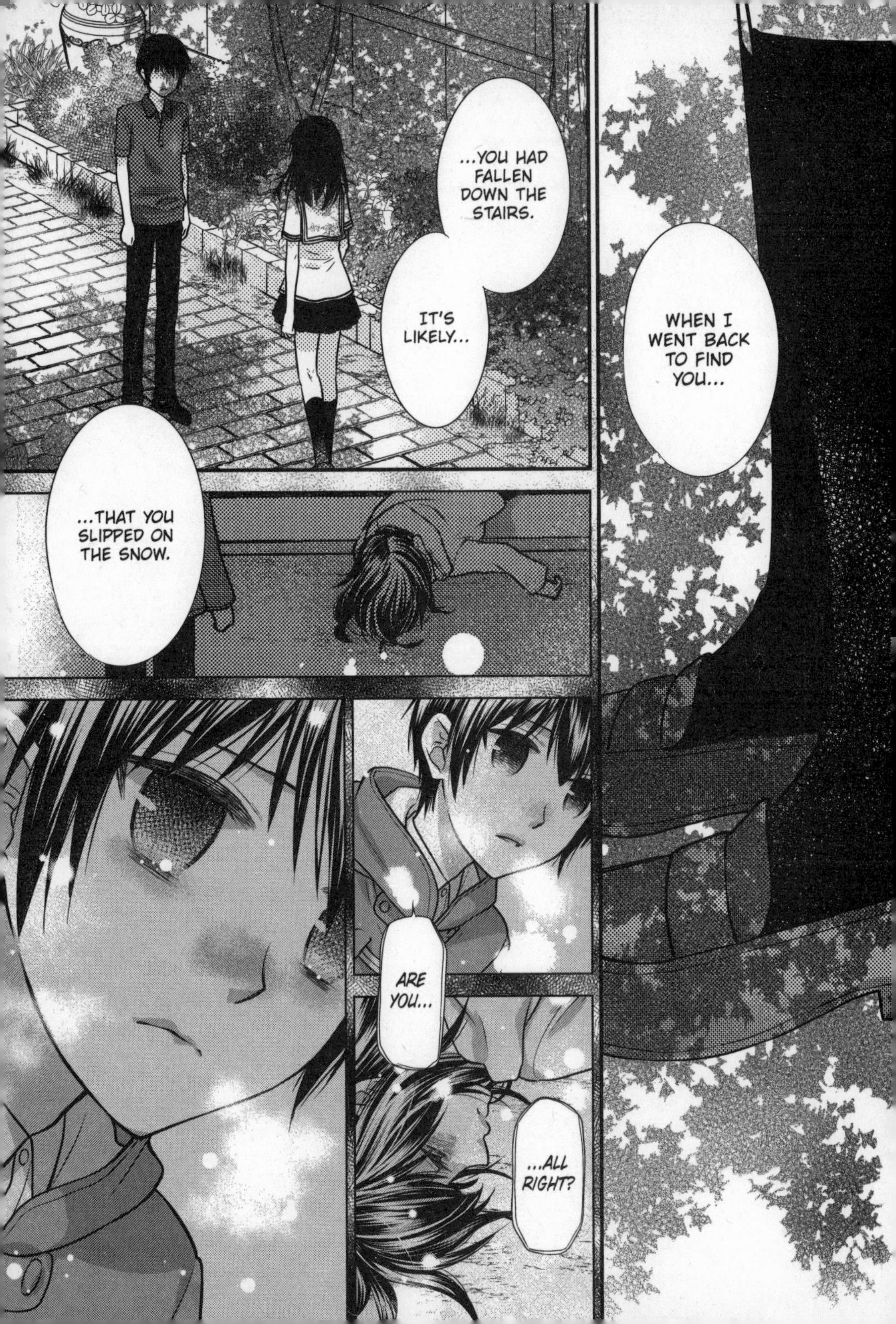
WHEN I WENT BACK TO FIND YOU...
...YOU HAD FALLEN DOWN THE STAIRS.
IT'S LIKELY...
...THAT YOU SLIPPED ON THE SNOW.
ARE YOU...
...ALL RIGHT?

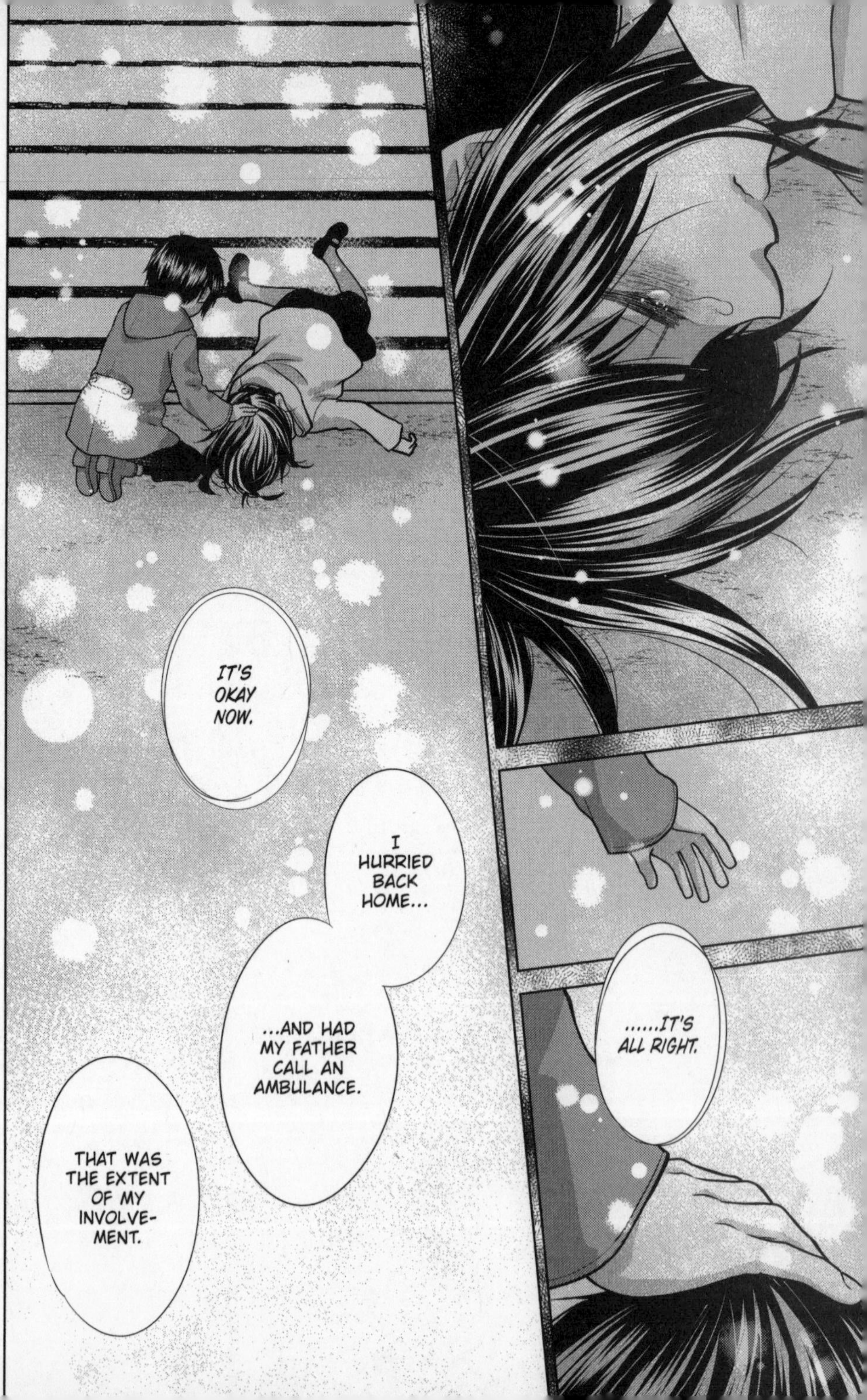
......IT'S ALL RIGHT.
IT'S OKAY NOW.
I HURRIED BACK HOME...
...AND HAD MY FATHER CALL AN AMBULANCE.
THAT WAS THE EXTENT OF MY INVOLVE-MENT.

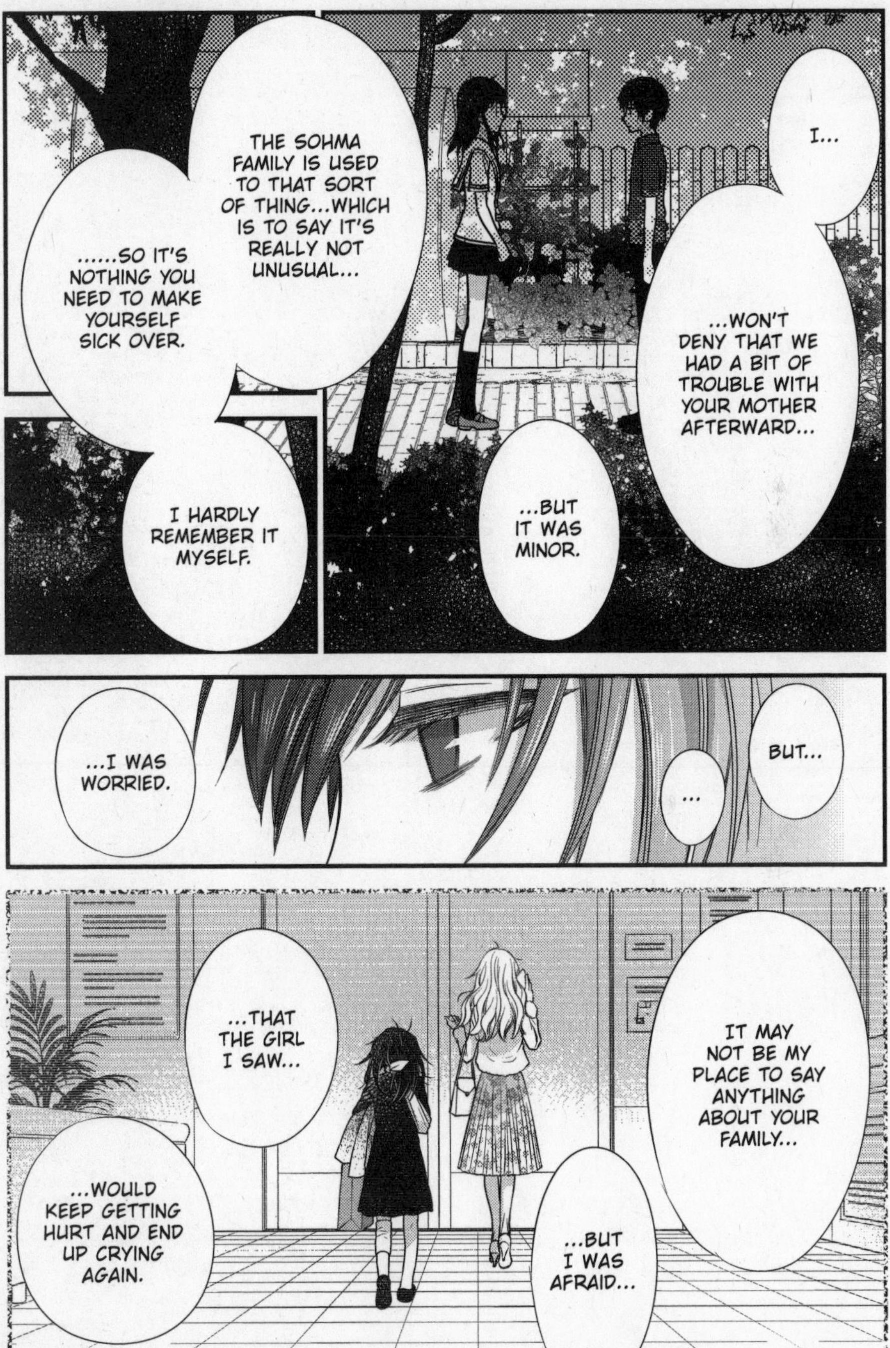
I...
...WON'T DENY THAT WE HAD A BIT OF TROUBLE WITH YOUR MOTHER AFTERWARD...
...BUT IT WAS MINOR.
THE SOHMA FAMILY IS USED TO THAT SORT OF THING...WHICH IS TO SAY IT'S REALLY NOT UNUSUAL...
......SO IT'S NOTHING YOU NEED TO MAKE YOURSELF SICK OVER.
I HARDLY REMEMBER IT MYSELF.
BUT...
...
...I WAS WORRIED.
IT MAY NOT BE MY PLACE TO SAY ANYTHING ABOUT YOUR FAMILY...
...BUT I WAS AFRAID...
...THAT THE GIRL I SAW...
...WOULD KEEP GETTING HURT AND END UP CRYING AGAIN.

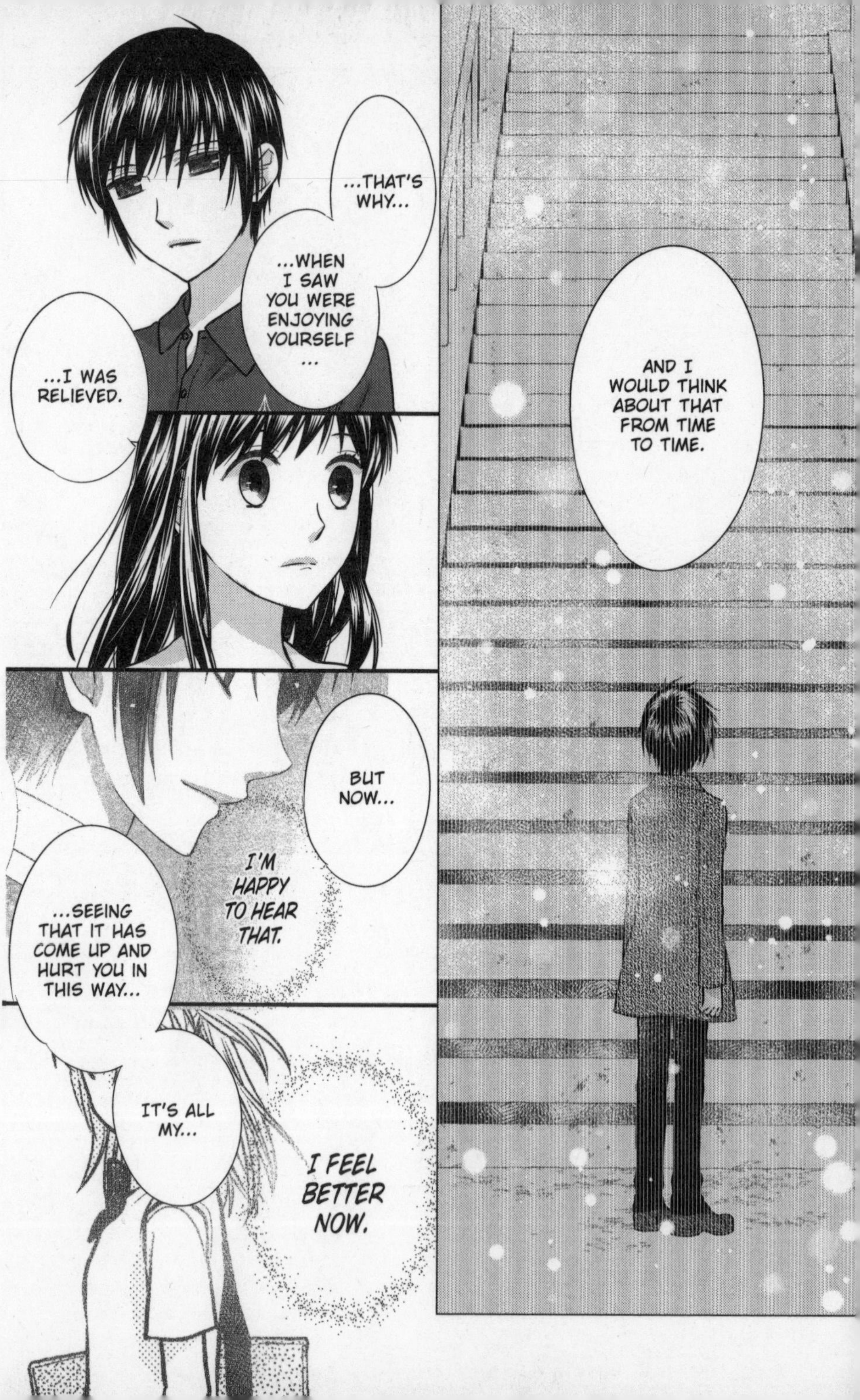
AND I WOULD THINK ABOUT THAT FROM TIME TO TIME.
...THAT'S WHY...
...WHEN I SAW YOU WERE ENJOYING YOURSELF ...
...I WAS RELIEVED.
BUT NOW...
I'M HAPPY TO HEAR THAT.
...SEEING THAT IT HAS COME UP AND HURT YOU IN THIS WAY...
IT'S ALL MY...
I FEEL BETTER NOW.

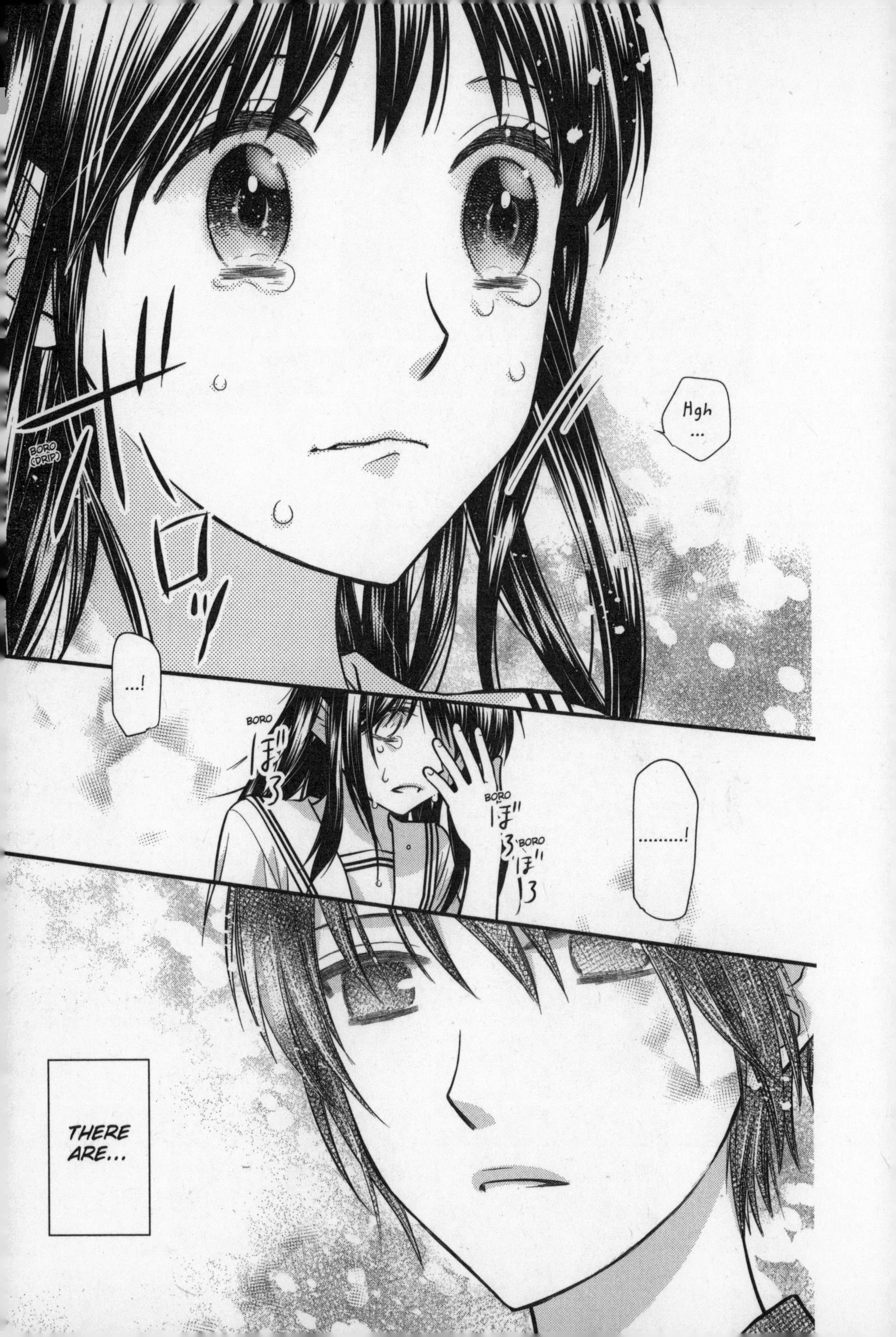
Hgh ...
BORO (DRIP)
..........!
BORO
BORO
BORO
...!
THERE ARE...

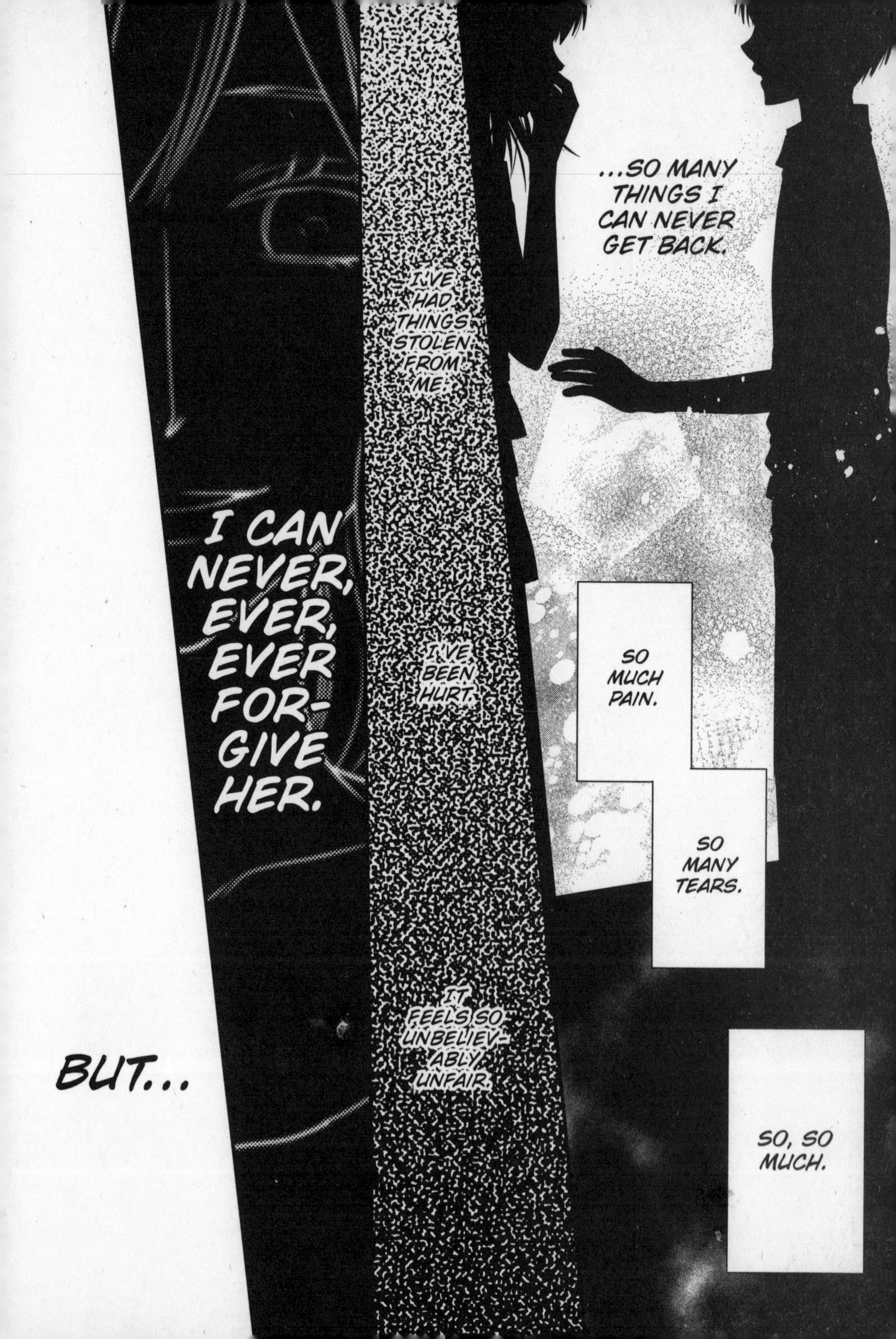
...SO MANY THINGS I CAN NEVER GET BACK.
SO MUCH PAIN.
SO MANY TEARS.
SO, SO MUCH.
I'VE HAD THINGS STOLEN FROM ME.
I'VE BEEN HURT.
IT FEELS SO UNBELIEV-ABLY UNFAIR.
I CAN NEVER, EVER, EVER FOR-GIVE HER.
BUT...

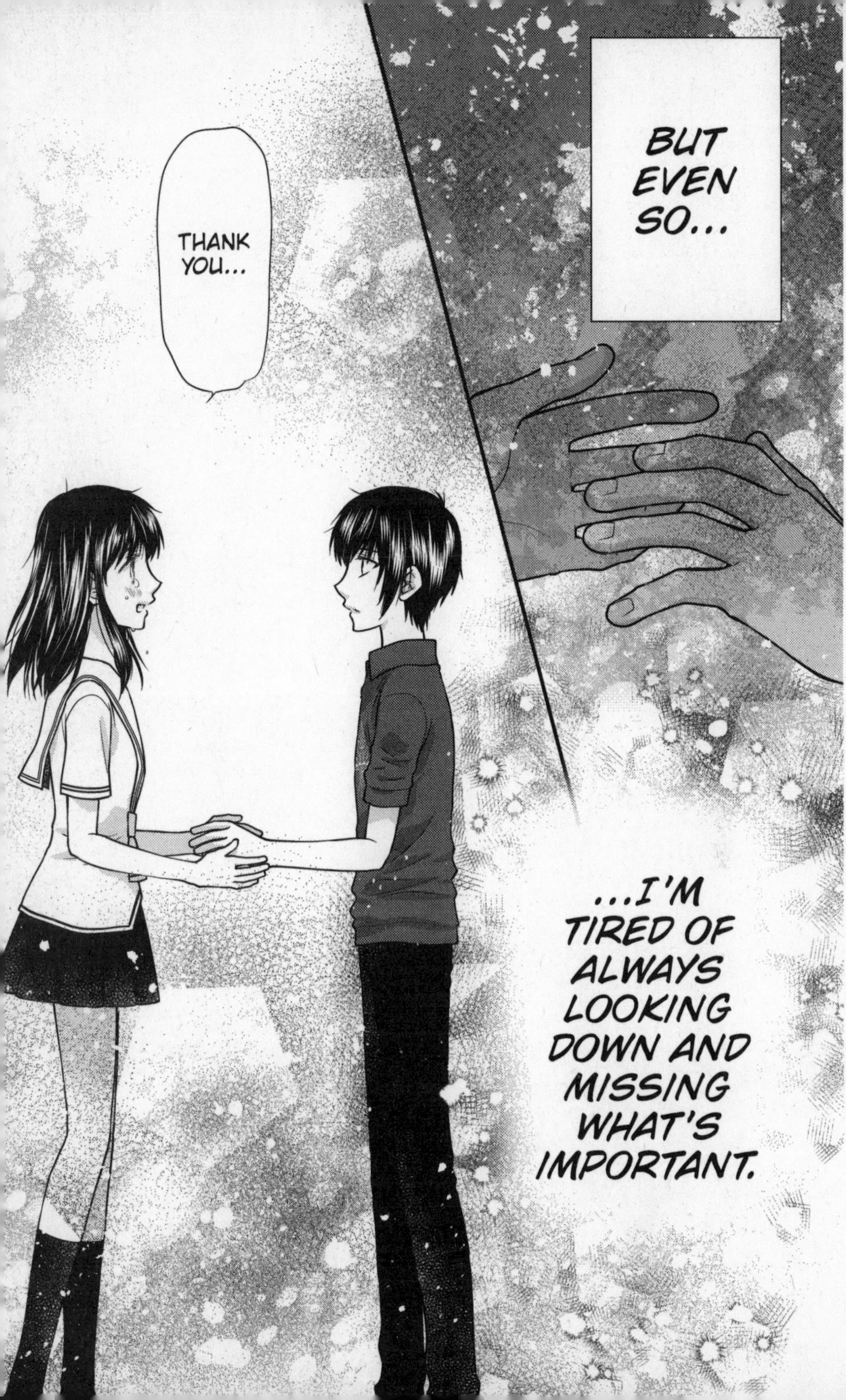
BUT EVEN SO...
THANK YOU...
...I'M TIRED OF ALWAYS LOOKING DOWN AND MISSING WHAT'S IMPORTANT.

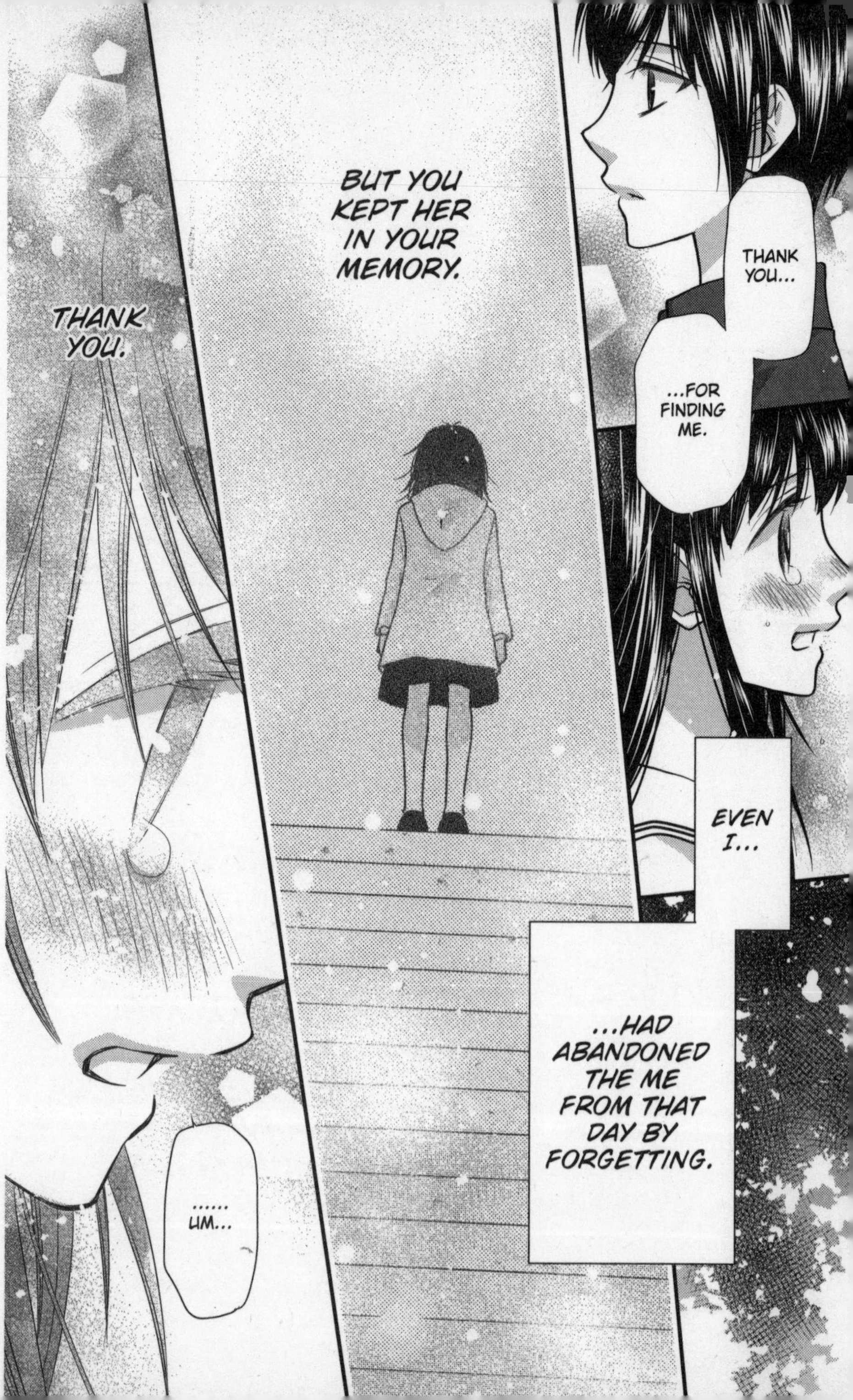
THANK YOU...
...FOR FINDING ME.
EVEN I...
...HAD ABANDONED THE ME FROM THAT DAY BY FORGETTING.
BUT YOU KEPT HER IN YOUR MEMORY.
THANK YOU.
...... UM...

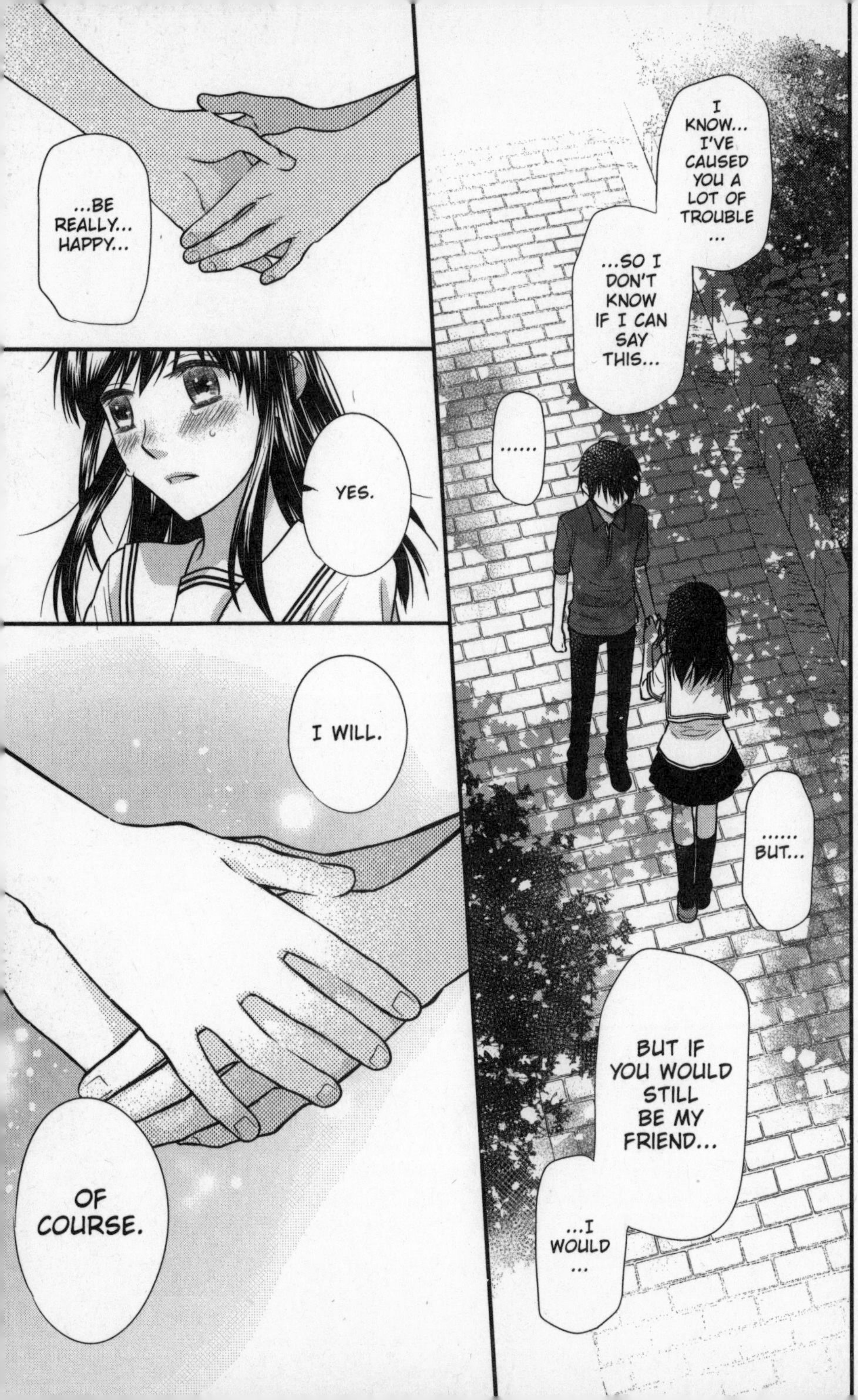
I KNOW... I'VE CAUSED YOU A LOT OF TROUBLE...
...SO I DON'T KNOW IF I CAN SAY THIS...
......
...... BUT...
BUT IF YOU WOULD STILL BE MY FRIEND...
...I WOULD...
...BE REALLY... HAPPY...
YES.
I WILL.
OF COURSE.

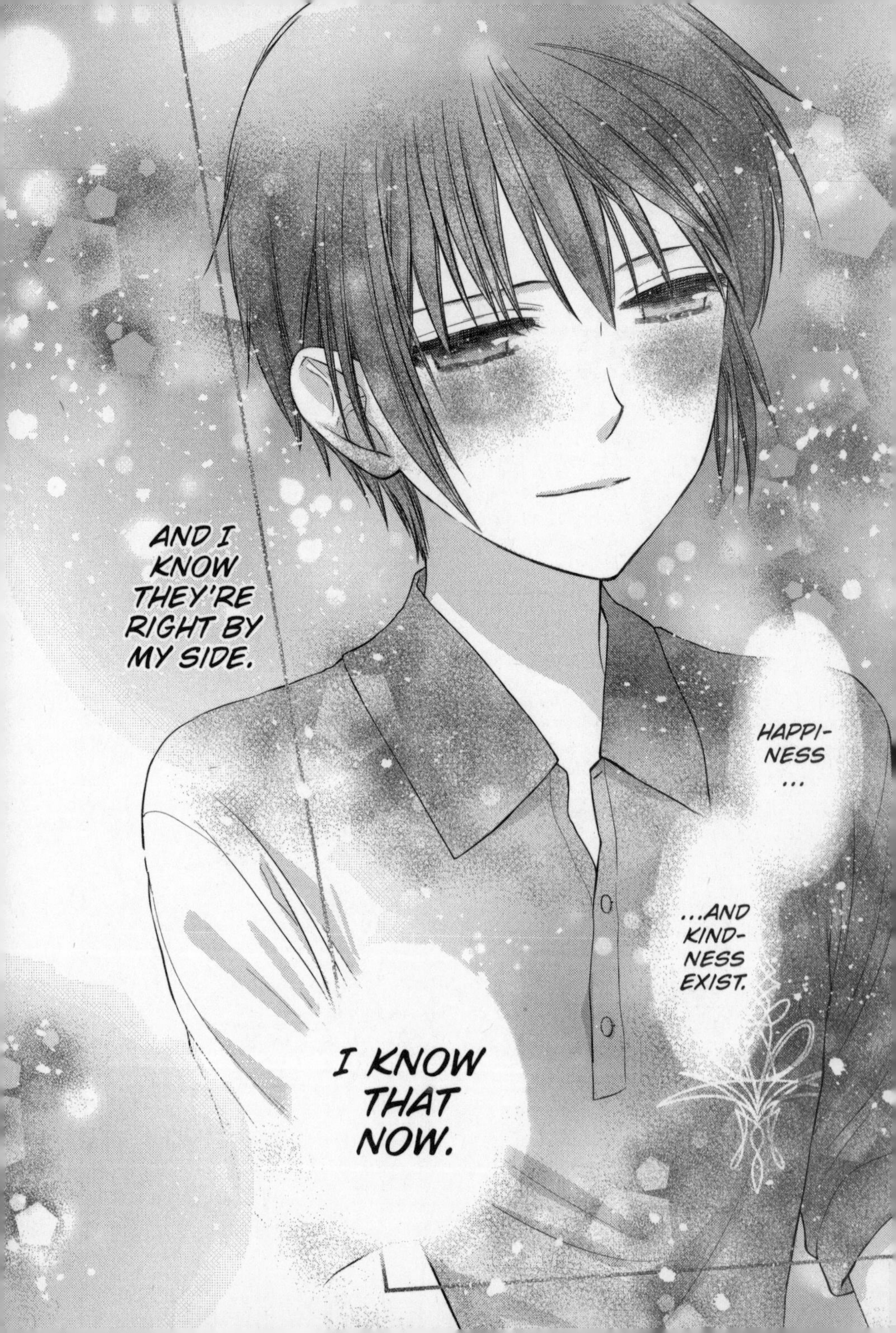
HAPPI-NESS...
...AND KIND-NESS EXIST.
I KNOW THAT NOW.
AND I KNOW THEY'RE RIGHT BY MY SIDE.

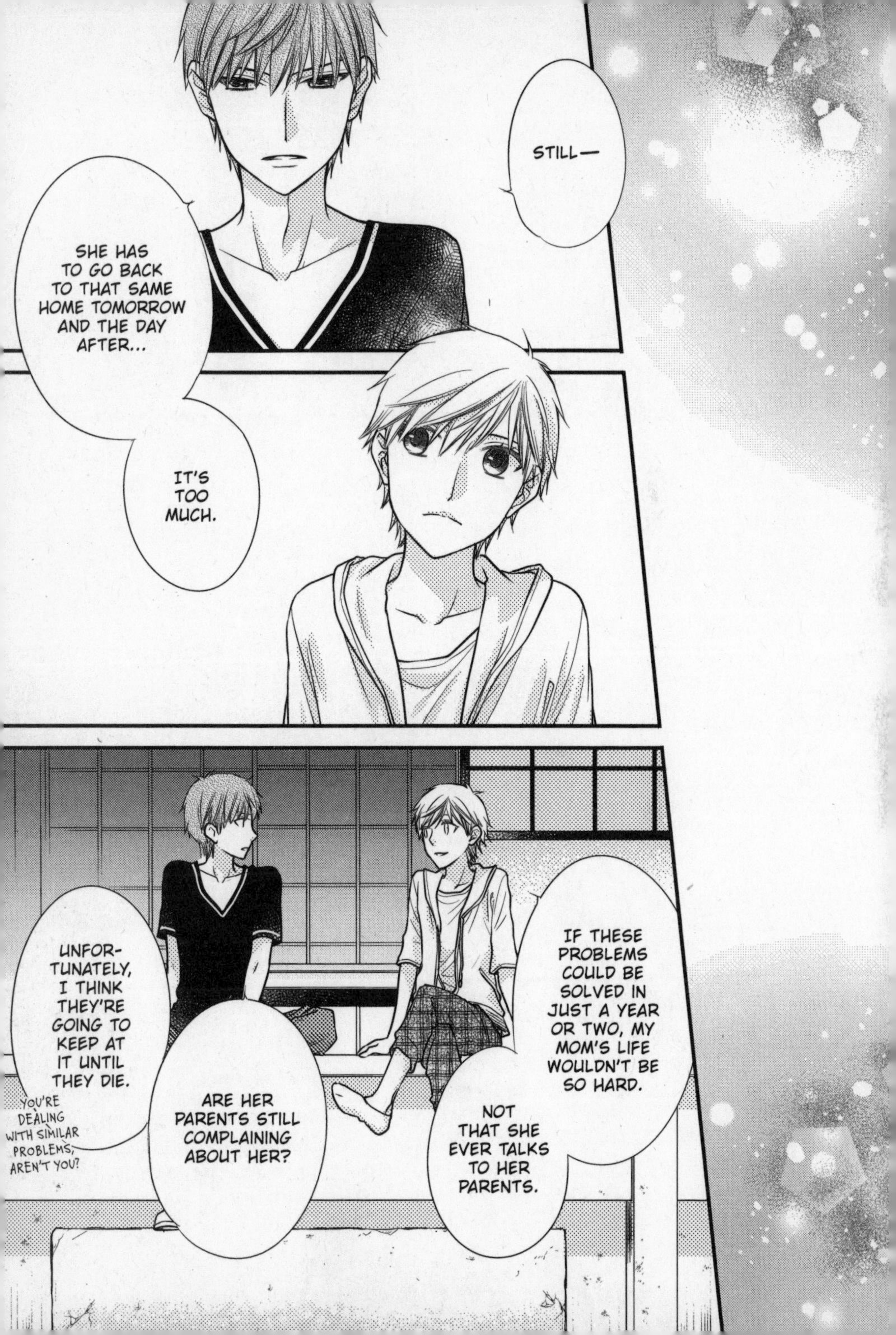
STILL—
SHE HAS TO GO BACK TO THAT SAME HOME TOMORROW AND THE DAY AFTER...
IT'S TOO MUCH.
ARE HER PARENTS STILL COMPLAINING ABOUT HER?
UNFOR-TUNATELY, I THINK THEY'RE GOING TO KEEP AT IT UNTIL THEY DIE.
IF THESE PROBLEMS COULD BE SOLVED IN JUST A YEAR OR TWO, MY MOM'S LIFE WOULDN'T BE SO HARD.
NOT THAT SHE EVER TALKS TO HER PARENTS.
YOU'RE DEALING WITH SIMILAR PROBLEMS, AREN'T YOU?

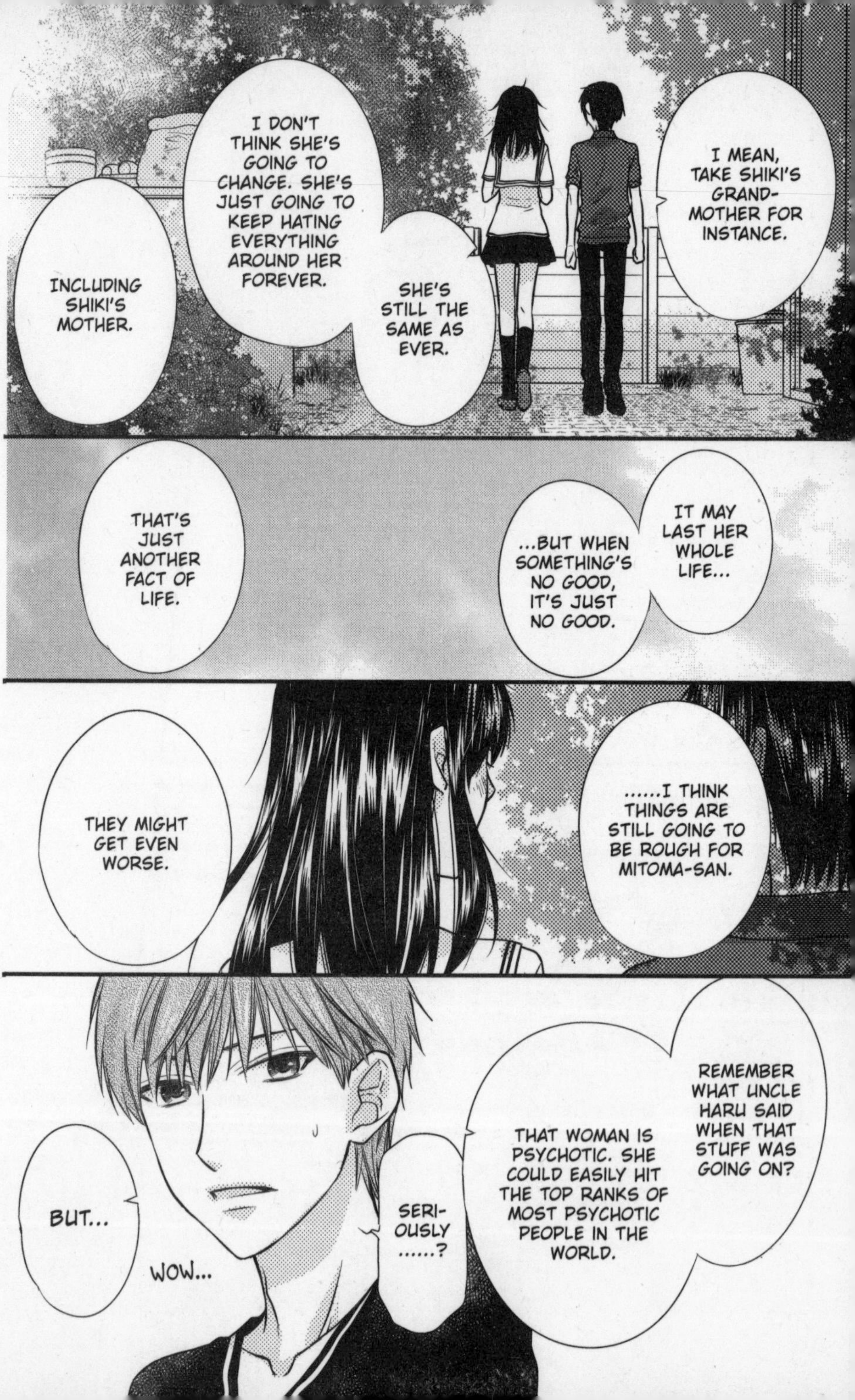
I MEAN, TAKE SHIKI'S GRAND-MOTHER FOR INSTANCE.
SHE'S STILL THE SAME AS EVER.
I DON'T THINK SHE'S GOING TO CHANGE. SHE'S JUST GOING TO KEEP HATING EVERYTHING AROUND HER FOREVER.
INCLUDING SHIKI'S MOTHER.
IT MAY LAST HER WHOLE LIFE...
...BUT WHEN SOMETHING'S NO GOOD, IT'S JUST NO GOOD.
THAT'S JUST ANOTHER FACT OF LIFE.
......I THINK THINGS ARE STILL GOING TO BE ROUGH FOR MITOMA-SAN.
THEY MIGHT GET EVEN WORSE.
REMEMBER WHAT UNCLE HARU SAID WHEN THAT STUFF WAS GOING ON?
THAT WOMAN IS PSYCHOTIC. SHE COULD EASILY HIT THE TOP RANKS OF MOST PSYCHOTIC PEOPLE IN THE WORLD.
SERI-OUSLY ......?
WOW...
BUT...

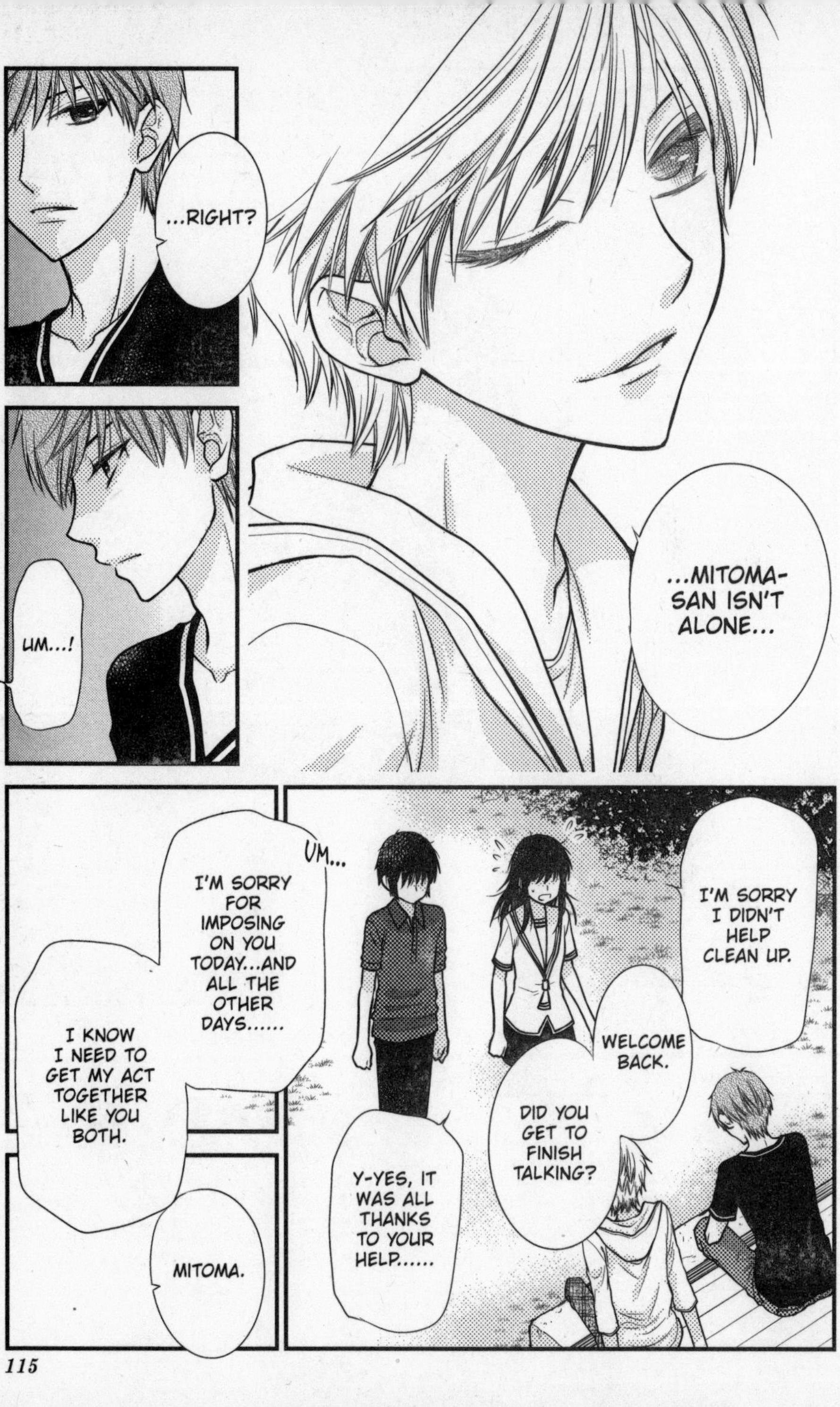
...MITOMA-SAN ISN'T ALONE...
...RIGHT?
UM...!
I'M SORRY I DIDN'T HELP CLEAN UP.
WELCOME BACK.
DID YOU GET TO FINISH TALKING?
Y-YES, IT WAS ALL THANKS TO YOUR HELP......
UM...
I'M SORRY FOR IMPOSING ON YOU TODAY...AND ALL THE OTHER DAYS......
I KNOW I NEED TO GET MY ACT TOGETHER LIKE YOU BOTH.
MITOMA.

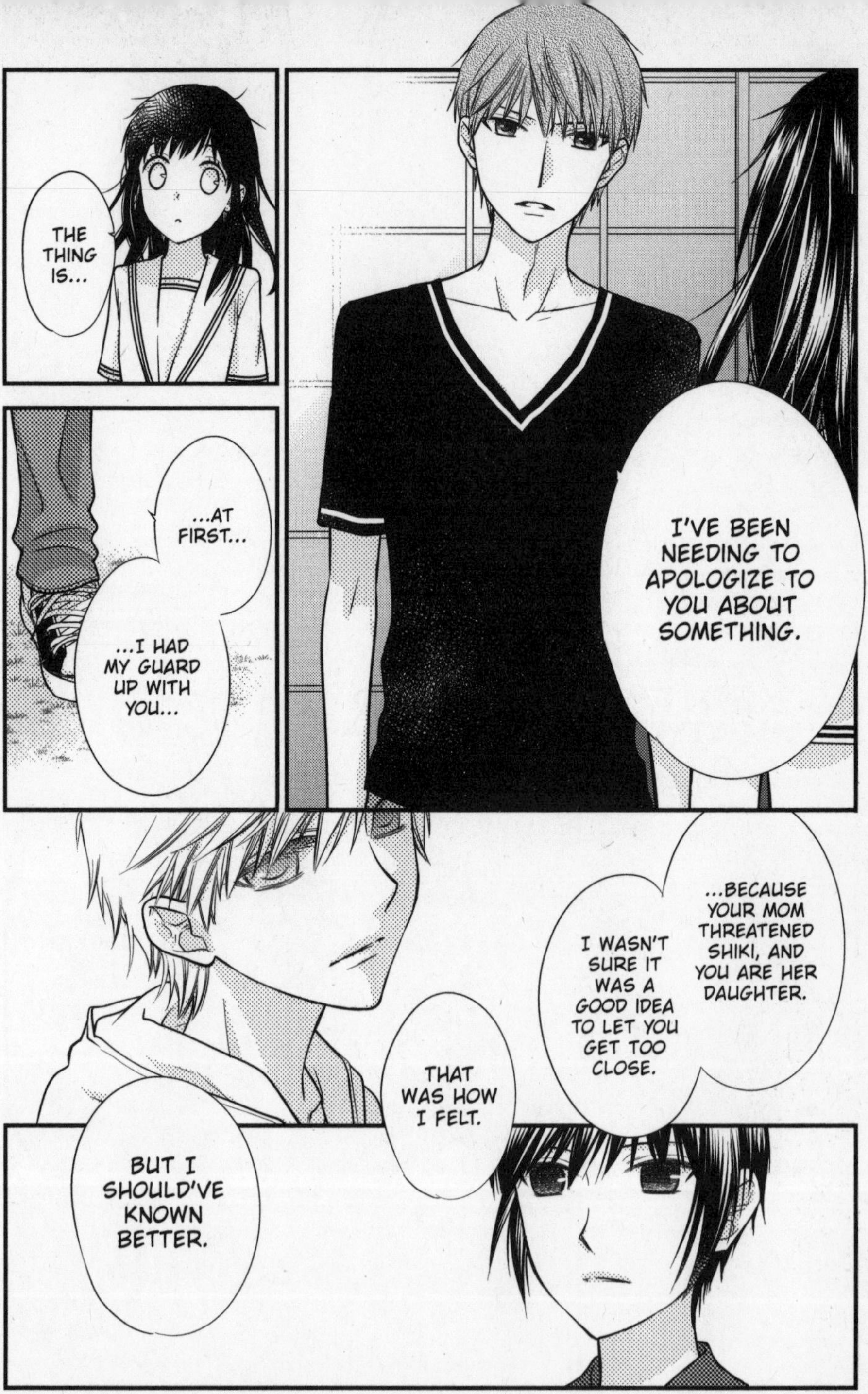
I'VE BEEN NEEDING TO APOLOGIZE TO YOU ABOUT SOMETHING.
THE THING IS...
...AT FIRST...
...I HAD MY GUARD UP WITH YOU...
...BECAUSE YOUR MOM THREATENED SHIKI, AND YOU ARE HER DAUGHTER.
I WASN'T SURE IT WAS A GOOD IDEA TO LET YOU GET TOO CLOSE.
THAT WAS HOW I FELT.
BUT I SHOULD'VE KNOWN BETTER.

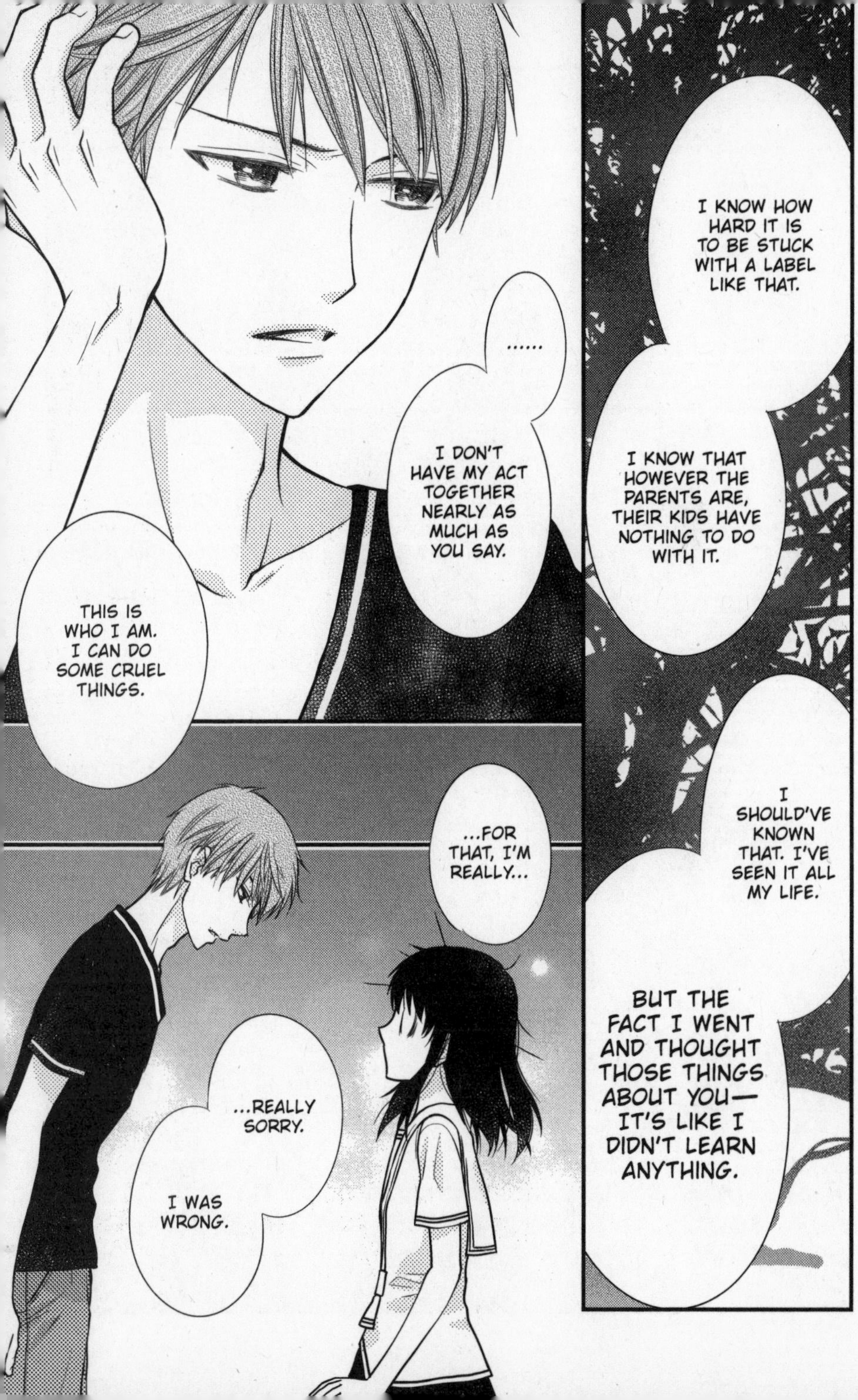
I KNOW HOW HARD IT IS TO BE STUCK WITH A LABEL LIKE THAT.
I KNOW THAT HOWEVER THE PARENTS ARE, THEIR KIDS HAVE NOTHING TO DO WITH IT.
I SHOULD'VE KNOWN THAT. I'VE SEEN IT ALL MY LIFE.
BUT THE FACT I WENT AND THOUGHT THOSE THINGS ABOUT YOU— IT'S LIKE I DIDN'T LEARN ANYTHING.
......
I DON'T HAVE MY ACT TOGETHER NEARLY AS MUCH AS YOU SAY.
THIS IS WHO I AM. I CAN DO SOME CRUEL THINGS.
...FOR THAT, I'M REALLY...
...REALLY SORRY.
I WAS WRONG.

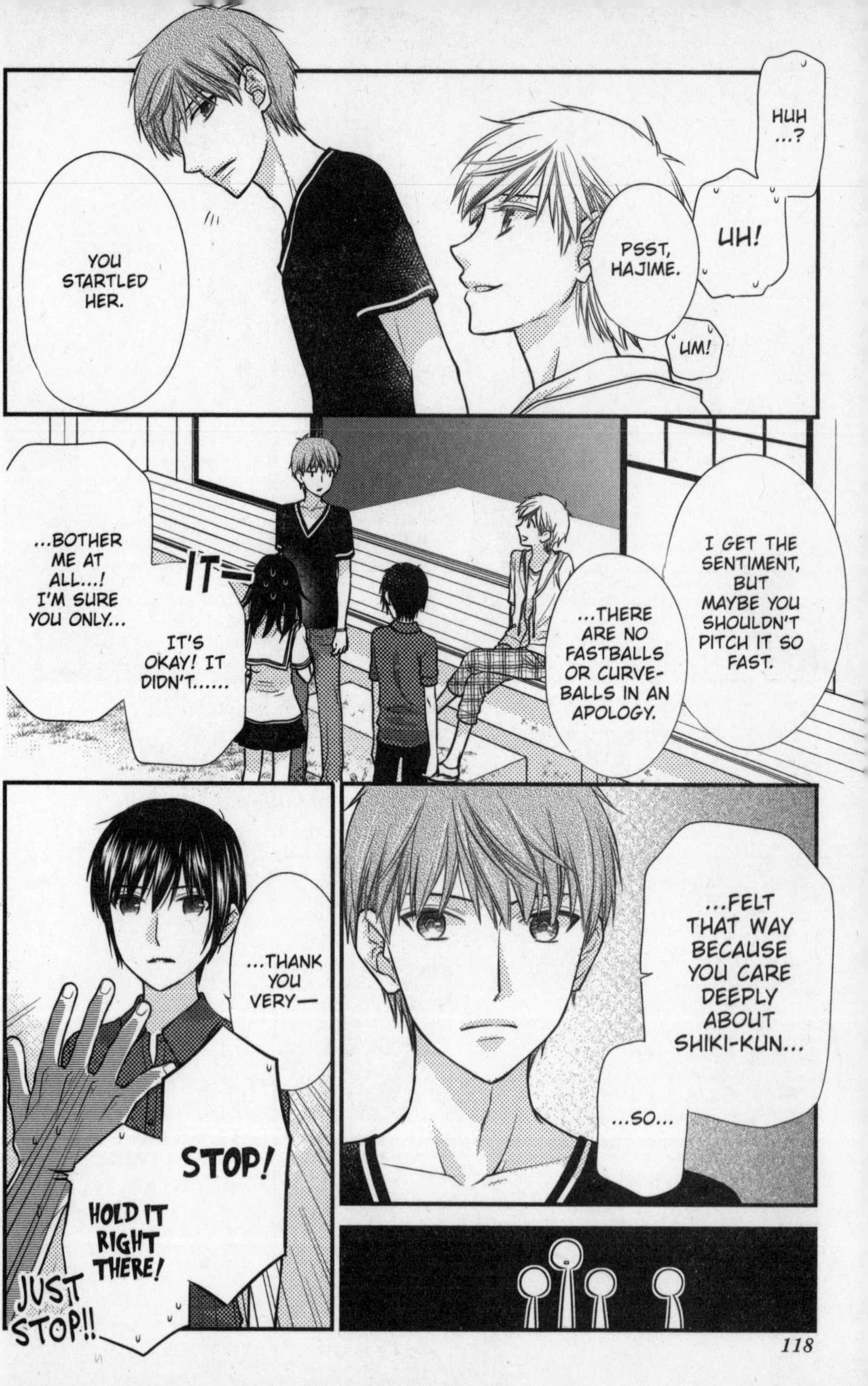
HUH ...?
PSST, HAJIME.
UH!
UM!
YOU STARTLED HER.
I GET THE SENTIMENT, BUT MAYBE YOU SHOULDN'T PITCH IT SO FAST.
...THERE ARE NO FASTBALLS OR CURVE-BALLS IN AN APOLOGY.
IT—
IT'S OKAY! IT DIDN'T......
...BOTHER ME AT ALL...! I'M SURE YOU ONLY...
...FELT THAT WAY BECAUSE YOU CARE DEEPLY ABOUT SHIKI-KUN...
...SO...
...THANK YOU VERY—
STOP!
HOLD IT RIGHT THERE!
JUST STOP!!

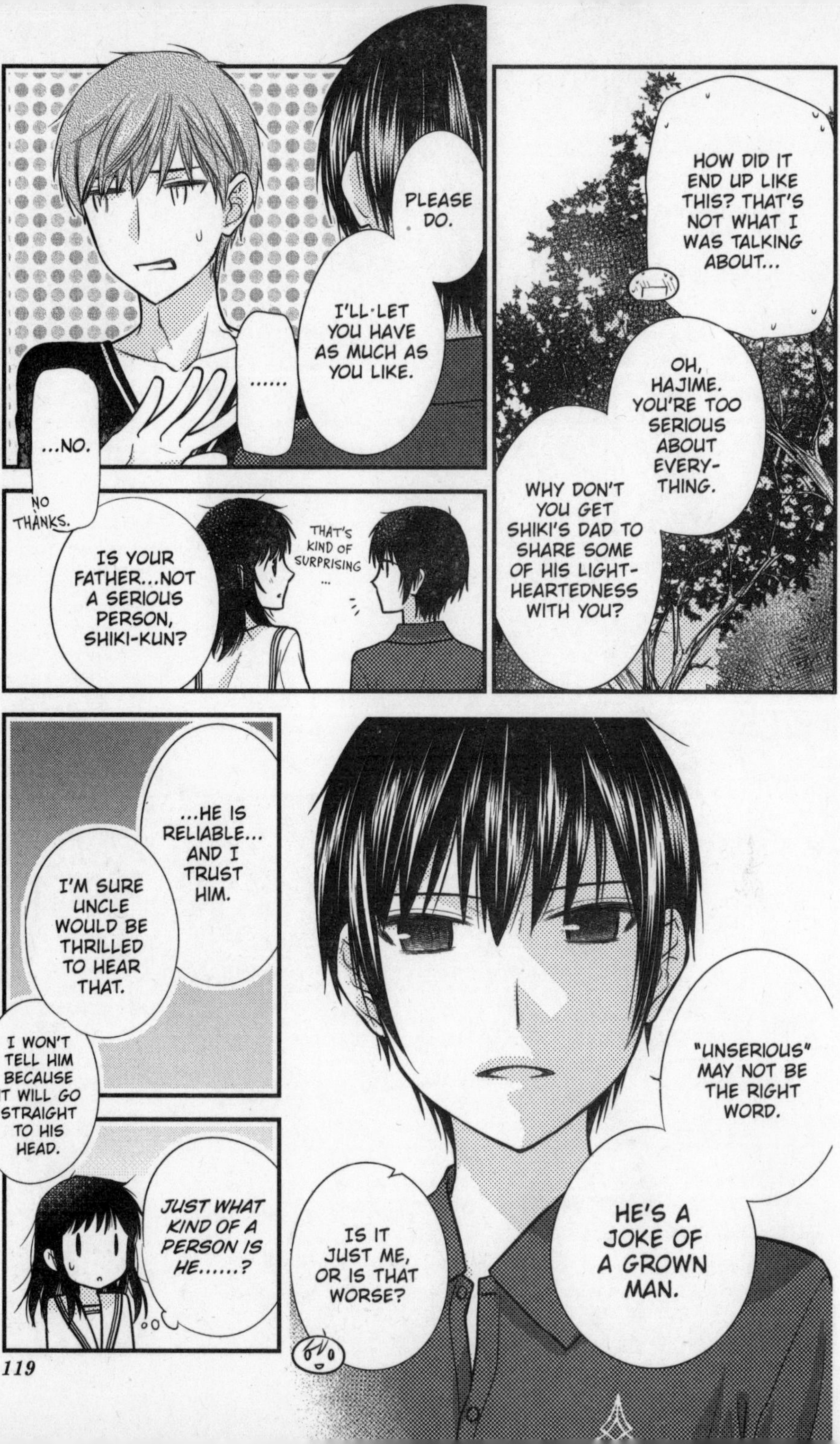
HOW DID IT END UP LIKE THIS? THAT'S NOT WHAT I WAS TALKING ABOUT...
OH, HAJIME. YOU'RE TOO SERIOUS ABOUT EVERY-THING.
WHY DON'T YOU GET SHIKI'S DAD TO SHARE SOME OF HIS LIGHT-HEARTEDNESS WITH YOU?
PLEASE DO.
I'LL LET YOU HAVE AS MUCH AS YOU LIKE.
......
...NO.
NO THANKS.
THAT'S KIND OF SURPRISING ...
IS YOUR FATHER...NOT A SERIOUS PERSON, SHIKI-KUN?
"UNSERIOUS" MAY NOT BE THE RIGHT WORD.
HE'S A JOKE OF A GROWN MAN.
IS IT JUST ME, OR IS THAT WORSE?
...HE IS RELIABLE... AND I TRUST HIM.
I'M SURE UNCLE WOULD BE THRILLED TO HEAR THAT.
I WON'T TELL HIM BECAUSE IT WILL GO STRAIGHT TO HIS HEAD.
JUST WHAT KIND OF A PERSON IS HE......?

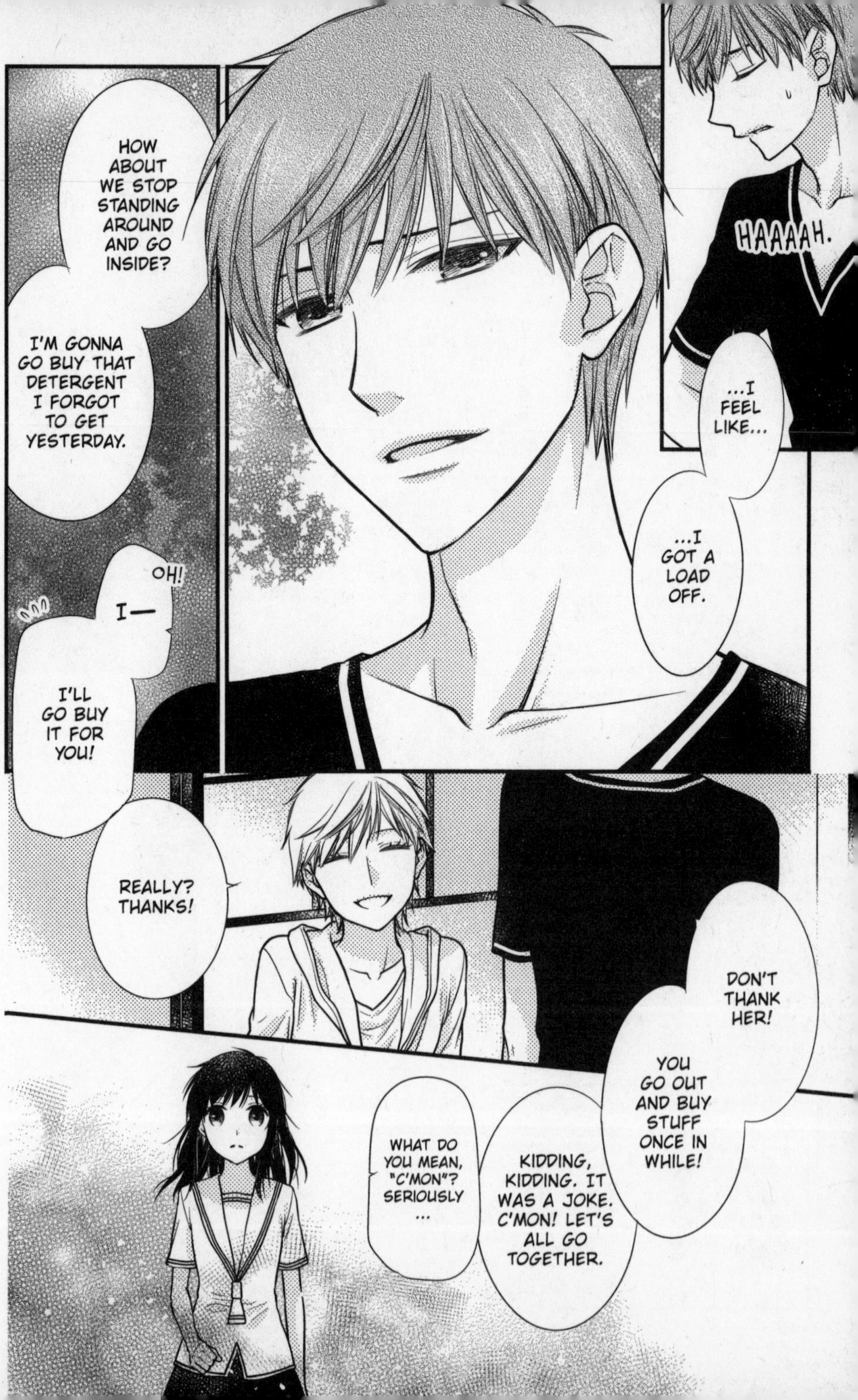
HAAAAH.
...I FEEL LIKE...
...I GOT A LOAD OFF.
HOW ABOUT WE STOP STANDING AROUND AND GO INSIDE?
I'M GONNA GO BUY THAT DETERGENT I FORGOT TO GET YESTERDAY.
OH! I—
I'LL GO BUY IT FOR YOU!
REALLY? THANKS!
DON'T THANK HER!
YOU GO OUT AND BUY STUFF ONCE IN WHILE!
KIDDING, KIDDING. IT WAS A JOKE. C'MON! LET'S ALL GO TOGETHER.
WHAT DO YOU MEAN, "C'MON"? SERIOUSLY ...

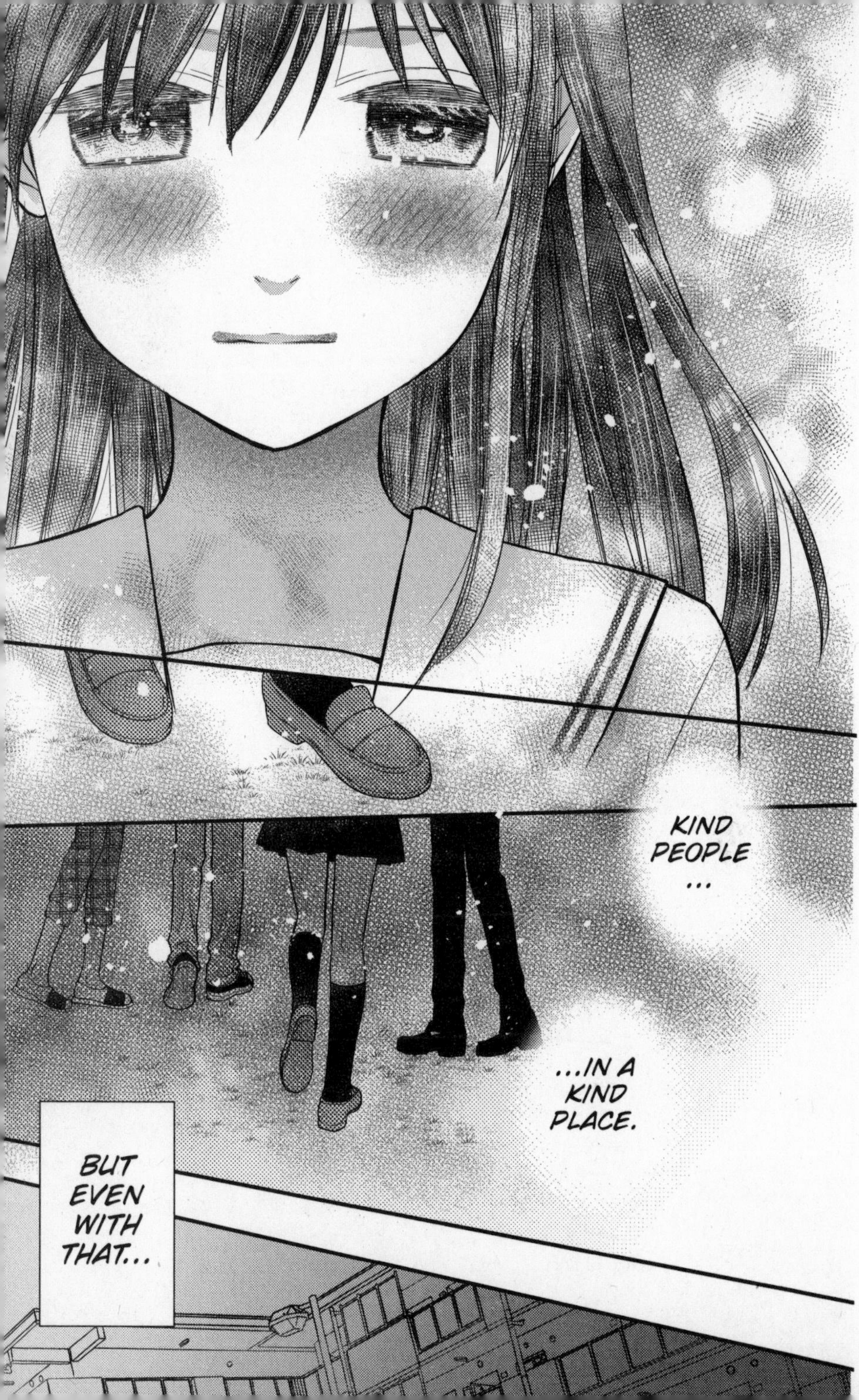
KIND PEOPLE ...
...IN A KIND PLACE.
BUT EVEN WITH THAT...

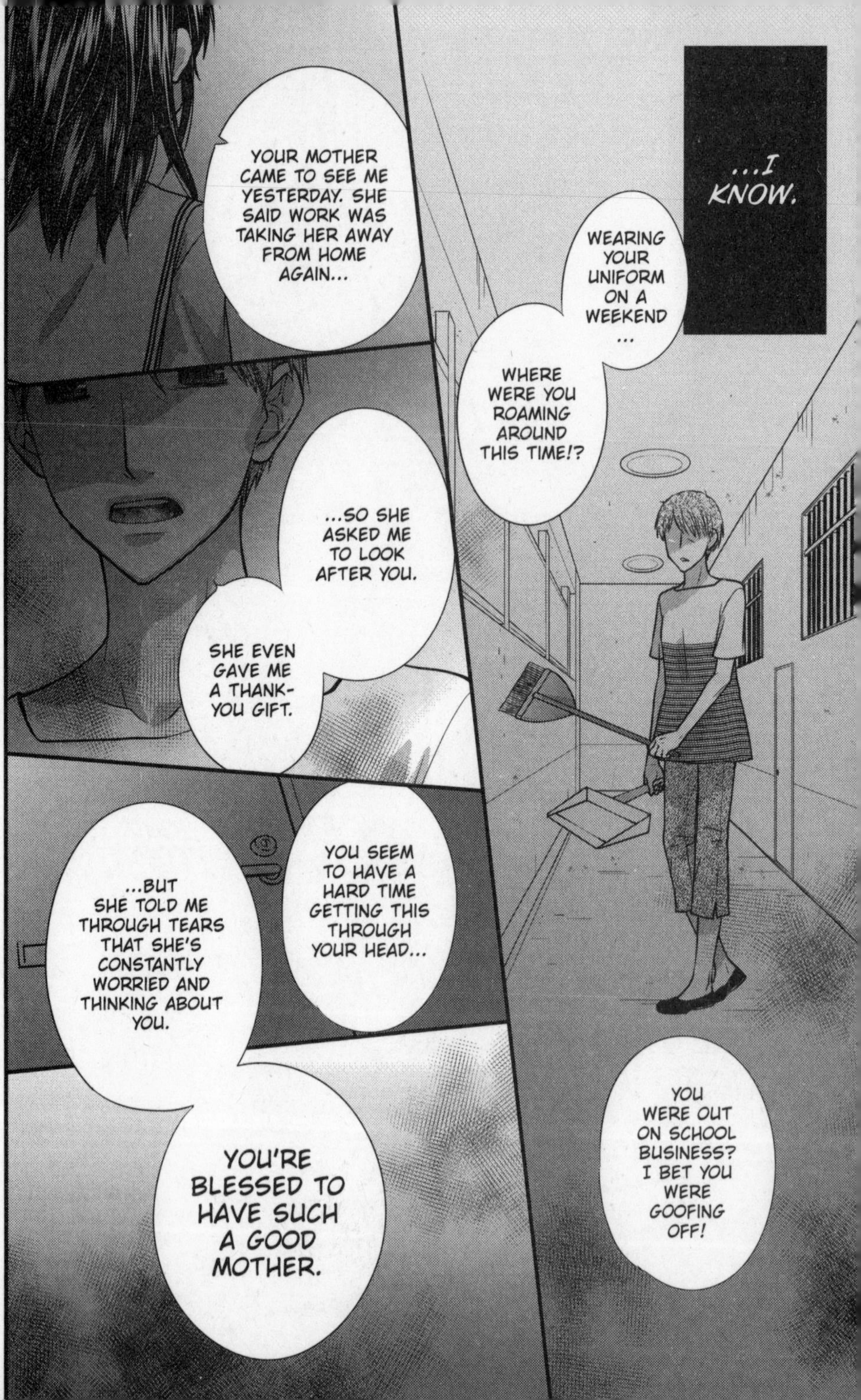
...I KNOW.
WEARING YOUR UNIFORM ON A WEEKEND...
WHERE WERE YOU ROAMING AROUND THIS TIME!?
YOU WERE OUT ON SCHOOL BUSINESS? I BET YOU WERE GOOFING OFF!
YOUR MOTHER CAME TO SEE ME YESTERDAY. SHE SAID WORK WAS TAKING HER AWAY FROM HOME AGAIN...
...SO SHE ASKED ME TO LOOK AFTER YOU.
SHE EVEN GAVE ME A THANK-YOU GIFT.
YOU SEEM TO HAVE A HARD TIME GETTING THIS THROUGH YOUR HEAD...
...BUT SHE TOLD ME THROUGH TEARS THAT SHE'S CONSTANTLY WORRIED AND THINKING ABOUT YOU.
YOU'RE BLESSED TO HAVE SUCH A GOOD MOTHER.

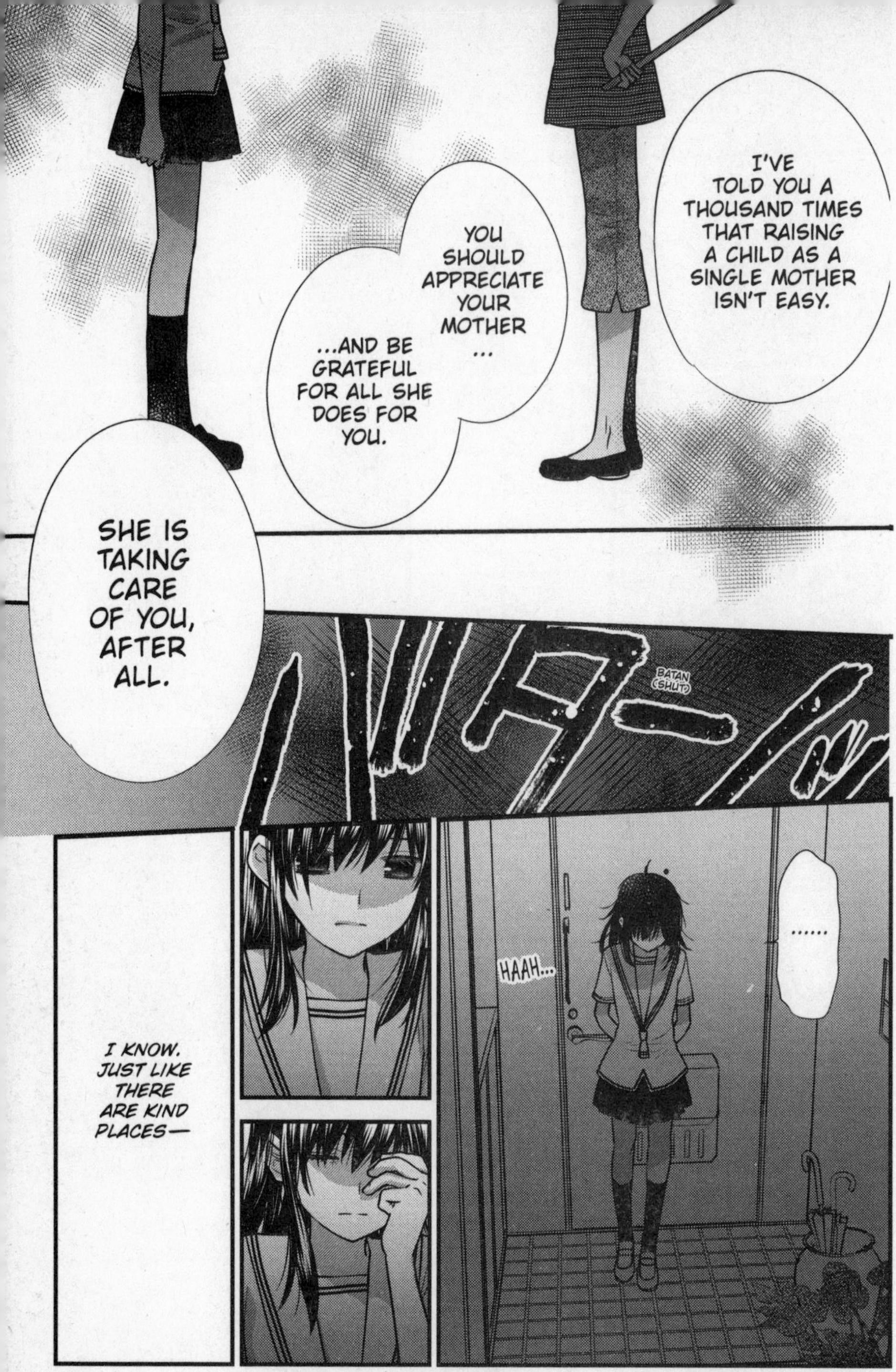
I'VE TOLD YOU A THOUSAND TIMES THAT RAISING A CHILD AS A SINGLE MOTHER ISN'T EASY.
YOU SHOULD APPRECIATE YOUR MOTHER ...
...AND BE GRATEFUL FOR ALL SHE DOES FOR YOU.
SHE IS TAKING CARE OF YOU, AFTER ALL.
BATAN (SHUT)
......
HAAH...
I KNOW. JUST LIKE THERE ARE KIND PLACES—

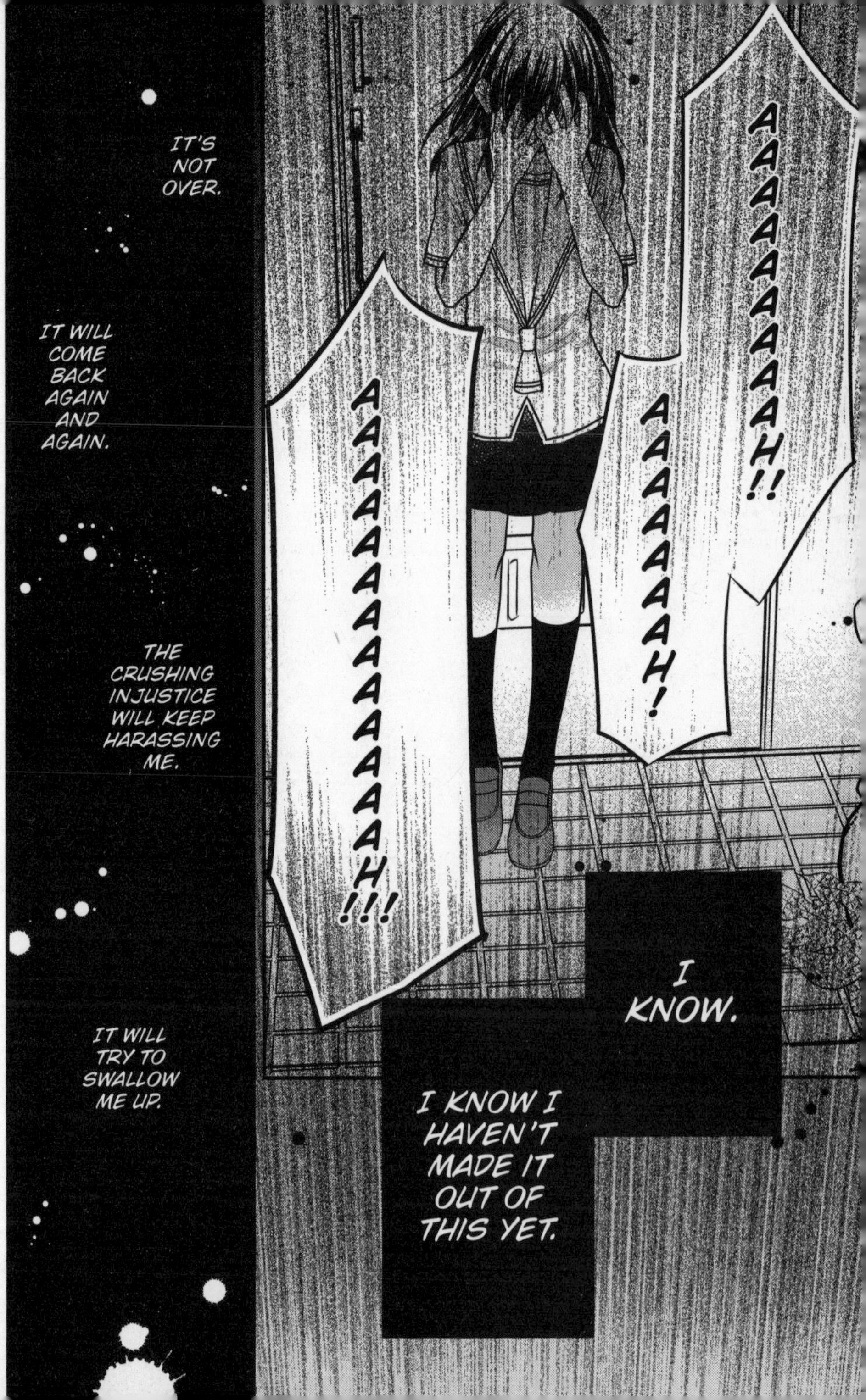

AAAAAAAAAAAAH!!
AAAAAAAH!
AAAAAAAAAAAAAAAAH!!!
I KNOW.
I KNOW I HAVEN'T MADE IT OUT OF THIS YET.
IT'S NOT OVER.
IT WILL COME BACK AGAIN AND AGAIN.
THE CRUSHING INJUSTICE WILL KEEP HARASSING ME.
IT WILL TRY TO SWALLOW ME UP.

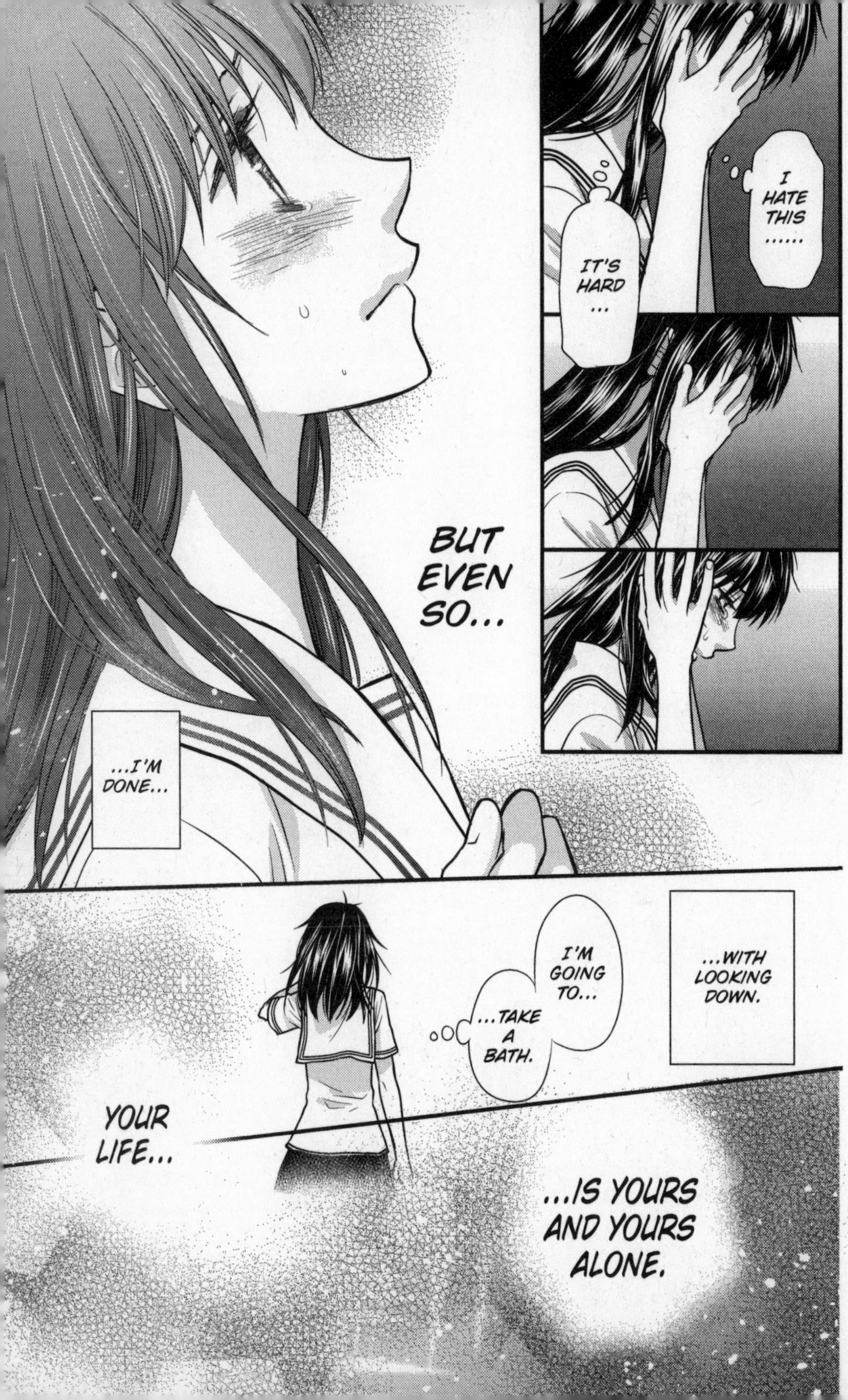
I HATE THIS ......
IT'S HARD ...
BUT EVEN SO...
...I'M DONE...
...WITH LOOKING DOWN.
I'M GOING TO...
...TAKE A BATH.
YOUR LIFE...
...IS YOURS AND YOURS ALONE.

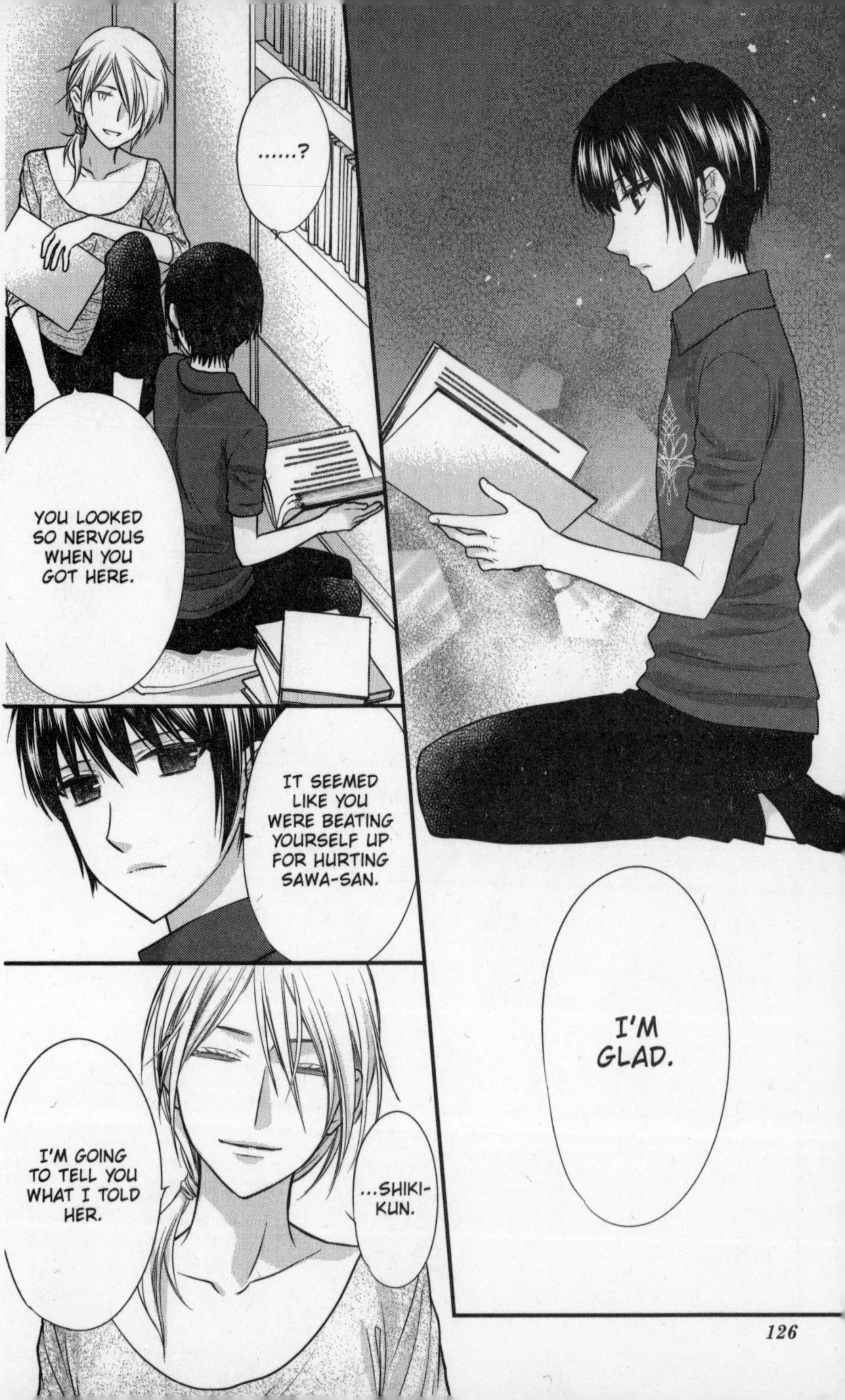
I'M GLAD.
......?
YOU LOOKED SO NERVOUS WHEN YOU GOT HERE.
IT SEEMED LIKE YOU WERE BEATING YOURSELF UP FOR HURTING SAWA-SAN.
...SHIKI-KUN.
I'M GOING TO TELL YOU WHAT I TOLD HER.

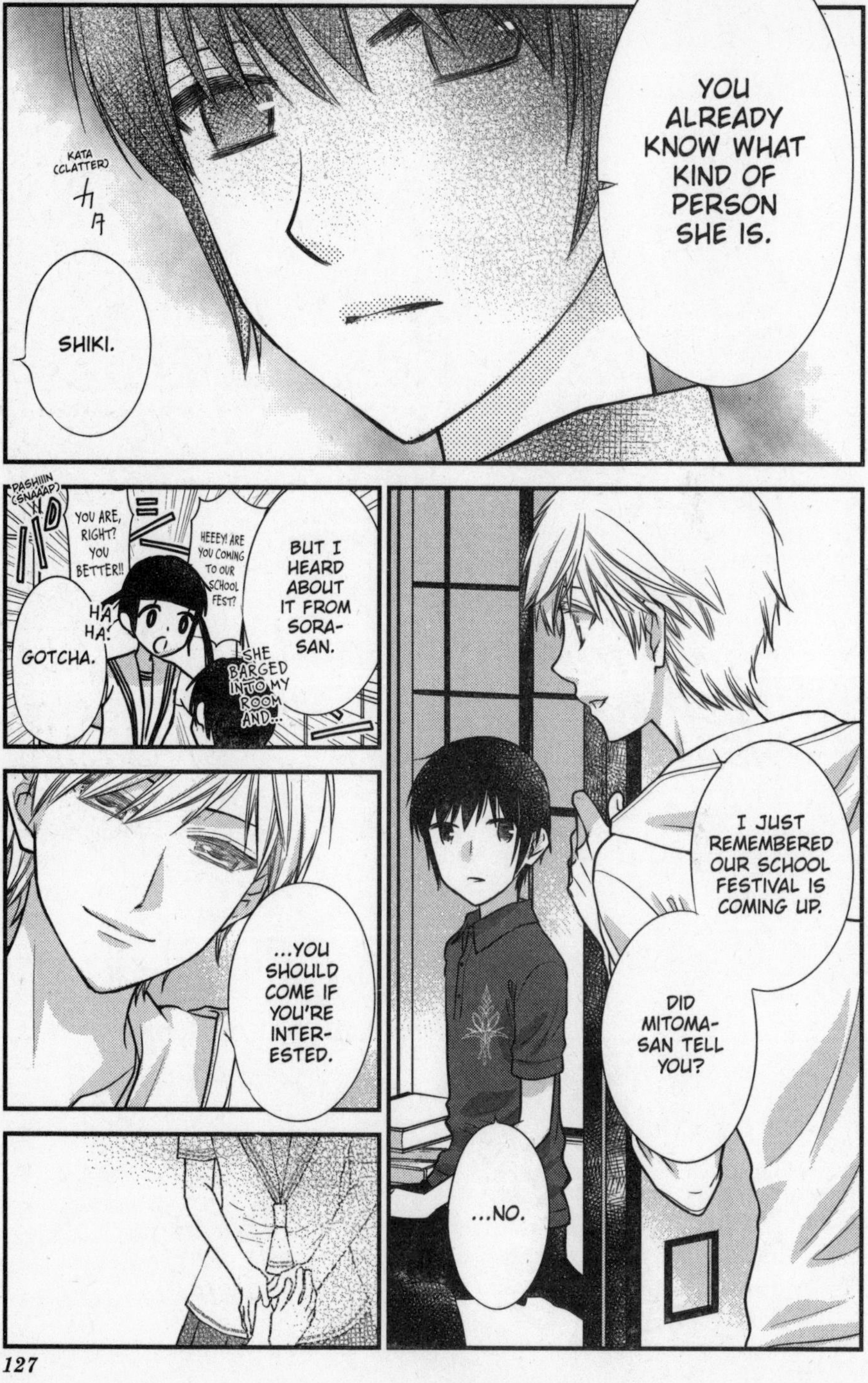
YOU ALREADY KNOW WHAT KIND OF PERSON SHE IS.
KATA (CLATTER)
カタ
SHIKI.
I JUST REMEMBERED OUR SCHOOL FESTIVAL IS COMING UP.
DID MITOMA-SAN TELL YOU?
...NO.
BUT I HEARD ABOUT IT FROM SORA-SAN.
SHE BARGED INTO MY ROOM AND...
HEEEY! ARE YOU COMING TO OUR SCHOOL FEST?
YOU ARE, RIGHT? YOU BETTER!!
PASHIIIN (SNAAAP)
HA HA!
GOTCHA.
...YOU SHOULD COME IF YOU'RE INTERESTED.

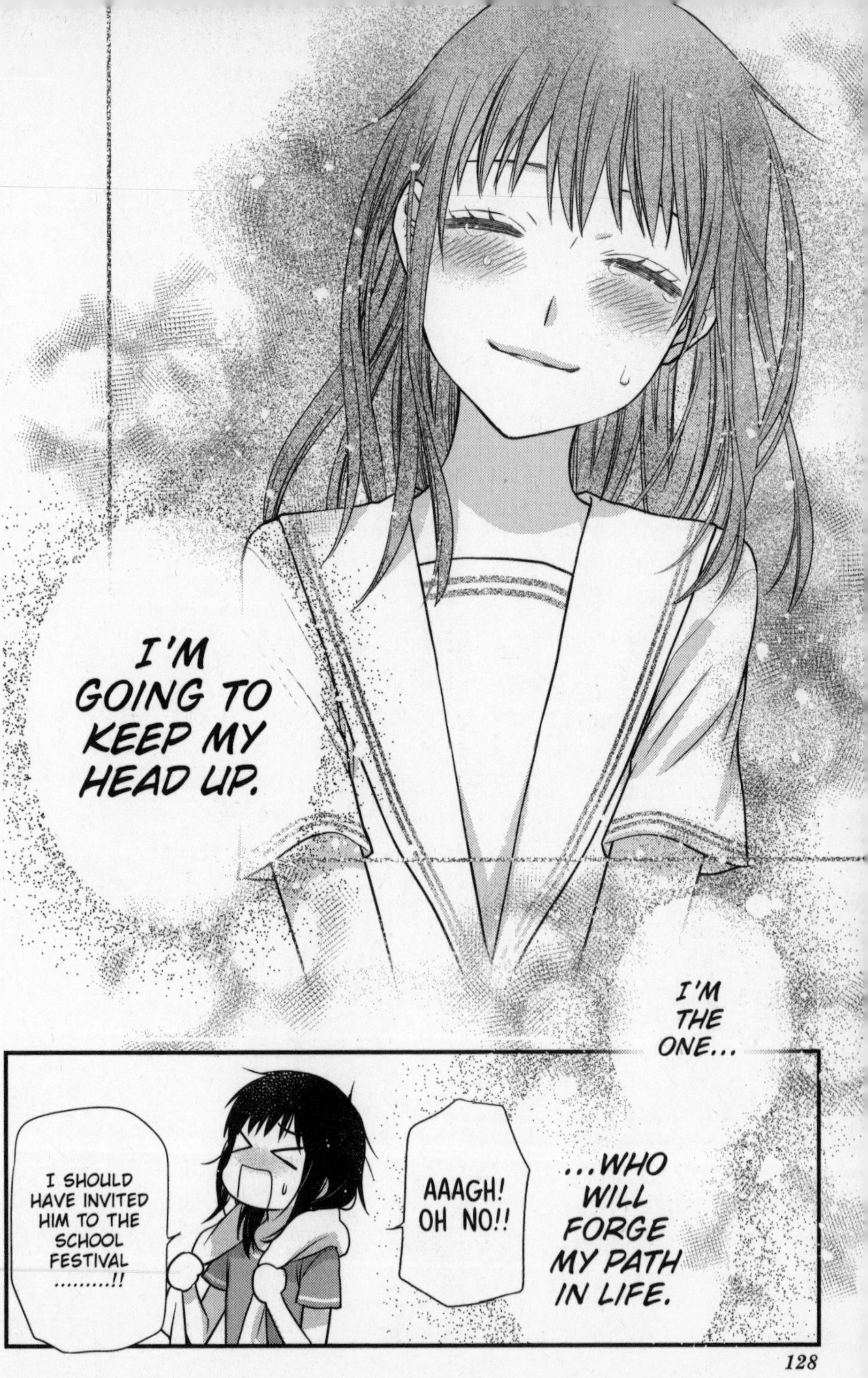
I'M GOING TO KEEP MY HEAD UP.
I'M THE ONE...
...WHO WILL FORGE MY PATH IN LIFE.
AAAGH! OH NO!!
I SHOULD HAVE INVITED HIM TO THE SCHOOL FESTIVAL ....!!

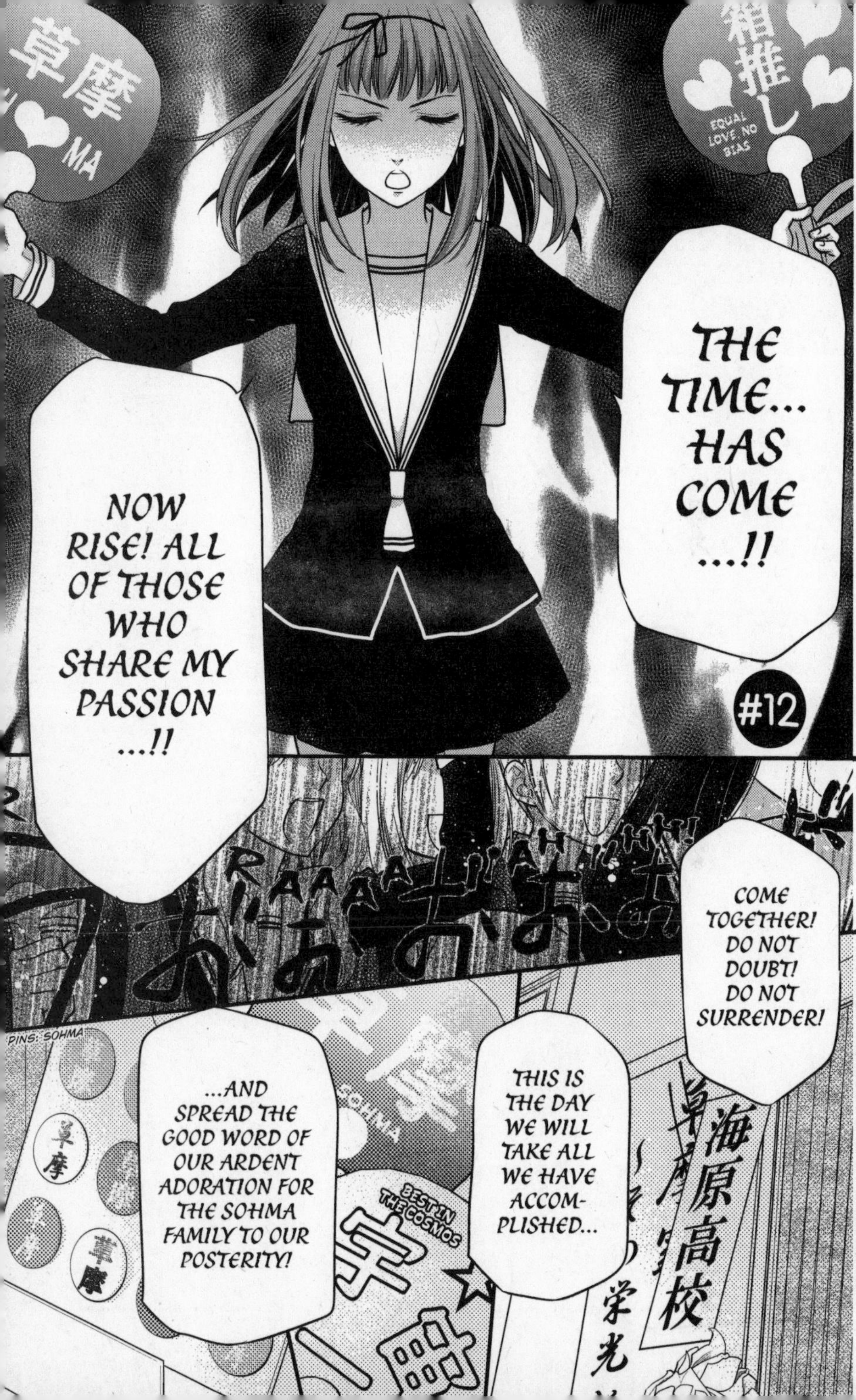

草摩
MA
箱推し
EQUAL LOVE NO BIAS
THE TIME... HAS COME ...!!
NOW RISE! ALL OF THOSE WHO SHARE MY PASSION ...!!
#12
RAAAAAHHH!
COME TOGETHER! DO NOT DOUBT! DO NOT SURRENDER!
THIS IS THE DAY WE WILL TAKE ALL WE HAVE ACCOMPLISHED...
...AND SPREAD THE GOOD WORD OF OUR ARDENT ADORATION FOR THE SOHMA FAMILY TO OUR POSTERITY!
海原高校
SOHMA
BEST IN THE COSMOS
PINS: SOHMA
SIGNS: KAIBARA HIGH SCHOOL, SOHMA FAMILY ~THE MIRACLE OF ITS GLORY AND SPLENDOR~

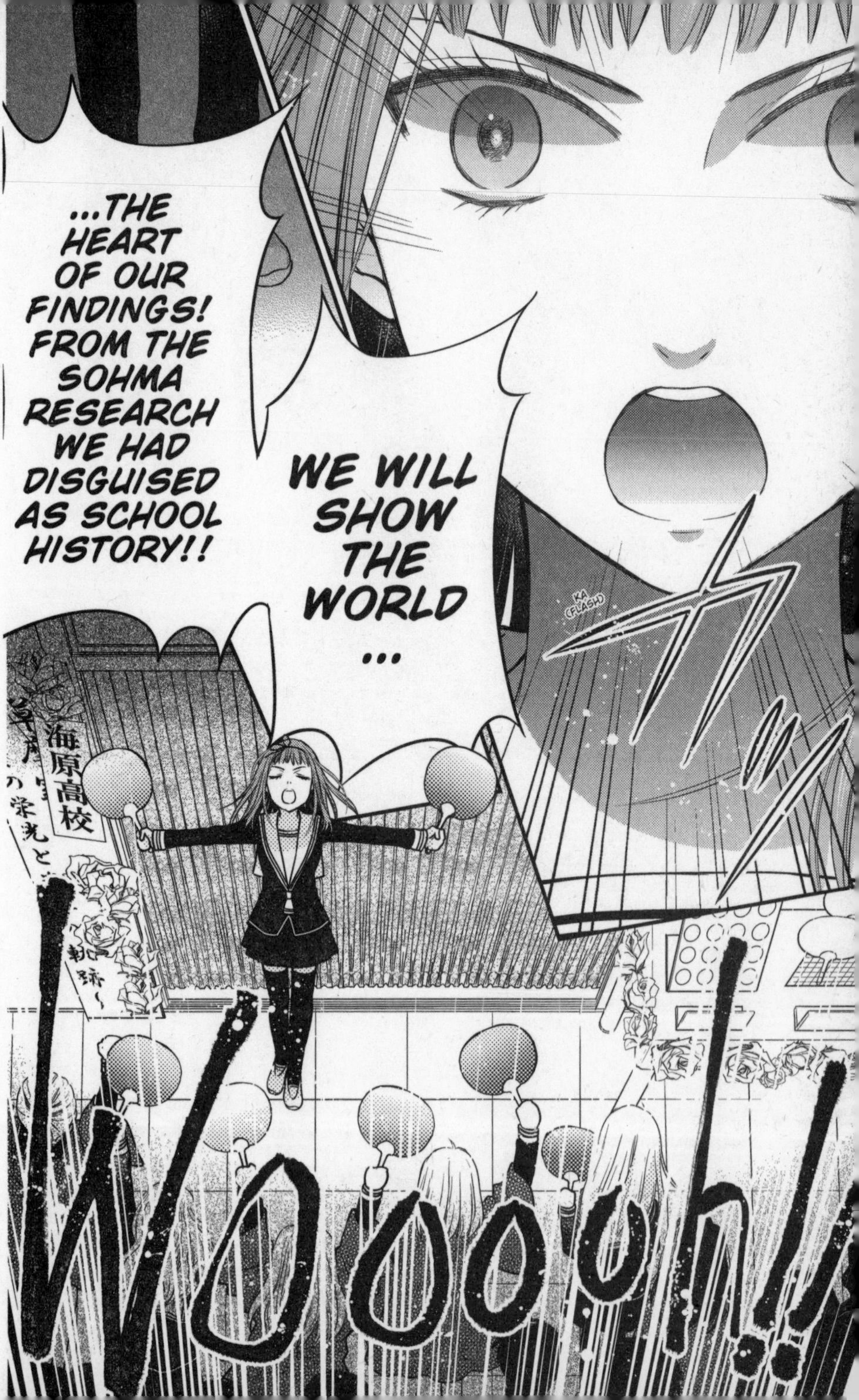
...THE HEART OF OUR FINDINGS! FROM THE SOHMA RESEARCH WE HAD DISGUISED AS SCHOOL HISTORY!!
WE WILL SHOW THE WORLD ...
KA (FLASH)
海原高校
Wooooh!!

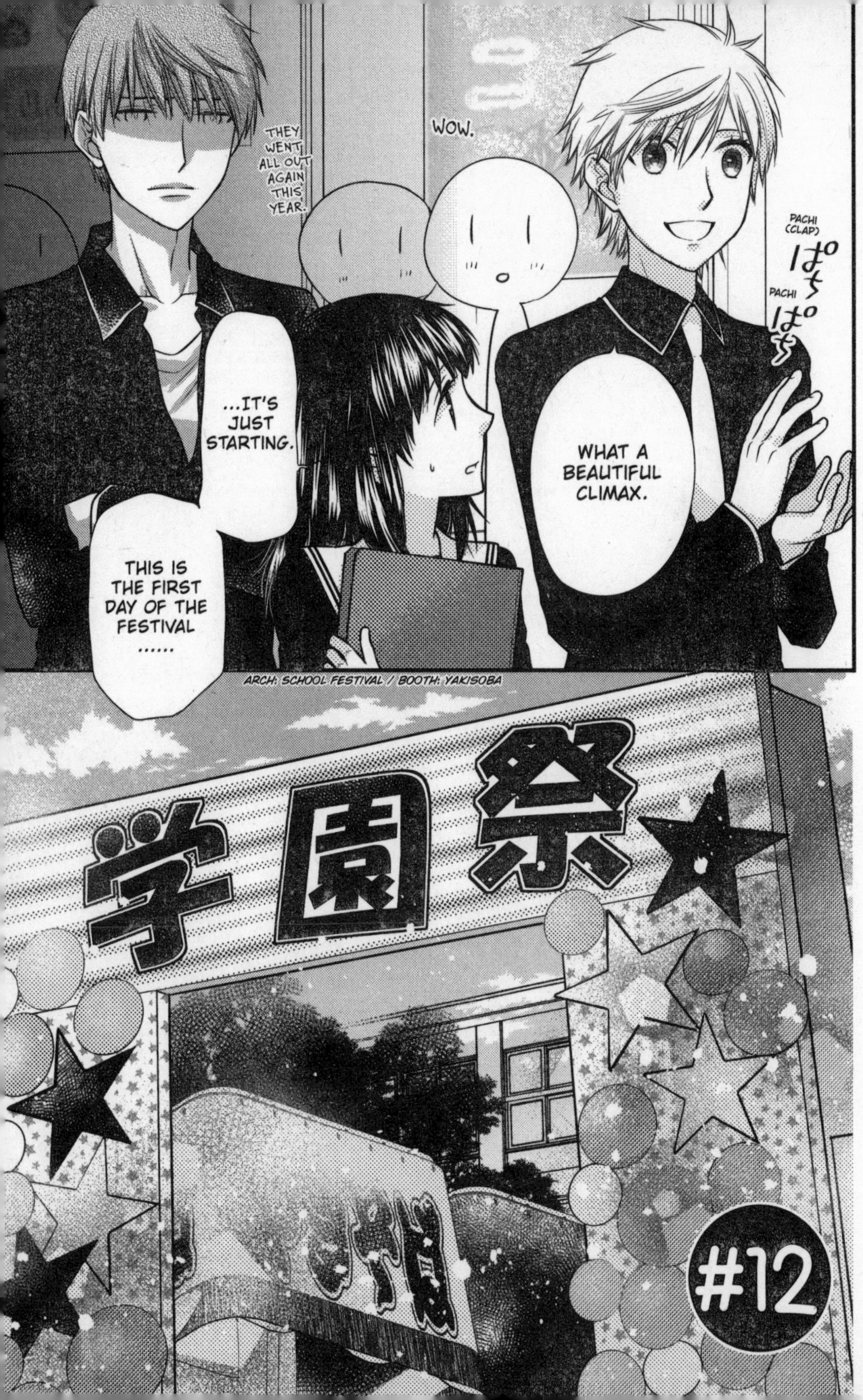
PACHI (CLAP)
ぱち
PACHI
ぱち
WHAT A BEAUTIFUL CLIMAX.
WOW.
THEY WENT ALL OUT AGAIN THIS YEAR.
...IT'S JUST STARTING.
THIS IS THE FIRST DAY OF THE FESTIVAL ......
ARCH: SCHOOL FESTIVAL / BOOTH: YAKISOBA
学園祭
#12

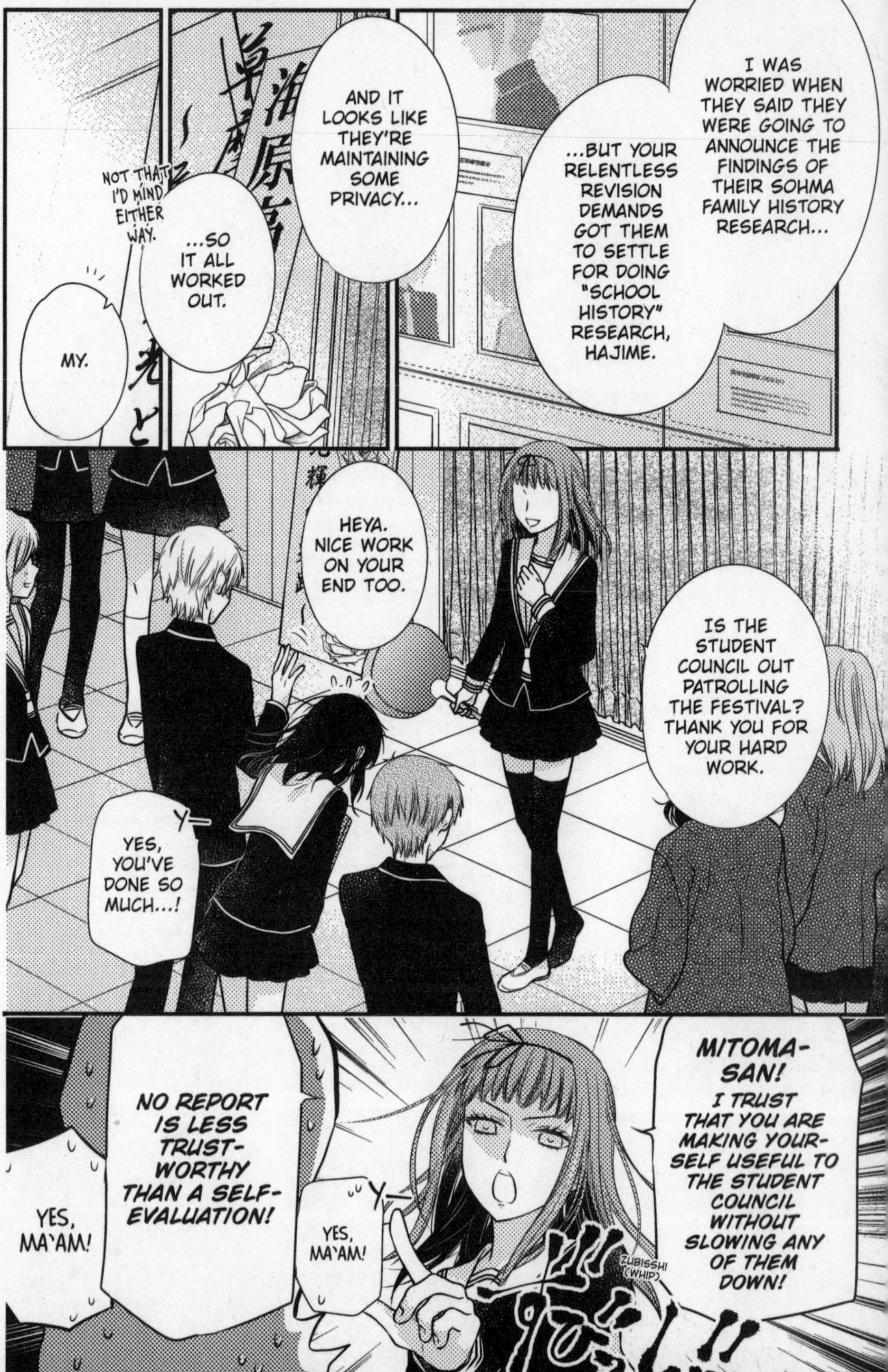
I WAS WORRIED WHEN THEY SAID THEY WERE GOING TO ANNOUNCE THE FINDINGS OF THEIR SOHMA FAMILY HISTORY RESEARCH...
...BUT YOUR RELENTLESS REVISION DEMANDS GOT THEM TO SETTLE FOR DOING "SCHOOL HISTORY" RESEARCH, HAJIME.
AND IT LOOKS LIKE THEY'RE MAINTAINING SOME PRIVACY...
...SO IT ALL WORKED OUT.
NOT THAT I'D MIND EITHER WAY.
MY.
IS THE STUDENT COUNCIL OUT PATROLLING THE FESTIVAL? THANK YOU FOR YOUR HARD WORK.
HEYA. NICE WORK ON YOUR END TOO.
YES, YOU'VE DONE SO MUCH...!
MITOMA-SAN! I TRUST THAT YOU ARE MAKING YOURSELF USEFUL TO THE STUDENT COUNCIL WITHOUT SLOWING ANY OF THEM DOWN!
ZUBISSHI (WHIP)
YES, MA'AM!
NO REPORT IS LESS TRUST-WORTHY THAN A SELF-EVALUATION!
YES, MA'AM!

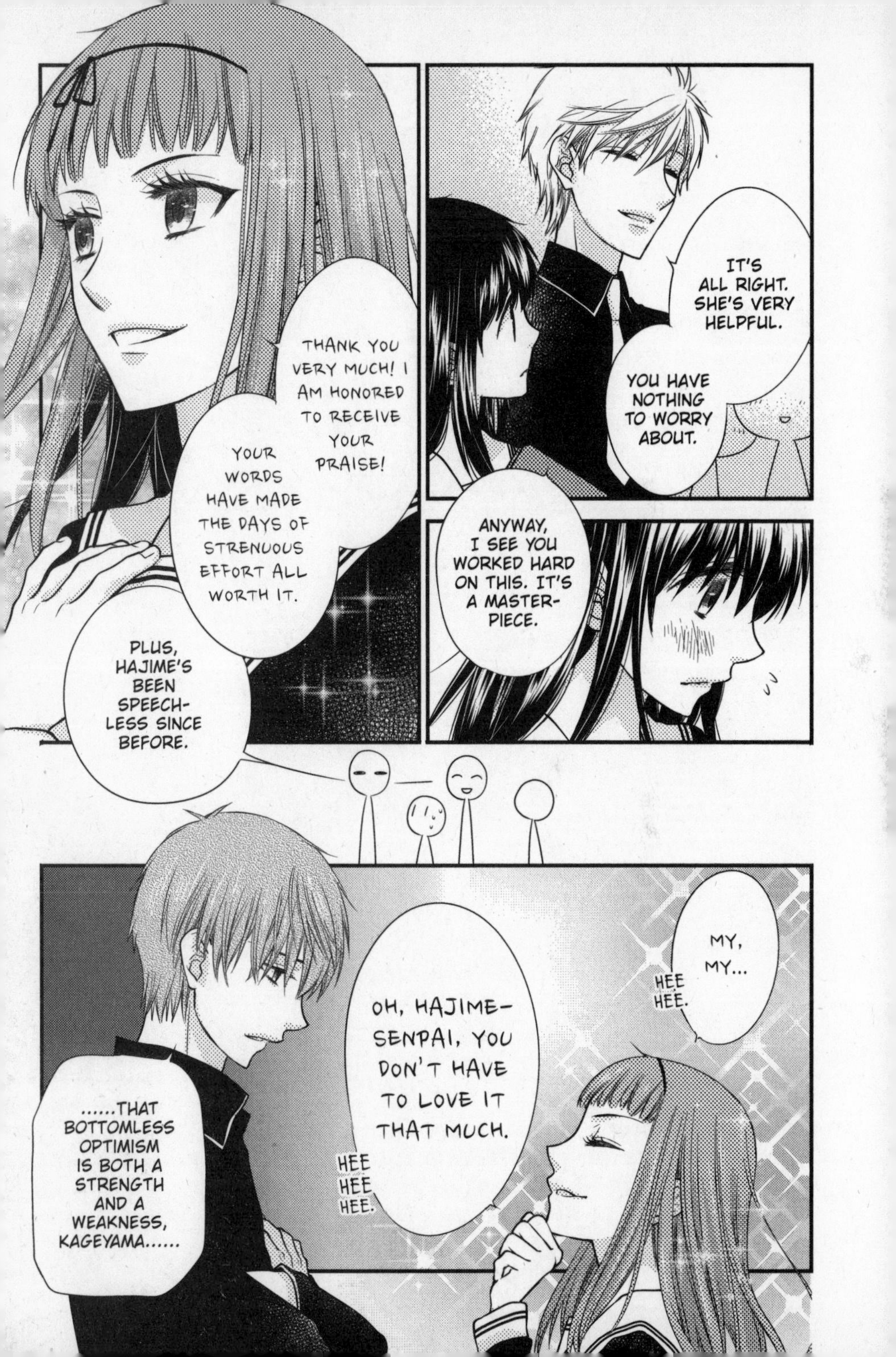
IT'S ALL RIGHT. SHE'S VERY HELPFUL.
YOU HAVE NOTHING TO WORRY ABOUT.
ANYWAY, I SEE YOU WORKED HARD ON THIS. IT'S A MASTER-PIECE.
THANK YOU VERY MUCH! I AM HONORED TO RECEIVE YOUR PRAISE!
YOUR WORDS HAVE MADE THE DAYS OF STRENUOUS EFFORT ALL WORTH IT.
PLUS, HAJIME'S BEEN SPEECH-LESS SINCE BEFORE.
MY, MY...
HEE HEE.
OH, HAJIME-SENPAI, YOU DON'T HAVE TO LOVE IT THAT MUCH.
HEE HEE HEE.
......THAT BOTTOMLESS OPTIMISM IS BOTH A STRENGTH AND A WEAKNESS, KAGEYAMA......

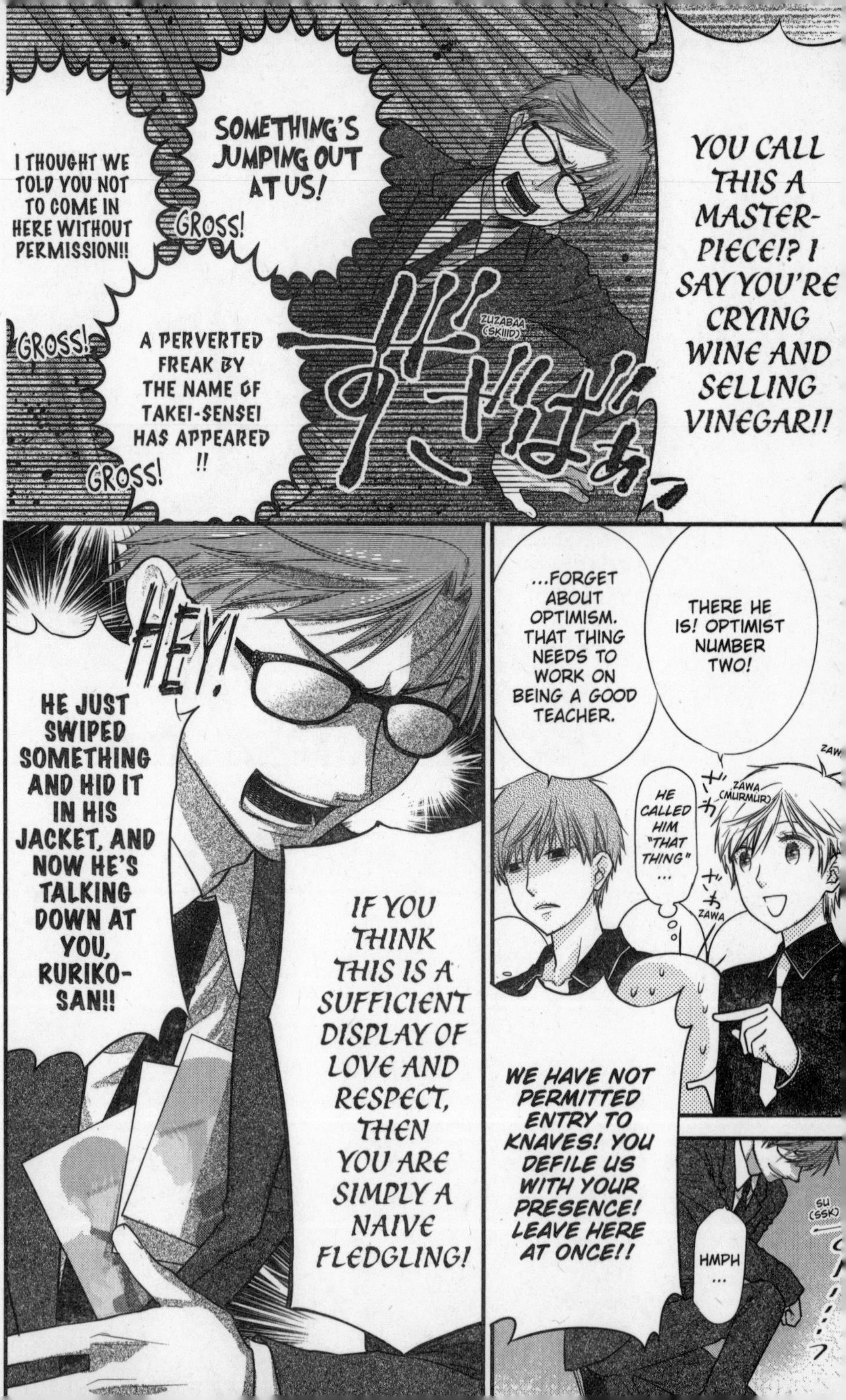
YOU CALL THIS A MASTER-PIECE!? I SAY YOU'RE CRYING WINE AND SELLING VINEGAR!!
ZUZABAA (SKIIID)
SOMETHING'S JUMPING OUT AT US!
GROSS!
I THOUGHT WE TOLD YOU NOT TO COME IN HERE WITHOUT PERMISSION!!
A PERVERTED FREAK BY THE NAME OF TAKEI-SENSEI HAS APPEARED!!
GROSS!
GROSS!
THERE HE IS! OPTIMIST NUMBER TWO!
...FORGET ABOUT OPTIMISM. THAT THING NEEDS TO WORK ON BEING A GOOD TEACHER.
ZAWA
ZAWA (MURMUR)
HE CALLED HIM "THAT THING"...
ZAWA
SU (SSK)
HMPH...
WE HAVE NOT PERMITTED ENTRY TO KNAVES! YOU DEFILE US WITH YOUR PRESENCE! LEAVE HERE AT ONCE!!
HEY!
IF YOU THINK THIS IS A SUFFICIENT DISPLAY OF LOVE AND RESPECT, THEN YOU ARE SIMPLY A NAIVE FLEDGLING!
HE JUST SWIPED SOMETHING AND HID IT IN HIS JACKET, AND NOW HE'S TALKING DOWN AT YOU, RURIKO-SAN!!

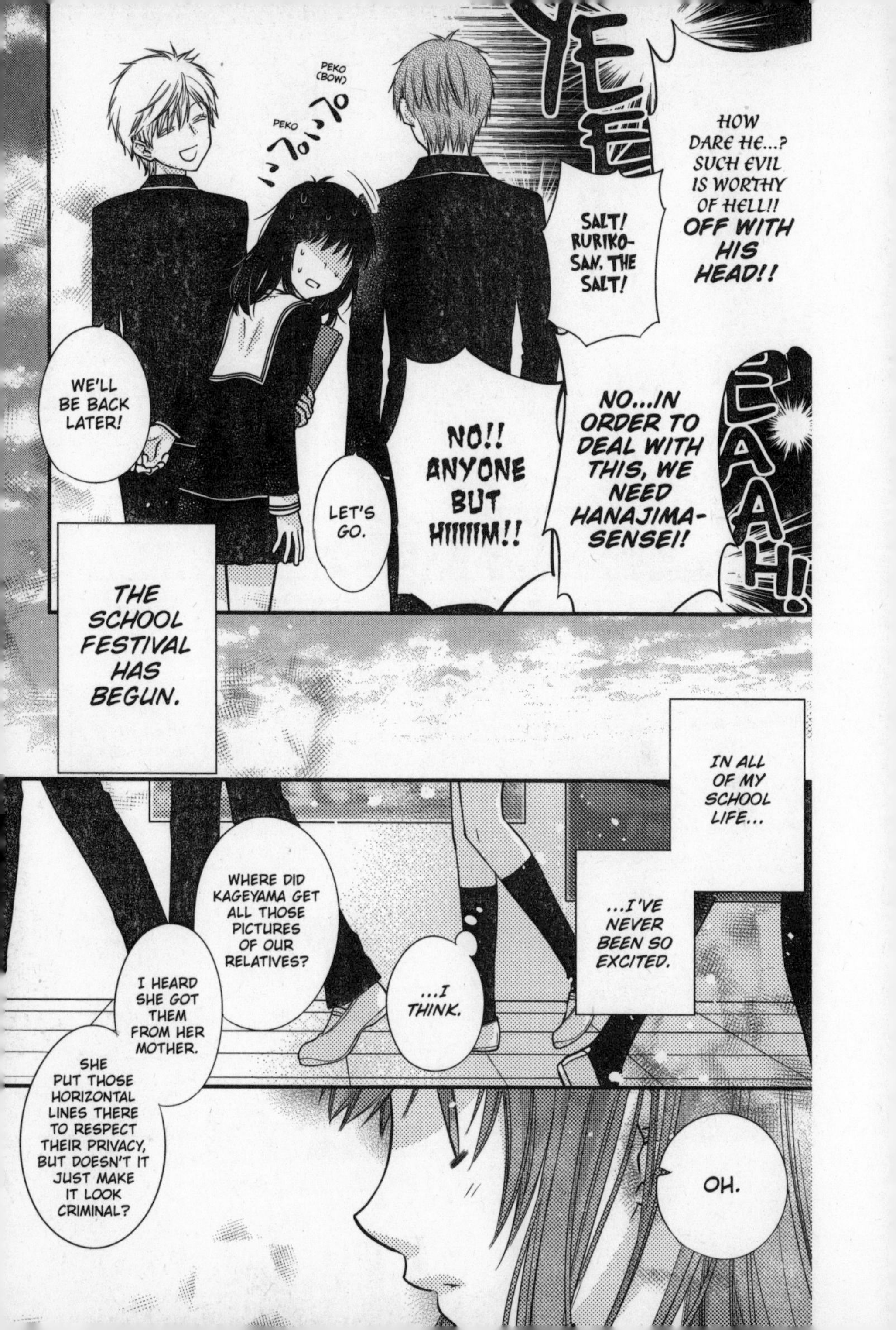
YEE
HOW DARE HE...? SUCH EVIL IS WORTHY OF HELL!! OFF WITH HIS HEAD!!
SALT! RURIKO-SAN, THE SALT!
EAAAH!!
NO...IN ORDER TO DEAL WITH THIS, WE NEED HANAJIMA-SENSEI!
NO!! ANYONE BUT HIIIIIM!!
LET'S GO.
PEKO (BOW)
PEKO
WE'LL BE BACK LATER!
THE SCHOOL FESTIVAL HAS BEGUN.
IN ALL OF MY SCHOOL LIFE...
...I'VE NEVER BEEN SO EXCITED.
...I THINK.
WHERE DID KAGEYAMA GET ALL THOSE PICTURES OF OUR RELATIVES?
I HEARD SHE GOT THEM FROM HER MOTHER.
SHE PUT THOSE HORIZONTAL LINES THERE TO RESPECT THEIR PRIVACY, BUT DOESN'T IT JUST MAKE IT LOOK CRIMINAL?
OH.

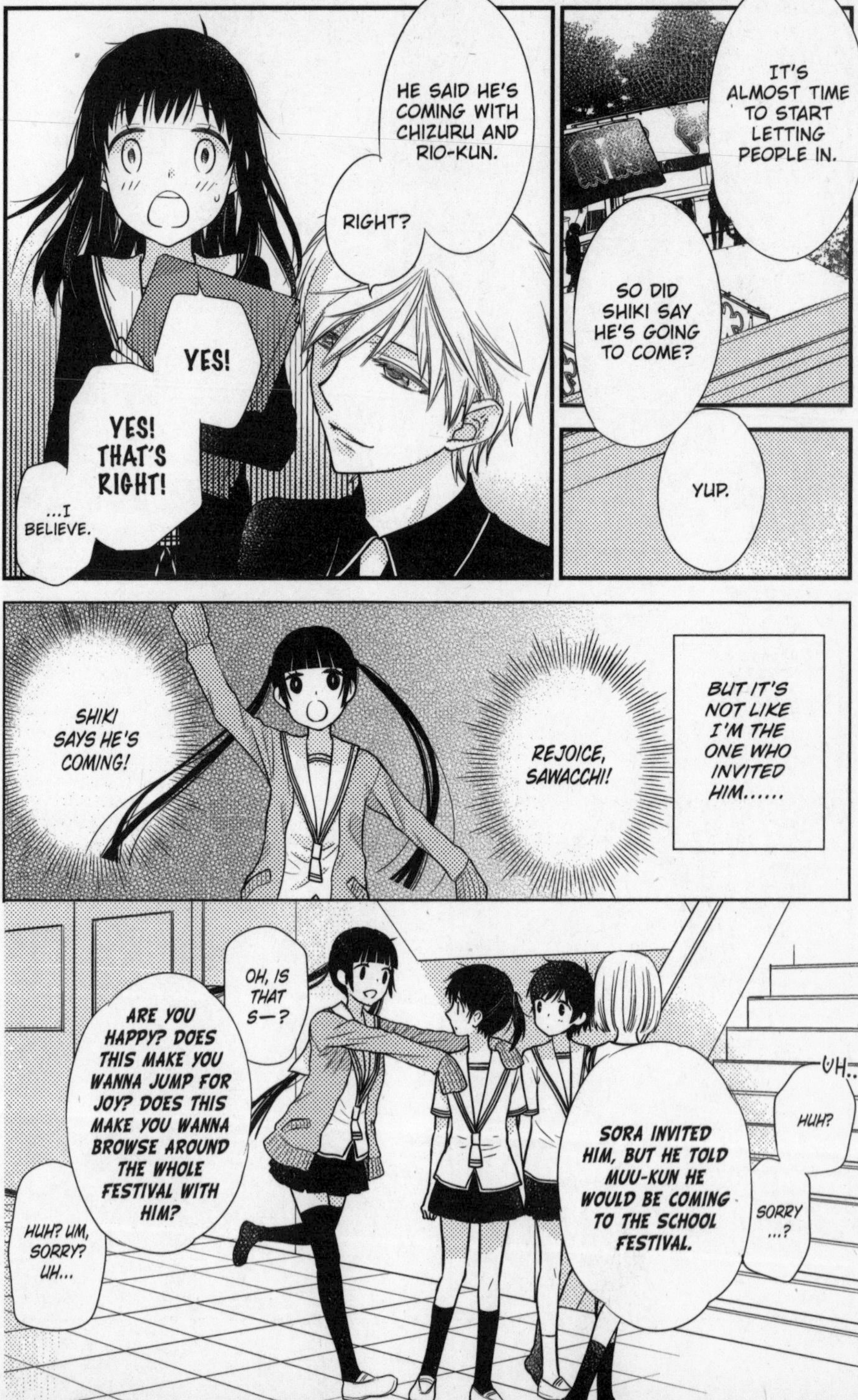

IT'S ALMOST TIME TO START LETTING PEOPLE IN.
SO DID SHIKI SAY HE'S GOING TO COME?
YUP.
HE SAID HE'S COMING WITH CHIZURU AND RIO-KUN.
RIGHT?
YES!
YES! THAT'S RIGHT!
...I BELIEVE.
BUT IT'S NOT LIKE I'M THE ONE WHO INVITED HIM......
REJOICE, SAWACCHI!
SHIKI SAYS HE'S COMING!
UH...
HUH?
SORRY ...?
SORA INVITED HIM, BUT HE TOLD MUU-KUN HE WOULD BE COMING TO THE SCHOOL FESTIVAL.
OH, IS THAT S—?
ARE YOU HAPPY? DOES THIS MAKE YOU WANNA JUMP FOR JOY? DOES THIS MAKE YOU WANNA BROWSE AROUND THE WHOLE FESTIVAL WITH HIM?
HUH? UM, SORRY? UH...

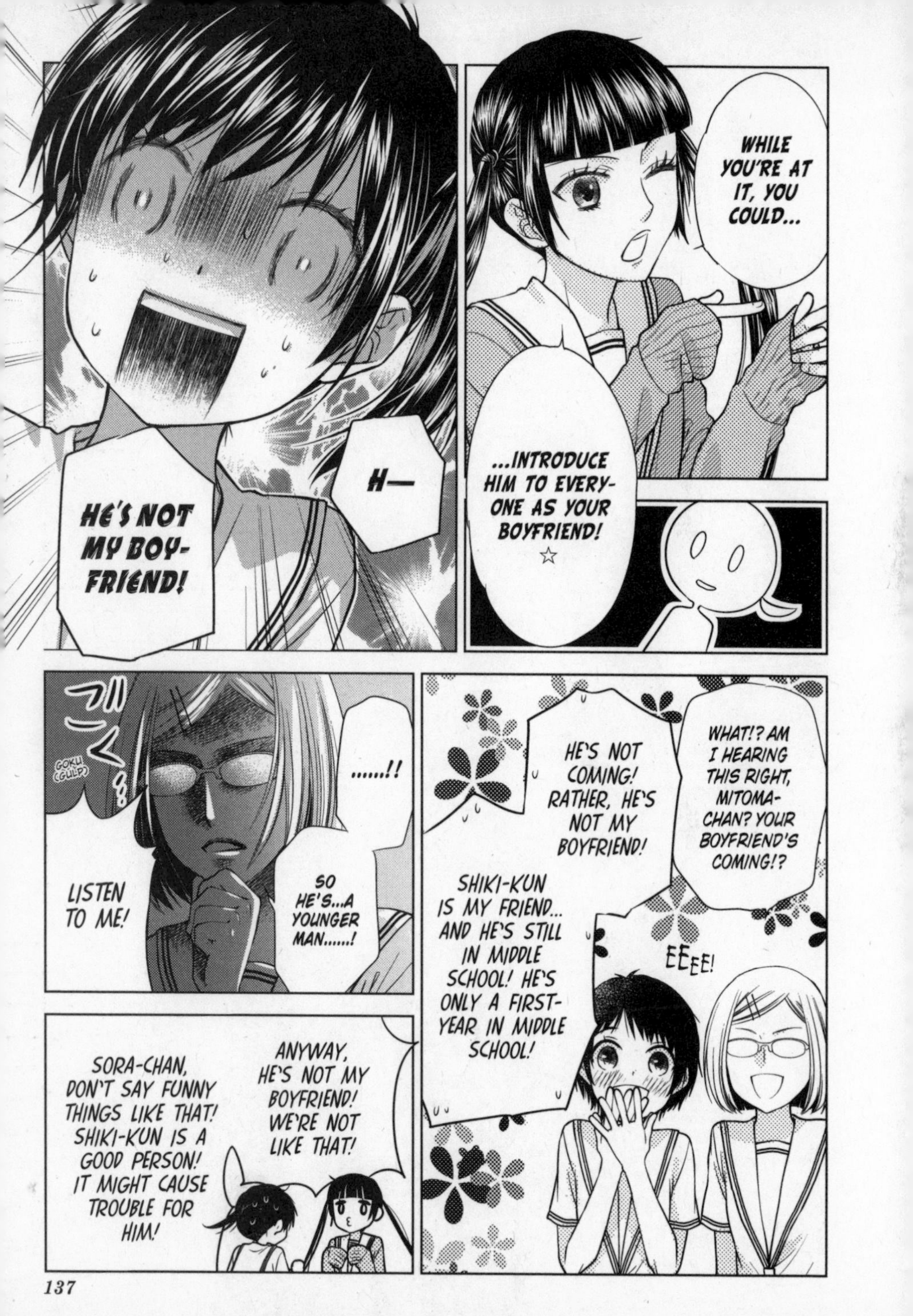
WHILE YOU'RE AT IT, YOU COULD...
...INTRODUCE HIM TO EVERYONE AS YOUR BOYFRIEND! ☆
H—
HE'S NOT MY BOY-FRIEND!
WHAT!? AM I HEARING THIS RIGHT, MITOMA-CHAN? YOUR BOYFRIEND'S COMING!?
HE'S NOT COMING! RATHER, HE'S NOT MY BOYFRIEND!
EEEE!
SHIKI-KUN IS MY FRIEND... AND HE'S STILL IN MIDDLE SCHOOL! HE'S ONLY A FIRST-YEAR IN MIDDLE SCHOOL!
GOKU (GULP)
......!!
SO HE'S...A YOUNGER MAN......!
LISTEN TO ME!
ANYWAY, HE'S NOT MY BOYFRIEND! WE'RE NOT LIKE THAT!
SORA-CHAN, DON'T SAY FUNNY THINGS LIKE THAT! SHIKI-KUN IS A GOOD PERSON! IT MIGHT CAUSE TROUBLE FOR HIM!

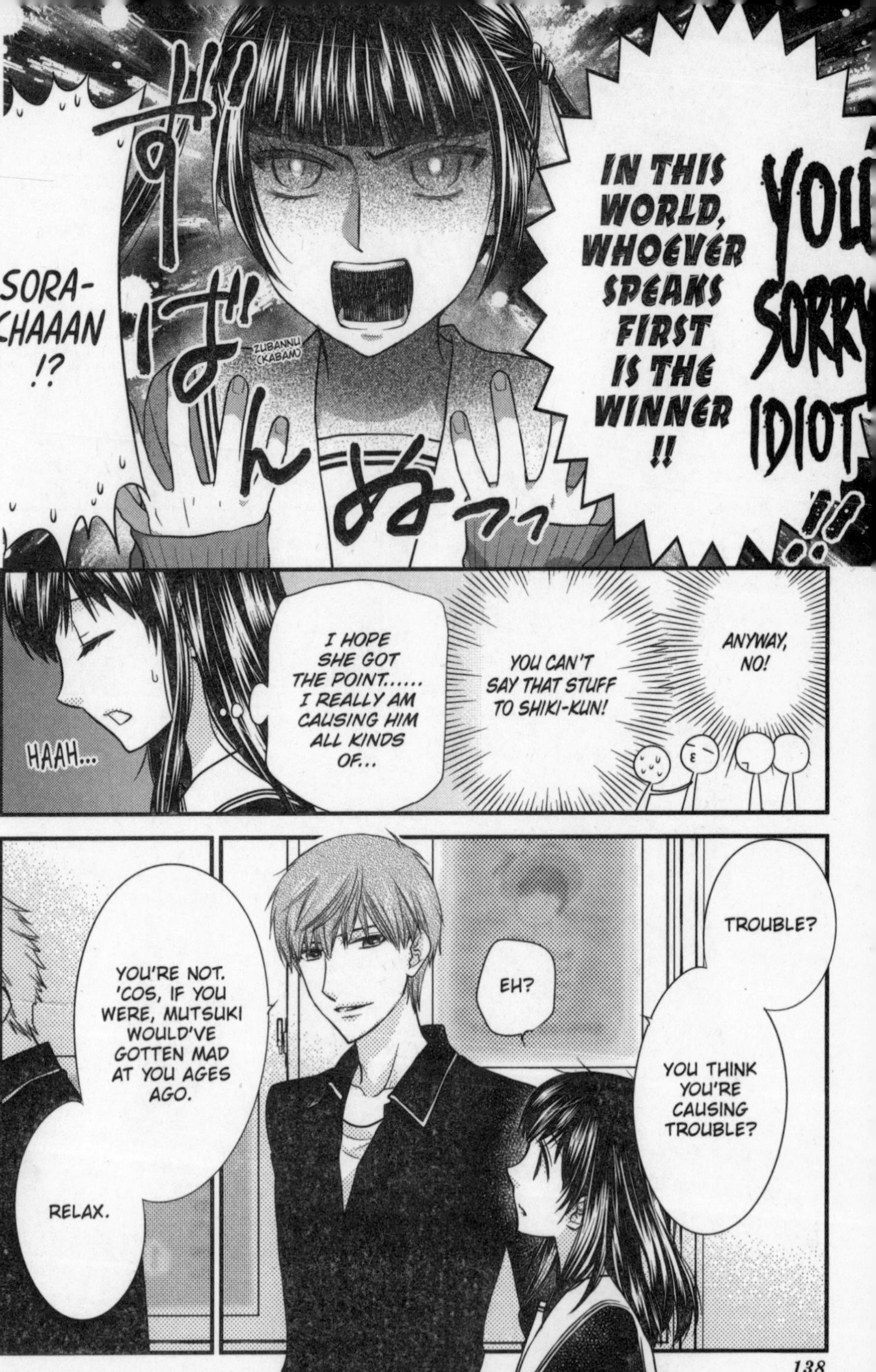
YOU SORRY IDIOT!!
IN THIS WORLD, WHOEVER SPEAKS FIRST IS THE WINNER!!
ZUBANNU (KABAM)
SORA-CHAAAN!?
ANYWAY, NO!
YOU CAN'T SAY THAT STUFF TO SHIKI-KUN!
I HOPE SHE GOT THE POINT...... I REALLY AM CAUSING HIM ALL KINDS OF...
HAAH...
TROUBLE?
YOU THINK YOU'RE CAUSING TROUBLE?
EH?
YOU'RE NOT. 'COS, IF YOU WERE, MUTSUKI WOULD'VE GOTTEN MAD AT YOU AGES AGO.
RELAX.

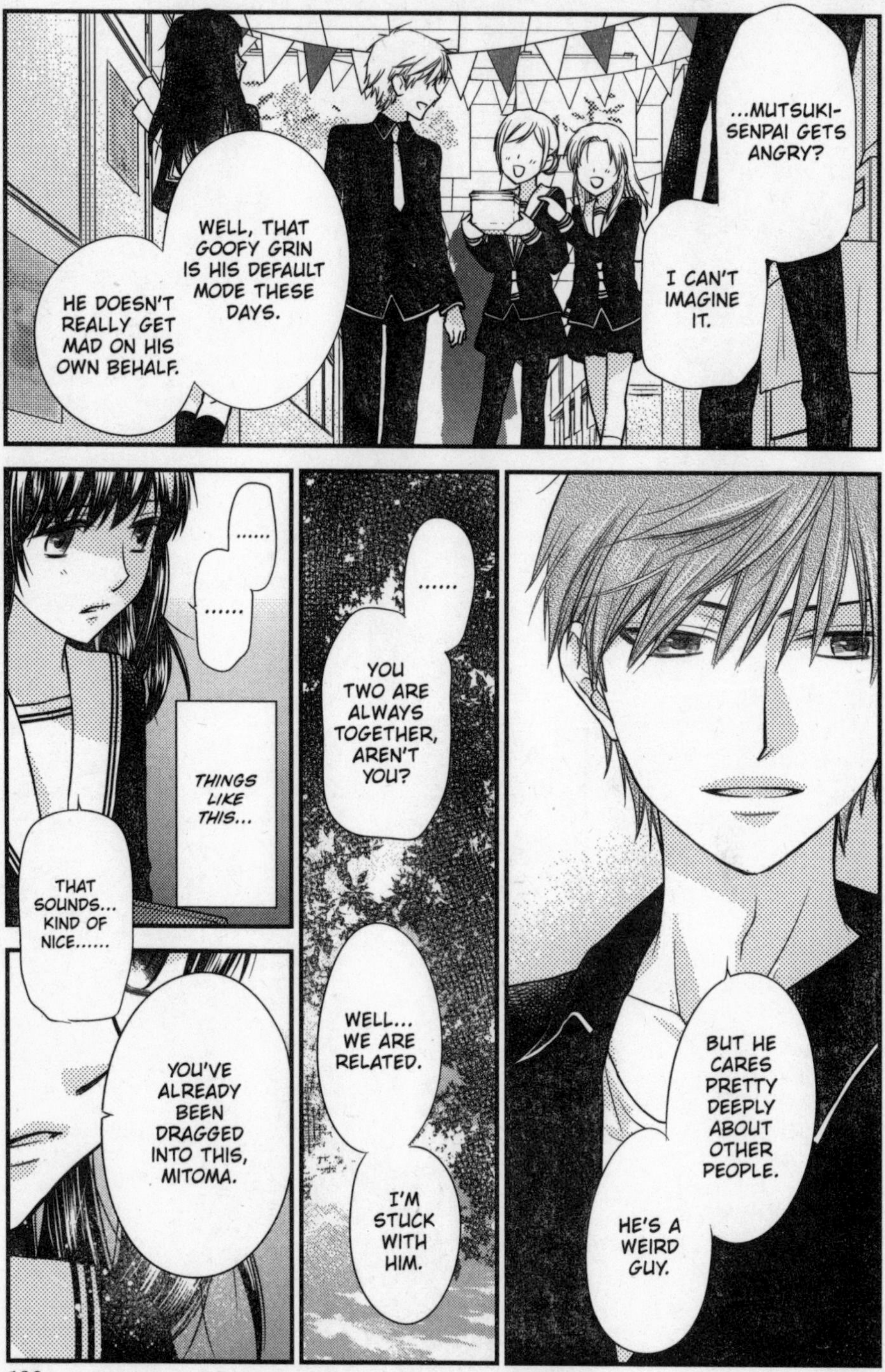
...MUTSUKI-SENPAI GETS ANGRY?
I CAN'T IMAGINE IT.
WELL, THAT GOOFY GRIN IS HIS DEFAULT MODE THESE DAYS.
HE DOESN'T REALLY GET MAD ON HIS OWN BEHALF.
BUT HE CARES PRETTY DEEPLY ABOUT OTHER PEOPLE.
HE'S A WEIRD GUY.
......
YOU TWO ARE ALWAYS TOGETHER, AREN'T YOU?
WELL... WE ARE RELATED.
I'M STUCK WITH HIM.
......
......
THINGS LIKE THIS...
THAT SOUNDS... KIND OF NICE......
YOU'VE ALREADY BEEN DRAGGED INTO THIS, MITOMA.

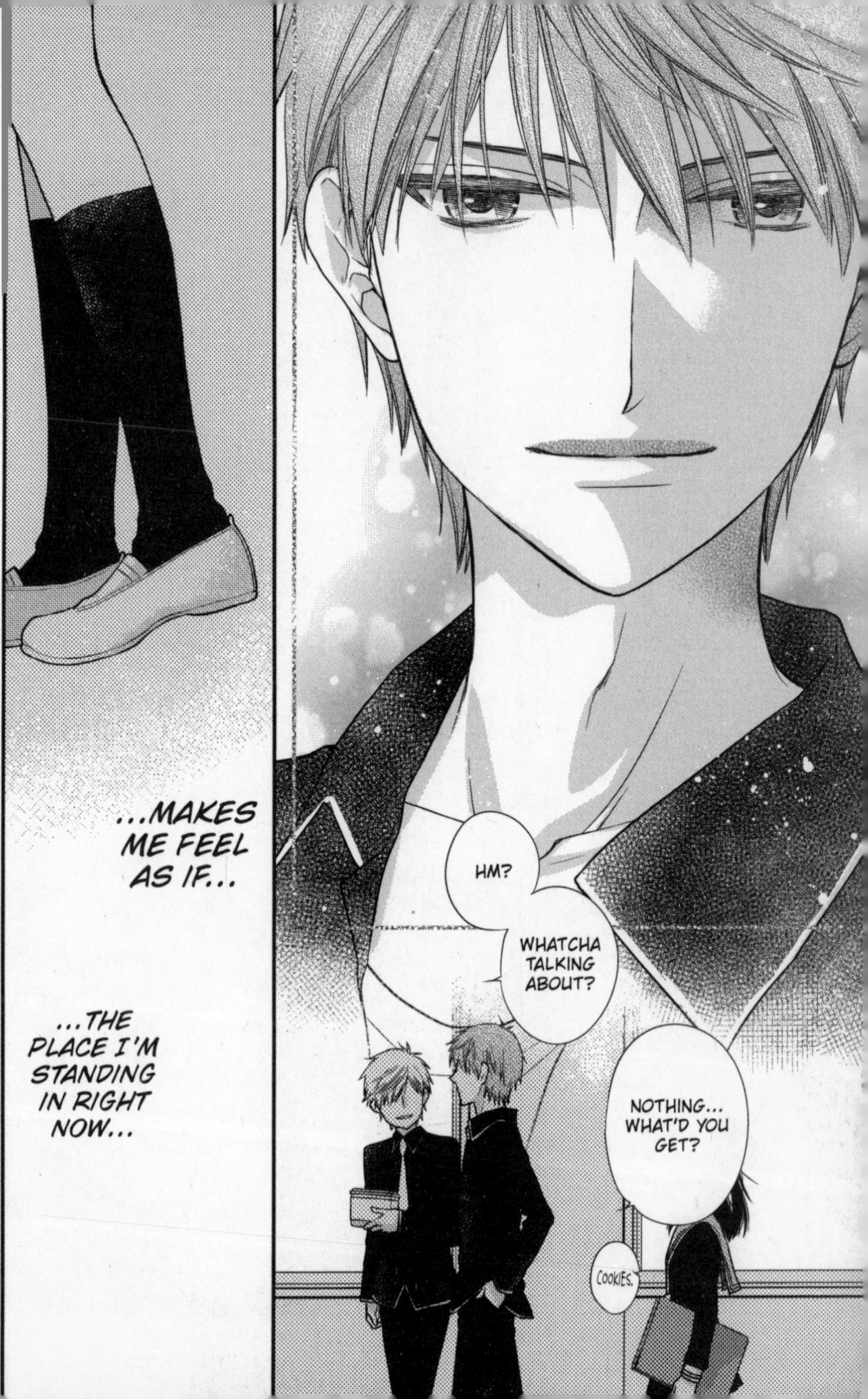
HM?
WHATCHA TALKING ABOUT?
NOTHING... WHAT'D YOU GET?
COOKIES.
...MAKES ME FEEL AS IF...
...THE PLACE I'M STANDING IN RIGHT NOW...

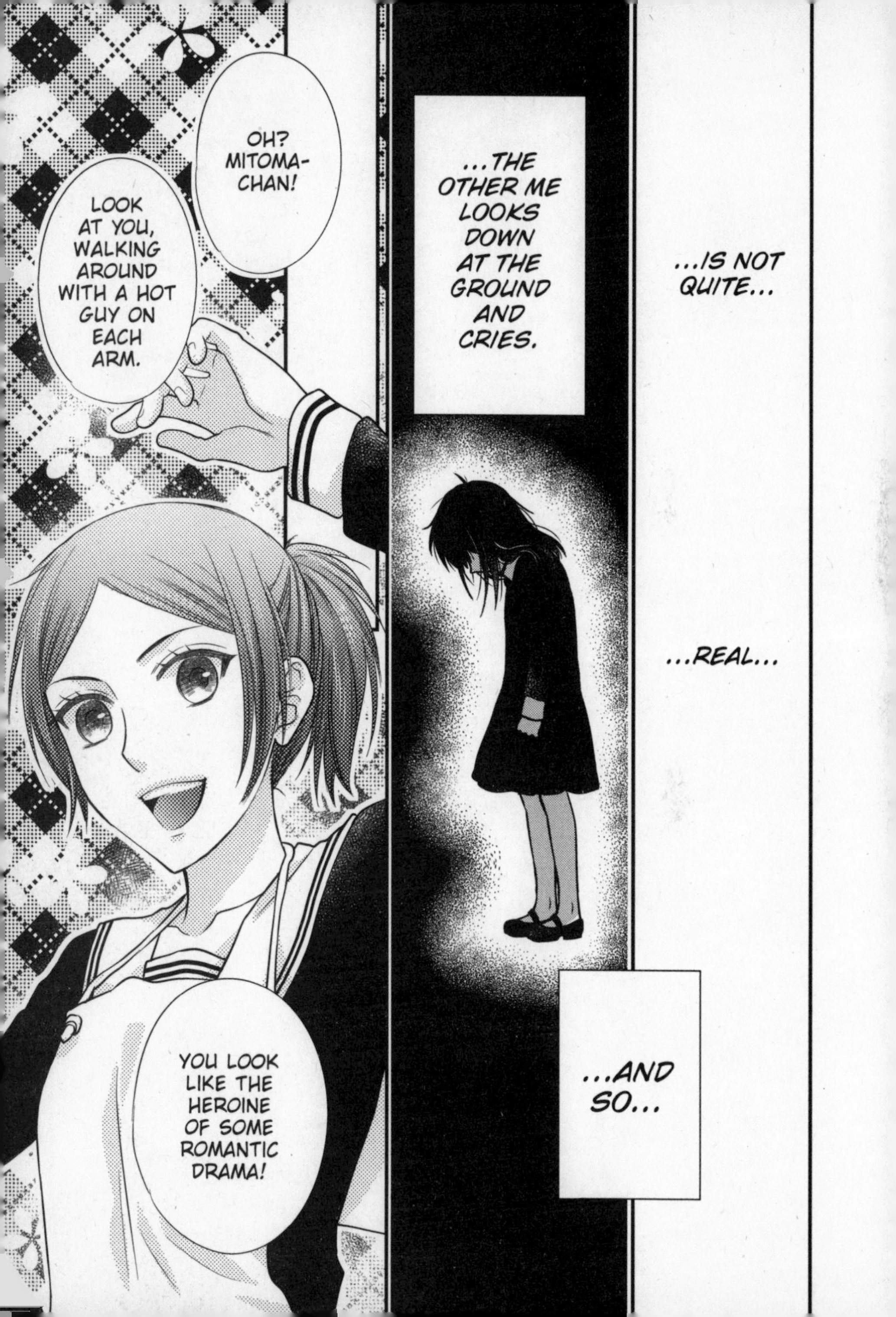
...IS NOT QUITE...
...REAL...
...THE OTHER ME LOOKS DOWN AT THE GROUND AND CRIES.
...AND SO...
OH? MITOMA-CHAN!
LOOK AT YOU, WALKING AROUND WITH A HOT GUY ON EACH ARM.
YOU LOOK LIKE THE HEROINE OF SOME ROMANTIC DRAMA!

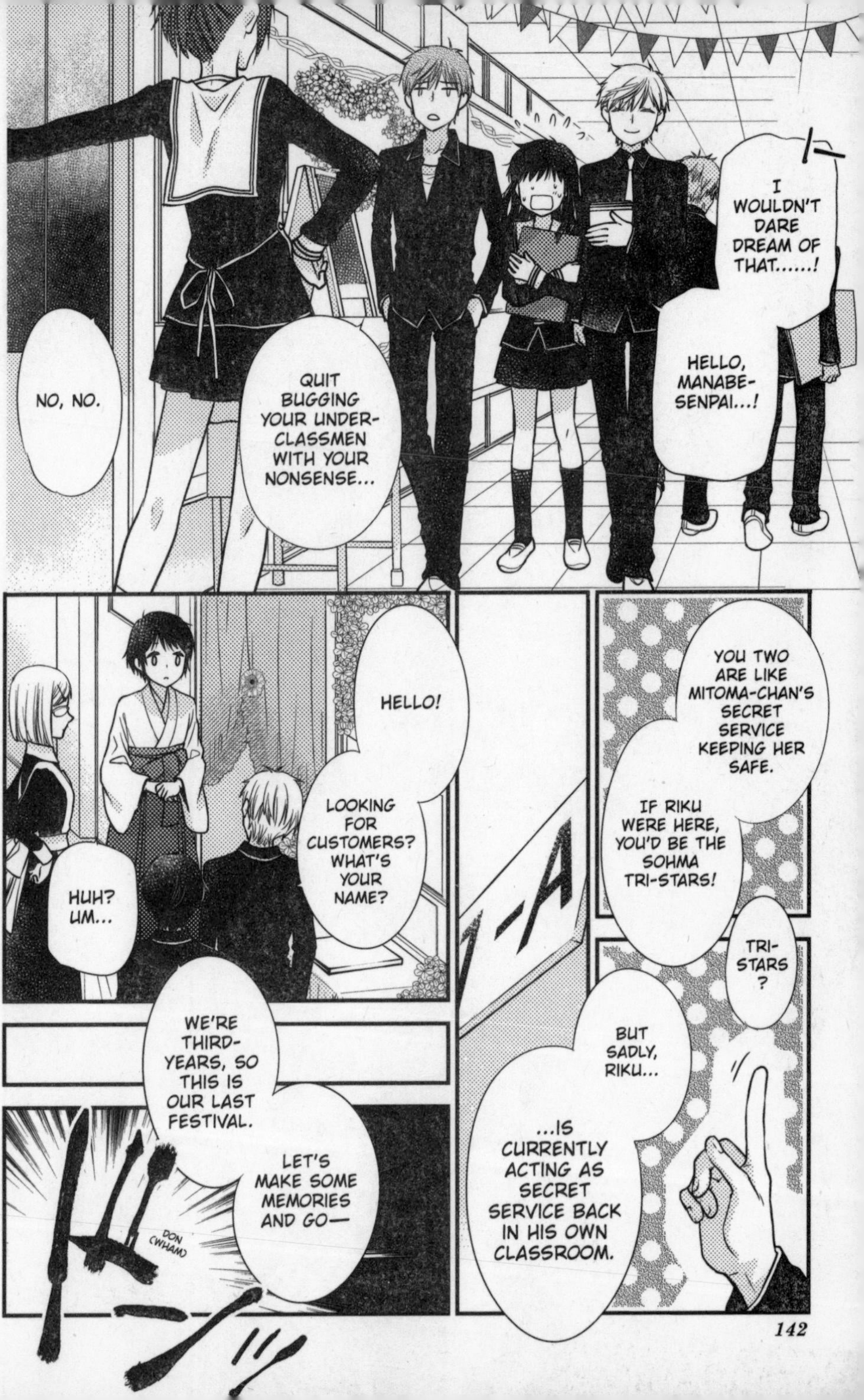
I WOULDN'T DARE DREAM OF THAT......!
HELLO, MANABE-SENPAI...!
QUIT BUGGING YOUR UNDER-CLASSMEN WITH YOUR NONSENSE...
NO, NO.
YOU TWO ARE LIKE MITOMA-CHAN'S SECRET SERVICE KEEPING HER SAFE.
IF RIKU WERE HERE, YOU'D BE THE SOHMA TRI-STARS!
TRI-STARS?
BUT SADLY, RIKU...
...IS CURRENTLY ACTING AS SECRET SERVICE BACK IN HIS OWN CLASSROOM.
HELLO!
LOOKING FOR CUSTOMERS? WHAT'S YOUR NAME?
HUH? UM...
WE'RE THIRD-YEARS, SO THIS IS OUR LAST FESTIVAL.
LET'S MAKE SOME MEMORIES AND GO—
DON (WHAM)

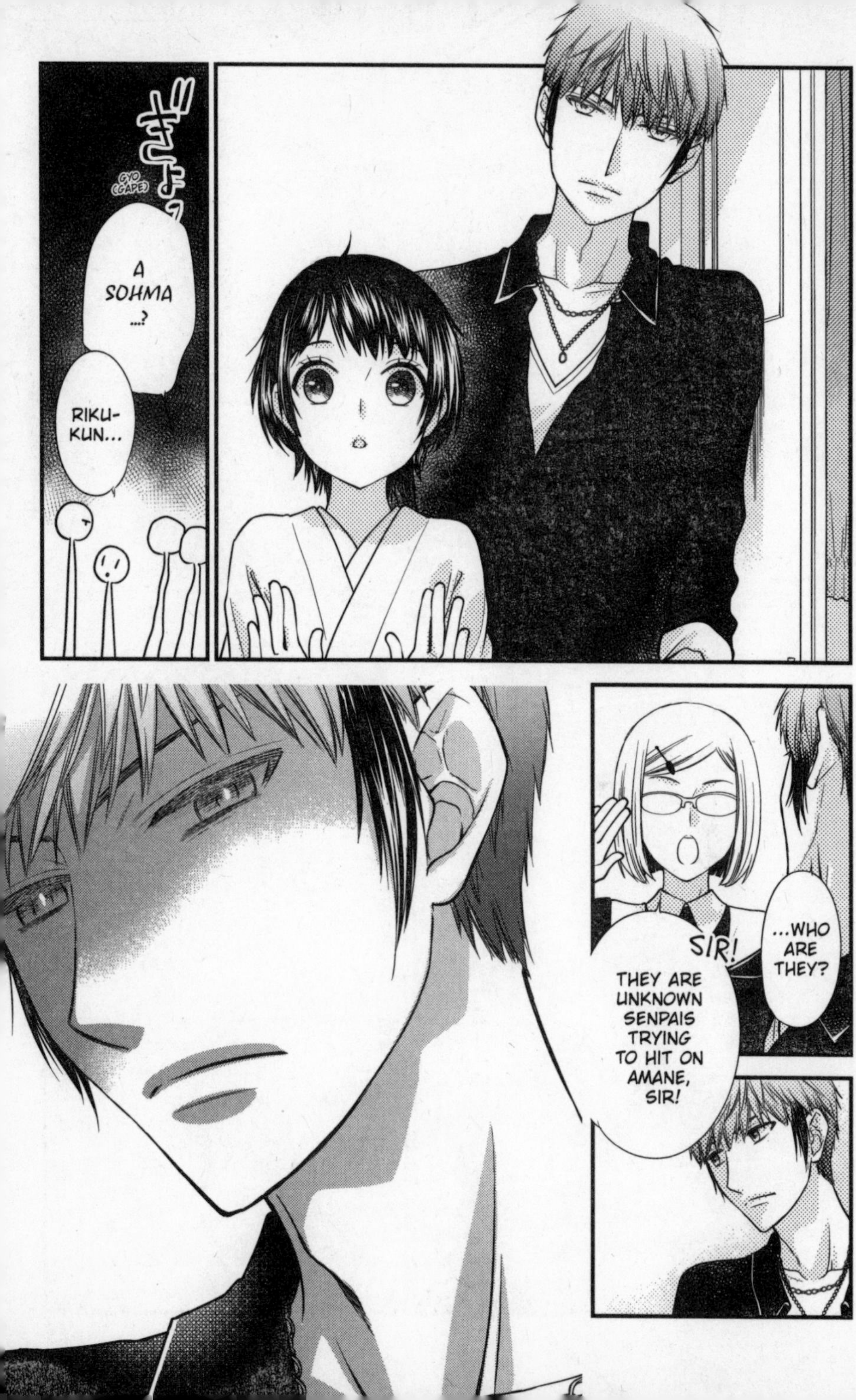
GYO (GAPE)
A SOHMA ...?
RIKU-KUN...
...WHO ARE THEY?
SIR!
THEY ARE UNKNOWN SENPAIS TRYING TO HIT ON AMANE, SIR!

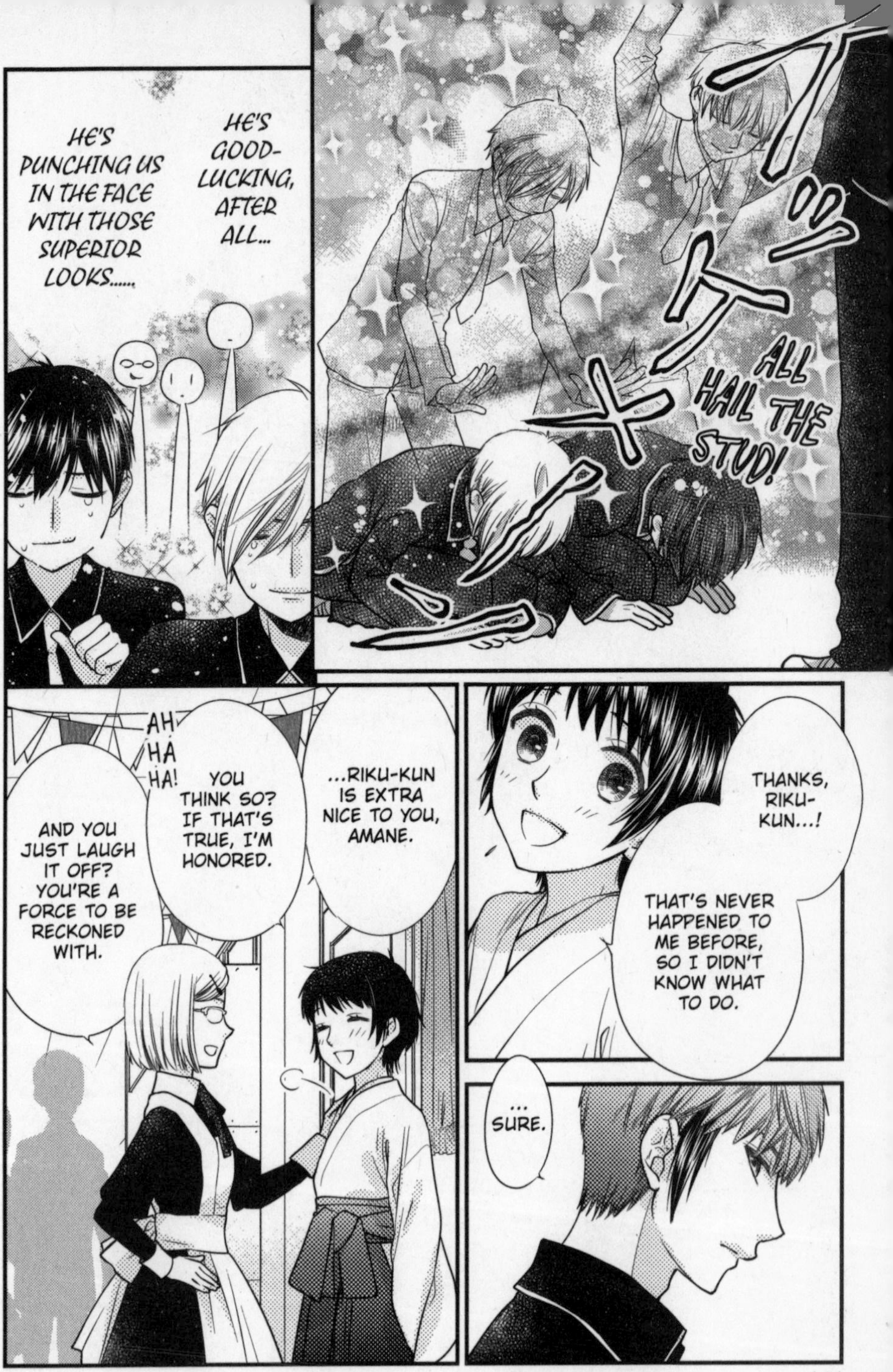
ALL HAIL THE STUD!
HE'S GOOD-LUCKING, AFTER ALL...
HE'S PUNCHING US IN THE FACE WITH THOSE SUPERIOR LOOKS......
THANKS, RIKU-KUN...!
THAT'S NEVER HAPPENED TO ME BEFORE, SO I DIDN'T KNOW WHAT TO DO.
... SURE.
...RIKU-KUN IS EXTRA NICE TO YOU, AMANE.
YOU THINK SO? IF THAT'S TRUE, I'M HONORED.
AH HA HA!
AND YOU JUST LAUGH IT OFF? YOU'RE A FORCE TO BE RECKONED WITH.

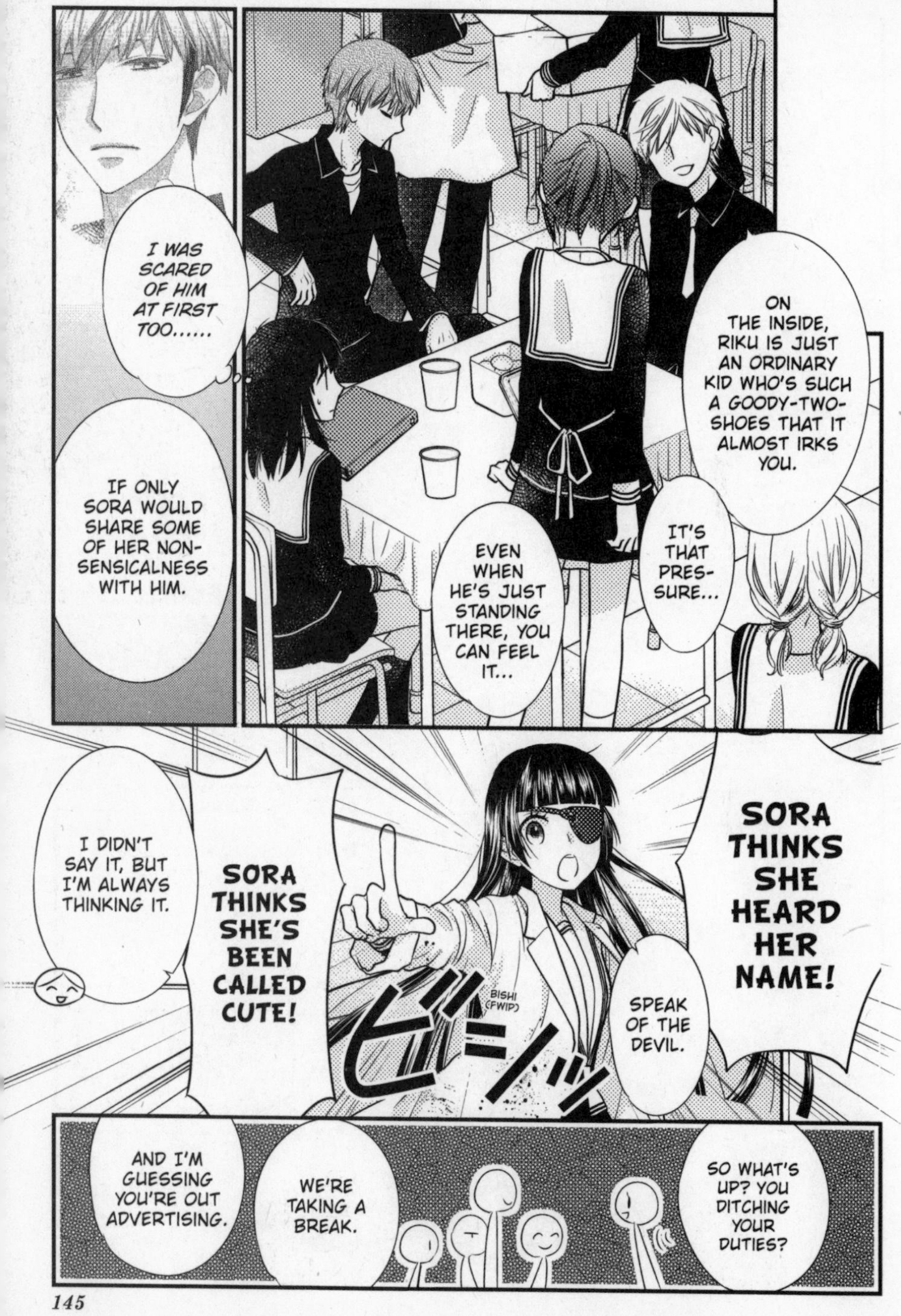
ON THE INSIDE, RIKU IS JUST AN ORDINARY KID WHO'S SUCH A GOODY-TWO-SHOES THAT IT ALMOST IRKS YOU.
IT'S THAT PRES-SURE...
EVEN WHEN HE'S JUST STANDING THERE, YOU CAN FEEL IT...
I WAS SCARED OF HIM AT FIRST TOO......
IF ONLY SORA WOULD SHARE SOME OF HER NON-SENSICALNESS WITH HIM.
SORA THINKS SHE HEARD HER NAME!
SPEAK OF THE DEVIL.
BISHI (FWIP)
ビシッ
SORA THINKS SHE'S BEEN CALLED CUTE!
I DIDN'T SAY IT, BUT I'M ALWAYS THINKING IT.
SO WHAT'S UP? YOU DITCHING YOUR DUTIES?
WE'RE TAKING A BREAK.
AND I'M GUESSING YOU'RE OUT ADVERTISING.

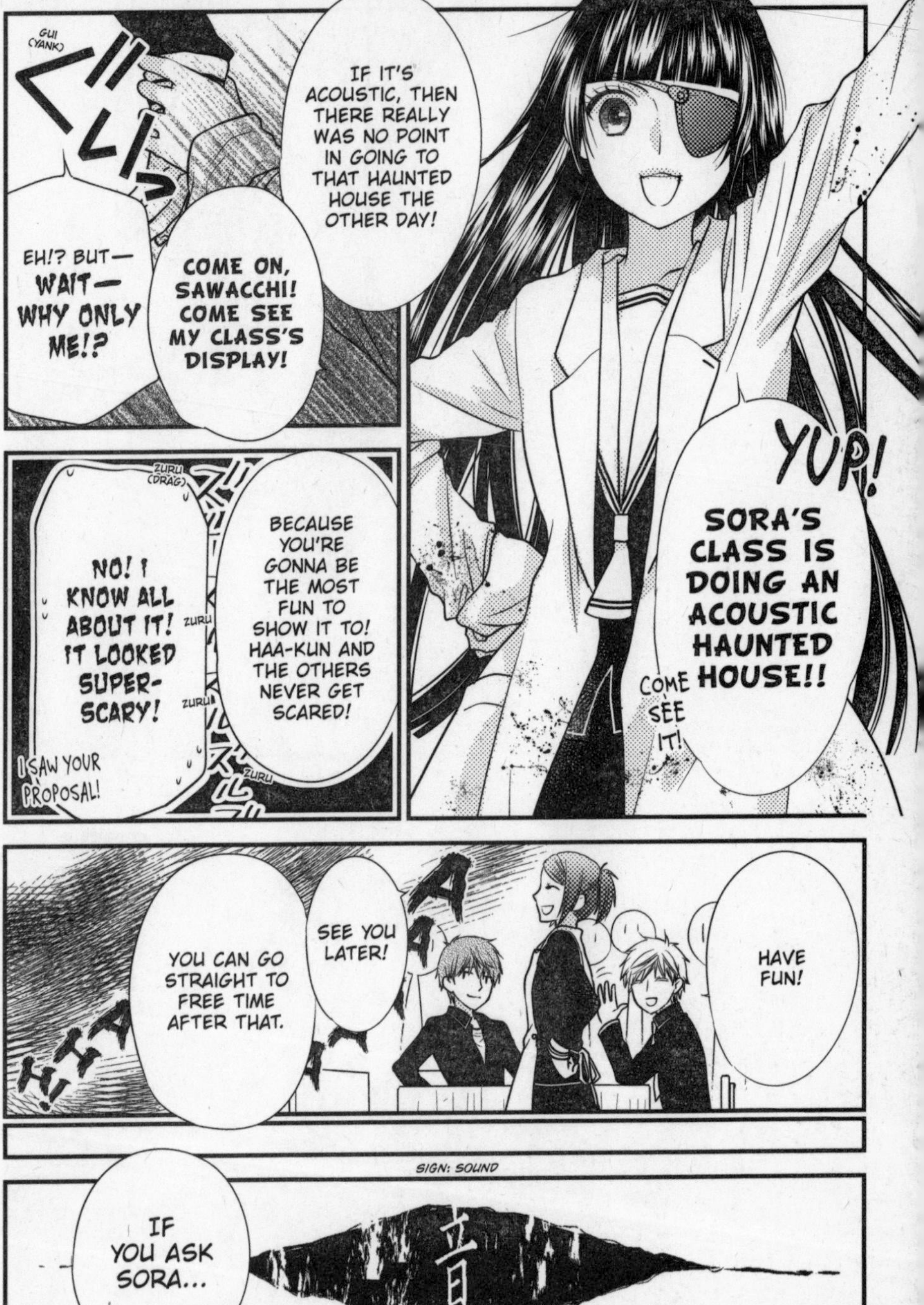
YUP!
SORA'S CLASS IS DOING AN ACOUSTIC HAUNTED HOUSE!!
COME SEE IT!
IF IT'S ACOUSTIC, THEN THERE REALLY WAS NO POINT IN GOING TO THAT HAUNTED HOUSE THE OTHER DAY!
COME ON, SAWACCHI! COME SEE MY CLASS'S DISPLAY!
EH!? BUT— WAIT— WHY ONLY ME!?
GUI (YANK)
ZURU (DRAG)
BECAUSE YOU'RE GONNA BE THE MOST FUN TO SHOW IT TO! HAA-KUN AND THE OTHERS NEVER GET SCARED!
NO! I KNOW ALL ABOUT IT! IT LOOKED SUPER-SCARY!
ZURU
ZURU
ZURU
I SAW YOUR PROPOSAL!
HAVE FUN!
SEE YOU LATER!
YOU CAN GO STRAIGHT TO FREE TIME AFTER THAT.
SIGN: SOUND
IF YOU ASK SORA...
音

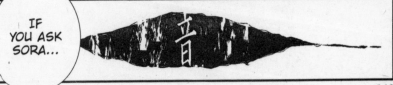

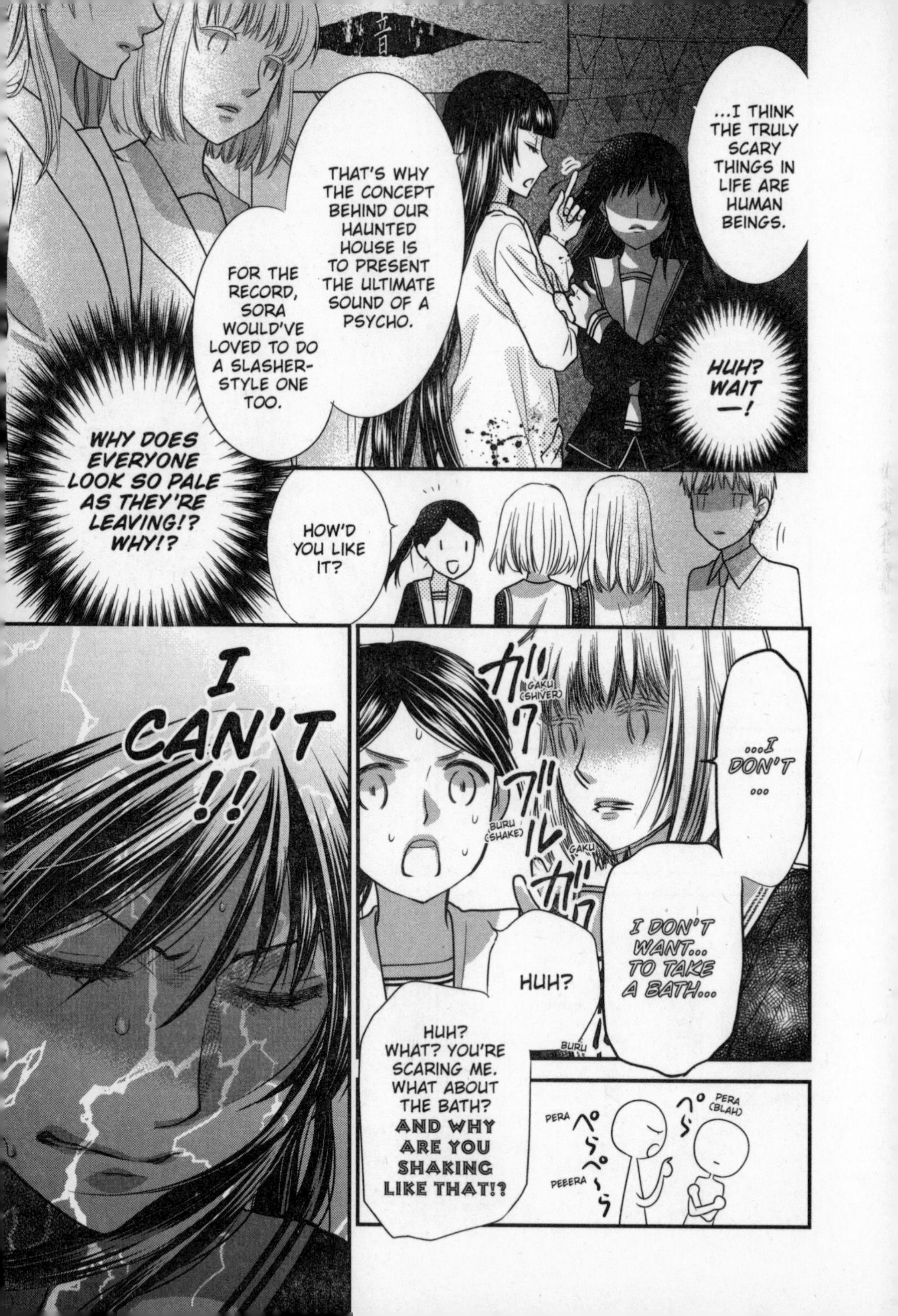
...I THINK THE TRULY SCARY THINGS IN LIFE ARE HUMAN BEINGS.
HUH? WAIT—!
THAT'S WHY THE CONCEPT BEHIND OUR HAUNTED HOUSE IS TO PRESENT THE ULTIMATE SOUND OF A PSYCHO.
FOR THE RECORD, SORA WOULD'VE LOVED TO DO A SLASHER-STYLE ONE TOO.
WHY DOES EVERYONE LOOK SO PALE AS THEY'RE LEAVING!? WHY!?
HOW'D YOU LIKE IT?
...I DON'T...
GAKU (SHIVER)
BURU (SHAKE)
GAKU
I DON'T WANT... TO TAKE A BATH...
HUH?
BURU
HUH? WHAT? YOU'RE SCARING ME. WHAT ABOUT THE BATH? AND WHY ARE YOU SHAKING LIKE THAT!?
PERA (BLAH)
PERA
PEEERA
I CAN'T!!

SIGN (RIGHT): WILL EAT AWAY AT YOUR SENSES
SIGNBOARD (LEFT): NO ENTRY

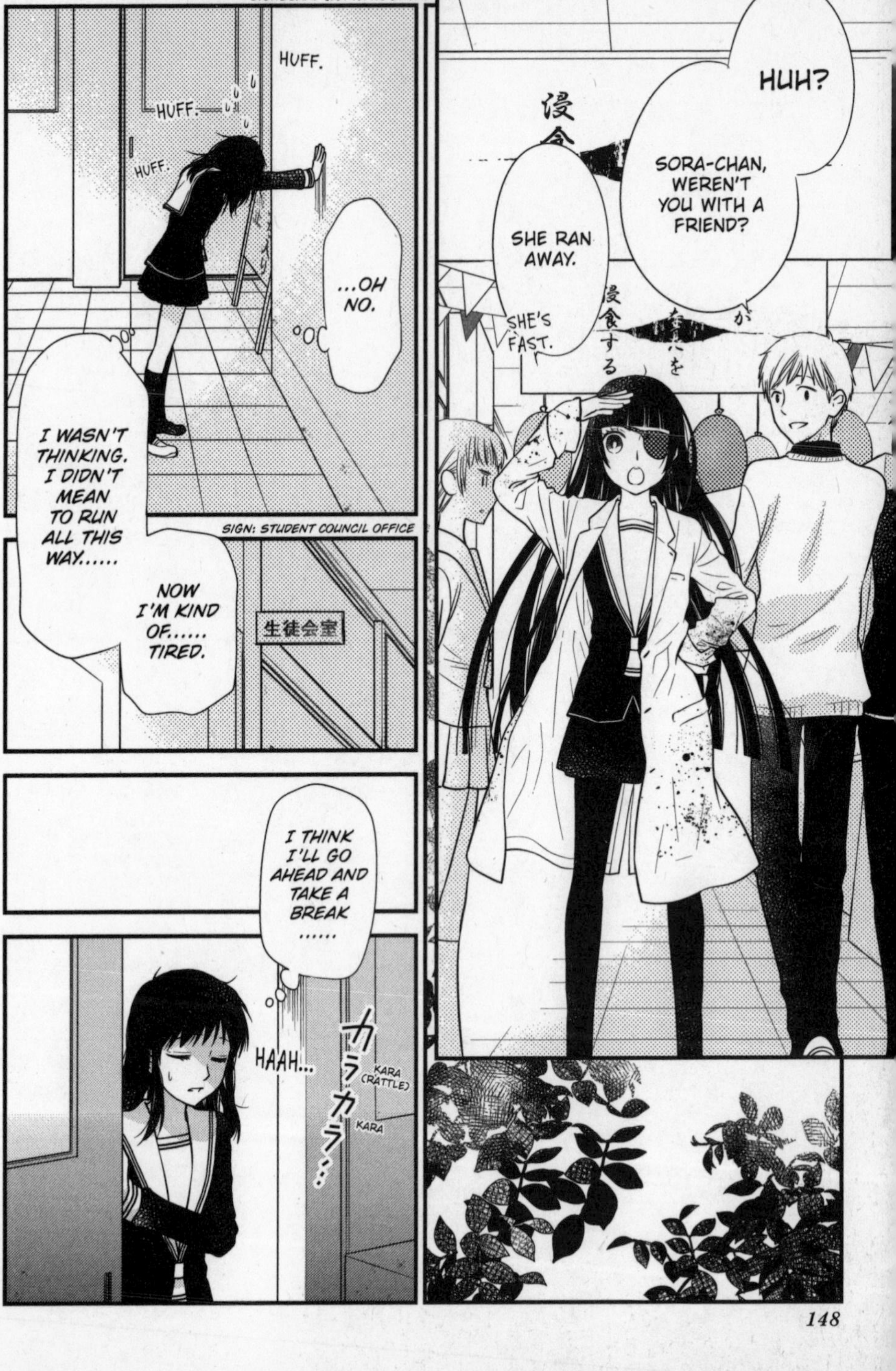
HUH?
SORA-CHAN, WEREN'T YOU WITH A FRIEND?
SHE RAN AWAY.
SHE'S FAST.
浸食する
HUFF.
HUFF.
HUFF.
...OH NO.
I WASN'T THINKING. I DIDN'T MEAN TO RUN ALL THIS WAY......
SIGN: STUDENT COUNCIL OFFICE
生徒会室
NOW I'M KIND OF...... TIRED.
I THINK I'LL GO AHEAD AND TAKE A BREAK ......
HAAH...
カラカラ
KARA (RATTLE)
KARA

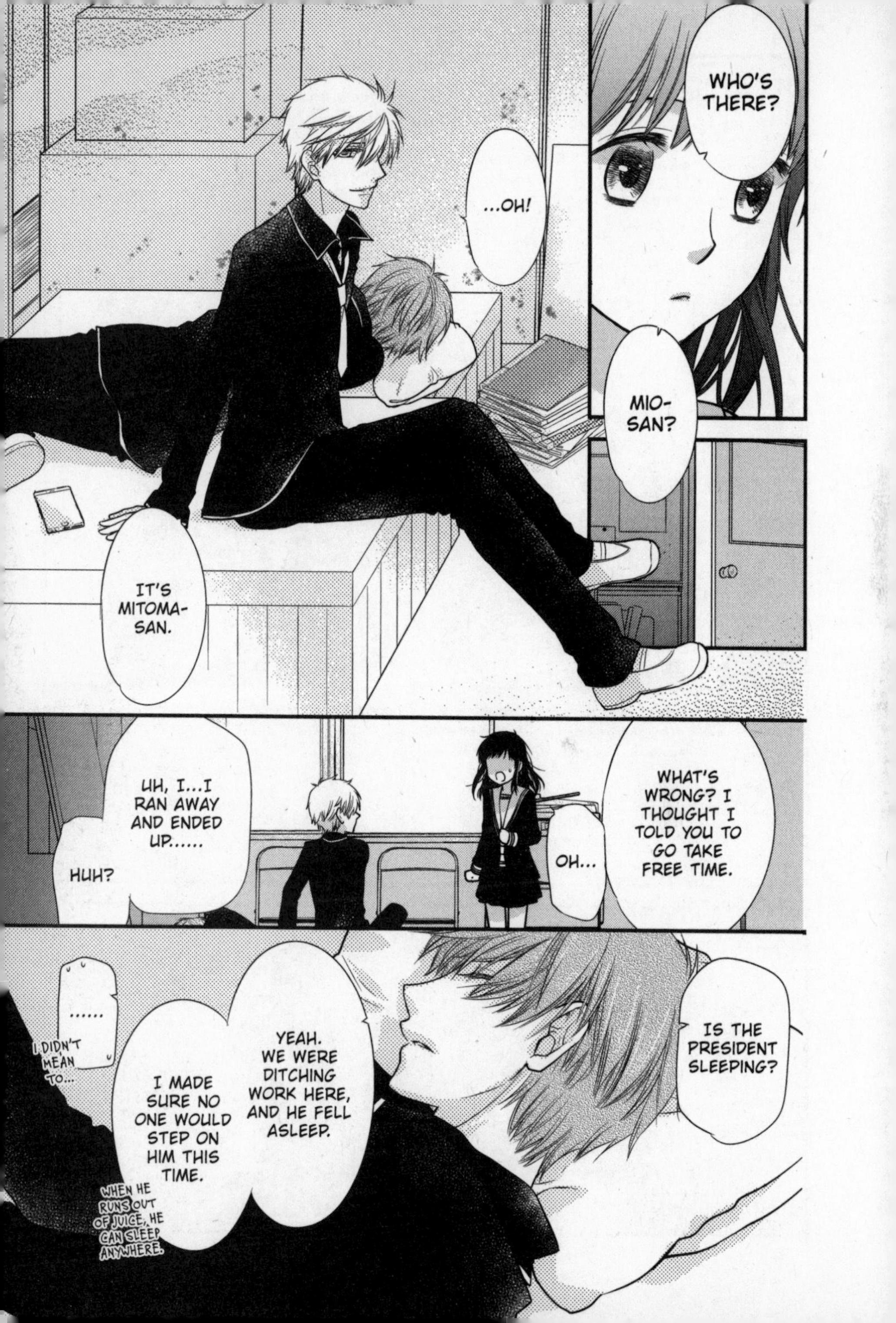
WHO'S THERE?
MIO-SAN?
...OH!
IT'S MITOMA-SAN.
WHAT'S WRONG? I THOUGHT I TOLD YOU TO GO TAKE FREE TIME.
OH...
UH, I...I RAN AWAY AND ENDED UP......
HUH?
IS THE PRESIDENT SLEEPING?
YEAH. WE WERE DITCHING WORK HERE, AND HE FELL ASLEEP.
I MADE SURE NO ONE WOULD STEP ON HIM THIS TIME.
......
I DIDN'T MEAN TO...
WHEN HE RUNS OUT OF JUICE, HE CAN SLEEP ANYWHERE.

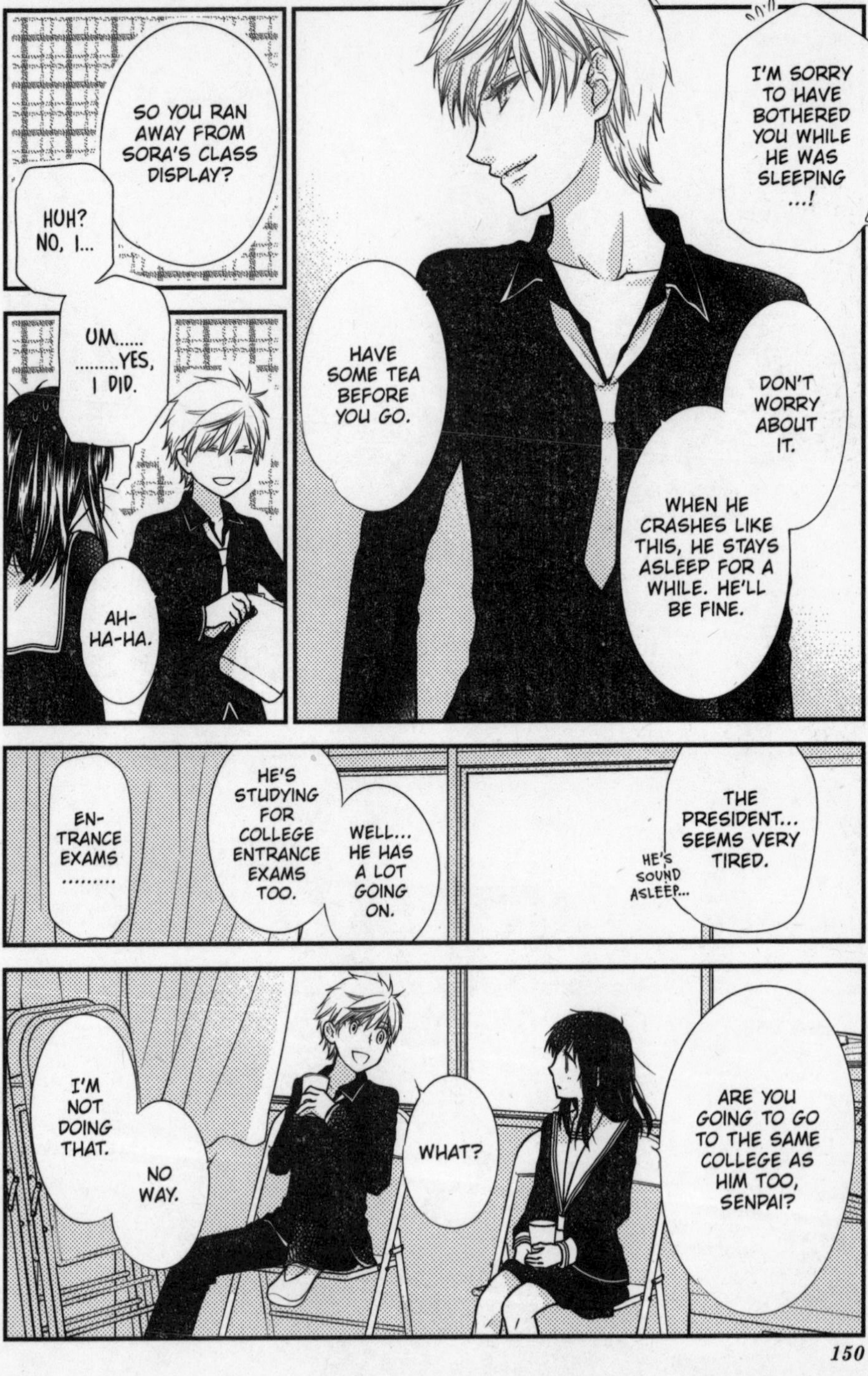
I'M SORRY TO HAVE BOTHERED YOU WHILE HE WAS SLEEPING ...!
DON'T WORRY ABOUT IT.
WHEN HE CRASHES LIKE THIS, HE STAYS ASLEEP FOR A WHILE. HE'LL BE FINE.
HAVE SOME TEA BEFORE YOU GO.
SO YOU RAN AWAY FROM SORA'S CLASS DISPLAY?
HUH? NO, I...
UM...... ....YES, I DID.
AH-HA-HA.
THE PRESIDENT... SEEMS VERY TIRED.
HE'S SOUND ASLEEP...
WELL... HE HAS A LOT GOING ON.
HE'S STUDYING FOR COLLEGE ENTRANCE EXAMS TOO.
EN-TRANCE EXAMS ....
ARE YOU GOING TO GO TO THE SAME COLLEGE AS HIM TOO, SENPAI?
WHAT?
I'M NOT DOING THAT.
NO WAY.

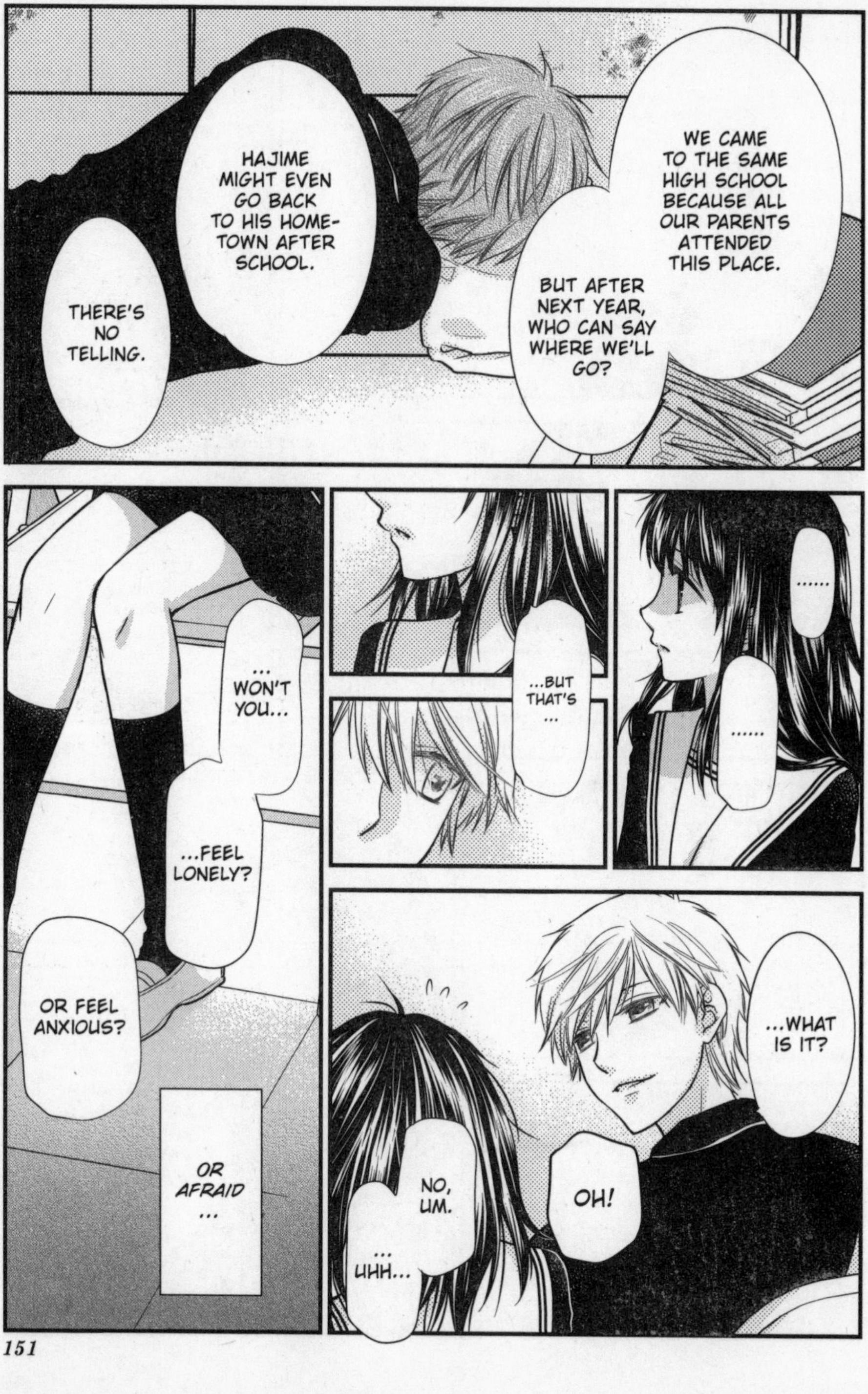
WE CAME TO THE SAME HIGH SCHOOL BECAUSE ALL OUR PARENTS ATTENDED THIS PLACE.
BUT AFTER NEXT YEAR, WHO CAN SAY WHERE WE'LL GO?
HAJIME MIGHT EVEN GO BACK TO HIS HOME-TOWN AFTER SCHOOL.
THERE'S NO TELLING.
......
......
...BUT THAT'S ...
...WHAT IS IT?
OH!
NO, UM.
... UHH...
... WON'T YOU...
...FEEL LONELY?
OR FEEL ANXIOUS?
OR AFRAID ...

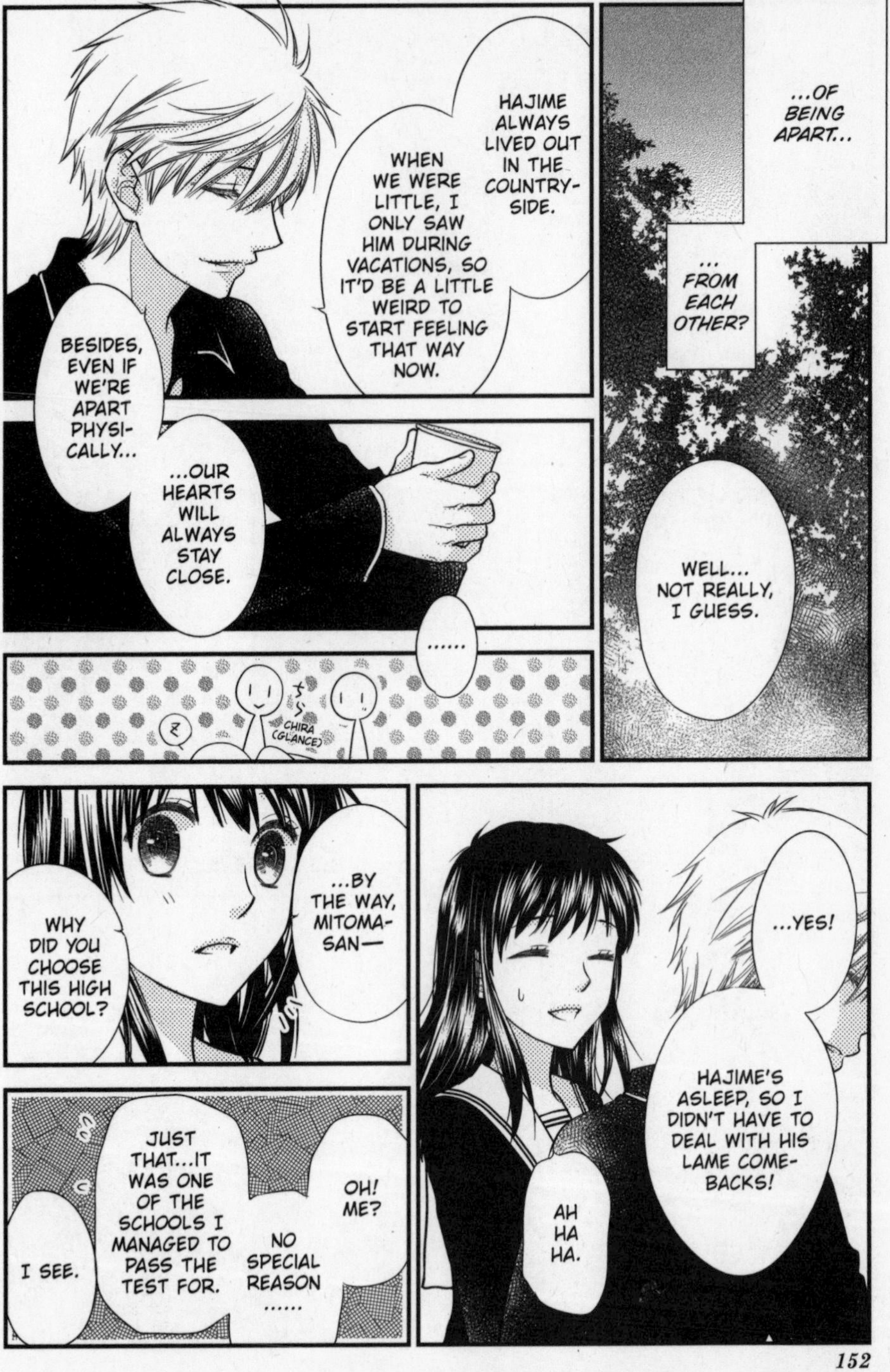
...OF BEING APART...
...FROM EACH OTHER?
WELL... NOT REALLY, I GUESS.
HAJIME ALWAYS LIVED OUT IN THE COUNTRY-SIDE.
WHEN WE WERE LITTLE, I ONLY SAW HIM DURING VACATIONS, SO IT'D BE A LITTLE WEIRD TO START FEELING THAT WAY NOW.
BESIDES, EVEN IF WE'RE APART PHYSI-CALLY...
...OUR HEARTS WILL ALWAYS STAY CLOSE.
......
CHIRA (GLANCE)
...YES!
HAJIME'S ASLEEP, SO I DIDN'T HAVE TO DEAL WITH HIS LAME COME-BACKS!
AH HA HA.
...BY THE WAY, MITOMA-SAN—
WHY DID YOU CHOOSE THIS HIGH SCHOOL?
OH! ME?
NO SPECIAL REASON ......
JUST THAT...IT WAS ONE OF THE SCHOOLS I MANAGED TO PASS THE TEST FOR.
I SEE.

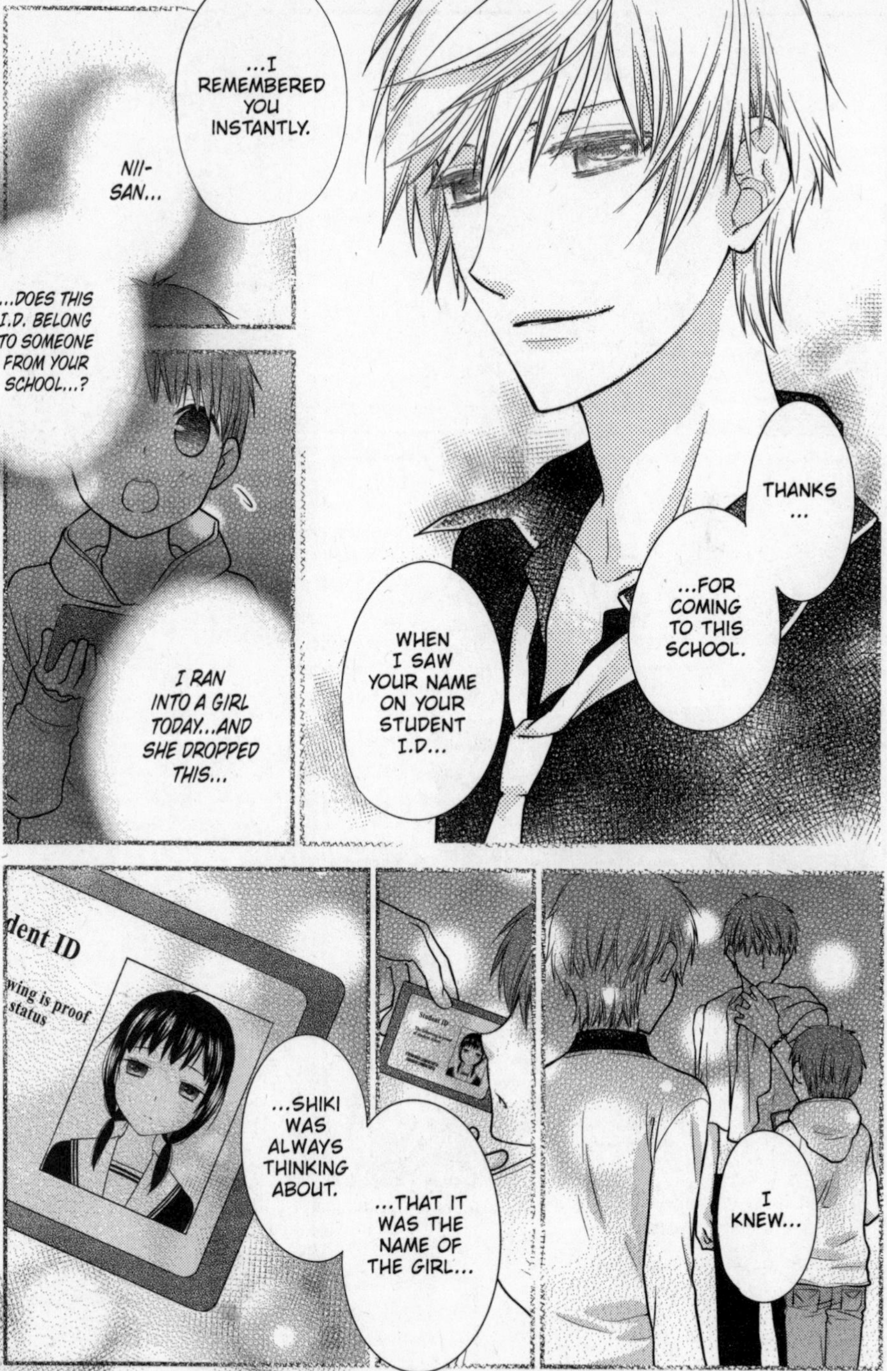
...I REMEMBERED YOU INSTANTLY.
THANKS...
...FOR COMING TO THIS SCHOOL.
WHEN I SAW YOUR NAME ON YOUR STUDENT I.D...
NII-SAN...
...DOES THIS I.D. BELONG TO SOMEONE FROM YOUR SCHOOL...?
I RAN INTO A GIRL TODAY...AND SHE DROPPED THIS...
I KNEW...
...THAT IT WAS THE NAME OF THE GIRL...
...SHIKI WAS ALWAYS THINKING ABOUT.
dent ID
wing is proof
status

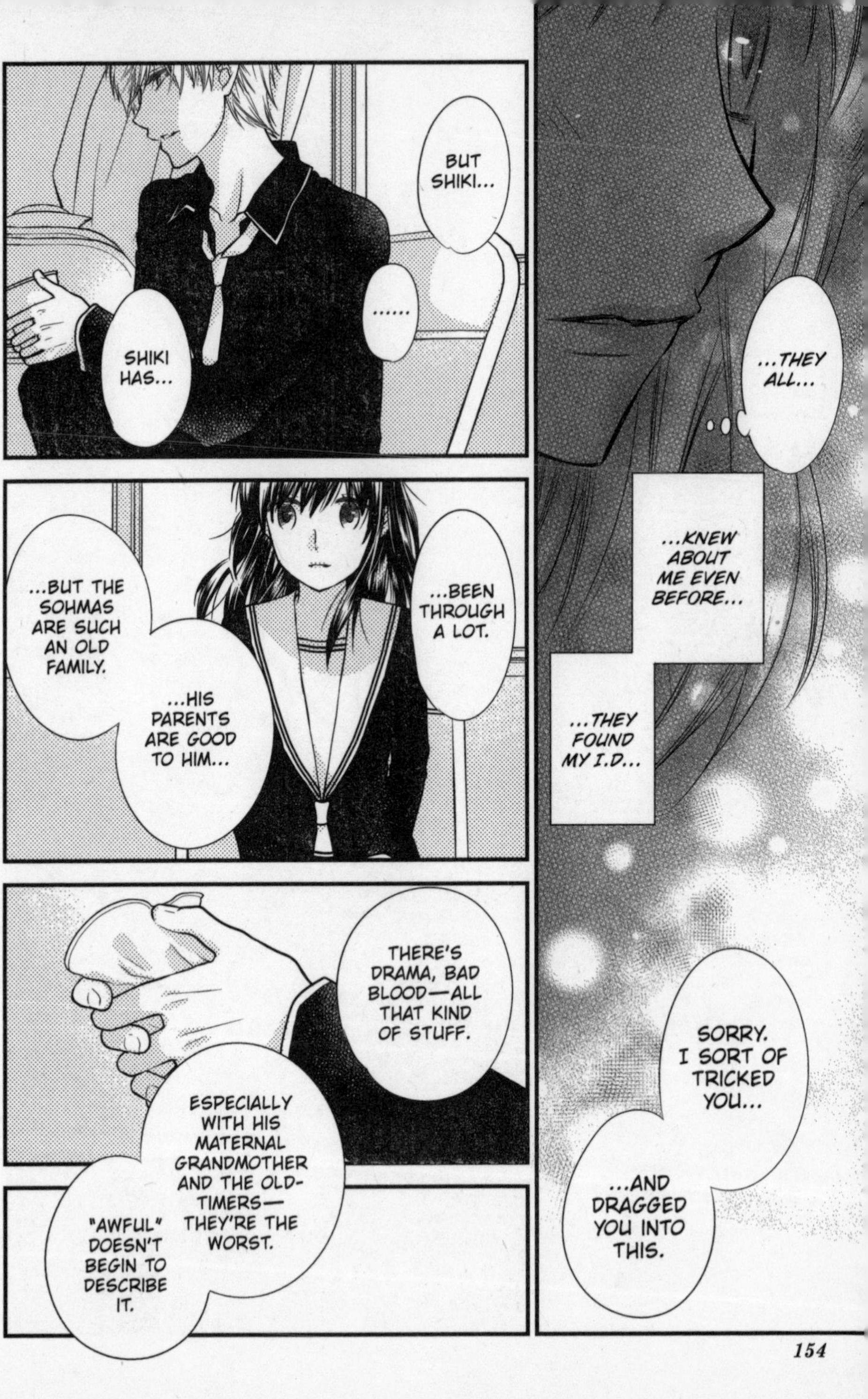
...THEY ALL...
...KNEW ABOUT ME EVEN BEFORE...
...THEY FOUND MY I.D...
SORRY. I SORT OF TRICKED YOU...
...AND DRAGGED YOU INTO THIS.
BUT SHIKI...
......
SHIKI HAS...
...BEEN THROUGH A LOT.
...HIS PARENTS ARE GOOD TO HIM...
...BUT THE SOHMAS ARE SUCH AN OLD FAMILY.
THERE'S DRAMA, BAD BLOOD—ALL THAT KIND OF STUFF.
ESPECIALLY WITH HIS MATERNAL GRANDMOTHER AND THE OLD-TIMERS—THEY'RE THE WORST.
"AWFUL" DOESN'T BEGIN TO DESCRIBE IT.

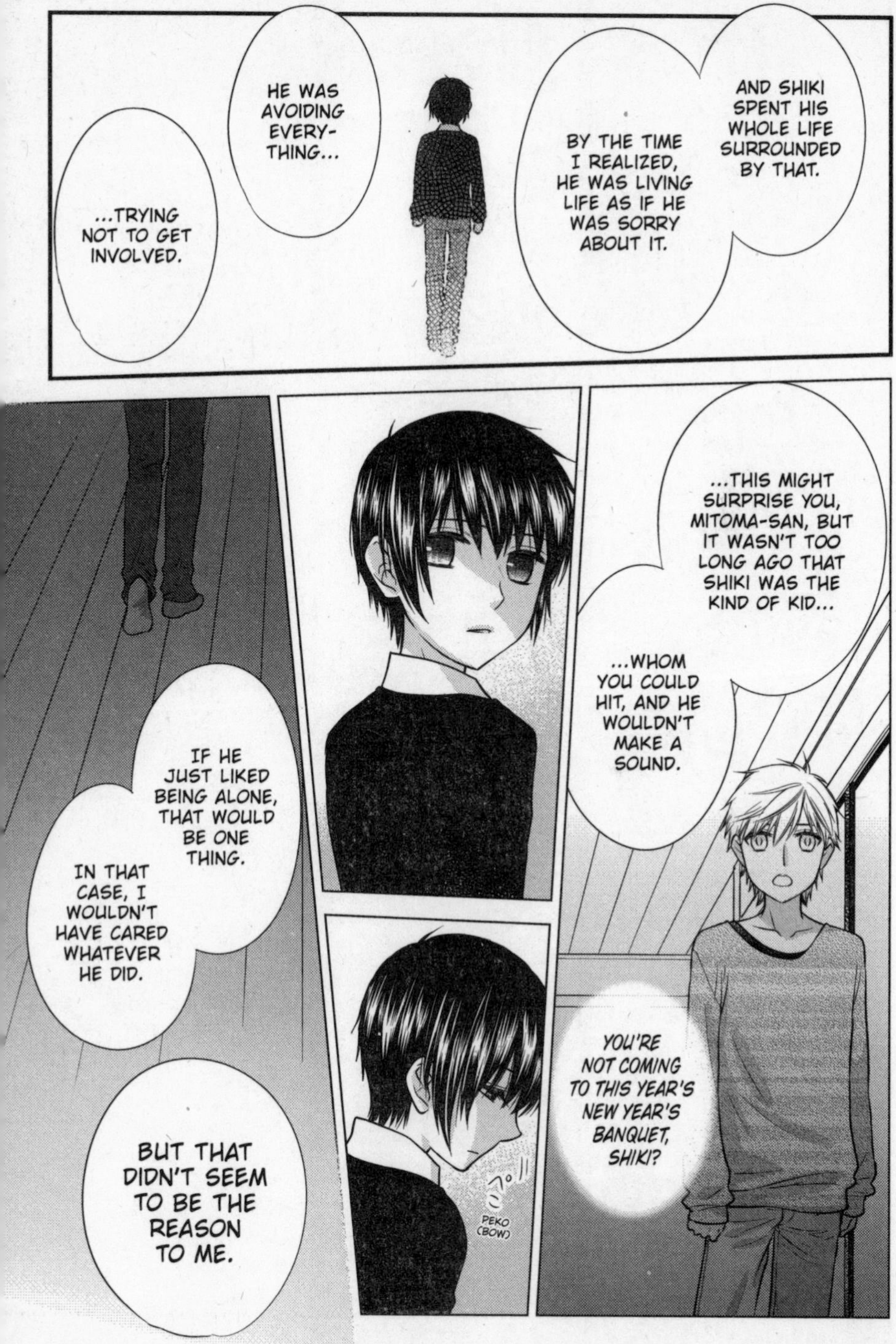
AND SHIKI SPENT HIS WHOLE LIFE SURROUNDED BY THAT.
BY THE TIME I REALIZED, HE WAS LIVING LIFE AS IF HE WAS SORRY ABOUT IT.
HE WAS AVOIDING EVERY-THING...
...TRYING NOT TO GET INVOLVED.
...THIS MIGHT SURPRISE YOU, MITOMA-SAN, BUT IT WASN'T TOO LONG AGO THAT SHIKI WAS THE KIND OF KID...
...WHOM YOU COULD HIT, AND HE WOULDN'T MAKE A SOUND.
YOU'RE NOT COMING TO THIS YEAR'S NEW YEAR'S BANQUET, SHIKI?
ぺこ
PEKO (BOW)
IF HE JUST LIKED BEING ALONE, THAT WOULD BE ONE THING.
IN THAT CASE, I WOULDN'T HAVE CARED WHATEVER HE DID.
BUT THAT DIDN'T SEEM TO BE THE REASON TO ME.

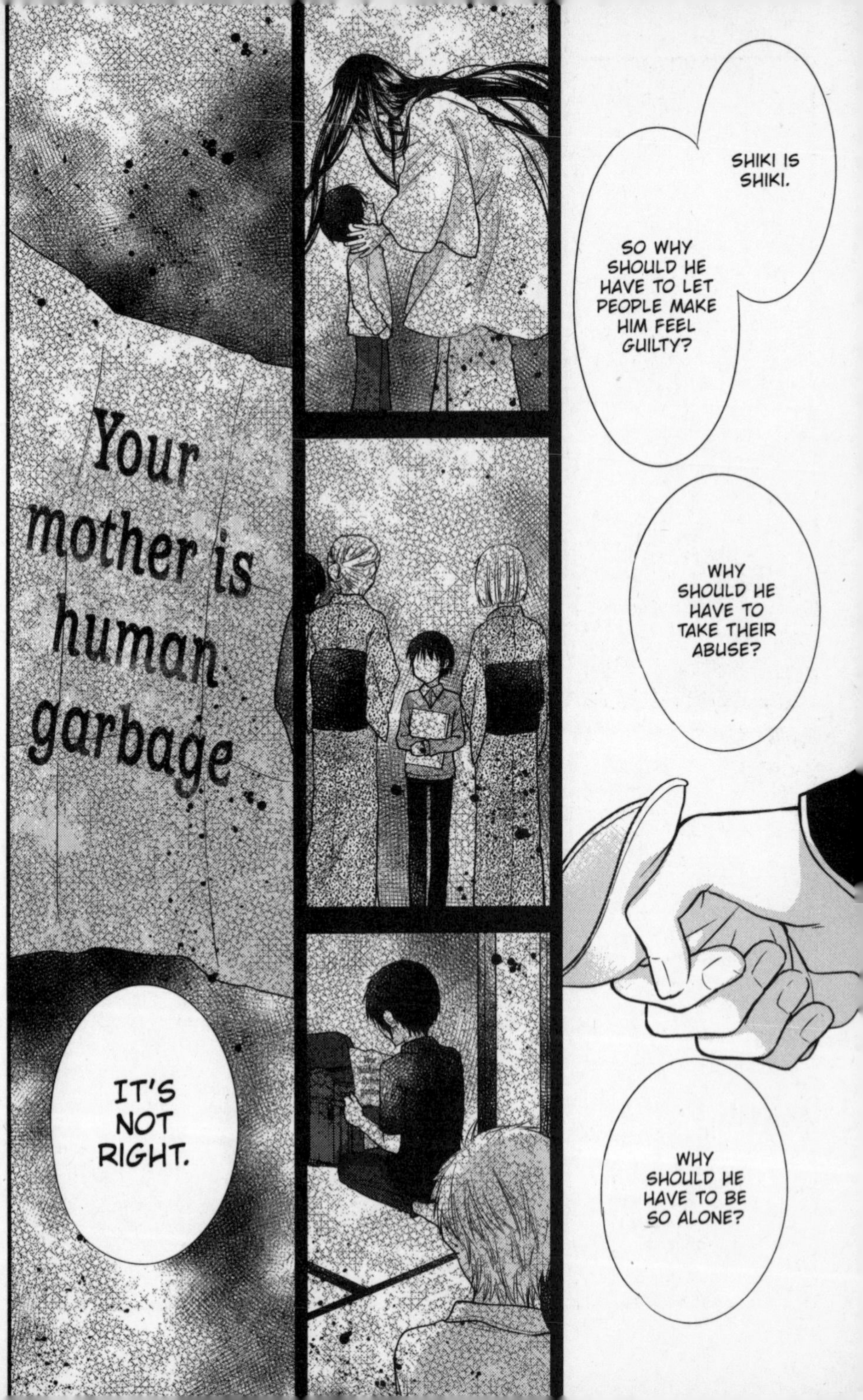
SHIKI IS SHIKI.
SO WHY SHOULD HE HAVE TO LET PEOPLE MAKE HIM FEEL GUILTY?
WHY SHOULD HE HAVE TO TAKE THEIR ABUSE?
WHY SHOULD HE HAVE TO BE SO ALONE?
Your mother is human garbage
IT'S NOT RIGHT.

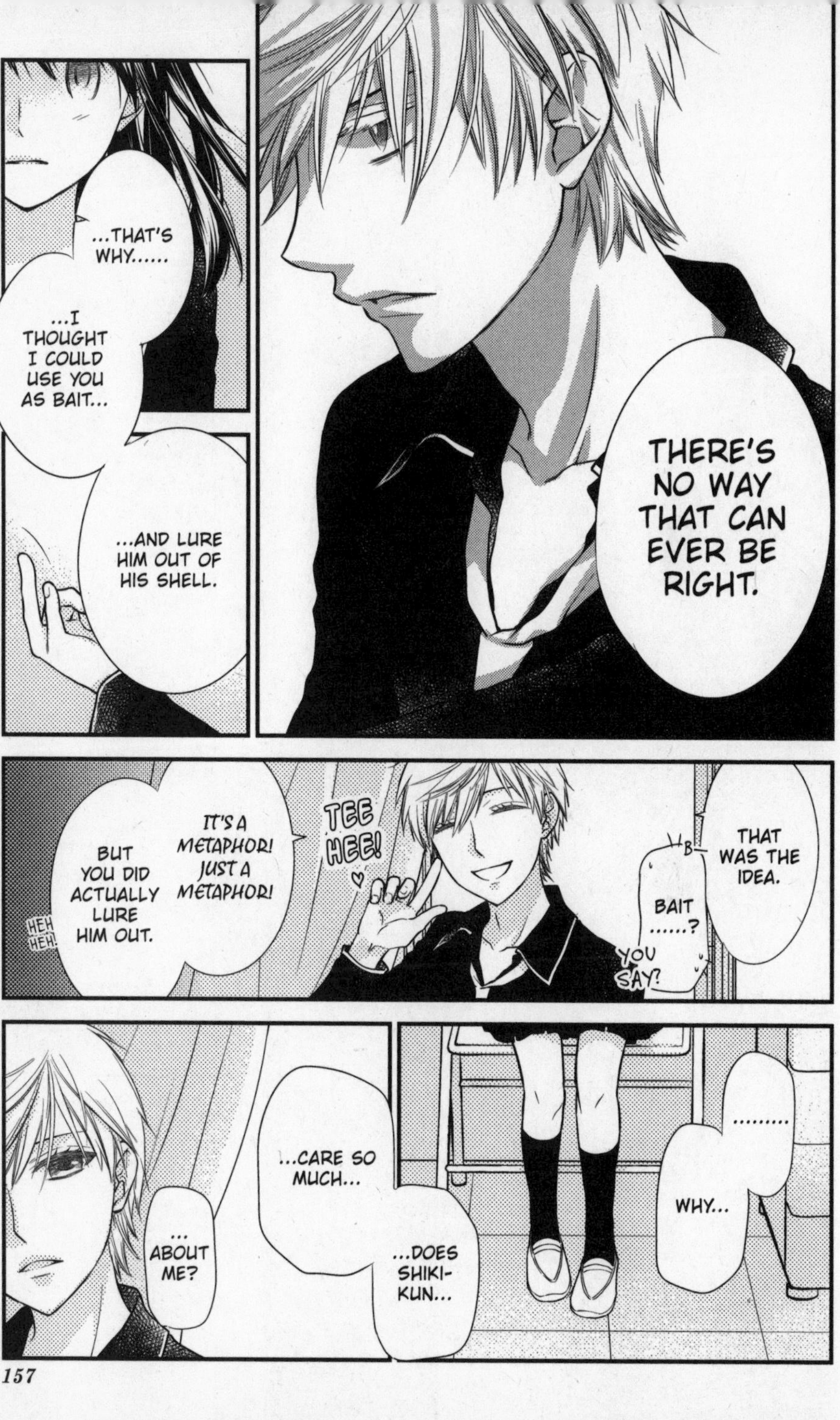
THERE'S NO WAY THAT CAN EVER BE RIGHT.
...THAT'S WHY......
...I THOUGHT I COULD USE YOU AS BAIT...
...AND LURE HIM OUT OF HIS SHELL.
THAT WAS THE IDEA.
BAIT ......?
YOU SAY?
TEE HEE!
IT'S A METAPHOR! JUST A METAPHOR!
BUT YOU DID ACTUALLY LURE HIM OUT.
HEH HEH!
....
WHY...
...DOES SHIKI-KUN...
...CARE SO MUCH...
... ABOUT ME?

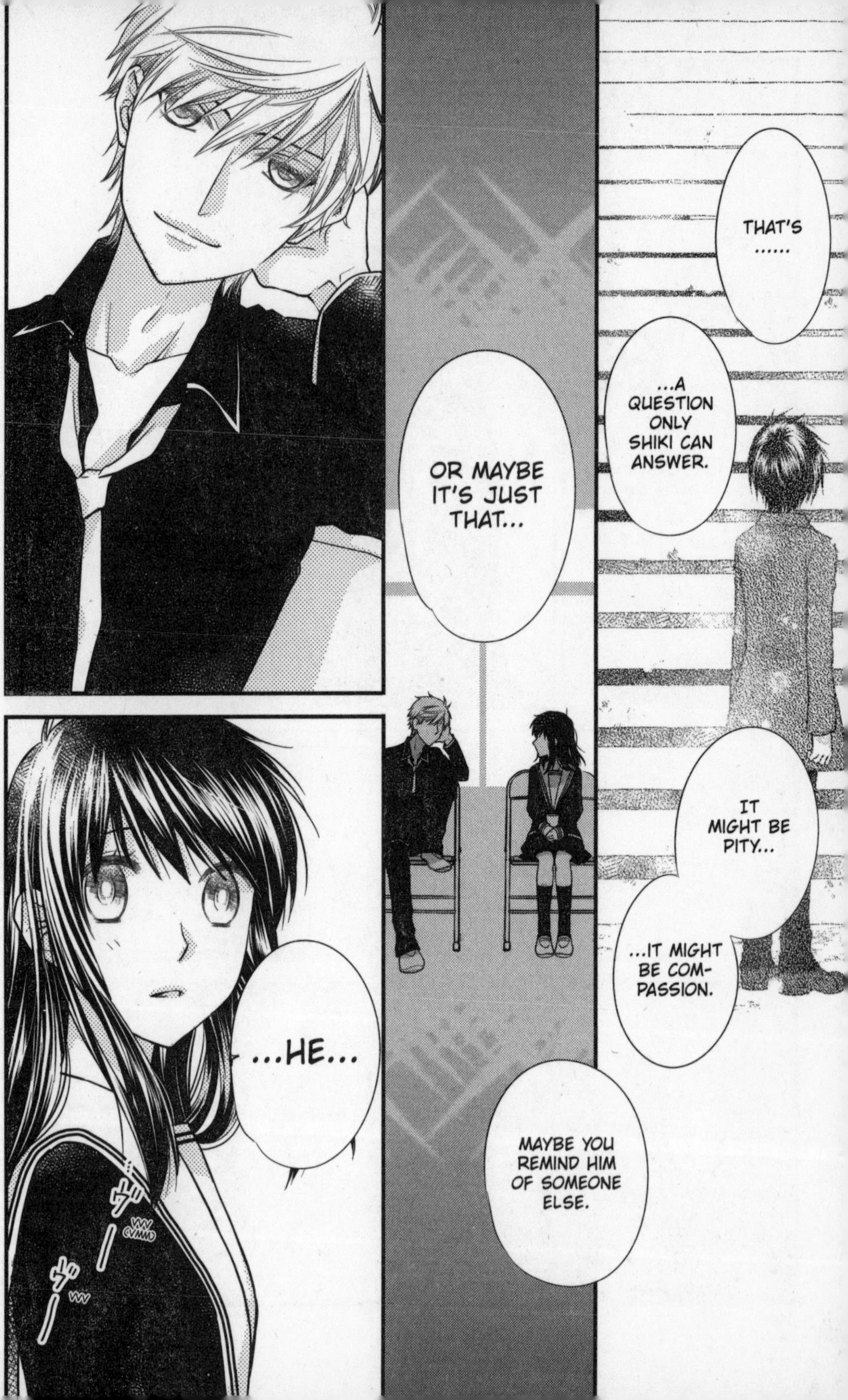
THAT'S ......
...A QUESTION ONLY SHIKI CAN ANSWER.
IT MIGHT BE PITY...
...IT MIGHT BE COM-PASSION.
OR MAYBE IT'S JUST THAT...
MAYBE YOU REMIND HIM OF SOMEONE ELSE.
...HE...

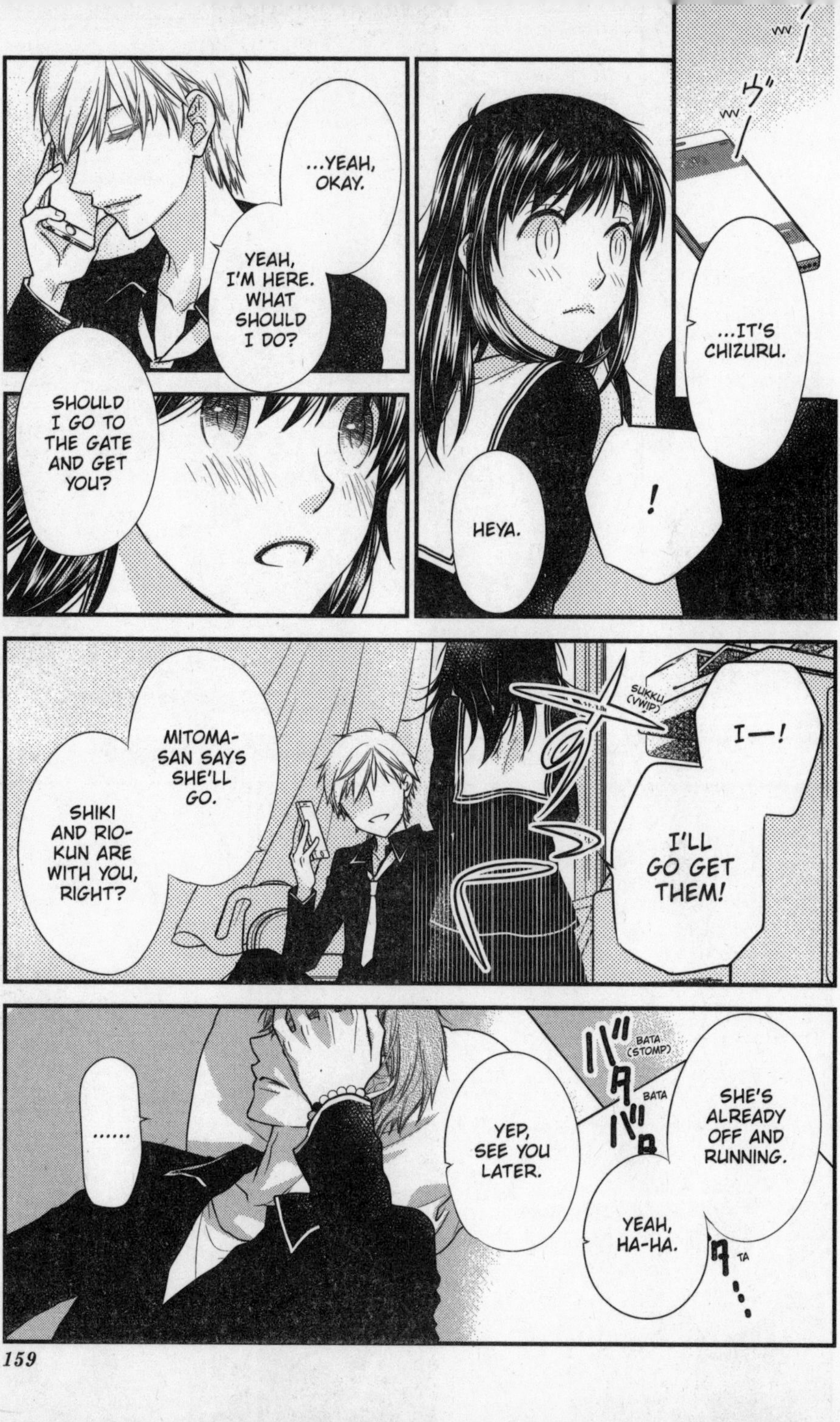
VVV
VVV
…IT'S CHIZURU.
!
HEYA.
...YEAH, OKAY.
YEAH, I'M HERE. WHAT SHOULD I DO?
SHOULD I GO TO THE GATE AND GET YOU?
SUKKU (VWIP)
I—!
I'LL GO GET THEM!
MITOMA-SAN SAYS SHE'LL GO.
SHIKI AND RIO-KUN ARE WITH YOU, RIGHT?
BATA (STOMP)
BATA
SHE'S ALREADY OFF AND RUNNING.
YEAH, HA-HA.
TA
YEP, SEE YOU LATER.
……

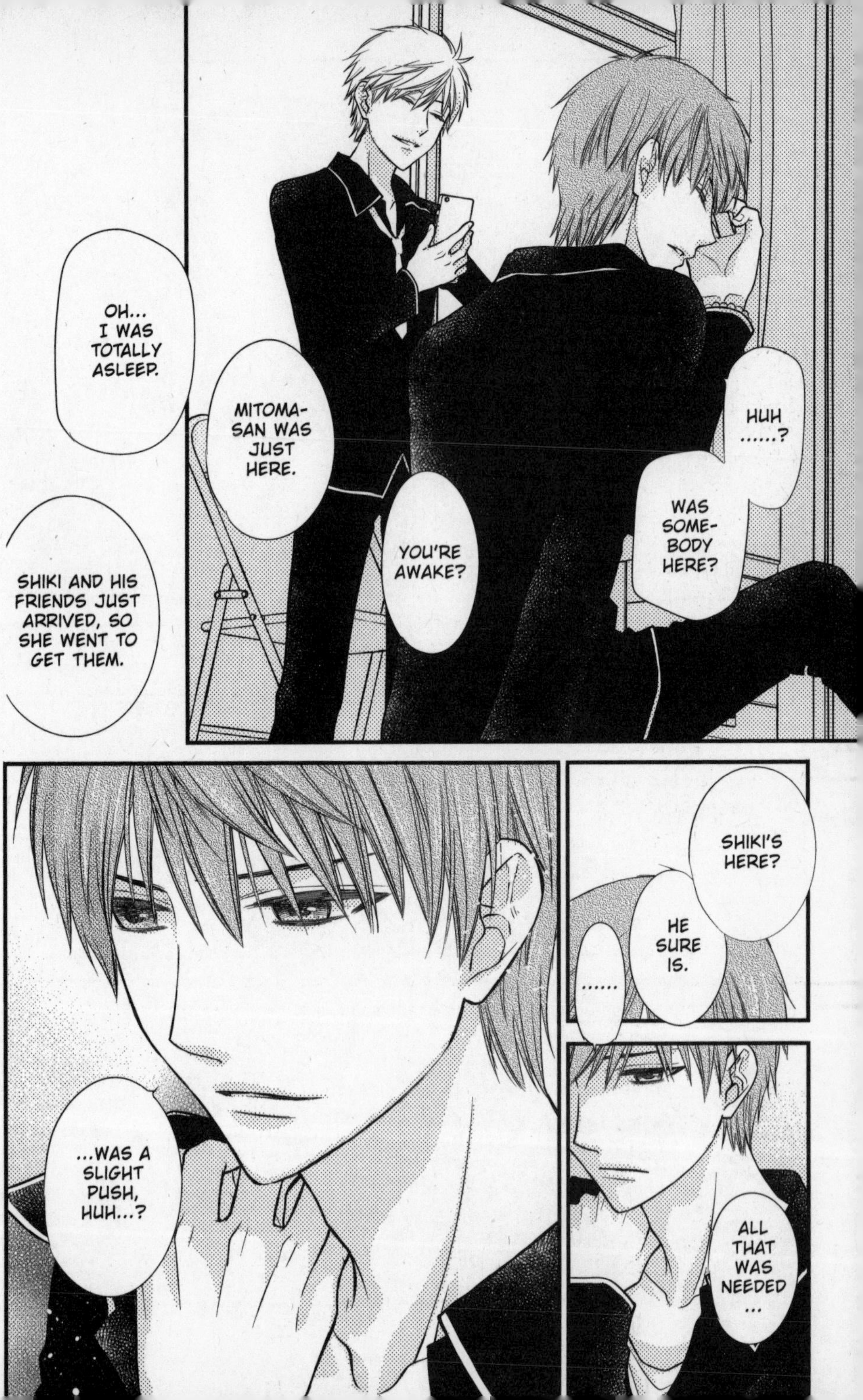
HUH ......?
WAS SOMEBODY HERE?
YOU'RE AWAKE?
MITOMA-SAN WAS JUST HERE.
OH... I WAS TOTALLY ASLEEP.
SHIKI AND HIS FRIENDS JUST ARRIVED, SO SHE WENT TO GET THEM.
SHIKI'S HERE?
HE SURE IS.
......
ALL THAT WAS NEEDED ...
...WAS A SLIGHT PUSH, HUH...?

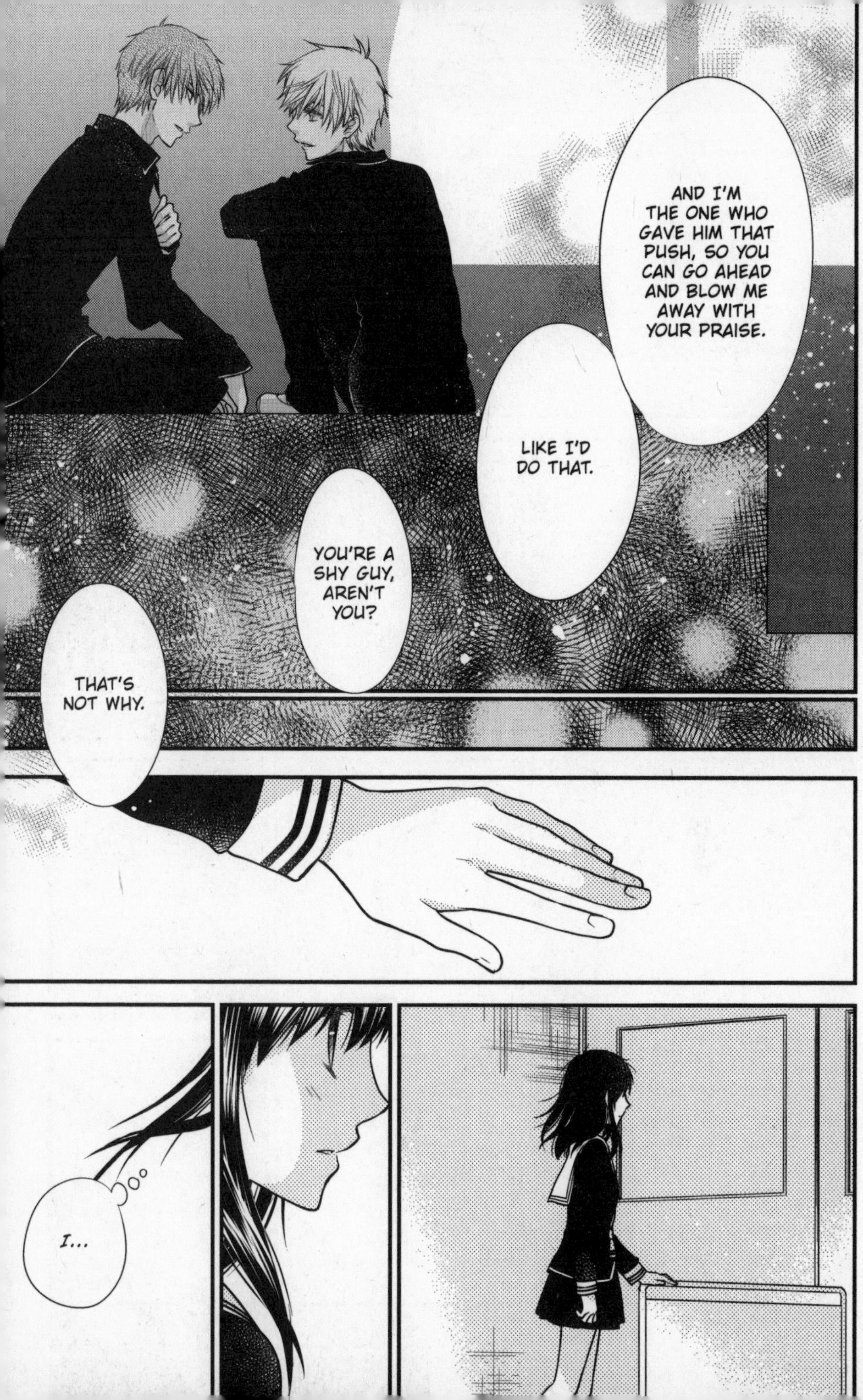
AND I'M THE ONE WHO GAVE HIM THAT PUSH, SO YOU CAN GO AHEAD AND BLOW ME AWAY WITH YOUR PRAISE.
LIKE I'D DO THAT.
YOU'RE A SHY GUY, AREN'T YOU?
THAT'S NOT WHY.
I...

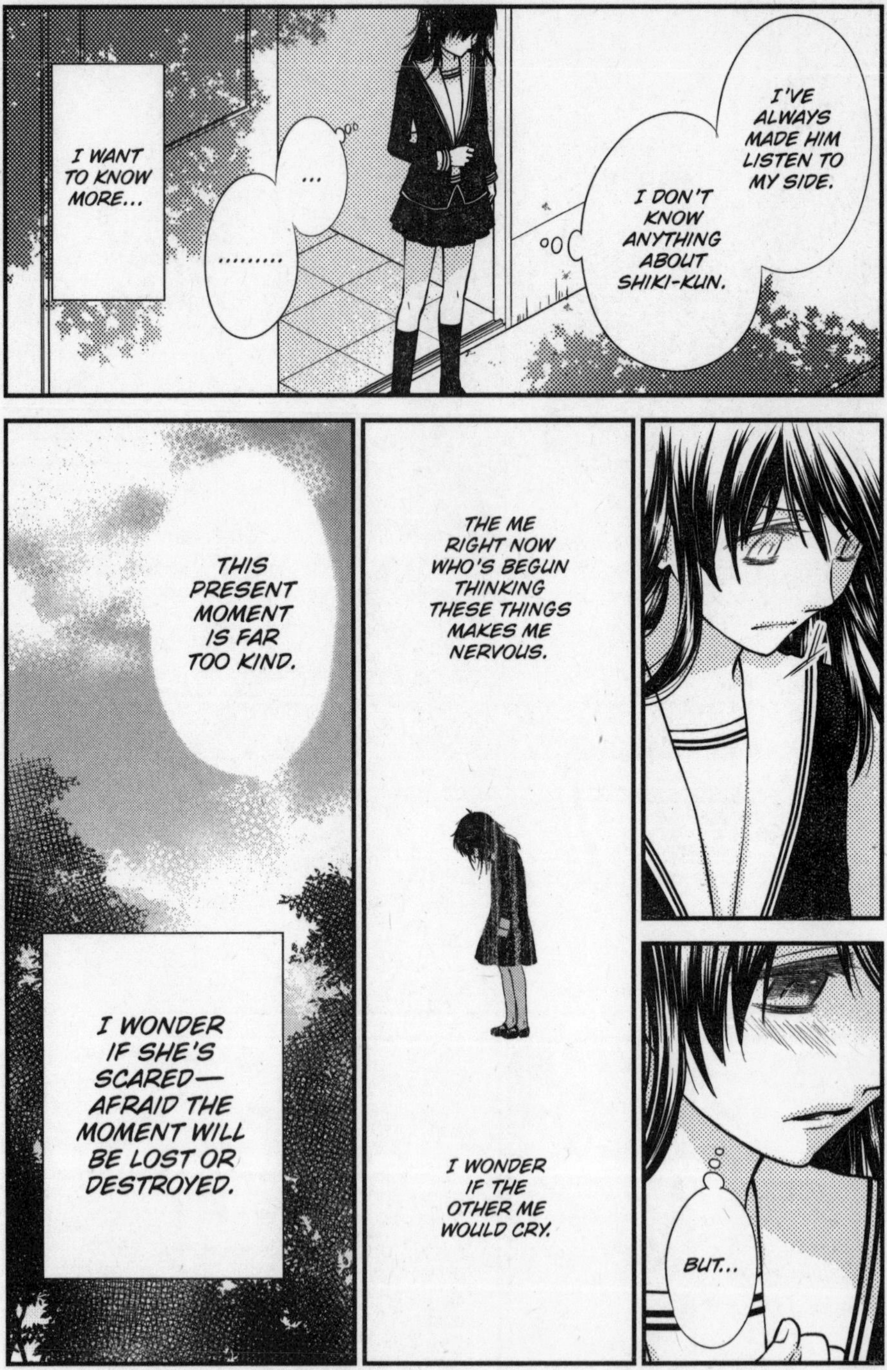
I'VE ALWAYS MADE HIM LISTEN TO MY SIDE.
I DON'T KNOW ANYTHING ABOUT SHIKI-KUN.
...
....
I WANT TO KNOW MORE...
BUT...
THE ME RIGHT NOW WHO'S BEGUN THINKING THESE THINGS MAKES ME NERVOUS.
I WONDER IF THE OTHER ME WOULD CRY.
THIS PRESENT MOMENT IS FAR TOO KIND.
I WONDER IF SHE'S SCARED—AFRAID THE MOMENT WILL BE LOST OR DESTROYED.

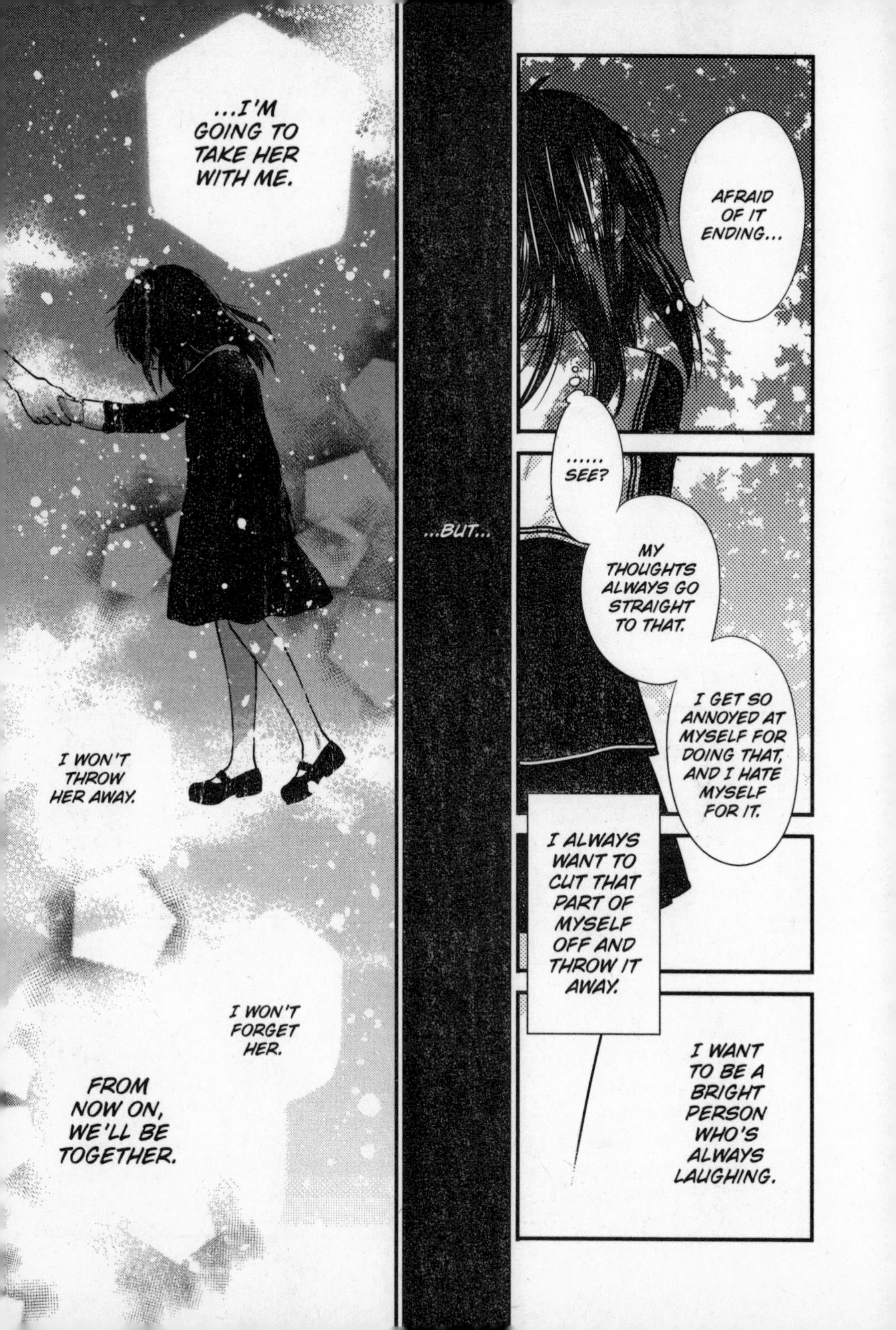
AFRAID OF IT ENDING...
......SEE?
MY THOUGHTS ALWAYS GO STRAIGHT TO THAT.
I GET SO ANNOYED AT MYSELF FOR DOING THAT, AND I HATE MYSELF FOR IT.
I ALWAYS WANT TO CUT THAT PART OF MYSELF OFF AND THROW IT AWAY.
I WANT TO BE A BRIGHT PERSON WHO'S ALWAYS LAUGHING.
...BUT...
...I'M GOING TO TAKE HER WITH ME.
I WON'T THROW HER AWAY.
I WON'T FORGET HER.
FROM NOW ON, WE'LL BE TOGETHER.

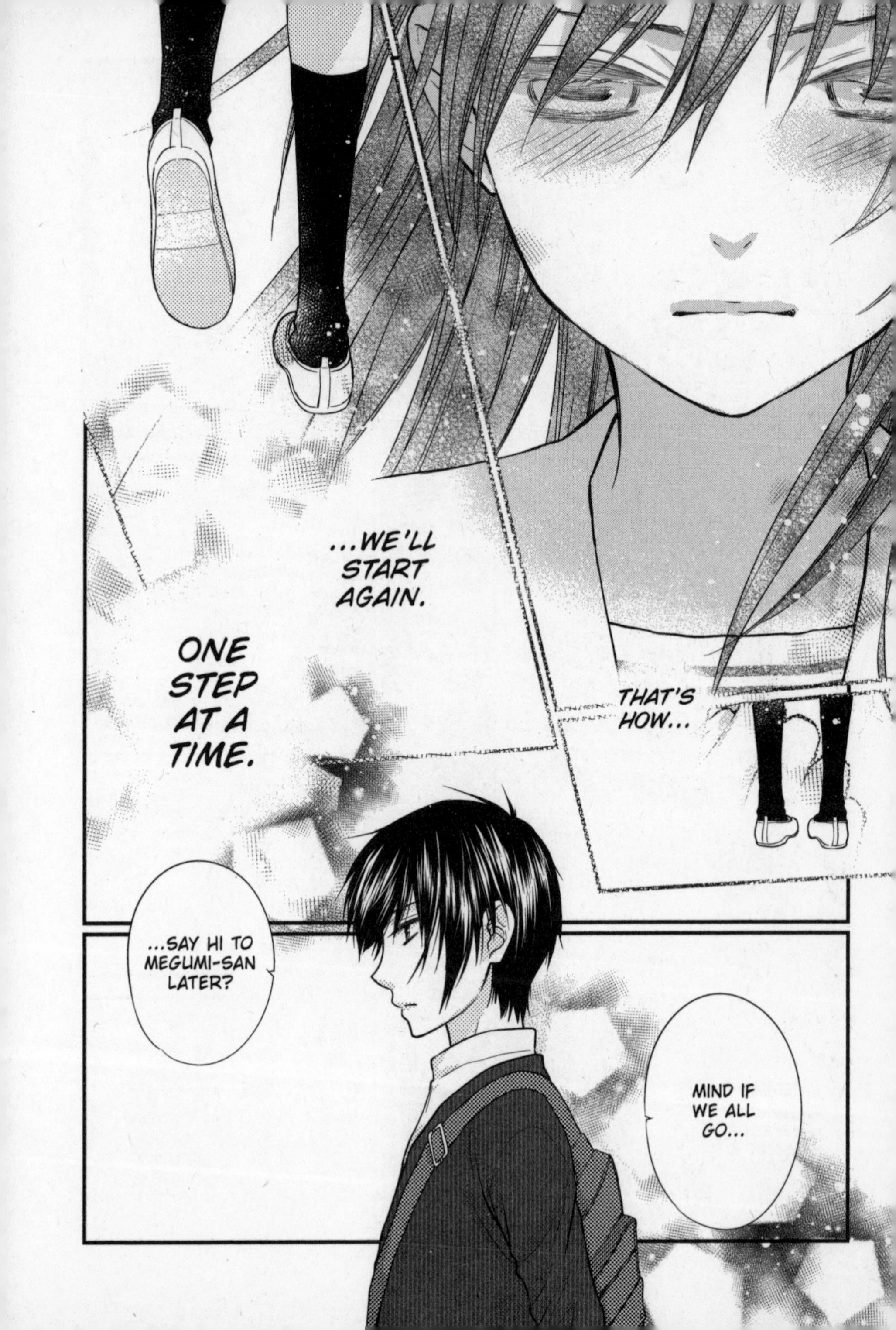
THAT'S HOW...
...WE'LL START AGAIN.
ONE STEP AT A TIME.
MIND IF WE ALL GO...
...SAY HI TO MEGUMI-SAN LATER?

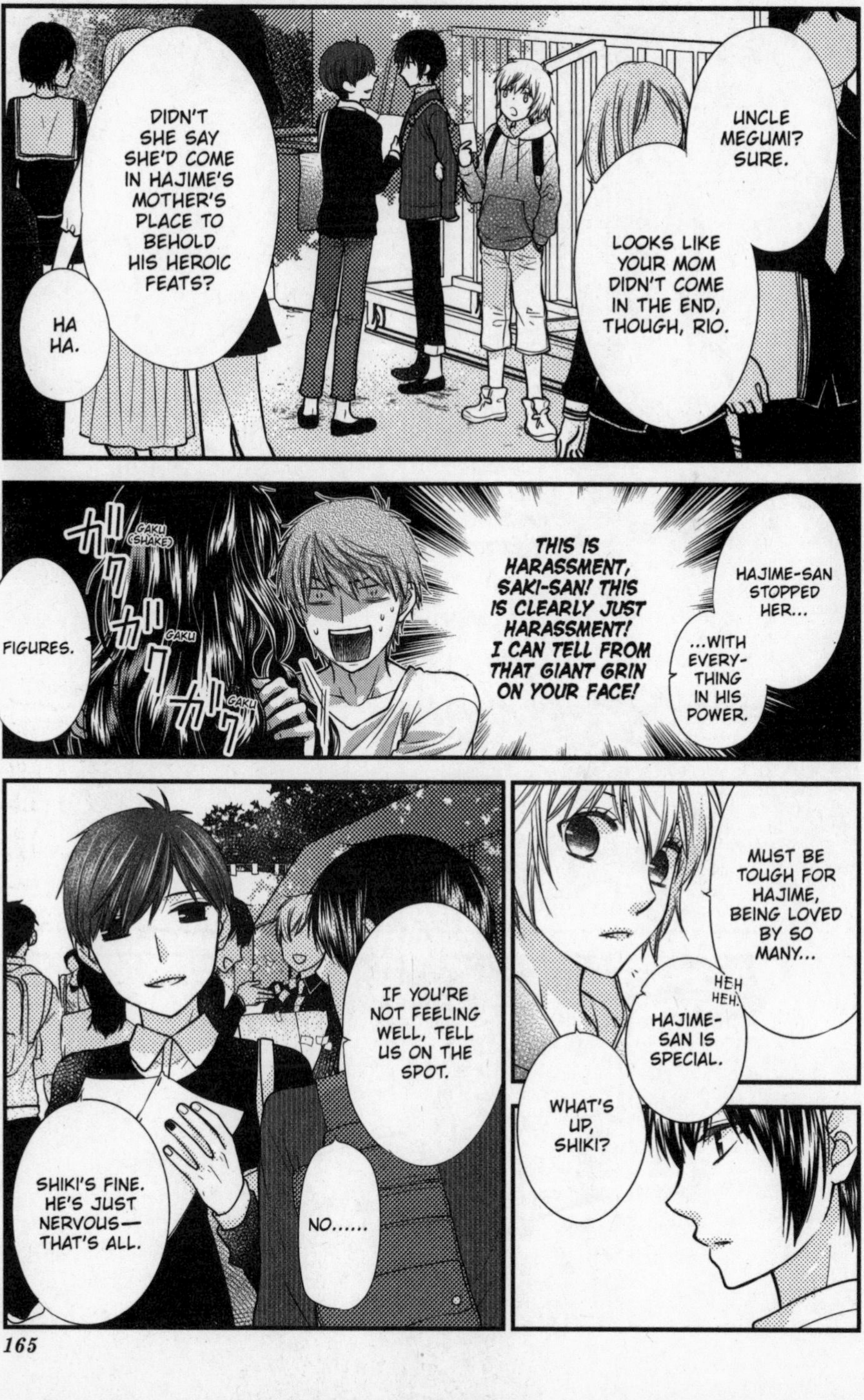
UNCLE MEGUMI? SURE.
LOOKS LIKE YOUR MOM DIDN'T COME IN THE END, THOUGH, RIO.
DIDN'T SHE SAY SHE'D COME IN HAJIME'S MOTHER'S PLACE TO BEHOLD HIS HEROIC FEATS?
HA HA.
HAJIME-SAN STOPPED HER...
...WITH EVERY-THING IN HIS POWER.
THIS IS HARASSMENT, SAKI-SAN! THIS IS CLEARLY JUST HARASSMENT! I CAN TELL FROM THAT GIANT GRIN ON YOUR FACE!
GAKU (SHAKE)
GAKU
GAKU
FIGURES.
MUST BE TOUGH FOR HAJIME, BEING LOVED BY SO MANY...
HEH HEH.
HAJIME-SAN IS SPECIAL.
WHAT'S UP, SHIKI?
IF YOU'RE NOT FEELING WELL, TELL US ON THE SPOT.
NO......
SHIKI'S FINE. HE'S JUST NERVOUS—THAT'S ALL.

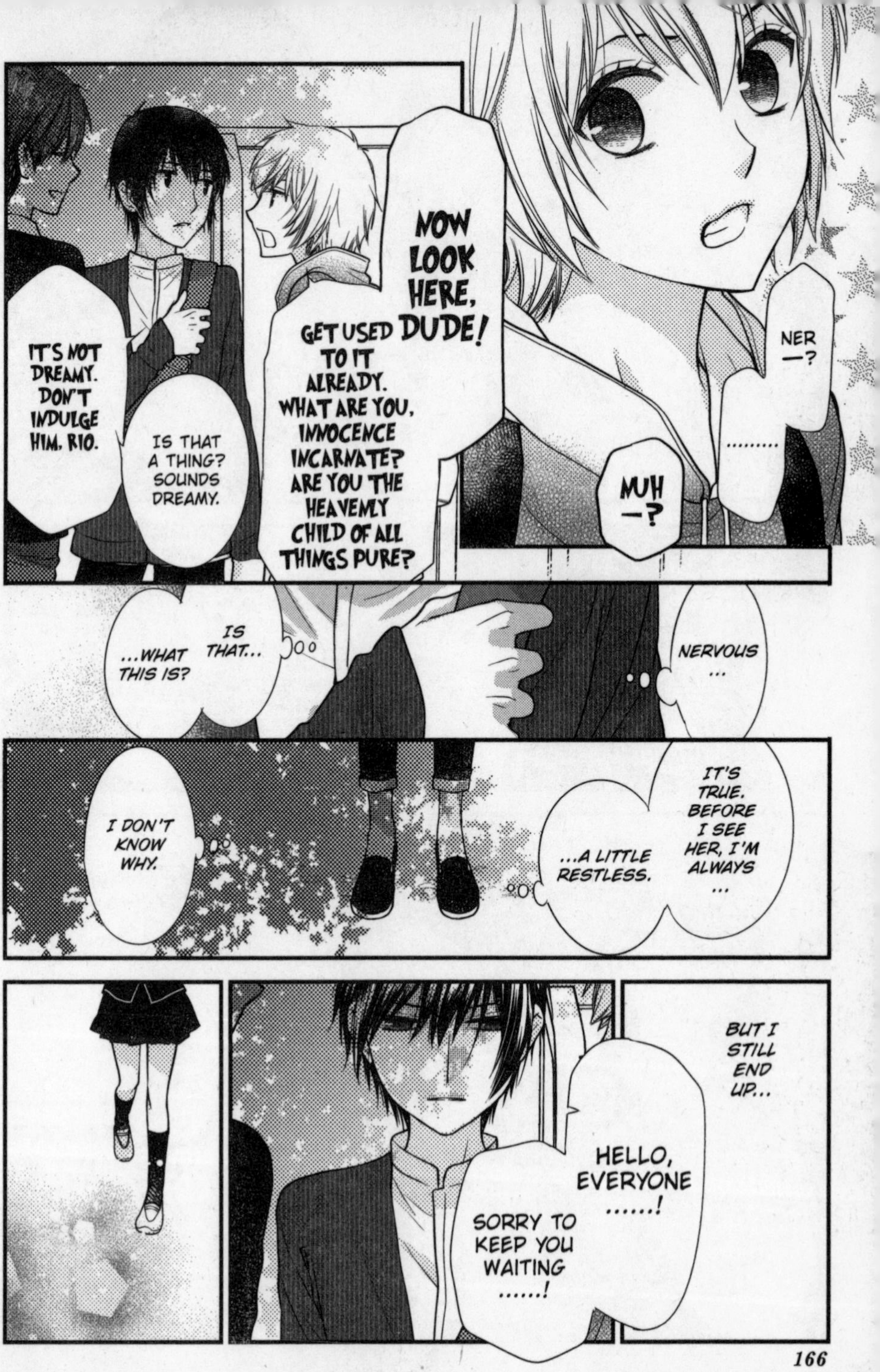
NER—?
....
MUH—?
NOW LOOK HERE, DUDE!
GET USED TO IT ALREADY. WHAT ARE YOU, INNOCENCE INCARNATE? ARE YOU THE HEAVENLY CHILD OF ALL THINGS PURE?
IS THAT A THING? SOUNDS DREAMY.
IT'S NOT DREAMY. DON'T INDULGE HIM, RIO.
NERVOUS...
IS THAT...
...WHAT THIS IS?
IT'S TRUE. BEFORE I SEE HER, I'M ALWAYS...
...A LITTLE RESTLESS.
I DON'T KNOW WHY.
BUT I STILL END UP...
HELLO, EVERYONE......!
SORRY TO KEEP YOU WAITING......!

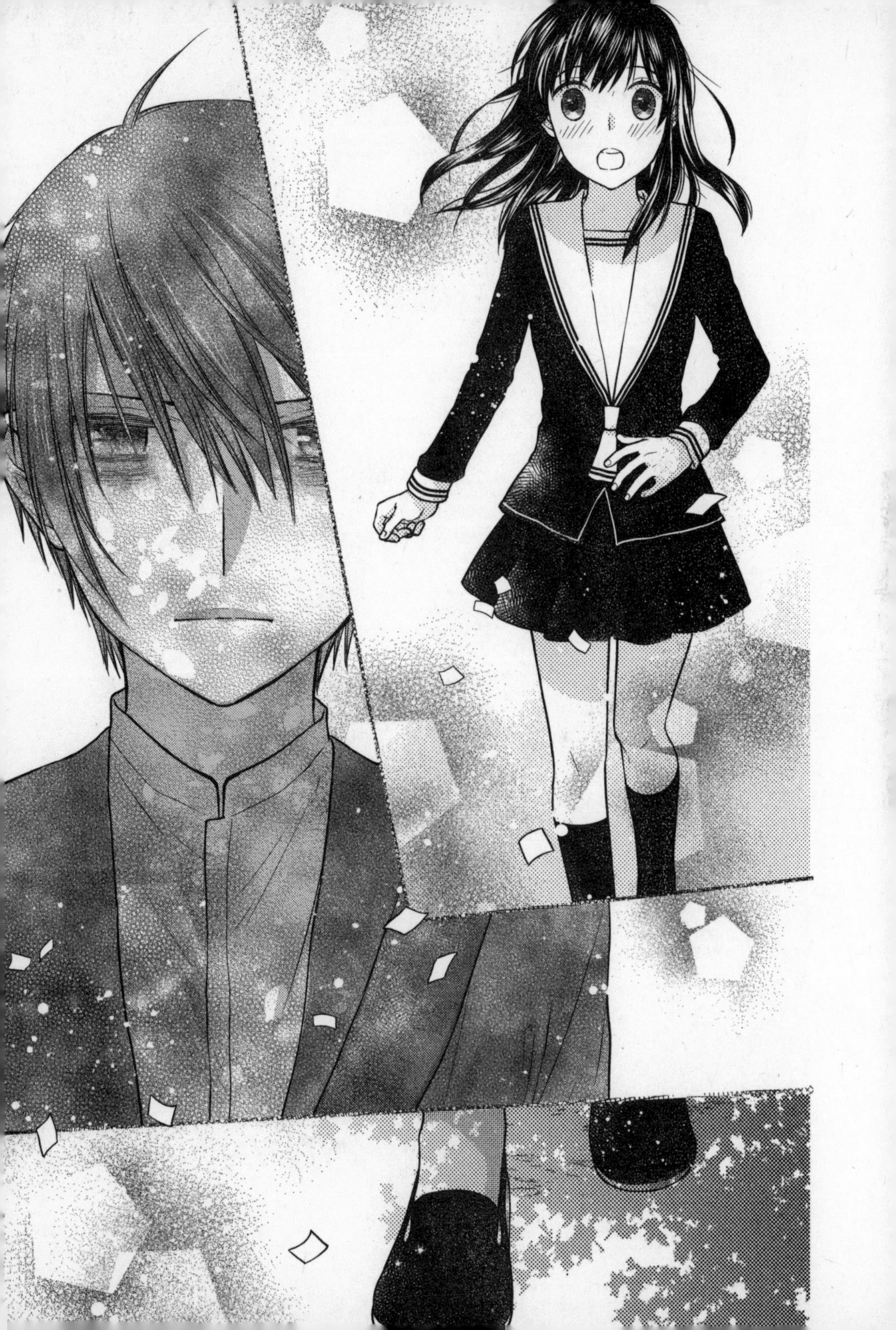

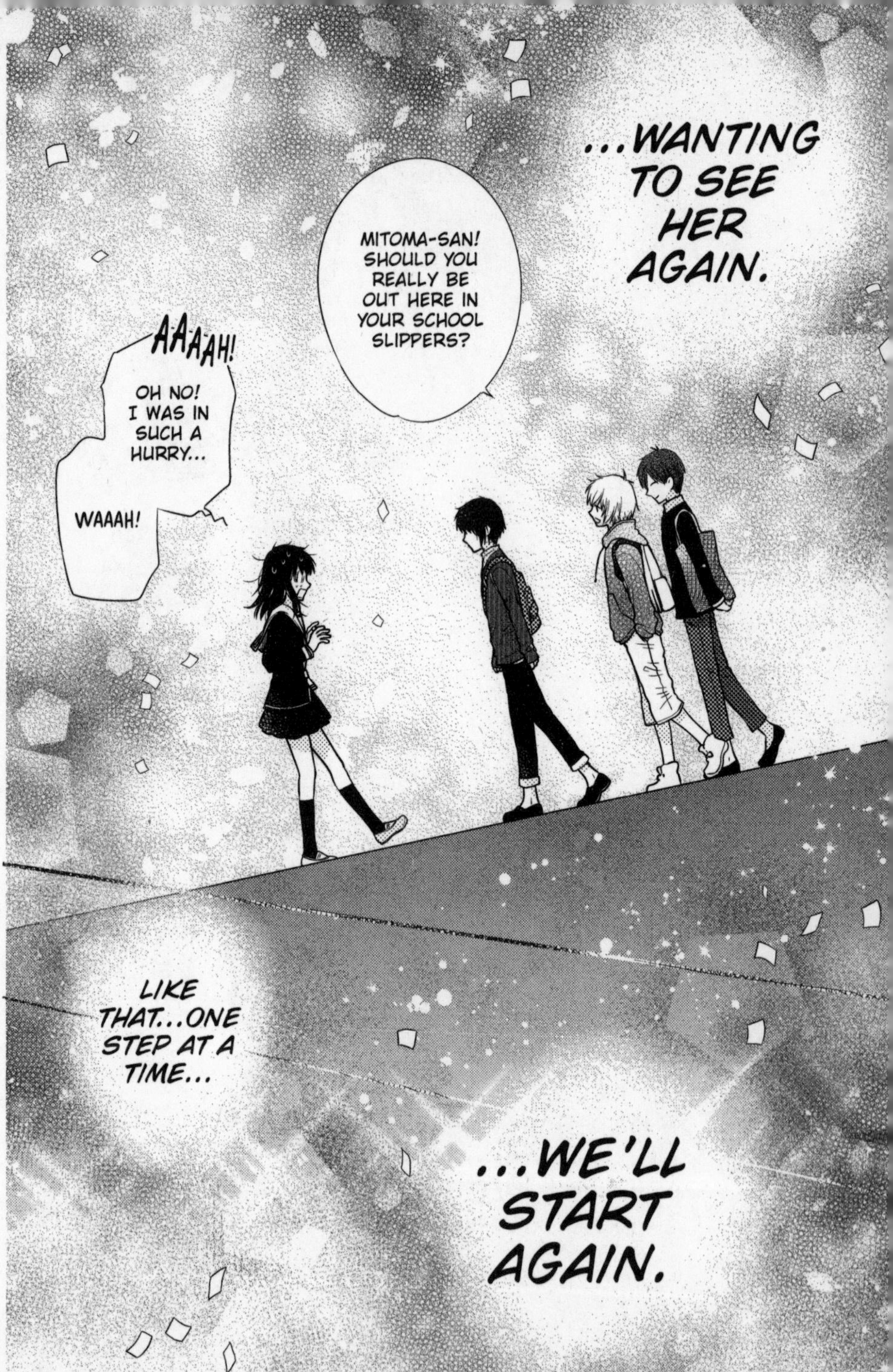
...WANTING TO SEE HER AGAIN.
MITOMA-SAN! SHOULD YOU REALLY BE OUT HERE IN YOUR SCHOOL SLIPPERS?
AAAAAH!
OH NO! I WAS IN SUCH A HURRY...
WAAAH!
LIKE THAT...ONE STEP AT A TIME...
...WE'LL START AGAIN.

FRUITS BASKET ANOTHER 3 THE END

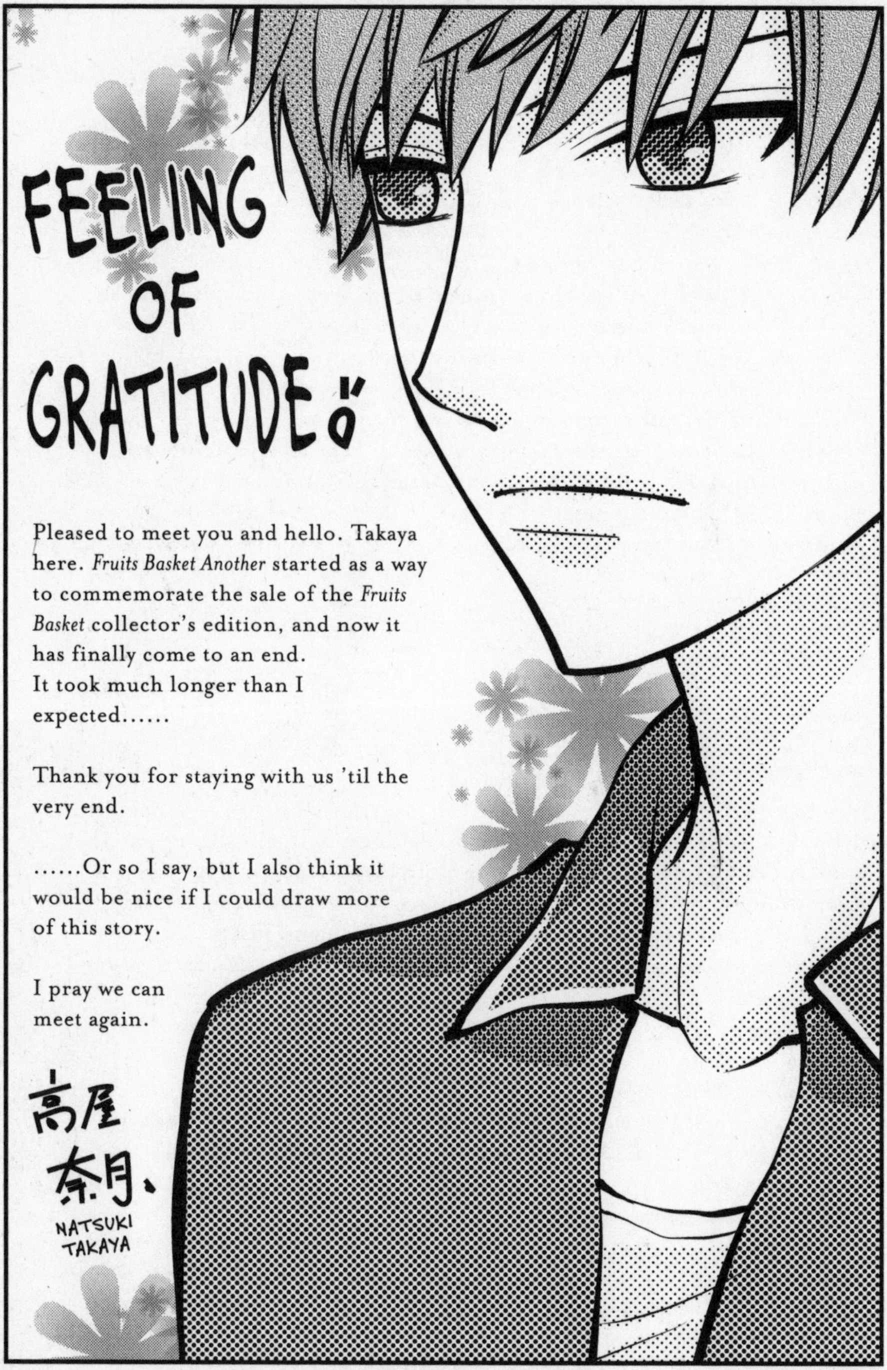

FEELING OF GRATITUDE

Pleased to meet you and hello. Takaya here. *Fruits Basket Another* started as a way to commemorate the sale of the *Fruits Basket* collector's edition, and now it has finally come to an end.
It took much longer than I expected......

Thank you for staying with us 'til the very end.

......Or so I say, but I also think it would be nice if I could draw more of this story.

I pray we can meet again.

高屋奈月、

NATSUKI TAKAYA

TRANSLATION NOTES

COMMON HONORIFICS

no honorific: Indicates familiarity or closeness; if used without permission or reason, addressing someone in this manner would constitute an insult.

-san: The Japanese equivalent of Mr./Mrs./Miss. If a situation calls for politeness, this is the fail-safe honorific.

-kun: Used most often when referring to boys, this indicates affection or familiarity. Occasionally used by older men among their peers, but it may also be used by anyone referring to a person of lower standing.

-chan: An affectionate honorific indicating familiarity used mostly in reference to girls; also used in reference to cute persons or animals of either gender.

-senpai: A suffix used to address upperclassmen or more experienced coworkers.

-sensei: A respectful term for teachers, artists, or high-level professionals.

onii-san/onii-chan/nii-san/nii-chan: Terms used to refer to one's older brother from most respectful to most casual. The first is more polite and can be used to refer to another person's brother while the rest are more exclusive to family members.

Page 16
Warte mal: The German phrase for "Hold on a second."

Page 34
Takoyaki: A popular Japanese festival and street snack sold at small vendors. The name literally translates to "fried octopus." The savory snack comes in a small, easily consumable ball shape. It contains minced octopus and tempura scraps in lightly cooked batter and is sprinkled with green onions, pickled ginger, and bonito flakes. Mayonnaise and Worcestershire sauce are also added for the finishing touch.

Page 44
Purikura: An abbreviation of the term "Print Club," or *purinto kurabu*, *purikura* is a kind of Japanese photo booth where people can go in with their friends or significant others to take pictures. Once the picture is taken, you can draw or edit the image digitally by adding backgrounds, borders, and effects. It is a very popular pastime among young Japanese students.

Page 45
Yukata: A simplified, more casual version of the kimono worn in the summer during festivals and in hot-spring resorts. The word translates to "bathing cloth," as it is also worn as a quick cover-up after bathing.

Page 45
Fireworks: In addition to the large fireworks that are often seen in the sky during celebratory events, there are also miniature handheld fireworks that can be bought for personal use in convenience stores throughout Japan.

Page 135
Salt: Salt is traditionally used in Japan for purification. Scattering salt around the perimeter of an area is believed to keep evil spirits away.

Page 168
School slippers: In Japanese schools, there are shoe lockers positioned near the entrance for students to change out of their outside shoes into school slippers, or *uwabaki*, for sanitary purposes. It is also a part of Japanese culture to remove one's shoes before entering a premise.

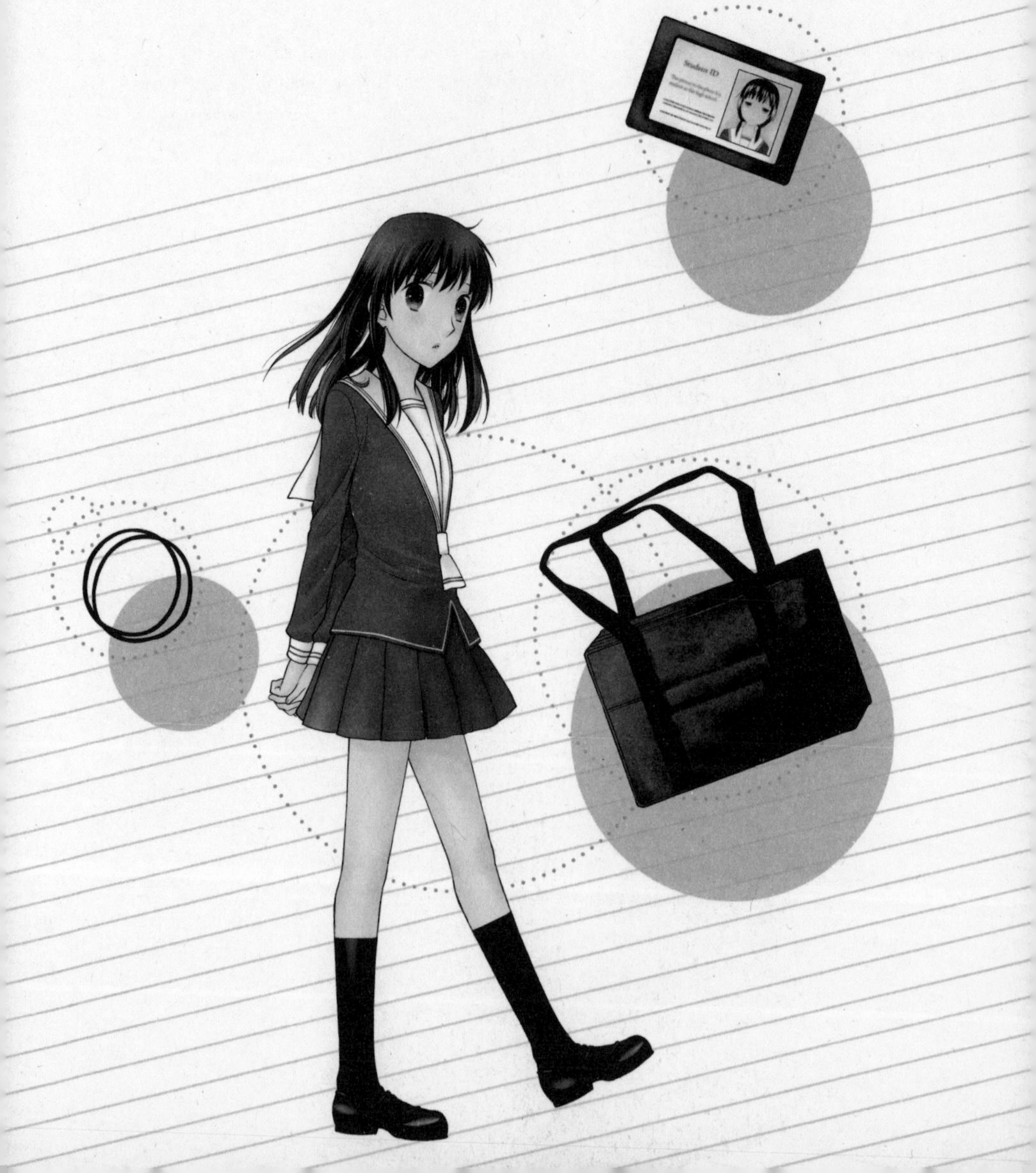
Student ID

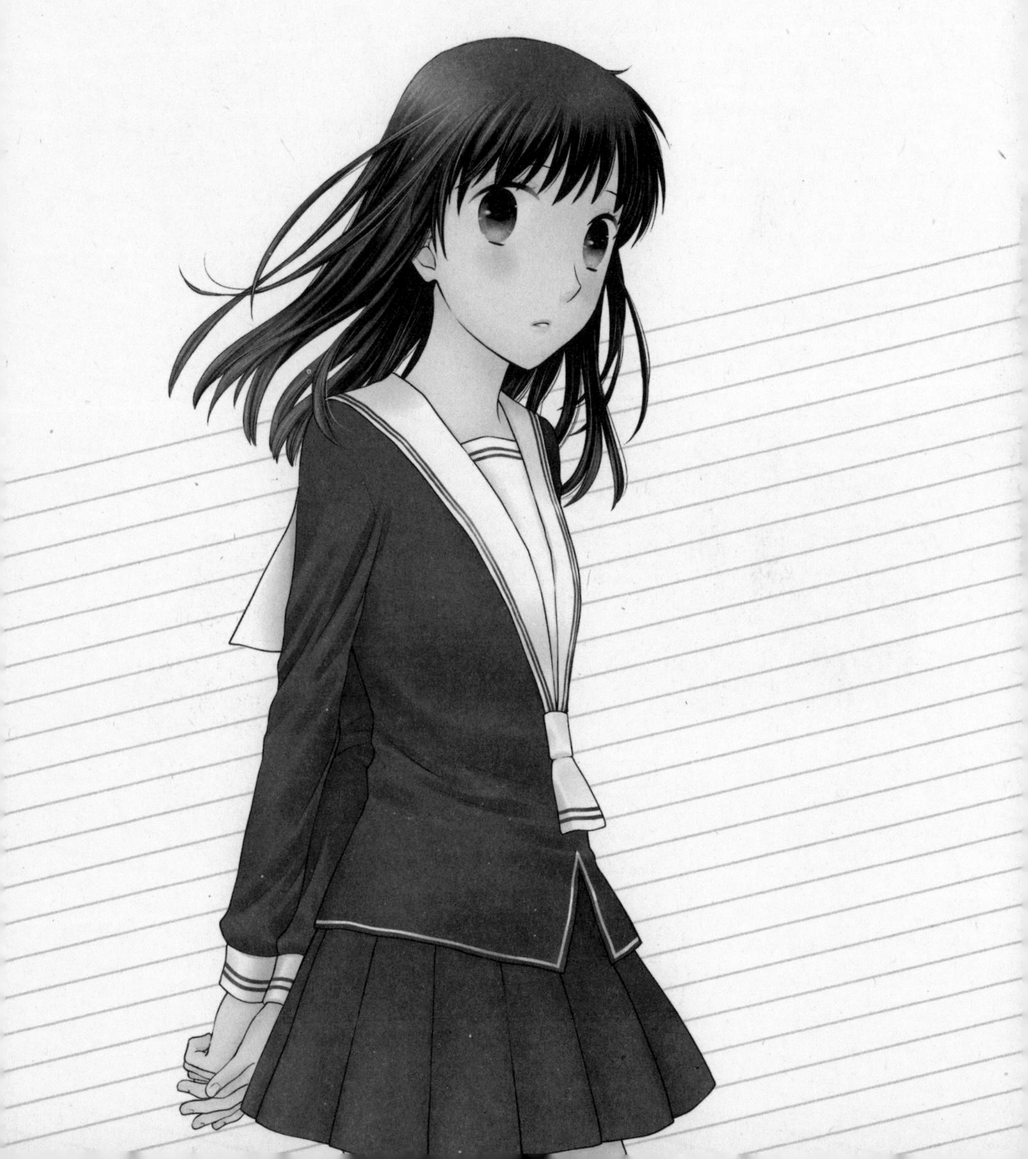

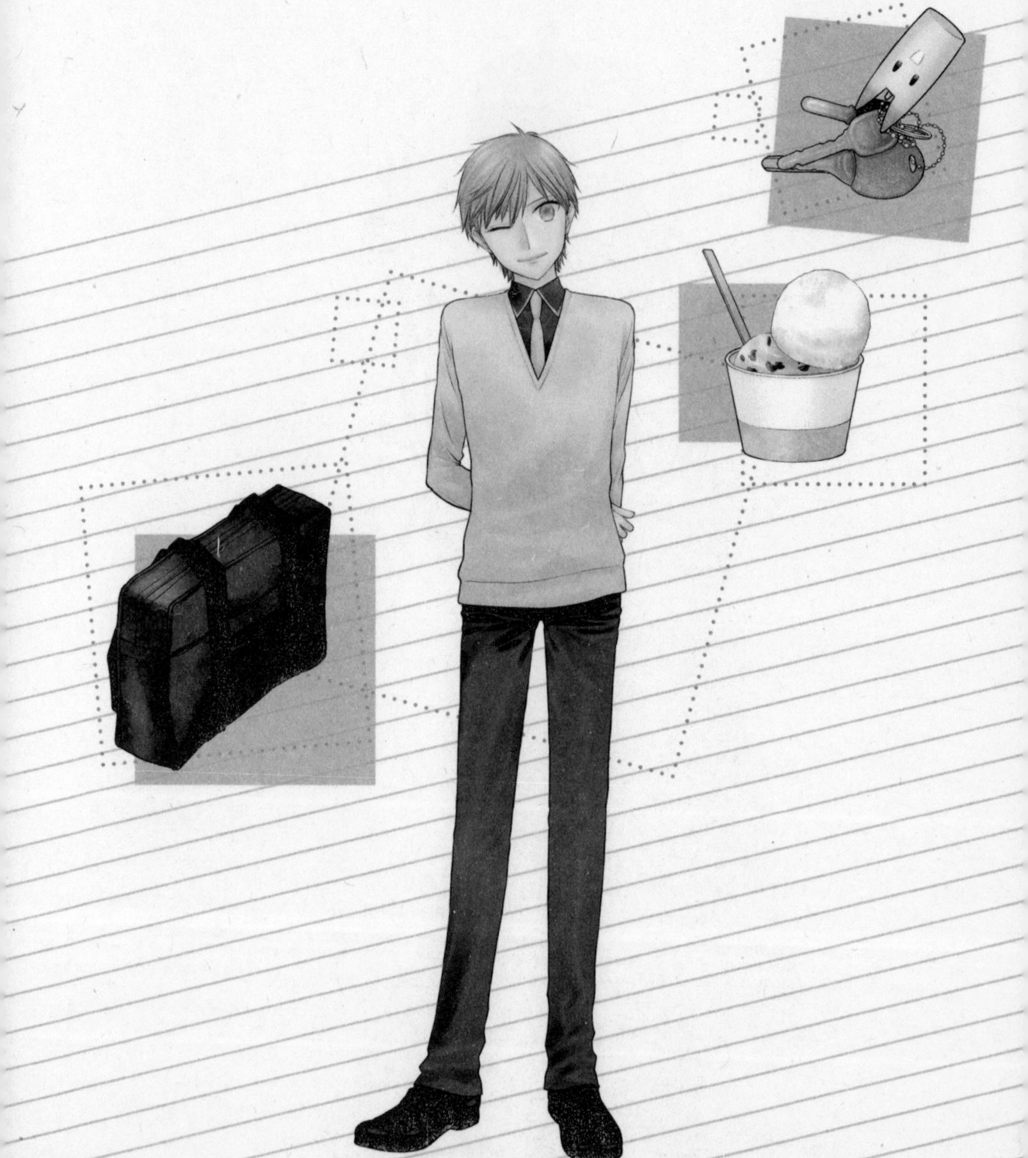

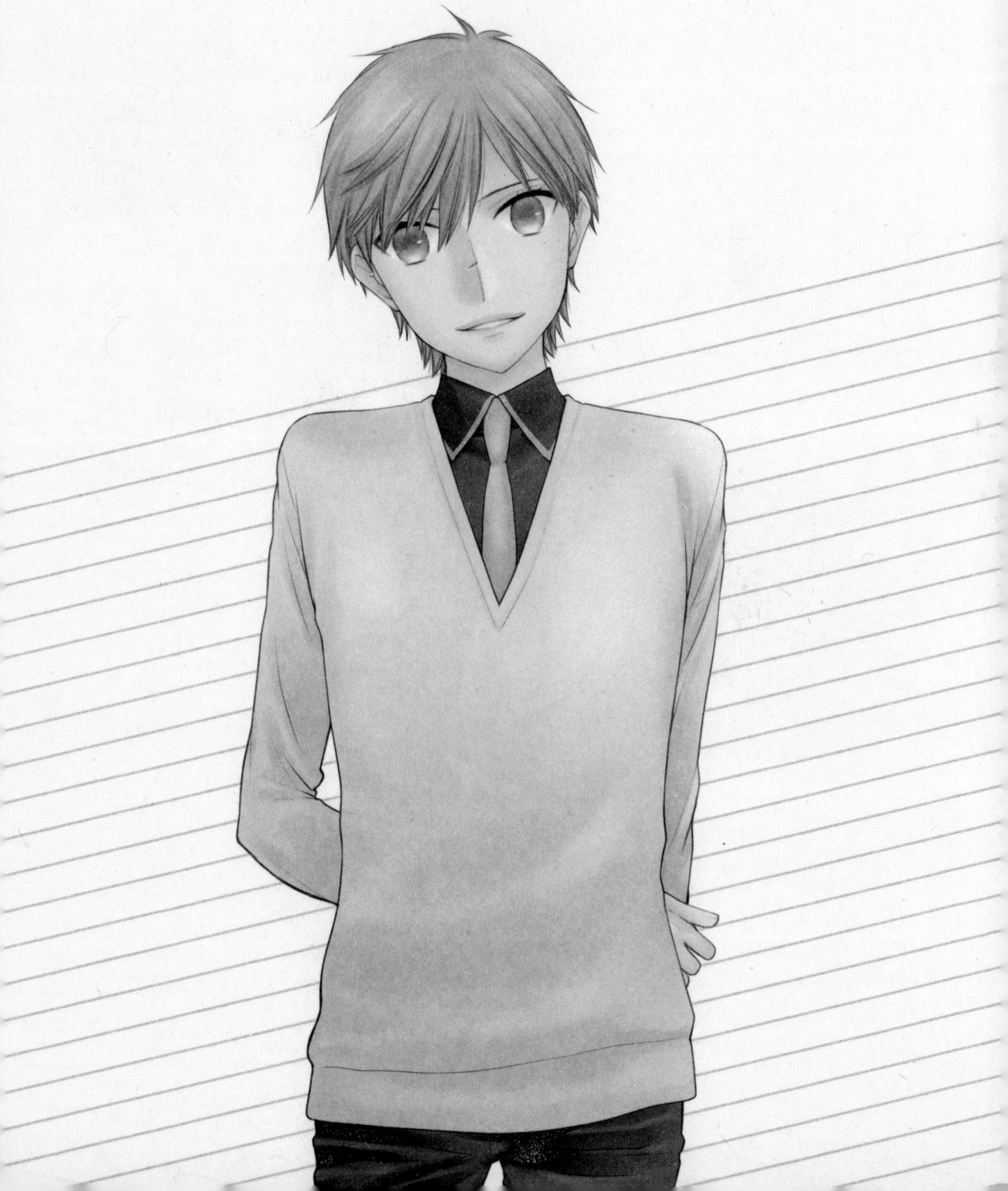

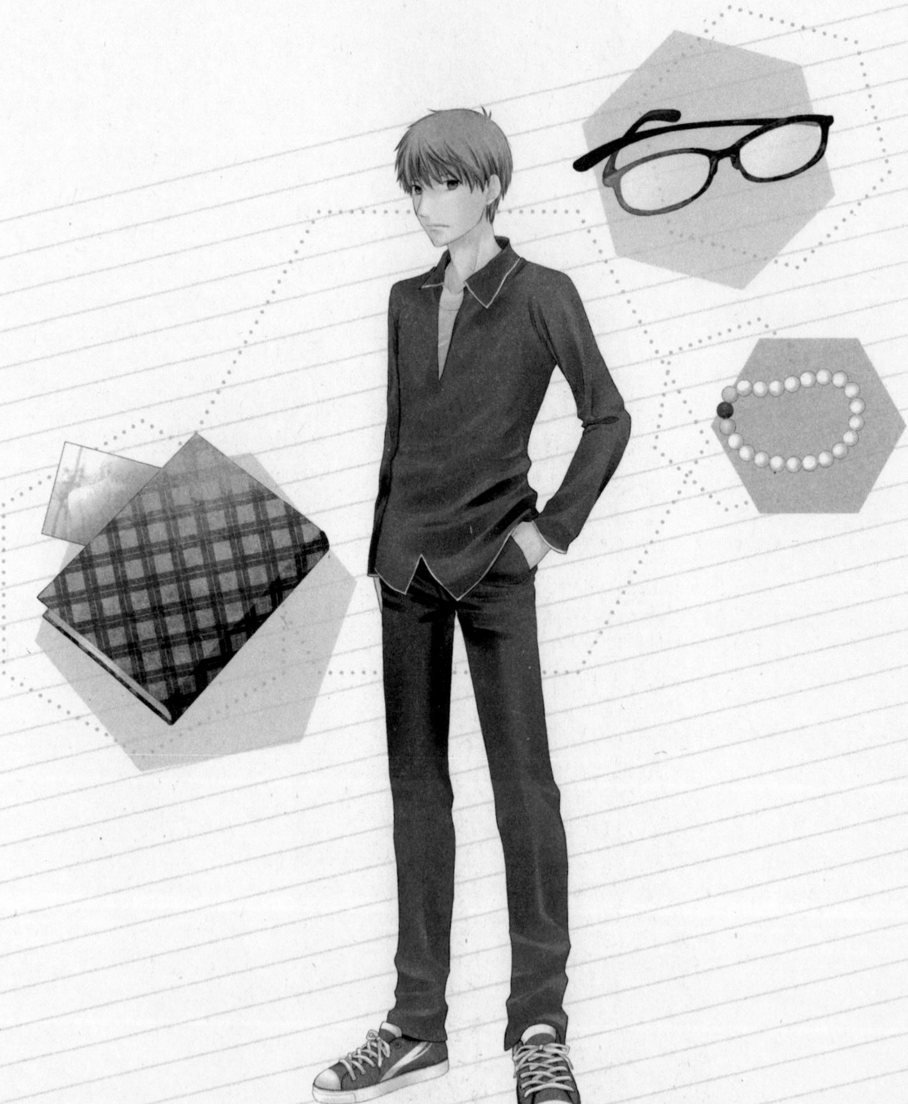

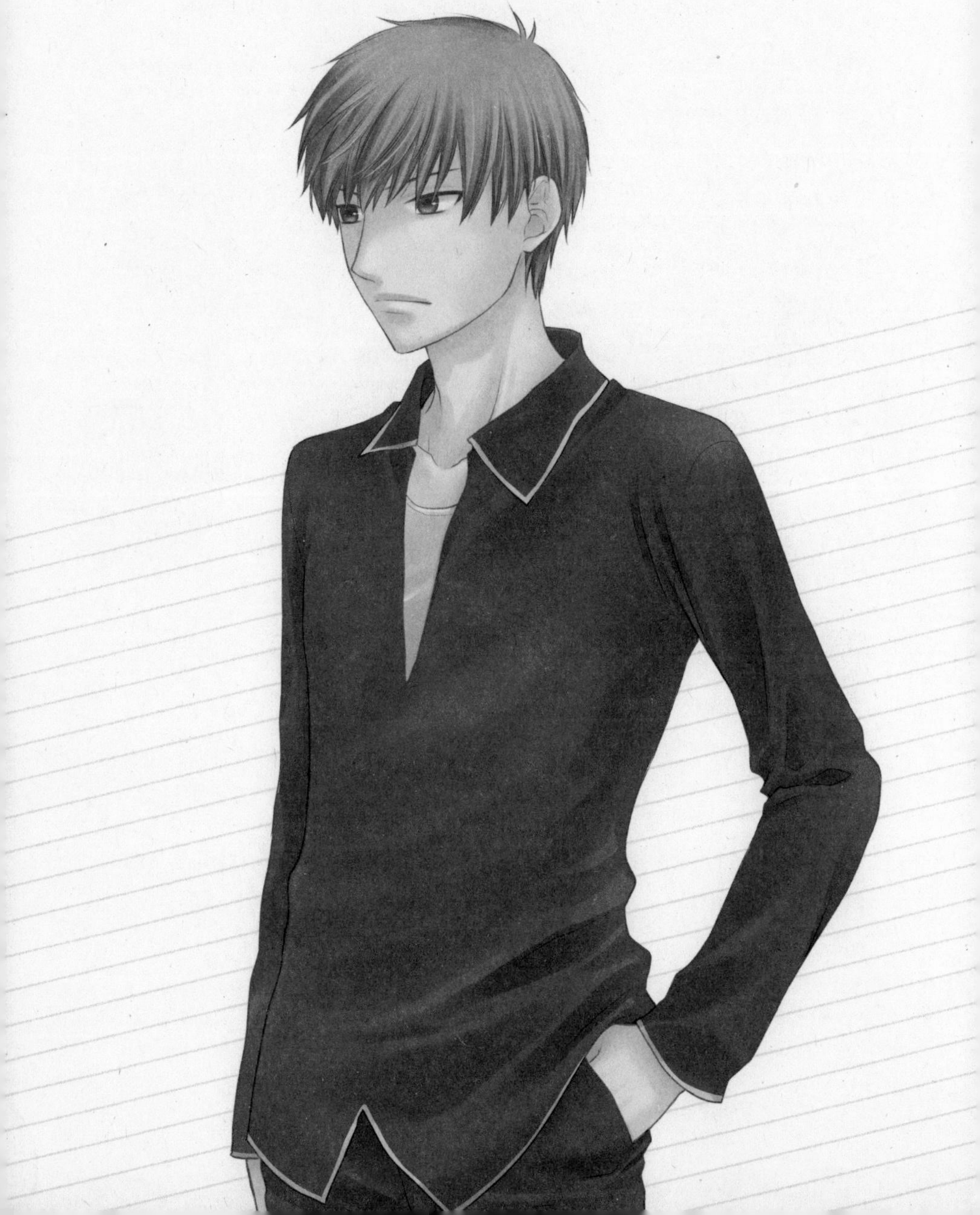

Fruits Basket another ③

NATSUKI TAKAYA

Translation: Alethea and Athena Nibley ✳ Lettering: Lys Blakeslee

Fruits Basket Another by Natsuki Takaya
© Natsuki Takaya 2019
All rights reserved.
First published in Japan in 2019 by HAKUSENSHA, INC., Tokyo.
English language translation rights in U.S.A., Canada and U.K. arranged with
HAKUSENSHA, INC., Tokyo through TUTTLE-MORI AGENCY, INC., Tokyo.

English translation © 2019 by Yen Press, LLC

Yen Press
150 West 30th Street, 19th Floor
New York, NY 10001

Visit us at yenpress.com
facebook.com/yenpress
twitter.com/yenpress
yenpress.tumblr.com
instagram.com/yenpress

First Yen Press Edition: October 2019

Yen Press is an imprint of Yen Press, LLC.
The Yen Press name and logo are trademarks of Yen Press, LLC.

Library of Congress Control Number: 2018939354

ISBNs: 978-1-9753-5859-4 (paperback)
       978-1-9753-5927-0 (ebook)

10 9 8 7 6 5 4 3 2 1

WOR

Printed in the United States of America